11/20/99
To Sharon,
Thanks for all you do,
Ken Goodman

Reflections and Connections

Essays in Honor of Kenneth S. Goodman's Influence on Language Education

Reflections and Connections

Essays in Honor of Kenneth S. Goodman's Influence on Language Education

edited by

Ann M. Marek
Nevada Department of Education

Carole Edelsky
Arizona State University

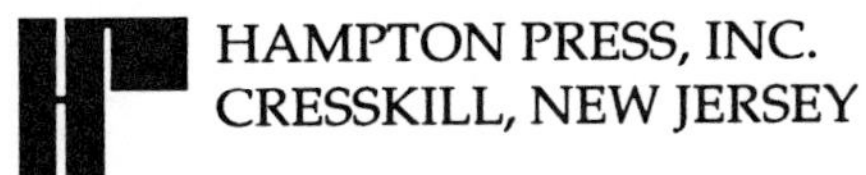

HAMPTON PRESS, INC.
CRESSKILL, NEW JERSEY

Printed in the United States of America

Library of Congress Cataloging-in-Publication Data

Reflections and connections : essays in honor of Kenneth S. Goodman's influence on language education / edited by Ann M. Marek, Carole Edelsky

p. cm.

Includes bibliographical references and index.

ISBN 1-57273-157-5. -- ISBN 1-57273-158-3 (ppb.)

1. Language and languages--Study and teaching. 2. Goodman, Kenneth S.--Influence. I. Marek, Ann M. II. Edelsky, Carole. III. Goodman, Kenneth, S.

P51.R36 1998

418'.007--dc21 98-31423

CIP

Hampton Press, Inc.
23 Broadway
Cresskill, NJ 07626

Contents

Introduction

Kenneth Goodman's transactional sociopsycholinguistic theory and model of the reading process has had a revolutionary impact on educators in the field of reading. Since the publication of his first research article in 1965, and the first iteration of his theory of the reading process in 1967, Goodman has developed, refined, and extended his model, which now includes not only conceptualizations of reading, but also writing and written texts. The theoretical insights Goodman reflects in his model are based in large part on an extensive body of research in miscue analysis, the reading evaluation instrument he pioneered in the 1960s and 1970s. The findings from miscue analysis have informed theorists, researchers, reading specialists, teachers, parents, and even students themselves. In a fundamental way, miscue analysis has taught us that what is meant by reading in the late 20th century in the Western world—that reading—is a language process. Thus, it is most effectively and efficiently learned if all the interrelated systems of information in language (graphophonic, syntactic, semantic, and pragmatic) are preserved in a meaningful, whole text, written and read for real purposes. This view of reading and the research from which it has been derived create a basic foundation for what is known today as *whole language.*

Whether in writing or in oral presentations, Goodman consistently emphasizes his concern for applying what we learn from observing language learners to the kinds of research we pursue, the sorts of curriculum we design, and the methods for instruction and evaluation that we select. His focus on applying knowledge in classrooms has led him to write primarily for an audience of teachers dedicated to supporting the literacy development of their students. But because he has openly and frequently criticized much of what passes for reading instruction and evaluation, he has also gained the attention of researchers, policymakers, publishers, and others whose direct or indirect influence has long (and in some cases, profitably) controlled the daily routine of classrooms. Goodman has attempted through his work to reverse the power in classrooms—from the teachers' manuals to the teachers themselves.

This book brings together the voices of teachers, researchers, and theoreticians whose own work has been significantly influenced by the work of Goodman. Because the influence of Goodman has been far-reaching, the topics of these individual chapters vary widely, but what unifies the chapters are the linkages to Goodman's foundational work in understanding language, learning, and teaching. Though they describe their own work, many of the contributors have also been affected by Goodman in personal ways over the years as they have examined, challenged, and changed what they believe about language, learning, and society. In this way, private and professional lives have become intertwined, and many of the authors share personal reflections as they describe their professional connections to the work of Kenneth Goodman.

The collection is divided into three major sections: *Foundations, Connections,* and *Extensions,* followed by a final piece which serves as a kind of *Epilogue.*

Foundations

The chapters within this section provide an introduction to the work of Kenneth Goodman. Collectively, they help readers understand the context within which he has been working (from both historical and personal perspectives), the scope of his work (including an emphasis on miscue analysis, the research paradigm he invented for studying reading), and the influence of other disciplines on his own research and theory building.

Carole Edelsky's chapter places the beginning of Goodman's work within the unique political and historical context of the 1960s. Early in her chapter, Edelsky reminds us that "it is not possible to understand theoretical arguments . . . without understanding what they were opposed to in particular historical settings." Through her words, we recall the behaviorist paradigm that dominated instruction and evaluation in the mid-1960s, and the unfortunate and damaging beliefs that children from minority and low socioeconomic groups were necessarily deficient as language learners. She deftly explains that these factors in school-culture at the time supported "a mainstream need to blame the children for failure." Clearly, this is one of the most important orientations that Goodman opposed—one that led him to debunk clinical, behaviorist explanations for teaching and learning, through describing and presenting what all kinds of real readers do when they read real texts.

Although circumstances placed Goodman at the right place at the right time, it is to his credit that he asked the right questions: What happens when we read? How can we find out? How will we interpret what we discover? How will this knowledge influence what happens in classrooms? Beginning with the first of these questions, Ann Marek traces the development and refinement of Goodman's model of reading since 1965, including a discussion of the miscue analysis studies which led to many of his conclusions.

A wide-ranging group of researchers, theorists, teachers, and readers have had a considerable impact on Goodman's thinking over the years, a fact he often acknowledges by saying he has learned much more from others than they could have from him. Among those colleagues is Dorothy Watson, whose chapter recalls the foundational miscue analysis work done at Wayne State University in the late 1960s and early 1970s. Her chapter puts the development of the whole language movement into a context that begins with those early research findings, followed shortly by the emergence of a few TAWL (Teachers Applying Whole Language) groups, and developing over the next two decades into a radically different conceptualization of teaching, learning, and curriculum so widely implemented in the United States and Canada that the Whole Language Umbrella organization was formed to provide a framework for continuing professional collaboration.

Systemic functional linguistics has been instrumental in what Goodman has described as the "vertical grounding of the transactional sociopsycholinguistic theory of reading, writing, and written texts" (1994, p. 1101); Fries's chapter is a clear presentation of the principles in systemic functional linguistics that connect to whole language. Like Goodman's model which attempts to describe what people actually do when they read, systemic functional linguistic theory attempts to describe the language people actually use when they interact. Fries's detailed systemic functional linguistic analysis of one advertisement shows the need for using a whole text as the primary unit of linguistic analysis and lends further support to a whole language argument for making whole texts a central feature of literacy education.

Miscue analysis has been at the core of the development and refinement of Goodman's theory of the reading process; everything readers are observed to do while reading has to be accounted for in his theory, every aspect of his theory must be validated in the observations of real readers. An extensive data base of readers' miscues has provided the foundation for his work, and miscue analysis has been used by other teachers and researchers for the past 30 years. In her chapter, Sharon Murphy notes that the ERIC database contains several hundred articles that use the term "miscue analysis"—in addition to other books and articles not indexed by ERIC. Murphy points out that "miscue analysis has become such a part of educational currency that it is often used without reference to its originator." As debates continue about teaching and learning reading, there is a heightened need for educators to be able to substantiate both the validity and reliability of miscue analysis as an indicator of readers' abilities. Her chapter presents what is arguably the most comprehensive review ever conducted of the literature documenting the validity and reliability of miscue analysis, and it will doubtless strengthen the credibility of the major miscue analysis research base underlying whole language.

The work described by Mark Sadoski, Robert Carey, and William Page is a more specific, in-depth presentation of the evidence of reliability and validity of miscue analysis as a measure of reading comprehension. The miscue data base they analyze includes readers from upper primary to secondary students in different geographic regions, reading different texts. Miscue analysis scoring systems used to evaluate these readers' comprehension of texts are then examined using professional standards for determining content validity, criterion-related validity, construct validity, validity as persuasive argument, and validity as circumstantial evidence. This "classical" analysis also examines reliability issues, focusing in particular on interrater reliability in the scoring of miscues, a subject often raised in critiques of miscue analysis research.

Understanding miscue analysis research is a key to understanding Goodman, and the chapter by David Bloome, David Landis, and John Villemaire on "reading reading miscue research" is a useful guide for delving into alternate "readings" of theoretical assumptions underlying miscue analysis. In their first "reading" of miscue research, they discuss the view of reading and the kinds of reasoning embedded in miscue analysis and research on readers' miscues. Their second "reading" of miscue research problematizes these embedded views. In so doing, Bloome, Landis, and Villemaire spotlight tentativeness, a central feature of Goodman's writing about the reading process and an important stance to take regarding the sociological character of reading practices.

Connections

The chapters in this section reflect the depth and variety of ways in which Goodman has influenced teachers and teacher educators. Brian

Cambourne talks about the need for those debating pedagogy to make their ideologies known—that is, to acknowledge and expressly articulate their beliefs about language and learning. Using himself (as a young man teaching in the 1950s) and a woman teaching in a whole language classroom in the 1990s, he makes a convincing argument that educational practices cannot, and should not, be understood apart from the personal philosophies that inspire (or tolerate) the practice. The connection between personal and professional lives is eloquently arrayed in Debra Goodman's chapter. She draws a compelling parallel between the struggles of a woman finding herself while becoming a teacher, and the struggles faced by young children becoming literate. Rare, poignant glimpses of her father, Kenneth Goodman, and her mother, Yetta Goodman, add depth to our understanding of the ways in which personal history becomes intertwined with professional choices.

The journey of Lois Bridges from teacher, to student, to teacher educator, is a narrative of learning itself; her chapter contains powerful and at times painful insights into the processes and tensions involved in professional growth. Her story reflects not only her own personal and professional growth, but also the ways in which what she learned about herself influenced the ways she interacted with other professionals involved in change. Jan Turbill also considers professional growth by tracing the evolution of her model for staff development over a 20-year period in Australia. Turbill maintains that the challenge in staff development is "to create learning programs and learning cultures" for teaching about whole language, as well as for supporting teachers making a paradigm shift to whole language. Like others in this volume, Turbill helps us understand that the knowledge being generated about how students learn language forced a new paradigm in literacy education.

Miscue analysis has played a key role in forcing that paradigm shift. As teachers learn to use miscue analysis, they often find themselves in a state of disequilibrium—what they previously believed about reading is undercut by the evidence of what readers really do. And for many, coming to understand reading through miscue analysis is a turning point in professional directions. Recognizing the power of miscue analysis to teach teachers about reading, Pat Long spent several years comparing forms of error analysis, attempting to determine whether a simplified and less time-consuming form could lead to the same depth in understand reading that the Reading Miscue Inventory produced. Her research is chronicled in her chapter, which also describes Goodman's influence on Australian teachers' views of reading.

The work of David Freeman and Yvonne Freeman is similarly concerned with facilitating a paradigm shift among teachers. Their chapter describes their work in teacher education aimed at those who teach second language learners, incorporating Goodman's principles for describing contexts in which learning is "easy" rather than "hard." In other words, they turn certain common sense assumptions on their heads, and they also articulate common concerns and recommended approaches in both mainstream and second language teaching.

Extensions

In the final section of the volume, we see the work of scholars who have extended Goodman's work in ways that hint at the power of his conceptualizations in language learning. Sandra Wilde's chapter describes the ways in which she has used the principles of miscue analysis to understand the linguistic strengths writers demonstrate in invented spellings. She shows that such spellings can be more or less literate, just as reading miscues can be of higher or lower quality. With many examples from young children's writing, Wilde argues that spellings are not simply right or wrong. Thus, teachers cannot be merely dispensers of correct spellings and correctors of wrong ones; they must become providers of opportunities and coaches who are knowledgeable about the full repertoire of strategies children use as they read and write.

Although miscue analysis has been a powerful tool for teachers and researchers, it has not yet been widely used by readers themselves. Yetta Goodman presents a technique called "retrospective" miscue analysis (RMA), which she uses to involve readers in analyzing their own reading in order to help them revalue themselves as readers. As she explains the assumptions of RMA and describes procedures and discussions in particular RMA sessions, she reveals how empowering these sessions are for the readers reflecting on their own reading. Yetta Goodman's work thus suggests that miscue analysis may be as valuable for readers as it has been for teachers and researchers.

Catherine Wallace's work uses miscue analysis in similar ways to explore what readers and teachers know about reading. In her chapter, Wallace describes her work with second language learners who are learning English literacy, yet who have little or no literacy in their first language. She uses miscue analysis in a traditional way as an evaluation tool for assessing the learners' progress in reading development. But she also uses the miscue analysis sessions to engage readers in discussions about their reading. Thus, the sessions provide insights into what the learners think about their miscues, as well insights into the nature of her "teacher intervention" as she and the readers discuss their reading.

In the opening pages of her chapter, Rudine Sims Bishop reminds readers that one of the most significant insights from miscue analysis studies is that "*what* students read could make a difference." In the large-scale study reported in 1978, students whose language was a stable rural dialect of English, or a language other than English, had higher retelling scores for "culturally relevant" stories than they did for other stories. Sims Bishop was involved in this research, and she recalls the fact that the task of *finding* culturally relevant stories was extremely difficult in the 1970s. She uses the miscue research as a springboard for her discussion of the value of African American children's literature, not only for developing literacy but for connecting "us all together as humans."

The next chapter, by Bess Altwerger and Barbara Flores, expands the notion that what students read makes a difference and moves the discussion into the realm of whole language as critical pedagogy. In a time when whole language is simplistically characterized as "learning to read naturally," or "literature-based reading," or "journal writing," Altwerger and Flores help us see whole language in perhaps its most compelling form—"a pedagogy in service of equity and justice for all people." In this chapter we hear the voices of students and teachers who have had the courage to use literacy to examine the worlds in which they live. It is this deliberate, critical inquiry in whole language classrooms that can lead students to "understand, critique, and even transform society."

The issue of "education as inquiry" is one of the themes explored by Jerome Harste, who takes us on a journey through whole language classrooms in New York, Indiana, and Hawaii, where teachers are struggling "to make curriculum more relevant as well as more critical." His chapter tells powerful stories of teachers working with other teachers in writing curricula, a process through which Harste says "our intuitive theories of instruction become articulated, are made public, and become a source of professional growth." Harste's observations and interactions with these teachers, their students, and the students' parents cause him to conclude that "inquiry still needs to be invented from the inside out through the hard work of curricular development, risk-taking, and reflection." The teachers he describes have clearly begun this hard work, and Harste urges holistic educators to "take heart"—whole language teachers are "writing a new identity not only for themselves, but for the profession."

Finally, in one of the more intriguing extensions of Goodman's principles, Steven Strauss brings together concepts from Vygotsky and Goodman in his work with individuals recovering from aphasia, who are "learning a first language for the second time." Strauss is a neurologist using what he calls "Goodman contexts" (natural, meaningful, social contexts that optimize rather than "control" performance) to study as well as rehabilitate aphasic language performance. His comparisons of aphasic responses to inauthentic texts in noncommunicative tasks with the same patients' responses to authentic texts and their communicative speech are both provocative theoretically and humanly touching.

Epilogue

Roger Shuy, linguist and colleague of Kenneth Goodman for 30 years, chose this opportunity to reflect on the evolution of his professional relationship with Goodman and to synthesize that evolution into several key points about "what it means to be a good colleague." Shuy talks directly and personally about the way he met Goodman, the ways they worked together over the years, and the ways in which their collegial relationship has endured. Shuy says, "Every academic comes to realize sooner or later that this work can be a lonely endeavor unless good colleagues can be found to share one's hopes, successes and struggles." Each of us who wrote for this volume to honor Ken Goodman, as well as hundreds more who are not explicitly represented here, are fortunate indeed to have Ken as a colleague.

This book is a kaleidoscope. The picture you see depends on your own focus, the angle through which you view, the stance you take. No attempt has been made to "standardize" these pieces, to homogenize them, as though there is a single, unified point each could or should make directly about the ways our work has been influenced by Kenneth Goodman. Goodman's influence is not an object, static and easily described; it is a process, dynamic and unique. Goodman has influenced each of us to varying degrees, in myriad ways, depending on the context within which we individually came to know his work. We took what we needed—what was engaging, relevant, useful—and incorporated it into the kaleidoscope of our own work. Although this volume is a tribute to Goodman's contributions to the field of language education, it exemplifies the nature and power of the work of the individual authors as well. Although he invented some of the tools, sketched the frameworks for interpretation, and shared his vision of classrooms where knowledgeable teachers make critical decisions, we asked our own questions, conducted our own research, and constructed our own knowledge. Goodman will say it is simply a tribute to ourselves. But we will know better.

Ann M. Marek, Reno, Nevada
Carole Edelsky, Phoenix, Arizona

FOUNDATIONS

Chapter One

*The Psycholinguistic Guessing Game: A Political-Historical Retrospective**

Carole Edelsky
Arizona State University

In 1967, when Ken Goodman made his first major public presentation of the psycholinguistic model of the reading process, I was living in Texas. My then-husband was in the army, stationed at Ft. Sam Houston, and for the first time in nine years we could afford to live in a small bungalow instead of cramming ourselves and our three babies, one of whom vomited all day and screamed all night, into a four-room apartment. In 1967, I had never heard of Ken Goodman and I told my neighbor (I was the authority because I had taught fourth grade) that as long as her kids learned to sound out words she would not have to worry; they would learn to read. After more than a quarter of a century, the screaming baby and the other two have grown up; so has my understanding of reading.

THEORIES ARE HISTORICAL

It is not just Ken Goodman's theoretical model of reading that is political

*This is a slightly revised version of a talk given at a symposium at the National Council of Teachers of English (NCTE), in November 1992, celebrating the 25th anniversary of Ken Goodman's presentation of reading as a psycholinguistic guessing game.

and historical. All theories in any field are situated historically; they are thought about and talked about in a milieu in which particular ideas and events condition and shape theory developments. Vygotsky's perspective on cultural transmission and sociohistorical bases for thinking and consciousness were certainly related to revolutionary conditions in Russia and intellectual concerns about building a new society. Psychology's focus in the United States on measurable differences between individuals was related to early 20th century capitalism's need to offer scientific explanations for social disparities, and the new discipline of psychology's need to establish itself as scientific at a time when science itself had just recently won its struggle with religion as the arbiter of truth and the guide for living. History also has to be accounted for in the appeals of oppositional theories. For example, whole language theory opposes direct instruction, and it uses a perspective on language acquisition to justify that opposition. Several generations back, Dewey also used a perspective on language acquisition in his arguments but not to oppose direct instruction. In fact, he was advocating at least some modicum of explicit instruction and opposing then-current attractions to Rousseau's radical laissez-faire approach to education (Dewey, 1916). It is not possible to understand theoretical arguments, in other words, without understanding what they were opposed to in particular historical settings.

THEORIES ARE POLITICAL

If all theories are situated, they are also political in the sense that they support or oppose particular power arrangements. Thomas Laquer details one intriguing example in a book called *Making Sex: Body and Gender from the Greeks to Freud* (cited in Smith, 1991). Apparently, from the 16th through the 18th centuries, Western philosophers, scientists, and social commentators believed in a one-sex model of anatomy. Females were considered to be inverted males. The advent of two-sex models placed men higher, not just morally but ontologically; external genitals were supposed to make men more active and warmer. Women, wearing some of their genitals inside, could be and were less active and colder (don't ask about the logic here!), therefore lower on the ontological ladder and less deserving of social privilege. Another twist on the idea that anatomy is destiny![1]

[1]Lest we feel superior about the "objective" and "true" nature of our anatomical understandings today (or at least in the 20th century), in a book-length discussion of the social construction of a medical fact (the fact of syphilis),

Social definitions also preceded and predetermined biological understanding when, in the 19th century, anthropologists, measuring the brains of Whites and Blacks, consistently found White brains to be bigger even though no such difference exists. Larger and therefore presumably more developed brains were assumed to be found in more developed races (and classes), both explaining and justifying greater rights and privileges, like the right of those with bigger brains to own those with smaller brains (Gould, 1981).

From a distance of 100 years or more, it is relatively easy to see that mainstream science back then was a social activity, reflecting the reigning ideology of the society in which it was carried out, the political exigencies of the time, and the personal prejudices of its practitioners. It is also easy to see that theories that challenged prevailing ones represented political as well as intellectual challenges (Lewontin, 1981). The politics at work in current scientific theory—both mainstream and oppositional theory—are much less obvious, however. But an appreciation of the historical and political nature of both Ken Goodman's theories and the mainstream educational science his work opposed in 1967 is essential in order to understand the richness of both the model as it was presented in 1967 and the complexity of the current scene in reading. And in order to appreciate the historical and political nature of Goodman's 1967 model, it is necessary to consider what was going on then, not just in reading but in education generally, in linguistics, and in the world.

THE SIXTIES AT LARGE

The 1960s was a decade of such exhilaration, turmoil, hope, and disillusionment that the mere mention of that decade still evokes strong reactions. By 1970, against a backdrop of economic surplus, radicals, liberals, and eventually many in the mainstream in America had forged a tenuous consensus about the repugnance of the war in Vietnam. Fewer, but still considerable numbers, were disgusted by racial and class disparities at home.

But the decade did not start that way. Todd Gitlin (1987) notes that "[h]istory rarely follows the decimal system as neatly as it did in 1960." With the election of John F. Kennedy, it was possible to anticipate a thaw, a shift in the climate of opinion from the 1950s, "the way spring

---

Ludwig Fleck (1979) offered evidence that medical textbook illustrators in the 1930s fictionalized their diagrams to correspond with prevailing theories in anatomy and physiology.

announces itself with scents and a scatter of birdsong before the temperature climbs to stay. And then it was as if, all over the country, young people had been waiting for just these signals" (p. 81). What some heroic Black (known then as Negro) youths did in this historical springtime was to sit down at a Woolworth's lunch counter in Greensboro, NC. Refusing to know their place, they touched off a wave of sit-ins at lunch counters across the South. Rejecting the snail's pace of desegregation and the persistent denial of their civil rights, courageous Blacks and a few White allies took action.

The Civil Rights Movement was a movement, something that moves, not just an intellectual position. It broke sharply with the mood of the 1950s which counseled "moderation at every turn" (Gitlin, 1987, p. 85). It was about action, "acting as if" segregation did not exist, reflexively "creating the condition it described" (p. 224). The sit-ins, supported by a tradition of Black liberation writing and activity in Southern churches, were quickly followed by Freedom Rides, during which civil rights crusaders had "their skulls cracked [and] their clothes set afire . . . for daring to take seriously a Supreme Court decision banning segregation in bus terminals" (pp. 136-137). In the next few years, organizers from the Student Nonviolent Coordinating Committee (SNCC) risked their own lives in rural Mississippi and Georgia trying to "coax sharecroppers to register to vote, knowing that all of them might be ambushed and shot to death for their pains" (p. 142). Until the Voting Rights Act of 1965, civil rights activists got almost no protection from federal law officials as Ku Klux Klansmen and others, including occasional local law enforcement personnel, beat the "troublemakers" who were "acting as if" Constitutional rights were a reality.

In the meantime, as the war in Vietnam escalated, so did anti-war activity. Not surprisingly, given the numbers of poor and Black young men sent to Vietnam, anti-racist themes resonated in work to end the war. By the mid-1960s, at growing numbers of meetings and demonstrations around the country, one heard slogans like "War on Poverty-Not on People" and "Freedom Now in Vietnam." An anti-war recruiting table set up on the Berkeley campus developed into the Free Speech Movement. Even pop culture sang Bob Dylan's lyrics, popularized by Peter, Paul and Mary, tying anti-war and civil rights themes: "How many times must a cannon ball fly before they're forever banned? . . . How many years can some people exist before they're allowed to be free? . . . The answer, my friend, is blowin' in the wind, the answer is blowin' in the wind."

Amid the sit-ins, love-ins, teach-ins, and be-ins, counter-institutions sprang up, mirroring the anti-establishment messages in songs: underground newspapers, hip radio stations, astrology networks, cooperatives, crash pads for runaways, free medical clinics, free schools. The media spun out the counter-culture as consumed with drugs, sex, and rock and roll. LSD was still legal in California. Public talk about sex, at least, was more common. And some rock and roll songs, borrowed from Black musical traditions, offered frankly political lyrics. Middle-class White young people metaphorically (but only apparently) burned their bridges behind them as they set off for the Bay Area and other hip spots. Some poor Blacks burned their neighborhoods literally. Oppression surrounded by change and movement, frustration mixed with the glimmer of possibility, set off riots, first in Watts, then Detroit and Newark. Radicals called these rebellions.

By 1967, the year of Ken Goodman's presentation of his psycholinguistic model of reading, there were 486,000 American troops in Vietnam and 15,000 had been killed. In that year, the United States defoliated 1.7 million acres in Vietnam (Gitlin, 1987). Huge majorities in Congress continued to appropriate money for the war. George Wallace was preparing to run for President. Black and Latino youths with growing political awareness and know-how had begun to organize and recruit for, respectively, the Black Panthers and the Brown Berets. Some people in various Movements (Black, Chicano, Women's, New Left) had developed thorough-going analyses, laying the blame for political, social, and economic injustice on capitalism's doorstep. In fact, by 1967, radicals argued that without an adequate analysis of the systemic sources of injustice—that is, without an adequate theory—a movement could not go far. Ken Goodman argued similarly: Without an examined and well-worked-out theory, the field of reading would not get far either.

As civil rights and anti-war activity intensified, it became clearer that activists were not just an alliance of Black youth and disaffected young college students. Early in the decade, boycotts in the South had been joined in large number by middle class, middle-aged Blacks. As the 1960s drew to a close, it was harder for the politicians, the mainstream press, and middle America to maintain that all the criticism was coming from merely one sector. Even—and especially—those fighting the war opposed it and began to make connections between the war and racism. In a show of disgust, Vietnam veterans threw their medals on the White House lawn and, during the November 1969 moratorium, it was soldiers, too, who were making peace signs. By the late 1960s, protest (e.g., draft card burning) was changing to resistance (e.g., trying to seal off U.S. Army induction centers). In other words, the more radical began (as the Quakers say) "speaking truth to power" in an ever louder voice. And official power came down hard. Among the victims was often youthful, often White, often privileged innocence. In 10 years, the world had changed.

Certain themes persisted throughout the 1960s. They appeared in major social movements, in theories in the academy (especially in linguistics), and also in the model Goodman presented in 1967 and his subsequent writing to flesh out that model. The themes, as might be imagined, were themselves political; they point to attempts at changing existing power relationships. One theme was revolution; or, if that is too strong, sharp departures from what had been, a no-turning-back to previous conceptions and social compacts. Closely connected was the theme of justice and increased democracy: civil rights, "power to the people." Whether "the people" were Black, Hispanic, female, poor, or language minority, the referent here was a group who had been dealt a lesser hand in power allocations. Love and peace were themes as well, related for many people at the time to themes of justice and rights. After all, if the people, the less powerful, deserved greater power and equal rights, it was because trusting the people, loving the people in the sense that heroes like Ghandi, Martin Luther King, and Che Guevara loved the people, was an article of faith in a democracy.

LINGUISTICS IN THE SIXTIES

Although the 1960s played everywhere, they had special billing on college campuses. It was there (prior to the Democratic Convention in Chicago in 1968) that the themes played loudest, there where the most active recruiting took place for various movement activity. Poor and minority constituencies, often living immediately around university campuses, demanded access to the higher education available (but not to them) right next door. Whether in response to these demands or to "cool out" and prevent further rebellions, higher education complied. Open admissions and the rise of community colleges were features of higher education in this decade.

Of course, the outdoor spaces on most campuses, as well as the classrooms and research offices in the social sciences, were not instantly converted to the spirit of the 1960s. They remained under the influence of the establishment culture. Behaviorism held the reins in psychology and educational psychology. But the scholarly work of academics in some disciplines at least was undergoing the same social quakes that were rocking the foundations outside the academy. Linguistics was one of those disciplines.

Throughout the late 1950s, the major theoretical perspective in American linguistics was structuralism. It was empiricist in the extreme, focusing on constituents in an actually spoken corpus. The way structural linguistics differentiated constituents was through functional contrasts, with the most basic of these being phonemic contrasts. Structural linguistics, compatible with other behaviorist theories of human activity, disdained any appeal to anything mental.

In the late 1950s, Noam Chomsky published *Syntactic Structures*, developing the idea of generative grammar. Instead of focusing on functional contrasts in speech behavior, Chomsky highlighted a finite system of tacit rules that allow people to generate and understand an infinite number of sentences, a system of rules residing somehow in the minds of speakers (Crystal, 1971). Meaning came into fashion. Whereas structuralists defined parts of speech on the basis of their formal properties, generative grammarians could define them on semantic grounds. Generative grammarians relied on intuitions to produce data and noted people's ability to understand each other despite mistakes and disfluencies, to reconcile actual and expected speech. As elaborated in the mid-1960s with the publication of Chomsky's *Aspects of the Theory of Syntax*, generative grammar emphasized a distinction between competence and performance. In so doing, it was part of the movement to value human agency, to trust people to think and know, to recognize, and in so doing, to give power to people.

Besides Skinner and the behaviorists, Chomsky had some major critics in the 1960s who were not behaviorists but who believed that linguists were looking at the wrong thing with the wrong lens. They argued that looking at actual activity (including how that activity was interpreted), not at invented sentences, was the way to understand language as well as social life. In particular, some anthropological linguists, sociologists interested in language, and philosophers of language disagreed with Chomsky's focus on linguistic rules for generating appropriate sentences and his lack of interest in actual speech in particular settings. Hymes (1972) argued, for instance, that appropriateness was not a property of sentences but of the relation between sentences and contexts. According to these critics, linguists should indeed take account of "mind," that is, of people as interpreters of what they say to each other. But linguists should take as their phenomena of interest people really saying things to each other, in particular places, for particular reasons, and with an eye out for particular conditions (like who has the power to do what in a situation).

The shift in linguistics—from functional and formal contrasts to meaning and mind, extended by sociolinguistics to interpretations and contexts (including political dimensions of contexts)—was a theoretical prerequisite for some important, socially conscious work on dialects. Structuralist linguists had established the linguistic equality of all linguistic varieties. Thus, both standard and nonstandard dialects had been phenomena of interest for linguists for many years. But events in and out of the academy now made nonstandard dialects—in particular, Black English—phenomena of more than academic interest. As the Civil Rights Movement was making racial disparities in housing, education, income, draft status, and so on a public issue, glaring inequalities became front-page stories. One question came up repeatedly: Why did non-White, poor, and working-class people do worse in school than White middle-class people? Many psychologists and sociologists in North America and Europe answered the question in ways that supported the established order. The most blatantly racist and victim-blaming answer was that Blacks were genetically inferior (Jensen, 1969). Only slightly more liberal answers (because they blamed environment rather than heredity) were that a culture of poverty, defined by how it failed to meet a middle-class standard, was at fault (Lewis, 1966); homes of minority youngsters either offered too little or too much stimulation (Moynihan, 1965); poor Black children had both language and cognitive deficits (there were debates about which deficit caused which) (Bereiter & Engelmann, 1966); working-class children's restricted codes and particularistic meanings, learned through the ways they were socialized, suited them poorly for the school's demands for elaborated codes and universalistic meanings (Bernstein, 1966).

Linguists' work describing Black English could be and was also used to support the status quo, to show that features that differed from standard English were the culprit in low educational status. But some linguists and sociolinguists deliberately asked the question differently—not why do poor minority children fail but how do schools fail poor minority children? (It would be some time after Ken Goodman presented his model of the reading process before educators could add to that question: Just what is it that minority [and other] children fail at in school and are those tasks what we want to spend our time on [Edelsky & Draper, 1987]? It would also be a long time before the original question would be not merely flipped or added to but radically reframed: Why is failure an issue in the first place and how is it accomplished by everyone in the setting [McDermott, 1992; McDermott & Hood, 1982]?)

With the new theoretical understanding that speakers of all dialects have linguistic competence and that children's verbal performance had to be considered in connection with how they were interpreting the contexts in which they were performing, linguists and sociolinguists produced landmark work. Labov (1969) demonstrated the "logic of nonstandard English" and with wit and eloquence (hallmarks of style in the 1960s for academics as well as for the audacious Yippies) demolished the arguments of Jensen and of Bereiter and Engelmann (at least for an academic audience but not for the general educational community). Other linguists studied the origins (Stewart, 1970), structure (Dillard, 1967), attitudes toward (Williams, 1970), and social embeddedness (Shuy, Wolfram, & Riley, 1967) of the dialects of Black Americans. Indeed, liberal language scholars paid so much attention to Black English that Sledd (1972) accused them of using Black English as the "mother lode" for "a lucrative new industry for white linguists" (p. 200). Sledd's critique at the time was a disdainful version of what Gitlin claimed from a greater distance in 1987. America, argued Gitlin, got its "juice" in the 1960s from Blacks; Black music provided the beat and Black calls for justice provided the ethical momentum.

EDUCATION IN THE SIXTIES

Outside the universities and community colleges, the predominant school culture continued as it had for decades, massively stable with minor concessions to changes in fashion. One of these new trends was to focus on the language of minority children, especially Black children, to explain their school failure. Only now, with the aid of scholarship from educational psychology and British sociology in particular, poor and especially Black children's language could be described scientifically as deficient, restricted, and also as remediable. Through in-service workshops and during their preservice teacher education, teachers were taught the behaviorist view that children learn words (the behaviorist equivalent of "language") through imitation and reinforcement but that lower class parents respond inappropriately to babies, using only monosyllables or nonverbal gestures. Thus, with the backing of the work of Bereiter and Engelmann and others, teachers were taught that the lower class child "doesn't learn how to be taught and so behaves as though he were mentally retarded or without language" (Boyd, 1970, p. 130). Though written accessibly, Labov's elegant sociolinguistic critique of Bereiter and Engelmann reached very few school districts; it did not fit the mainstream need to blame the children for failing. But Bereiter and Engleman's description did. Thus, teachers learned that Black children often spoke in "some amalgam," in giant words with no distinct usable words. "Read me a book" might become "re-ih-bu" (Boyd, 1979, p. 133). Some scholars (e.g., Bernstein, 1972) complained that their work was perverted in order to support blame-the-victim educational policies. Others, like Bereiter and Engelmann, were eager enough to blame Black children for getting poor educations that they developed commercial products like Distar which schools snapped up, simultaneously demonstrating their concern (for the welfare of the children? for the consciences of educators?) and their desire to appear scientific.

It was this mainstream school culture, though not necessarily the criticism of poor minority language cultures, that was countered by educational progressives in the 1960s. Articles on informal education in Britain appeared in major U.S. media (e.g., Featherstone, 1967). O'Neill, Holt, Kozol, Kohl, Herndon, and others spoke and wrote about the evils of authoritarian education and the promise of what came to be known in the United States as open education. Piaget was discovered by American academics, lending scientific support to calls for child-centered education. Schools with frankly political agendas were established to help organize newly registered Blacks in the South (Shannon, 1990). Some, like the Highlander Folk School, anti-authoritarian in organization and political in intent, had been in existence for some time, though their continued existence was a struggle (Horton, 1990). By 1970, the demand for alternative approaches in public education prompted Charles Silberman to write about what precipitated that demand: a "crisis in the classroom." The source of the crisis, according to Silberman (1970), was mindlessness—a failure to think about what the schools should be doing. Other commentators, however (e.g., Kozol, 1972; Mann, personal communication, 1970), argued that the mindlessness was only apparent, and schools were doing exactly what they were supposed to be doing. They just were not acknowledging it. They were sorting and ranking people in order to prepare a stratified labor market for capitalist use.

READING IN THE SIXTIES

And they were doing it especially well through reading instruction. By 1960, basals were nearly universal in United States classrooms (Goodman, Shannon, Freeman, & Murphy, 1988). With their ranked reading groups, materials based on supposedly scientific reading levels, and focus, for those of lowest status, on what is least meaningful, they helped accomplish, behind a mask of scientific objectivity, the sorting tasks the system needed. Frequently, basals were supplemented with phonics programs to quell the anxieties of educators and parents who thought that in relation to phonics basals offered too little too late. Some basal series written by structural linguists went to great lengths to group words in "stories" according to contrasting spelling patterns (rat, rate; can, cane). The idea was that children would discover the relationship between sounds and letters as they read words whole rather than having to "sound" and "blend" (Chall, 1967). Basals were not in every classroom, however. A few schools used the Language Experience Approach for teaching younger children and Individualized Reading for older ones.

The conception of reading underlying both basal technology and even many interpretations of the Language Experience Approach was behaviorist. Though varying notions floated around about what reading was, none were based on any developed theory or model. Instead, they all invoked—to a greater or lesser extent—some of the following behaviorist ideas: language is made up of discrete components, parts add up to make wholes, individual parts retain the same characteristics they have in the whole, skills are arranged in hierarchies, and words are the basic building blocks in reading (Edelsky, Altwerger, & Flores, 1990). According to a survey by Chall (1967), basal authors believed reading to consist of word perception, word recognition, and then comprehension. Phonics program authors tended to agree. Authors of linguistic series believed reading was recognizing words; meaning, however, was part of language study and, therefore, comprehension was not part of reading per se. Even Language Experience Approach proponents urged teachers to use the words from children's dictated stories in order to work with separate components of language. In many cases, the difference between progressives and traditionalists in reading had little to do with their conception of reading. Rather, the dividing line concerned classroom organization and materials. Progressives were opposed to whole class teaching and standardized materials; traditionalists favored such arrangements.

When reading was so widely considered to be a matter of "getting the words," no wonder the concerns of teachers, researchers, and people who wrote about reading revolved around methods for teaching children to "get the words." No wonder there was such interest in finding optimal materials for presenting words, and even so much interest in finding optimal words. (See Nila Banton Smith's [1965] lengthy discussion in which reading is defined by materials.) No wonder Chall was able to establish the grounds of "the great debate" on reading as two different ways of "getting words": a phonics way and a look/say way. Whether "getting the words" was the best conception of reading in the first place was never questioned. With such a word-bound view of reading, it is also no wonder that viewing Black children as speaking in giant run-together words was tantamount to seeing their language as a barrier to reading; that is, to "getting the words."

Such was the world in 1967 when Ken Goodman presented his model of the reading process. The various movements in the 1960s—civil rights, anti-war, and so on—were obviously political. It may not have been obvious, but the underpinnings of both acknowledged and unacknowledged theories in linguistics, education, and reading were political too.

THE POLITICS OF BEHAVIORISM

Behaviorism was the major theory embedded in both educational practice and a variety of theories in the social sciences in the 1960s. It was and remains a convenient partner in efforts to rationalize everyday life; that is, to make both public and private life predictable in order to reduce the risk of capital investment (Shannon, 1989). Dividing life and activity into component external behaviors, proposing behaviors or responses as under the control of stimuli, and eschewing meaning and mind are political as well as intellectual moves. They help create a mentality that views people as lacking in agency, a mentality that accepts that some people will control others, a mentality that refuses to consider questions of value such as: Should some control others and who should have that right? These premises underestimate human capabilities (e.g., ignoring people's predilection to invent and interpret) and trivialize learning (reducing it to nothing more than a strengthened response or a change in behavior). In all these ways, behaviorism legitimizes policies and practices that depend on passivity and obedience.

In the field of reading, the effect of behaviorist theory was pernicious, even by the 1960s. Conceiving of language as consisting of bits—researchable, teachable, and testable bits—behaviorism gave rise to tests of language bits which were then used as gatekeepers against people. It also created a climate in which test scores, seemingly objective but always biased, became the only criterion for success in school and also the main way of operationalizing (and presumably learning about) phenomena in research. Thus, an out-dated view of language, embodied in test scores—especially reading test scores—is at the heart of almost all of what is known about school achievement (as well as much of what is known [from research] about learning and thinking). The tests based on this view of language—and the view itself—emphasize the most surface and easily measurable features of language, those most likely to differ from dialect to dialect and those that can only be learned fully through membership in a speech community. Not surprisingly, the tests are keyed only to standard dialects. In fundamental ways, therefore, reading tests underrepresent and misrepresent the achievement of those who speak nonstandard dialects.

Skills hierarchies at the center of behaviorist notions of reading allowed for different goals for different learners and for different instructional stances, "slowing it down and making it more concrete" for the slower students, thus isolating "language components" even further (Allington, 1991). The net result was that behaviorism promoted sorting out students and allocating reading "skills" differentially: full literacy for some and lesser literacy for others. The sorting that schools had been able to do more efficiently once reading had been transformed from a moral virtue to a cognitive skill during the first half of the century became even more refined in the 1960s with the growing acceptance of behaviorist skills hierarchies. Now, in addition to three reading groups, additional divisions were added: gifted, remedial, and special education (Allington, 1991). Behaviorism made it scientific to track students for life.

POLITICS IN THE LINGUISTIC CHALLENGE TO BEHAVIORISM

The theoretical upheaval in linguistics that began in the late 1950s and gathered momentum in the 1960s was a forerunner in breaking the hold of behaviorism and in lending theoretical legitimacy to more progressive work in other fields. That upheaval was a double one: a shift from structuralism to generative grammar and later the rise of socially constituted studies of language (e.g., sociology of language, sociolinguistics, ethnomethodology, and philosophy of language with a social slant). Chomsky's positing of a distinction between linguistic competence and linguistic performance was critical. If linguistic competence is in the mind, if being a native speaker of a language means having linguistic competence (even if performance is marred by hesitations or slips of the tongue; indeed even if one is sleeping and there is no performance at all), that honors not just individuals but the species as a whole. That is, if human beings learn language and if knowing a language means having linguistic competence, then in a nontrivial sense, all god's children got competence. Moreover, if knowing a language means having linguistic competence, then that competence is shared with others who also know the language. Thus, competence, is social, not just mental. That means in order to study language, it is not necessary to do laboratory research on large numbers under controlled conditions (the behaviorist format for research); studies of even a single individual's competence can reveal the linguistic system for speakers of that language. It is competence that allows people to ignore surface differences that do not matter (e.g., the difference in pitch when I say "good morning," and when you say "good morning" or the difference between pronouncing the /p/ at the end of "cup" or not pronouncing it and simply closing the lips). It is competence that allows people to abstract underlying differences that do matter in what appears the same on the surface (e.g., ambiguities like "flying planes can be dangerous" [planes that fly / to fly a plane]). It is the idea that competence is shared that eventually opened the way (20 years later) for seeing "mind" as social (Cole, 1990). A theory that foregrounded such a competence/performance distinction and the accompanying distinction between deep and surface levels of language at a time when behaviorism held sway also foregrounded human agency. It did not merely devalue external control of human beings; it implied that total external control of surface performance was not only ultimately impossible, it was also irrelevant because deep structure and underlying competence was "where it's at."

The move among some linguists, anthropologists, sociologists, and philosophers of language to discount made-up sentences as data (favorite sources of data for generative grammarians) and to prefer instead actually occurring everyday activity was also political. In legitimizing diverse and common folks' everyday lives (including how daily activity was interpreted), in trying to understand what ordinary activity meant to the people involved (rather than measure it against a dominant out-group standard), this sociolinguistically sophisticated perspective enhanced the standing of diverse, ordinary people.

POLITICS IN GOODMAN'S PSYCHOLINGUISTIC MODEL OF READING

Civil rights, Woodstock, the fatal bombing in Madison, San Francisco State, police shootouts with Black Panthers, the Chicago Convention, Charles Manson, Black power, Women's power, State power, Kent State, open classrooms, Chomsky, behaviorism, My Lai, language deficits, race and genetic inferiority, Tet offensive, Distar, Make Love Not War, assassinations, Where Have All the Flowers Gone, decode first make sense later, sound it out, sound it out.

Ken Goodman's work is located in and grew out of that swirl. It gets its revolutionary flavor from what it opposed, what it supported, what it leaned on, what it transformed. It opposed racist depictions of diversity and societal hierarchies. It supported movements for minority power, for trusting ordinary people as they did ordinary things (like learn and use language). It leaned on new theories in linguistics and critiques and discoveries in sociolinguistics. And through transformed conceptions of reading, it transformed the school lives of millions.

Let me be specific by discussing the political implications of a few major features of the Goodman model: reading as a process, reading as a language process, miscues have qualities, and arguing through down-home examples.

Reading as a Process

A key assertion in this model is that reading is a process, with comprehending, supported by predicting and confirming, its major overall activity. In 1966, Goodman talked of comprehending, something someone is doing—fluid, open, multiple, and active—rather than comprehension—a solid object, a thing, standardizable. A major problem in contemporary life in the United States is the tendency to reify, to turn abstractions into concrete objects, converting ideas about intelligence, for example, into the score on an IQ test. At first, when processes and relationships are reified we sometimes resist, feeling "thingified" or even commercially commodified. The tendency to reify is strong, however, and after awhile, the reification is widely accepted so that we come to understand intelligence as an object or we see a basal series as a teacher. As Shannon (1989, p. 53) noted, "what are really transactions among people (past and present labor) are understood as transactions among things."[2] In 1967, reading had long been reified as word recognition and reading comprehension. Goodman's claim that comprehending was what was interesting, not the reified comprehension, was political. It put human activity above objects.

If reading is a process and comprehending is a process, then understandings are processed, fabricated, constructed. That means there is no single understanding, no one truth out there somewhere, so that to comprehend would be to "get it." If people create understandings, they create them from a perspective, a vantage point, a viewpoint. Because no one stands everyplace simultaneously, all understandings are partial and necessarily biased. I do not understand what I read bare and unfiltered. I understand it through the lens of a middle-aged, White, Jewish, middle-class heterosexual woman with a particular worldview who has raised three children in the Southwest in the late 20th century and who is reading whatever I am reading for particular purposes in a particular situation. If any of that were different, my understanding of what I read would be different. The philosopher Gilbert Ryle once quipped there is no such thing as immaculate perception. To see comprehending as a process with understandings as produced rather than "got" means being able to look critically at "official" understandings. It means giving credence to "unofficial" understandings. And that is certainly political.

---

[2]As I write this chapter, I am reifying Goodman's model and his writings, the theory of behaviorism, the decade of the 1960s, generative grammar, and a variety of other abstractions, making it seem as though the model or the theories or the decade were doing the arguing, the promoting, the preventing, the enabling. Rhetorical conventions are responsible (another reification); that is, I am as enculturated through language conventions as anyone else.

Reading As a Language Process

The Goodman model not only claimed reading was a process, it emphasized that it was a language process. If it is a language process, then written language is language. Because humans are language learners par excellence, there is no reason to assume language learning should be especially difficult and every reason to assume everyone can learn written language; that is, that everyone can learn to read.[3] Thus, Goodman's model denied the category of "at risk" even before it was so labeled. Instead, like parents acting as if babies can take part in conversations and thus creating the conditions that allow babies to take part and learn to talk, Goodman's model urges us to act as if children are readers. By "acting as if" (tactically similar—but for different motives—to civil rights activists acting as if lunch counters were already desegregated), we let children learn written language as language is learned; that is, we trust learners to learn written language. The less we trust, the more we try to control, the more we try to exert power over another. Trusting learners, in others words, is political.

It is not only a tactical alignment with the civil rights movement's "acting as if" and it is not only the trusting that is political in this theoretical notion. If written language is language and people learn written language the way language is learned, then they do not learn through practice exercises. Such a position delegitimizes the basal technology that depends on exercises (word recognition exercises, word attack skill exercises, and comprehension exercises) no matter the quality of the literary selections the basal offers. Delegitimizing basals means cutting into the power of publishers and district and state administrators over teachers and students. It also means cutting into the profits of the textbook publishing industry. Though it took more than a decade for the impact of this position to be felt widely in the publishing industry and in school districts, it was still political in 1967 and even more so today.

Moreover, if written language is language and it is learned like language, it is learned as it is used in particular situations with particular people (Goodman, 1970). Each set of situations and people provide grist for the language learning mill; what will be learned are (in today's terms) the discourse practices the child participated in. Language learning in any discourse situation is evidence of language strength. We can expect people to have learned different language conventions because they come to school having participated in different language situations. Such diversity is not a problem to be

---

[3]Asserting that everyone can learn to read does not imply that everyone can learn that peculiar activity known as reading instruction.

overcome; it is evidence of human capacity. By seeing all situations and all interlocutors as potential sources of language learning and all language learning as evidence of language strength that can serve further (written) language learning, Goodman's model discounts the idea that speakers of some dialects who have learned language in particular situations are linguistically disadvantaged. It takes some of the privilege away from those who are usually privileged. It evens things up a bit.

When Goodman claimed reading was a language process, he also claimed that without understanding how language works, one could not understand reading. The model and the writings explaining the model go on to show just how reading is a language process by highlighting certain characteristics of language as understood in 1967. Of special importance were the distinction between competence and performance, the centrality of meaning, and the simultaneous presence of interacting cueing systems. When language depends on an underlying competence, shared to be sure but necessarily residing in the mind, when people can be shown to be ignoring similarities to get to underlying differences in meaning and surface differences to count paraphrases, for example, as the same, then surface behavior or performance loses its unwarranted importance. Attention to behavioral objectives which amount to attempts to change performance seem misplaced because it is underlying competence that schools should be building (Goodman, 1970).

In language, meaning is fundamental. So it is in reading. Meaning is what readers go after and the making of meaning is how they get it. Meaning making is a negotiation between what readers bring and what writers offer. Meanings accumulate as a reader reads and tentative meanings get pinned down; retrospective thinking and language processing lets those meanings wash back and forward over an entire text. By building on generative grammarians' revolutionary understandings of language, Goodman could mount a theoretically principled and highly political attack on behaviorism in reading. In providing evidence that foregrounded mind (shaped by social arrangements but ultimately independently active), he was countering behaviorists' ideas about responses being under control of stimuli. Thus, instead of buttressing educational arrangements based on one party controlling another, as behaviorism does, his model supported the active agency of all. And by emphasizing meaning making—nonlinear, tentative, and often idiosyncratic—as the mind's chief activity in language learning and use, Goodman's work legitimized educational activity based on trusting people to think and make meaning.

The behaviorist view was that knowing a language meant knowing a hierarchy of skills. Goodman borrowed from new linguistic theory to argue against the existence of separate language skills and a skills hierarchy. Because language subsystems are present simultaneously, interacting with each other, language is both redundant and predictable. To process language, whatever skills are involved must be used simultaneously, in concert with the text-in-situation's offering of cues from simultaneously appearing cueing systems. Whoever has learned to talk has learned all the "skills"; there are no higher or lower skills necessary for knowing a language reserved for higher and lower talkers or for higher and lower readers, just more or less experience with one general skill: making meaning through integrating cues from all systems. Goodman's model made it theoretically untenable to continue to follow prevailing educational practice in 1967 (and today); that is, to allot full literacy (all the skills) to some and partial literacy (fewer skills) to others.

Miscues Have Qualities

Another major feature of Goodman's model with political implications is the proposal that miscues have a range of quality. The notion of unidimensional error—undifferentiated wrongness—underestimates human capacity. It ignores the different cueing systems a reader is attending to and the reasonableness of a reader's hypotheses. In language acquisition research in the 1960s, the serious, respectful analysis of children's errors revealed the hypotheses they were working with. Even more pertinent to the present discussion, they revealed that hypothesizing was the most apt way to think about what is going on when people learn language. After all, a child is not imitating anyone when she or he says "I goed." That error reveals a hypothesis that overgeneralizes the most common convention for forming the past tense in English. Serious consideration of miscues, as the model urged, offers the same benefit: a glimpse at an underlying process, which, once glimpsed, further discredits behaviorist notions of reading.

Moreover, analytic attention to miscues, as advocated in 1967, presumed that humans are actively engaged in psychological and linguistic processes influenced by social arrangements, even during their ordinary everyday lives. Along with scholars like Goffman and Garfinkel in sociology and Hymes in sociolinguistics, Goodman was prodding the field of reading to move toward the study of reading in the everyday world, to leave the laboratory and its pretense of superior knowledge.

Trying to take the reader's perspective in determining the source of different miscues allows a view of a strategic reader with language strengths. Taking the reader's perspective seriously diminishes power differences between readers and those analyzing their reading (e.g., teachers or researchers)—another move to lessen hierarchies.

Some of the data that showed that all miscues are not equal demonstrated that in important ways, people are. Miscues that were actually translations from one dialect to another offered strong evidence to oppose dominant views in the 1960s that some people were linguistically and cognitively deficient. In this respect, Goodman's model was a major contribution from the field of reading to the Civil Rights movement. It said Black children who read "I asked her if I could go" as "I aksed her could I go" were anything but inferior if they could use semantic and syntactic systems to override graphophonic cues and thus translate from one dialect to another so fluently. It said, look to oppressors (human or structural), not to victims, for explanations of minority groups' low status in school and elsewhere.

Arguing Through Down-home Examples

A stylistic feature of Goodman's model and his presentations of that model is the nature of the examples he used. When explaining or arguing, he gave examples that show young children and adults, rich and poor, doing the same thing when it comes to language processing. He gave examples of how he, too, has difficulty reading a contract, not because of unknown words but because known words are being used in unknown ways. His examples make us acknowledge that proficiency is situational, that even professionals, not just young inexperienced students, find themselves in written language situations that are beyond their capabilities. He used examples about himself, his family, and his profession, not to put himself forward but to put himself back, to get people to rethink the distinction between beginning and fluent readers, younger and older readers, better and worse readers. Goodman's examples do not ask us to completely eliminate these distinctions; they ask us to lessen them and the hierarchy they imply by looking honestly at what we ourselves do, removing the halo we hold around our own reading.

Sometimes, Goodman used examples from languages other than English, trying to crack the ethnocentrism of educators. Often after trying to widen the circle and put a dent in racism, classism, and sexism, he spelled out such a string of particularities, including even size-ism and able-ism, that he anticipated postmodern writings: "A flexible, relevant reading curriculum would capitalize on the strengths of children of both sexes and of all shapes, sizes, colors, ethnic and cultural backgrounds, dispositions, energy levels, and physical attributes" (Goodman, 1970, p. 28). Some of his examples poked holes in conventional wisdom about print, showing that decisions about creating a new paragraph in published materials, for instance, is often determined by the need for more white space on the page than by the need to show a shift in topic. It is as though Goodman was trying to demystify written language to reveal its secrets and provide easier access so everyone could partake.

RESPONSE TO THE MODEL

All of this constituted a radical departure from what was going on in reading during the 1960s. Instead of trying to answer old questions in new ways, Ken Goodman changed the questions; indeed he changed the subject altogether. His model implied that researchers should get out of the laboratory, that they should acknowledge the subjectivity—the interpretive character—of all analyses (not just the analysis of miscues) and stop pretending to a theoretically impossible objectivity. His writing about the model and its implications was explicitly anti-behaviorist. Moreover, that writing often aimed at a nonresearcher audience, was accessible, and frequently witty and passionate rather than aloof. It was as though Eisner had already spoken in 1967 (instead of in 1990) about the fallacy of separating thought and feeling. (If you think something without feeling, you know it. The way you know it is by how it feels.)

Lemke (1990) proposed that a new theory is always somebody's way of talking about a topic. A new theory, as well as old theories, also always supports particular interests and power arrangements. Goodman's theory opposed stratification and supported diverse but ordinary people's quest for justice, inclusion, and democracy. It fit the spirit of the 1960s. To enter the conversation using Goodman's way of talking about reading, therefore, meant being in sympathy with that spirit and wanting to support those interests.

In a recent deconstructionist analysis, critical legal scholar Gary Peller (1987) demonstrated how dichotomies like subjectivity/objectivity, passion/reason, partiality/impartiality, and rational/irrational embody a discourse of power for legitimizing social hierarchies. Peller's article is entitled "Reason and the Mob." To mainstream behaviorist reading researchers, Ken Goodman's work and the research tradition it was a part of represented the mob, an unruly challenge to a tight but rarely acknowledged hold on power. The typical way the American mainstream greets cultural challenges to business-as-usual is twofold: to domesticate them, adopting the surface (often limited to the jargon) without the substance; or to withhold press coverage, trying to render them invisible. Ken Goodman's model was (and still is) treated to both. The term "miscue" has been inserted into behaviorist in-service workshops. A recent review of research on reading comprehension instruction (Dole, Duffy, Roehler, & Pearson, 1991) in the most prominent journal for reviews in education discussed the shift in this century from behaviorist conceptions of reading to cognitive views emphasizing the interactive and constructive nature of comprehension. This "comprehensive" review failed to even mention Goodman or his revolutionary model.

Of course there are now a significant number of literacy researchers who do know the intellectual debt they owe Ken Goodman. But mostly, fittingly, it is "the people" who use the model—thousands of teachers, organizing themselves into a grass roots teachers' movement, who recognize a theory that serves their interests as well as the interests of learners in a democracy. And their number is growing. As Ken Goodman has said referring to whole language, he did not found the whole language movement; whole language teachers found him. Or rather, his model. For good reason.

REFERENCES

Allington, R. (1991). The legacy of "slow it down and make it more concrete." In J. Zutell & S. McCormick (Eds.), *Learner factors/teacher factors: Issues in literacy research and instruction, 40th Yearbook of the National Reading Conference* (pp. 19–29). Chicago: National Reading Conference.

Bereiter, C., & Engelmann, S. (1966). *Teaching disadvantaged children in the pre-school.* Englewood Cliffs, NJ: Prentice-Hall.

Bernstein, B. (1966). Elaborated and restricted codes: Their social origins and some consequences. In A. G. Smith (Ed.), *Communication and culture.* New York: Holt, Rinehart & Winston.

Bernstein, B. (1972). A critique of the concept of compensatory education. In C. Cazden, V. John, & D. Hymes (Eds.), *Functions of language in the classroom* (pp. 135–151). New York: Teachers College Press.

Boyd, G. (1970). *Teaching communication skills in the elementary school.* New York: D. Van Nostrand.

Chall, J. (1967). *Learning to read: The great debate.* New York: McGraw-Hill.

Cole, M. (1990). *On socially shared cognition.* Unpublished manuscript, Laboratory for Comparative Human Cognition, UCSD, La Jolla.

Crystal, D. (1971). *Linguistics.* Baltimore: Penguin.

Dewey, J. (1916). *Democracy and education.* New York: Macmillan.

Dillard, J. (1967). Negro children's dialect in the inner city. *The Florida Foreign Language Reporter, 5,* 7-10.

Dole, J., Duffy, G., Roehler, L., & Pearson, P. D. (1991). Moving from the old to the new: Research on reading comprehension instruction. *Review of Educational Research, 61,* 239-264.

Edelsky, C., Altwerger, B., & Flores, B. (1991). *Whole language: What's the difference*? Portsmouth, NH: Heinemann.

Edelsky, C., & Draper, K. (1987). Reading/"reading"; writing/"writing"; text/"text". *Reading-Canada-Lecture, 7,* pp. 201-216.

Eisner, E. (1990). *Address.* Annual meeting of The National Council of Teachers of English, Atlanta.

Featherstone, J. (1967, August 19). Schools for children: What's happening in British classrooms, *The New Republic.*

Featherstone, J. (1967, September 2). How children learn, *The New Republic.*

Featherstone, J. (1967, September 9). Teaching children to think, *The New Republic.*

Fleck, L. (1979). *The genesis and development of a scientific fact.* Chicago: University of Chicago Press.

Gitlin, T. (1987). *The sixties: Years of hope, days of rage.* New York: Bantam.

Goodman, K. (1970). Behind the eye: What happens in reading. In K. Goodman & O. S. Niles (Eds.), *Reading process and program* (pp. 3–38). Urbana, IL: National Council of Teachers of English.

Goodman, K., Shannon, P., Freeman, Y., & Murphy, S. (1988). *A report card on basal readers.* New York: Richard C. Owen.

Gould, S. J. (1981). *The mismeasure of man.* New York: Norton.

Horton, M. (1990). *The long haul.* New York: Doubleday.

Hymes, D. (1972). The scope of sociolinguistics. In R. Shuy (Ed.), *Report of the Twenty-third Annual Roundtable Meeting on Linguistics and Language Studies, GURT* (pp. 313–333). Washington, DC: Georgetown University Press.

Jensen, A. (1969). How much can we boost IQ and scholastic achievement? *Harvard Educational Review, 39,* 1-123.

Kozol, J. (1972). *Free schools.* New York: Bantam.

Labov, W. (1969). The logic of nonstandard English. In J. Alatis (Ed.), *Report of the Twentieth Annual Roundtable Meeting on Linguistics and Language Studies, GURT* (pp. 1–43). Washington, DC: Georgetown University Press.

Lemke, J. (1990). *Talking science.* Norwood, NJ: Ablex.

Lewis, O. (1966). *La vida*. New York: Random House.

Lewontin, R. (1981). The inferiority complex. *New York Review of Books*, pp. 12-16.

McDermott, R. (1992, October 23). Reading, language and culture [workshop]. University of Arizona, Tucson.

McDermott, R., & Hood, L. (1982). Institutionalized psychology and the ethnography of schooling. In P. Gilmore & A. Glatthorn (Eds.), *Children in and out of school*. Washington, DC: Center for Applied Linguistics.

Moynihan, D. (1965). *The Negro family: The case for national action*. Washington, DC: US Department of Labor.

Peller, G. (1987). Reason and the mob: The politics of representation. *Tikkun*, 2(3), 28-31, 92-95.

Shannon, P. (1989). *Broken promises*. Granby, MA: Bergin & Garvey.

Shannon, P. (1990). *Struggle to continue*. Portsmouth, NH: Heinemann.

Shuy, R., Wolfram, W., & Riley, W. (1967). *Linguistic correlates of social stratification in Detroit speech*. Washington, DC: US Office of Education Cooperative Research Project No. 6-1347.

Silberman, C. (1970). *Crisis in the classroom*. New York: Random House.

Sledd, J. (1972). Bi-dialectalism: The linguistics of White supremacy. In H. Funk & D. Triplett (Eds.), *Language arts in the elementary school: Readings* (pp. 199–207). Philadelphia: J. B. Lippincott.

Smith, B. (1991). Power in the groin. *Tikkun*, 6(4), 72-73.

Smith, N. B. (1965). *American reading instruction*. Newark, DE: International Reading Association.

Stewart, W. (1970). Toward a history of American Negro dialect. In F. Williams (Ed.), *Language and poverty* (pp. 351–379). Chicago: Markham.

Williams, F. (1970). Language, attitude, and social change. In F. Williams (Ed.), *Language and poverty* (pp. 380–399). Chicago: Markham.

Chapter Two

Making Sense of Kenneth Goodman

Ann M. Marek

LOOKING BACK

The professional odyssey that has shaped Kenneth Goodman's influence on the work of language educators began in 1962 when he asked himself the question, "What happens when we read?" It was a question many thought had been answered, at least in detail sufficient to inform curriculum and instruction designed to teach children to read. Curriculum, instruction, and evaluation were chiefly based on the theory that reading was a matter of recognizing words in sequence, identifying the meanings of the words, and through understanding and organizing the meanings of the words, acquiring an understanding of the text. Words were identified by applying several kinds of skills. In the more purely phonics-based approaches, the application of phonics rules was emphasized in attacking words. If the words were successfully pronounced, then it was believed they were identified and meaning could be ascribed. Other, more eclectic approaches combined phonics instruction with instruction focused on establishing sight word vocabularies and teaching skills for discerning word spelling patterns and recognizing visual configurations. In addition to word identification techniques, instruction included a focus on grammar: knowing the parts of speech, diagramming sentences, understanding phrase and clause structures, and so on—clearly a vestige of the days when most students were taught to read Latin. And comprehension instruction, based as it was on the premise that the reader must *acquire* the author's meaning, focused on directing the reader to identify the meaning in the author's text by defining words; identifying facts, characters, and events; and, to some extent, inferring cause-and-effect relationships and themes. Essentially, though, instruction concentrated on word recognition and vocabulary development because good readers were thought to be those who recognized the words and knew their meanings. Spache (1964) said: "Thus, in its simplest form, reading may be considered a series of word perceptions" (p. 12). The familiar phrase of a friend echoes through my mind: "It's pretty to think so." But was it true?

In 1962, most U.S. school children were learning to read with basal reading programs containing these elements of instruction. Readability formulas and word frequency counts were the "technologies" of the day that dictated text development for beginning readers. Texts were tightly controlled across grade levels by manipulating sentence length and structure, word selection and frequency, and other features of text, resulting in that stupefying written language genre, Dick-and-Jane-ese. The basal series were supplemented with thick workbooks, designed to reinforce the myriad skills children purportedly needed to learn in order to become readers. Many will recall these kind of exercises as having been the foundation of the reading instruction they received as children. Millions of children were learning to read in these classrooms. Goodman's children were learning to read in these classrooms; so was I, though even from my vantage point as a child in a two-room schoolhouse in rural California, I knew well those classmates who were not. And so we may wonder what led him to pose the question. What did he know or suspect that others did not? What was the nature of his dissatisfaction with what was known and accepted as the explanation for this thing called reading?

The answer is relatively simple—the theory did not fit reality. When Goodman observed children reading, he noticed that they read in ways that were incompatible with the popular theory. Word recognition did not seem to be the only, or at times even the primary skill they relied on in processing text. In fact, he observed readers who substituted words that had similar meanings but quite dissimilar letters and patterns (like "day" for "morning"). If reading essentially involved visual identification of words, how could readers seemingly ignore the visual display yet seem to make sense of the text? If good readers were those who consistently, accurately recognized words, how could these observations be explained? More importantly, how could reading instruction and evaluation be improved unless reading itself was better understood?

UNDERSTANDING READING

Cues and Miscues

Goodman began his inquiry into reading with what he has since described as the simplest task he could imagine (Goodman, 1992a). He gave students a text to read that they had not seen before. He asked them to read the text out loud, without any assistance, just as if they were reading alone. Tape recordings of those readings captured thousands of responses he expected them to make, and hundreds that were unexpected. It is critical to note that he assumed from the beginning that the unexpected responses were made using the same process the reader had used to make responses Goodman expected. This assumption—and the belief that any useful explanation of expected behavior would have to also explain unexpected behavior—became a cornerstone in building his theory of reading as a single, unitary process. Goodman and others used the unexpected responses, dubbed "miscues," to infer the process readers use in making *all* responses. Though Goodman is frequently credited with having done so, he did not coin the term *miscue*; rather, he gave it new meaning through its use in the field of reading. Miscues became for him "windows" on the reading process, and much of his work in the 1960s and 1970s was devoted to the development and refinement of miscue analysis, an instrument for analyzing readers' unexpected responses which was used to understand not only readers, but the reading process itself.

The first of his miscue studies was described in 1965 in an article he wrote for *Elementary English*, a journal of the National Council of Teachers of English. The study quantified his and other teachers' intuitions that children could read words in context that they could not read in isolation on lists. He studied groups of first-, second-, and third-grade students who read a list of words from a basal reader story, followed by reading the story itself. To begin, each student was presented with a list of words derived from a story at about grade level. If the child missed too many words, a story which appeared earlier in the basal series was given because it was presumed to be easier. If, however, the child missed few or no words, a more advanced story was given. As a result, within each grade level students read different texts depending on the apparent difficulty of the text and the relative ability of the student. After the students read the story aloud, they were asked to share an oral retelling as an indication of comprehension.

Goodman compared the average number of words the students missed in the lists to the average number of words missed in the stories, and presented findings supporting the notion that reading text is easier than reading words in isolation. Critics have pointed out over the years that as an experiment this study was not scientifically rigorous, nor were the findings particularly remarkable. Goodman (1992b) himself has stated: "Neither I nor anyone else at the time was impressed that the study supported [the] common belief that kids could read words in context that they couldn't read on lists" (p. 192). Ironically, some of the criticism about the research design turned out to illuminate rather than controvert Goodman's conclusions. Critics suggested that because students in each grade did not all read the same story, the dependent variables were insufficiently controlled. Over the years, Goodman and others have come to understand that no two readers ever construct a real text in exactly the same way, nor does a repeat reading of the same text ever evoke the exact same response in a given reader. In fact, Goodman's transactional sociopsycholinguistic theory of the reading process posits that there are at least two texts present when writers write and when readers read. For the writer, there is the entire "text" of meaning that exists in his or her mind; and there is a parallel text that becomes reflected as written language. Readers transact with the written text to construct yet another text: the meanings that exist in the mind of the reader, meanings that may expand or change over time, long after the written text is gone from view. Writers construct meaning and so do readers. Therefore, texts are not as static as one might think; there is not a simple relationship between the words placed on a page and a reader's construction of meaning. Goodman explains:

> In a transactional view, both the knower and the known are transformed in the process of knowing. The reader is transformed as new knowledge is assimilated and accommodated. The reader's conceptual schemata and values are altered through reading comprehension. Because the published text is a reality that does not change its physical properties as a result of being read, how can it change during reading? The answer is that the reader is constructing a text parallel and closely related to the published text. It stays the same yet is a different text for each reader. The reader's text involves inferences, references, and coreferences based on schemata that the reader brings to the transaction. And it is this reader's text that the reader comprehends and on which any later retelling is based. (Goodman, 1994, p. 1114)

This concept undercuts the research of experimentalists who believe that two texts can be made comparable through the mere control of word and sentence length (common methods for assigning a readability level) and who assume that when texts are similar across these dimensions, they evoke the same reading experiences for readers.

More important than the results of this modest study, though, are the ideas Goodman expresses that capture his orientation toward reading at the time and which were the genesis for much of what is now conceptualized in his theory of reading. Below, are some of the premises Goodman relates in this early piece. These premises clearly separate his emerging theories from what were then commonly accepted orientations toward reading research and instruction. For me, a focused, deliberate rereading of his words evokes a sense of their revolutionary power.

> In this study, reading has been defined as the active reconstruction of a message from written language.

The suggestion that readers are engaged in "active reconstruction" heralds a major theoretical shift in understanding reading. Goodman challenges the belief that reading is essentially a word identification task, in which readers passively recognize words (or do not), and in which the accurate recognition of words is a prerequisite for comprehension. In a few short years, Goodman would revise the term "reconstruct" to "construct," but as early as 1965 he was proposing that readers engage in a constructive process as language users. Readers construct meaning; the meaning does not reside in the text itself.

> Reading must involve some level of comprehension. Nothing short of this comprehension is reading.

This statement clearly discounts instructional practices in which reading is taught as a series of subdivided skills, with comprehension merely one of those skills. It also raises questions about the viability of so-called linguistic reading approaches that used nonsensical sentences (e.g., A man ran a tan van) in an attempt to teach beginning reading skills, for without a sensible text, readers cannot construct meaning. Goodman understood that comprehension is central to reading and that any instruction or assessment of reading without an integrated focus on comprehension is untenable.

> I have assumed that all reading behavior is caused. It is cued or miscued during the child's interaction with written language.

Aligned with Goodman's emerging theory that readers are active language users is this notion that miscues are caused by the same linguistic cues as the expected responses to the text. Goodman sensed that miscues are *caused*, that is, there are linguistic explanations for them. This assumption defied the traditional view that errors are random events caused by the reader's lack of skill or outright carelessness.

> Reading is a psycholinguistic process.

These five words, embedded as they are in the opening paragraph of Goodman's 1965 article, today seem somehow ordinary and obvious. But they signaled what was to become the key principle in Goodman's work: *Reading must be understood as a process of integrating thought and language.* It is this process that is explicated by Goodman in his transactional sociopsycholinguistic model of the reading process. This model, which explains reading in ways that render indefensible much of what passes for reading instruction in classrooms, has provoked controversy and debate for the past three decades.

At the close of the article, Goodman suggests several contentious and far-reaching implications for instruction based on this very early attempt to understand reading as a process. These implications are revisited below.

> Introducing new words out of context before new stories are introduced to children does not appear to be necessary or desirable.

Yet thousands upon thousands of teachers were beginning each reading lesson doing just that. In this single statement, Goodman's influence on the research-based dismantlement of traditional basal reading instruction had begun.

> Prompting children or correcting them when they read orally also appears to be unnecessary and undesirable in view of the self-correction which language cues in children.

And the battle began. The suggestion that teachers should abandon the practice of giving students words and correcting students' errors provided the most direct challenge to the primacy of teaching word recognition skills in reading.

> Shotgun teaching of so-called phonics skills to whole classes or groups of at the same time seems highly questionable in view of the extreme

> diversity of the difficulties children displayed in this study. No single difficulty seemed general enough to warrant this approach. In fact, it is most likely that at least as many children are suffering from difficulties caused by overusing particular learning strategies in reading as are suffering from a lack of such strategies.

Could *teaching* actually be getting in the way of *learning*? Did we perhaps know so little about individual children's abilities as language users that we caused as many difficulties as we corrected?

Other clues to understanding Goodman's influence are apparent in this early work. Even though the article focused chiefly on a small study, his orientation to research has from the beginning been inextricably woven into issues of classroom instruction. He has consistently made explicit statements about the direct application of knowledge gleaned from research to the choices teachers make in practice. Moreover, those explicit statements are often deliberately provocative. Consider this final implication:

> Eventually, I believe we must abandon our concentration on words in teaching reading and develop a theory of reading and a methodology that puts the focus where it belongs: on language.

Goodman eventually concluded that reading is most easily learned in natural, meaningful contexts in which the process is not short-circuited by material that artificially limits and manipulates language (Goodman & Goodman, 1979). Yet basal texts were deliberately written to control word length, sentence length, and the choices and repetitions of vocabulary items. These contrived texts crowded the shelves of elementary schools in 1965 and consumed budgets which might otherwise have been used to purchase children's literature, periodicals, nonfiction material, and other texts providing authentic literacy experiences for students (Edelsky & Smith, 1984). Furthermore, assessments of students' reading abilities were dominated by norm-referenced tests and other narrowly focused indicators of reading proficiency. But Goodman believed that when we limit language, we limit language users. Only when reading real language for meaningful purposes could readers move beyond those limits. Unwilling, unable to deny the challenge of reinventing reading, his life's work had begun.

Though it has been 30 years since this study was published, it continues to be cited by those who wish to discredit Goodman's research and theories (Nicholson, Lillas, & Rzoska, 1988), as though by maligning one early iteration of miscue analysis, all subsequent work can summarily be dismissed. Goodman (1992a) says that the reason this study retains prominence is that it is "the only thing I've ever done that experimentalists recognize as research." It merits attention, however, because it provides a very early glimpse into the directions Goodman pursued in constructing theory, designing research, and linking theory and research to instructional practice.

Arguably, if there is a single element of Goodman's work which distinguishes it from others whose work has also been influential, it is that he conceptualizes reading as language. This view seems self-evident today, and indeed it may have been obvious to some researchers, theorists, and educators in 1965. But Goodman's unique contribution is his insistence that we confront and deal with the complex reality of reading as language and abandon those classroom practices that endure merely on the basis of tradition. If reading is language, then all we know about language learning must be taken into account in the formulation of research questions and paradigms, the development of instructional materials and methods, and the design of evaluation tools.

It was an ambitious undertaking, this confrontation with reality. It forced Goodman over the next three decades to look for insights in fields that had been relatively unexplored by reading educators. He turned first to structural, descriptive linguistics, and found in Charles Fries's (1952) work explanations of the grammatical functions of words within the language system which were useful in the formulation of miscue analysis. Chomsky (1957) helped him understand how readers infer deep structure as they process surface features of text, remaining tentative, flexible, while going beyond the words to construct meaning.

Vygotsky's work in psychology dating from the 1930s was just becoming known in the United States in the 1960s. His theories about the interrelationships between thought and language extended Goodman's understanding of reading as a sociopsycholinguistic process, made easier when learned in the context of its use (1962) and when supported by curriculum that activates zones of proximal development for learners (1978). Goodman was also influenced by Piaget (1971), who held that language is critical in children's development from egocentricity to an objective, socialized, adult point of view. Piaget's conceptualization of assimilation and accommodation in the development of language was useful to Goodman in understanding the tensions between the personal (invention) and social (convention) forces that affect children learning to read and write (Goodman, 1994). More recently, Goodman has also incorporated key concepts from Halliday (1975, 1978), whose systemic-functional linguistics connects to and helps ground Goodman's theory that reading, writing, and written texts are literacy events that cannot be understood apart from the sociocultural contexts in which they exist.

Ferreiro and Teberosky, Piagetian scholars working in Buenos Aires in the 1970s, confirmed Goodman's belief that reading instruction should be grounded in an understanding of learners as "creative, active, and intelligent" rather than "passive, receptive and ignorant" (Ferreiro & Teberosky, 1982, pp. 14, 15). As a result of his pursuit of knowledge generated outside the United States, Goodman was also influenced by Cambourne's (1988) naturalistic theories about both the learning and teaching of literacy, Rosen's theory of the fundamental role of narrative in literacy learning (Rosen & Rosen, 1973), and Margaret Meek's (1988) exploration of how texts teach. Though he was unaware of Clay's (1972) work when he first began studying miscues, her analyses of oral reading behavior from a qualitative, rather than quantitative vantage point supported the underlying premises of miscue analysis.

And, significantly, he discovered the extensive work of Louise Rosenblatt (1938/1976, 1978) who understood that reading is essentially a transactive process, one in which, as Dewey suggested, both the known and the knower are transformed through the experience. Throughout its development, Goodman's model has clearly been transdisciplinary, connecting the insights from several scientific fields of study into an integrated theory, in this case, a transactive sociopsycholinguistic theory of the reading process.

The Psycholinguistic Guessing Game

In 1967, Goodman made the first public presentation of his emerging model of the reading process at the meeting of the American Educational Research Association. The presentation was transformed into an article published later that year by *The Journal of the Reading Specialist*. If any tentativeness could be sensed in the phrasing of his beliefs in the 1965 article, no such interpretation can be drawn here. The article begins:

> As scientific understanding develops in any field of study, preexisting, naive, common sense notions must give way. Such outmoded beliefs clutter the literature dealing with the process of reading. They interfere with the application of modern scientific concepts of language and thought to research in reading. They confuse the attempts at application of such concepts to solutions of problems involved in the teaching and learning of reading. The very fact that such naive beliefs are based on common sense explains their persistent and recurrent nature. To the casual and unsophisticated observer they appear to explain, even predict, a set of phenomena in reading. This paper will deal with one such key misconception and offer a more viable scientific alternative.

> Simply stated, the common sense notion I seek here to refute is this: "Reading is a precise process. It involves exact, detailed, sequential perception and identification of letters, words, spelling patterns and large language units." (p. 126)

What follows these opening paragraphs is the analysis of a series of miscues made by a fourth grader and a first grader. Each miscue is used as evidence to support Goodman's characterization of reading as a psycholinguistic guessing game, a term inspired by Noam Chomsky's description of reading as "tentative information processing" (Goodman, 1994). And as he methodically dismantles the simplistic decoding model of reading, he presents an early version of his model of reading as a psycholinguistic process, based on five years of studying reading using miscue analysis. Certainly others had done error analysis, but because they conceptualized reading as primarily a perceptual task, evaluation of reading proficiency was connected to accuracy—readers either said the word correctly or they did not. Because Goodman conceptualized reading as language, he had to analyze oral reading in a way that revealed the systems of language at work.

Miscue analysis provided the vehicle for that analysis. For every miscue, Goodman analyzed the extent to which the miscue was similar to the expected response in graphophonic and syntactic form (including grammatical function), and whether a similar meaning was being expressed. He described omissions, insertions, substitutions, and reversals. He explored the relationships between miscues and the information in the reader's peripheral field of vision. He noted the extent to which miscues fit portions of sentences (either leading to or following the miscue), but not within the entire sentence or text as a whole. Because dialect variability was believed at the time to adversely affect reading comprehension, he analyzed the extent to which miscues appeared to be influenced by features of the reader's dialect (e.g., sound, vocabulary, and syntactic variations).

He paid attention to what readers do when they make miscues, describing the instances in which they regress, reprocess the language, and overtly make self-corrections. He described complex miscues, in which syntax is transformed by readers who make several interrelated miscues within a single portion of text.

Importantly, every miscue was analyzed with a focus on language: What do we know about language, language learning, and language use that explains what readers are doing and why they are doing it? Relying on the evidence revealed in this careful observation and analysis of what readers were doing within a framework of language use, Goodman crafted his first model of the reading process:

readers, knowledgeable about language and about the world, selectively use cueing systems (graphic, phonic, syntactic, and semantic) and strategies (selecting, predicting, confirming, self-correcting) in a cyclical interaction with text. Goodman (1967) summarizes the theory in this way:

> Reading is a selective process. It involves partial use of available minimal language cues selected from perceptual input on the basis of the reader's expectation. As this partial information is processed, tentative decisions are made to be confirmed, rejected, or refined as reading progresses.
>
> More simply stated, reading is a psycholinguistic guessing game. It involves an interaction between thought and language. Efficient reading does not result from precise perception and identification of all elements, but from skill in selecting the fewest, most productive cues necessary to produce guesses which are right the first time. (pp. 126-127)

The notion of selectivity is critical. Not all cues have equal importance at any one point in the process; not all strategies are useful at any particular juncture. Therefore, Goodman suggests that teachers must design instruction to help readers "select the most productive cues, to use their knowledge of language structure, to draw on their experiences and concepts. They must be helped to discriminate between more and less useful available information" (1967, p. 134). New roles for teachers were being envisioned. After all, if reading and learning to read were being understood in new ways, so must teaching.

Goodman could have titled this article any number of things. But the deliberate choice to call reading a "guessing game" was guaranteed to attract the attention and quite possibly the ire of those who subscribed to the notion that proficient reading was the result of the careful application of a sequence of segmented skills. Surely they would take notice of someone suggesting that such a seemingly haphazard technique as "guessing" was an apt description of what readers do. Of course, Goodman was actually asserting that the rules of the psycholinguistic guessing game are extremely complex, and that we had failed to understand and appreciate the linguistic accomplishment of children who learn to play this guessing game. He closes the article with these words:

> I offer no apologies for the complexity of this model. Its faults lie, not in its complexity, but in the fact that it is not yet complex enough to fully account for the complex phenomena in the actual behavior of readers. But such is man's destiny in his quest for knowledge. Simplistic folklore must give way to complexity as we come to know. (p. 135)

For the next decade, miscue analysis research added considerably to what was known about readers, writers, and their transactions with text. The depth and complexity of that knowledge, based on real readers reading real texts, was beginning in many ways to reach classroom teachers who had found the same dissatisfaction Goodman had in traditional classroom reading instruction and evaluation.

The Miscue Analysis Studies: Windows on the Reading Process

In the years from 1967 until 1978, Goodman and his colleagues at Wayne State University in Detroit, and subsequently at the University of Arizona in Tucson, were supported through major grants by the U.S. Department of Heath, Education, and Welfare and the National Institute of Education to conduct extensive studies of the reading process, utilizing miscue analysis as the primary tool for coming to understand readers' transactions with texts (Goodman, 1968; Goodman & Burke, 1969, 1973; Goodman & Goodman, 1978). Perhaps nowhere else in language education do we find a research instrument and a theory so tightly woven together. Every phenomenon miscue analysis reveals must somehow be explained within Goodman's theory; every aspect of his theory must be examined for its integrity given the evidence in miscue analysis of what readers—all readers—really do.

Much of this work was done using Goodman's Taxonomy of Reading Miscues, a procedure first published by Goodman and Burke in 1973 and refined in subsequent years. In the decade from 1967 to 1978, data were collected from "hundreds of readers reading thousands of pages producing many thousands of miscues and a huge number of bits of data. (As many as 29 decisions were made about each miscue.)" (Goodman, 1992b, pp. 192-193). Throughout these studies, readers were asked to read relatively challenging texts they had not read previously, with no assistance from the teacher/researcher. Readers were told that no help would be given and that at the conclusion of the reading they would be asked to retell what they could remember about the text. A variety of reader response formats have been explored over the years, but oral retellings were used primarily in these early major studies.

The research was focused on Goodman's central question: What happens when we read? But the theory and the research became symbiotic—the analysis of the readers informed his emerging theory about the reading process; and the emerging theory in turn suggested new questions to ask, new approaches for analysis, and new ways of interpreting findings. And, of course, the refinements of the analyses added depth to the theory. Miscue analysis became, in Goodman's metaphor, a "window on the reading process" (1973, p. 3). It has been used to study readers of all ages, with varying linguistic, cultural, and socioeconomic backgrounds, in classrooms with varying methodological emphases, and in both rural and inner-city settings. Those thought to be the most accomplished readers have been studied as have those who describe themselves as illiterate nonreaders, with every conceivable level of proficiency in between (Brown, Marek, & Goodman, 1996).

A less rigorous and time-consuming method for analyzing miscues, the Reading Miscue Inventory (RMI), was formulated by Y. Goodman and Burke in 1972 and revised by Y. Goodman, Watson, and Burke in 1987. The RMI was devised principally as a tool for teacher/researchers to use when evaluating the proficiency of readers and designing relevant strategy lessons, but it has also been widely used as a research tool. In addition to the Taxonomy, there are now four versions of the RMI, each varying in complexity and in the depth of the information produced.

Although the technical aspects of miscue analysis have been modified over time (Y. Goodman & Burke, 1972; Y. Goodman, Watson, & Burke, 1987), Goodman never deviated from his initial assumption that observing and analyzing readers' transactions with texts would be the most useful means through which we could come to understand the process. This kind of sociopsycholinguistic analysis is light years away from the kind of quantitative, pejorative error analysis that dominated the field when Goodman began working in the early 1960s. And although some educators cling to the notion that reading is essentially a word recognition task (Adams, 1990), even those who have criticized aspects of Goodman's work often acknowledge that after hearing a presentation on miscue analysis (based on a real reader reading a real text), they never listened to a child read in the same way again. This phenomenon has been called "growing miscue ears," and those who understand and apply the principles of miscue analysis in their research and teaching have used their miscue ears to develop an extraordinary appreciation for the accomplishments of readers as language users.

This decade of exhaustive research established a solid foundation for Goodman's theory of the reading process. Key findings presented in 1976 include:

> To summarize, what we know of how readers operate is something like this: First of all, more proficient readers make better miscues; they're better miscues not in the sense that we like them but in terms of their effect. They're less likely to produce unacceptable grammar. Furthermore, more proficient readers have an ability to recognize when their miscues need correction. When a reader is correcting a lot of miscues that don't change the meaning and not correcting a lot that do change the meaning, there is a pretty powerful insight that he's

> operating on a wrong model, that in effect he's not very efficient because he's wasting a lot of time trying to achieve accuracy that's unnecessary, while not being able to handle the situation where he loses the meaning.
>
> The difference between more and less proficient readers is not a difference in the reading process but in how well they are able to use it. Our research has made it possible to infer from their miscues the control that readers are exercising over the reading process. It should also provide a basis for instructional procedures designed to improve that control. (Goodman, 1976, p. 70)

A Single Reading Process

What emerges from three decades of research is Goodman's theory that reading is a single process. Readers, writers, and texts vary, but the essential process of reading remains the same. In 1984, Goodman argued for "a unified theory of reading based on theory and research from the past and present in a wide range of fields . . . [integrating] the knowledge that is emerging concerning the reading process, based on the premise that, regardless of differences in vantage point and focus, the phenomena of reading are the same for all who study them" (p. 80). As he explains:

> It is not possible to read without using the strategies and cycles discussed above. It is not possible to read without engaging oneself in a transaction with a text and seeking to make sense of it. These are universal essentials to reading across text types, styles, languages, purposes, and orthographies. Readers develop special strategies and schemata for dealing with different text types, different purposes, different languages with different orthographies. . . .
>
> All this requires flexibility and variability within a single process which has universal characteristics required to make sense of print.
>
> And making sense of print is what reading is all about. (p. 112)

Goodman hoped that the evidence of reading as a single process would compel those in diverse fields to begin working together in transdisciplinary ways in order to make research, instruction, and evaluation more congruent and ultimately more useful. Ten years later he was less confident of that prediction:

> In 1984, I had great hopes that what I saw as an emerging consensus in theory and research on the nature of written language in key fields would lead to more collaboration across disciplines and multidisciplinary agreement on the issues needing exploration. Instead,

> since that time research in some fields has tended to turn away from comprehensive theories and to focus on narrow perspectives within disciplines. (Goodman, 1994, p. 1102)

Goodman goes on to cite a number of discouraging trends. He mentions the rebirth of behaviorism in psychology, which is leading to new kinds of reductionist research. He is frustrated by the willingness of those in artificial intelligence to call what they can teach computers "reading and writing," when in fact they have been unable to teach computers how to read and write in the ways humans can. He criticizes those researchers who use highly reduced language contexts to suggest that some children lack phonemic awareness, despite the fact that as users of oral language, these children necessarily are aware of the significant perceptual sound units of language. He talks about the narrow perspective of some linguists who continue to see oral language as innate and written language as learned in a behavioral way, leading to the conclusion that reading and writing cannot be learned in natural ways. Finally, although he recognizes the importance of children coming to understand and be flexible and strategic in their use of different language genres, he objects to the suggestion that children must be directly taught systemic-functional analysis as a way to impart what are being termed the "genres of power."

And yet he acknowledges that despite these nonproductive lines of research, the knowledge about language and language learning has grown significantly since his work began:

> In the 25 years since I began building a model of the reading process a lot has been learned. Those concerned with literacy and the development of written language have an integrated and increasingly powerful knowledge base about reading, text and writing to draw upon. All of this is meaningless, however, if the knowledge is not shared and used by the professionals whose job it is to help people—particularly young people—become literate. Fortunately, teaching as a profession is coming of age. Not only are teachers aware of and making use of this knowledge base, but they are also taking responsibility for translating it into practical pedagogy and authentic literacy experiences for their pupils. Teachers are not satisfied being told by researchers or by basal textbook authors what to do and when to do it. They are making professional decisions on behalf of their pupils. They are designing curriculum and inventing methodology consistent with the sociopsycholinguistic transactional understanding of literacy processes. Knowledge is being produced at the chalk-face of education, where teachers and pupils confront the realities of teaching and learning. (Goodman, 1994, pp. 1128-1129)

Goodman maintains, "I was, and have remained through all my work, an educationist and a teacher educator . . . my constant motivation has been to understand reading and other language processes in order to contribute to the improvement of teaching and learning" (1982, p. viii). Consistent with this motivation, Goodman has translated volumes of research into insights and applications that continue to inform the classroom decision making of teachers, curriculum developers, reading specialists, and administrators.

Whole Language Teaching

In 1973, Goodman edited a collection of papers based on miscue research entitled "Miscue Analysis: Applications to Reading Instruction." Topics ranged from classroom organization to teacher education; from clinical applications to the development of instructional materials; from non-native speakers of English to students in special education classrooms. In his opening essay, Goodman announced:

> Now we are at a point in our research where we feel we know enough about how reading works that we can share with teachers and other practitioners some of our insights and their implications for reading instruction. Had our research not been reality oriented and rooted in our concern for the practical, this task of translating research into application might have been more difficult. Because we worked with real kids reading real books in real schools, the practical applications of the lessons we have learned and even the research procedures we used are more evident. Everything we know we have learned from kids. Our purpose here is to show our fellow teachers how they also may learn from kids. (p. 3)

"Findings of Research in Miscue Analysis: Classroom Implications" (1976) further describes the application of miscue analysis to reading instruction, both in general terms (designing strategy lessons and materials) and in special areas of investigation (for example, dialect influences, testing, learning disabilities, diagnosis, and readability). Also in 1976, Goodman along with Meredith and Smith published the second edition of *Language and Thinking in Schools*, described as a language-thought centered view of teaching and learning. The purpose of the book was to

> synthesize some modern views of language and linguistics, of literature and semiotics, and of thinking and knowing that are pertinent to education . . . [and] to suggest new views of the teaching of reading,

> writing and the language arts rooted in the best intuitions of the past and strongly based on modern scholarship and research. (1987, p. v)

The third edition, published in 1987, contains what is arguably Goodman's most comprehensive translation of knowledge into practice. It is essential reading for anyone interested in how Goodman envisions classrooms that support language learners—a vision drawn in large part from classrooms already in existence but also drawn from the considerable research base that provides the foundation for a whole language curriculum in which students not only learn to read and write, they read and write to learn.

As teachers and others learned about miscue analysis and other ground-breaking research, they increasingly demanded that reading and language arts curriculum be reinvented. Influenced by Goodman, but also informed by the work of Frank Smith, Carolyn Burke, Yetta Goodman, Dorothy Watson, Jerry Harste, Don Graves, Rudine Sims Bishop, Janet Emig, Don Holdaway, Charlotte Huck, Marie Clay, and others, by the mid-1980s teachers/researchers across the United States and in other countries like Canada, Australia, and New Zealand, were initiating their own classroom revolutions. In the United States, these teachers rejected a basal reader tyranny that systematically denies teachers their rights and obligations to make professional decisions about curriculum and instruction for their students. Years of research had given these teachers a scientific basis on which they could argue against curriculum that conflicted with knowledge about language, language learning, and language evaluation, and they refused to perpetuate what they knew to be misguided practices.

These efforts got a substantial boost in 1988 with the publication of the *Report Card on Basal Readers* by Goodman, Shannon, Freeman, and Murphy. Their study was initiated by the Commission on Reading of the National Council of Teachers of English in order to examine the dominance of basal reading programs in elementary school classrooms. The volume contains a thorough analysis of basal readers and the institutionalized instruction which had resulted from decades of mandatory use of the basal in reading curriculum. Echoes of the implications Goodman posed in earlier decades are found in this piece, but they are much more extensively, and politically, treated. The authors describe the historical development of basal readers as the cornerstone of reading instruction in the United States. The historical context helps us understand why basal readers were considered valuable in assuring that students received consistent and "correct" instruction from teachers who were generally not well educated, in schools that were not well funded, and in a climate that tolerated (even expected, for some students) school failure. But according to the authors, decisions about classroom materials and reading instruction in the 1980s continued to be controlled by a few large publishers, even though the contexts that led to their dominance no longer existed.

In reality, teachers have never been more knowledgeable and professional than they are today. Sources for reading material proliferate, and society now expects a high level of literacy for all citizens, many of whom would have simply been excluded from the school system in earlier times. The *Report Card* makes the following recommendations for immediate policy implementation:

> 1. Teachers should not be required to use any program they find professionally objectionable.
> 2. No adoption of any basal should exclude the possibility of teachers modifying its use or using alternate materials and methods.
> 3. Publishers should immediately discontinue the practice of revising and censoring selections from children's literature.
> 4. Publishers should change the way teachers are treated in teachers' manuals of basals. They should be addressed as professionals and be supported in their exercise of professional judgment.
> 5. School authorities should establish criteria for reading instructional materials and make no adoptions if materials offered do not meet their criteria.
> 6. In all aspects of development, selection, and use of basals and alternate methods and materials the needs and welfare of students must be placed above all other considerations.
> 7. School authorities, legislatures, foundations, professional organizations, and others should encourage innovation within and without basals through funding research and experimental programs in schools. (Goodman et al., 1988, p. 153)

Many of these recommendations were implemented in school districts across the United States, probably more often the result of pressure brought by teachers and parents than as a direct result of the *Report Card* itself. By 1994, Goodman was encouraged by what he saw as the influence of knowledgeable teachers on the content of published materials for teaching and assessing reading:

> The knowledge is now so widely shared and implemented that it has shaken the foundations of two of the educational institutions most resistant to change and new knowledge: the textbook-publishing and test-publishing industries. Both are aware that teachers are so knowledgeable that they will no longer accept the old basals and the old tests. (pp. 1128-1129)

For the past 20 years, whole language teachers have found support for their knowledge, beliefs, and practices in Kenneth Goodman's research and theories. One might think that the complexity of his model of the reading process would seem overwhelming and irrelevant to classroom teachers, but in fact the opposite is true. Because Goodman's work has been based on the study of real readers, reading real texts, his observations and interpretations resonate among teachers who are also keen observers of students as language users. They are insulted by oversimplification of what they know to be complicated issues, and they actively seek the work of those willing to confront the complex reality of helping students become more proficient readers. Goodman makes sense to teachers who are trying to make sense of reading.

MOVING FORWARD

In a career that has now moved into its fourth decade, Goodman continues in his writing and speaking to confront issues which keep him at the center of much debate. In the *Whole Language Catalog* (1991), Goodman, Bridges Bird, and Y. Goodman edited an ambitious collection of theory, research, anecdotes, ideas, evaluations, practical tips, and much much more, all intended as a professional resource for whole language educators. But it is not organized like a typical curriculum guide, and by its very design and content the book frustrates teachers who want to be told "what to do on Monday morning." The resources in the *Catalog* simply cannot be understood from that vantage point. In *I Didn't Found Whole Language* (1992b), Goodman denounces the portrayal of him as a cult leader of whole language fanatics—and he does so by pointing out, among other things, that this characterization is singularly degrading to whole language teachers who are knowledgeable professionals and who selectively find elements of his work that are useful to them in their own work. *Phonics Phacts* (Goodman, 1993) examines the linguistic aspects of the graphophonic features of text and makes a scientific, reasoned argument for the role of developing students' knowledge about phonics within a whole language paradigm—a construct no doubt surprising to those who have simplistically assumed that whole language and phonics are mutually exclusive terms.

Goodman has recently completed a book that in some sense brings him full circle. Titled *Ken Goodman On Reading* (1996), it frames the issues in reading in ways he has always framed them: based on sound theory, supported by research, validated by the real experiences of teachers and readers, and aggressively challenging instruction and evaluation that ignore what we know about reading. He has been writing this book for nearly 20 years, continuing to cycle back through the manuscript draft, revisit the conceptual framework, and update the theory and research. Given what Goodman believes about the construction of multiple texts, it is interesting to imagine how many texts of this work have existed in his mind and how many interpretations will be made of the text that is published. Clearly, it is a book that was eagerly anticipated by those whose own work as language educators has for years been enriched and stimulated by Goodman. For new professionals, it may be their first experience seeing the issues through Ken Goodman's eyes, and whether they agree or disagree with his views, it will doubtless have an impact. It is a book whose time has come.

I recently attended a Town Hall meeting in my local community, sponsored by the State Department of Education, and designed to gather community input into the State's efforts to participate in the national Goals 2000 initiative. On a chilly January night, I met a number of earnest and well-prepared folks who oppose any efforts to establish national or state standards for education, believing instead that such matters are properly the purview of local officials who must answer to local parental voices and votes. (Goodman opposes these standards as well, but for somewhat different reasons, see Goodman, 1995a.) Their opposition to Goals 2000 is two-fold: They object to the process of state planning that derives from federal legislation, in which parents are only tangentially involved in decision making. They also object to the content they anticipate will be present in such plans: values clarification, multicultural exploration, sex education, and, indeed, whole language. Some of these folks could be dismissed as extremists who are the carefully rehearsed mouthpieces of the Eagle Forum and other far-right naysayers in the current educational reform movement. But some of what they have to say cannot be so easily ignored—that schools must be safe places from which children and young adults emerge as competent learners who possess the knowledge and skills necessary to be responsible, productive citizens in a democracy. They are suspicious of what they describe as the current cop-out mentality among educators and bureaucrats: Because students do not do well on tests, the tests must be invalid; because students do not know how to add, computation skills are trivial; because students do not know who George Washington was, it is more important to know how to find out. One of the women I met at this meeting loaned me a videotape of a lecturer ostensibly speaking to a group of parents and teachers, blaming whole language and other so-called progressive education movements for the decline of intellect, morality, and discipline among young people in the United States today. She wanted my reaction to the film and some days later I shared it, although I doubted it would have much impact. I told her I never taught reading the way the video demonstrated it is taught in whole language classrooms and even went so far as to show her why one of the video presenter's examples was fallacious. But arguing the points of the film seemed a shallow, combative posture to take; and clearly sending her an article or two by Kenneth Goodman was not likely to have the result I wanted either. This woman had been told a great deal about what is wrong with whole language, via newsletters, talk radio, and other seductively simplistic media presentations. I decided that the only possible way to balance that scale was to encourage her to visit and discover first-hand what a whole language classroom is really like—what students in that kind of supportive, rich environment actually know and are able to do. Children have the power and potential to influence her, even if I do not.

This is not an isolated incident. Political leaders in California are in the midst of attempting to dismantle its holistically oriented language arts framework, accusing the framework and whole language in general of causing the perceived decline in reading and spelling achievement test scores (Goodman, 1995b). In Arizona, the Governor has recently called for the abolishment of the state board of education and the process for licensing teachers, urging a return to local control over educational decision making (Arizona Daily Star, September 29, 1995). Similar controversies are emerging, and similar battles are being waged in towns, cities, and states throughout the United States.

And so it occurs to me that as we move for a period of time into a conservative, back-to-basics orientation in educational politics, the influence of Goodman will be felt as he described, at the chalk-face, through teachers who are more informed about language and language learning than ever before, and who express that knowledge with clarity to colleagues, parents, community members, and, indeed, students themselves. If we are, in fact, in the midst of a sea change, one that will find more control of education at the school building level, then whole language teachers will be well positioned to influence the continuing debate. There has never been a time when teachers were more able, more willing to assume that role. Theirs are the voices that will be heard, theirs is the influence that will endure, and Kenneth Goodman will smile softly and nod.

REFERENCES

Adams, M. J. (1990). *Beginning to read: Thinking and learning about print.* Cambridge, MA: MIT Press.

Brown, J., Marek, A., and Goodman, K. S. (1996). *An annotated chronological bibliography of miscue analysis.* Newark, DE: International Reading Association.

Cambourne, B. (1988). *The whole story.* Sydney, Australia: Ashton Scholastic.

Chomsky, N. (1957). *Syntactic structures.* The Hague, Netherlands: Mouton.

Clay, M. (1972). *Reading: The patterning of complex behaviour.* Auckland, New Zealand: Heinemann Educational Books.

Edelsky, C., & Smith, K. (1984). Is that writing—Or are those marks just a figment of your curriculum? *Language Arts, 61*(1), 24-32.

Ferreiro, E., & Teberosky, A. (1982). *Literacy before schooling.* Exeter, NH: Heinemann.

Fries, C. (1952). *The structure of English.* New York: Harcourt Brace.

Goodman, K. S. (1965). A linguistic study of cues and miscues in reading. *Elementary English, 42*(6), 639-643.

Goodman, K. S. (1967). Reading: A psycholinguistic guessing game. *The Journal of the Reading Specialist, 6*(4), 126-135.

Goodman, K. S. (1968). *Study of children's behavior while reading orally* [Contract No. OE-6-10-136]. Washington, DC: U.S. Department of Health, Education and Welfare.

Goodman, K. S. (1973). Miscues: Windows on the reading process. In K. S. Goodman (Ed.), *Miscue analysis: Applications to reading instruction* (pp. 3-14). Urbana, IL: ERIC and the National Council of Teachers of English.

Goodman, K. S. (1976). What we know About reading. In P. D. Allen & D. Watson (Eds.), *Findings of research in miscue analysis: Classroom implications* (pp. 57-69). Urbana, IL: ERIC and National Council of Teachers of English.

Goodman, K. S. (1982). Foreword. In F. V. Gollasch (Ed.), *Language and literacy. The selected writings of Kenneth S. Goodman, Volume I. Process, theory, research* (pp. vii-ix). Boston, MA: Routledge & Kegan Paul.

Goodman, K. S. (1984). Unity in reading. In A. C. Purves & O. Niles (Eds.), *Becoming readers in a complex society* (83rd yearbook of the National Society for the Study of Education, Part I, pp. 79-114). Chicago, IL: University of Chicago Press.

Goodman, K. S. (1992a, November). *Reading as a psycholinguistic guessing game: 25 years later.* Presentation at the National Council of Teachers of English Annual Convention, Louisville, KY.

Goodman, K. S. (1992b). I didn't found whole language. *The Reading Teacher, 46*(2), 188-199.

Goodman, K. S. (1993). *Phonics phacts.* Portsmouth, NH: Heinemann.

Goodman, K. S. (1994). Reading, writing, and written texts: A transactional socio-psycholinguistic view. In R. B. Ruddell, M. R. Ruddell, & H. Singer (Eds.), *Theoretical models and processes of reading* (pp. 1093-1130). Newark, DE: International Reading Association.

Goodman, K. S. (1995a). *Standards—NOT!* Unpublished manuscript. University of Arizona, Tucson.

Goodman, K. S. (1995b). The report of the California Reading Task Force: Forced choices in a non-crisis. *Fax Sheets for the Press on Whole Language,* No. 3. University of Arizona, Tucson.

Goodman, K. S. (1996). *Ken Goodman on reading.* Richmond Hill, Ontario: Scholastic Canada & Portsmouth, NH: Heinemann.

Goodman, K. S., Bridges Bird, L., & Goodman, Y. M. (1991). *The whole language catalog.* Santa Rosa, CA: American School Publishers.

Goodman, K. S., & Burke, C. L. (1969). *A study of oral reading miscues that result in grammatical retransformations* [Contract No. OEG-0-8-070219-2806 (0101)]. Washington, DC: U.S. Department of Health, Education and Welfare.

Goodman, K. S., & Burke, C. L. (1973). *Theoretically based studies of patterns of miscues in oral reading performance* [U.S.O.E. Project No. 90375. Grant No. OEG-09-320375-4269]. Washington, DC: U.S. Department of Health, Education, and Welfare.

Goodman, K. S., & Goodman, Y. M. (1978). *Reading of American children whose language is a stable rural dialect of English or a language other than English* [Final Report, Project NIE-C-00-3-0087]. Washington, DC: National Institute of Education.

Goodman, K. S., & Goodman, Y. M. (1979). Learning to read is natural. In L. B. Resnick & P. A. Weaver (Eds.), *Theory and practice of early reading* (pp. 137-55). Hillsdale, NJ: Erlbaum.

Goodman, K. S., Shannon, P., Freeman, Y.S., & Murphy, S. (1988). *Report card on basal readers.* Katonah, NY: Richard C. Owen Publishers.

Goodman, K., Smith, E. B., & Meredith, R. (1976). *Language and thinking in school* (2nd ed.). New York: Holt, Rinehart & Winston.

Goodman, K., Smith, E. B., Meredith, R., & Goodman, Y. M. (1987). *Language and thinking in school.* (3rd ed.). Katonah, NY: Richard C. Owen Publishers.

Goodman, Y. M., & Burke, C. L. (1972). *RMI Manual. Procedures for diagnosis and evaluation.* Katonah, NY: Richard C. Owen Publishers.

Goodman, Y. M., Watson, D. J., & Burke, C. L. (1987). *Reading miscue inventory: Alternative procedures.* Katonah, NY: Richard C. Owen Publishers.

Halliday, M. A. K. (1975). *Learning how to mean: Explorations in the development of language.* London: Edward Arnold.

Halliday, M. A. K. (1978). *Language as social semiotic: The social interpretation of language and meaning.* London: Edward Arnold.

Meek, M. (1988). *How texts teach what readers learn.* England: The Thimble Press.

Nicholson, T., Lillas, C., & Rzoska, M. A. (1988). Have we been misled by miscues? *The Reading Teacher, 42,* 6-10.

Piaget, J. (1971). *Psychology and epistemology.* New York: Grossman.

Rosen, C., & Rosen, H. (1973). *The language of primary school children.* Baltimore: Penguin Press.

Rosenblatt, L. M. (1976). *Literature as exploration.* New York: The Modern Language Association of America. (Original work published 1938)

Rosenblatt, L. M. (1978). *The reader, the text, the poem.* Carbondale: Southern Illinois University Press.

Spache, G. (1964). *Reading in the elementary school.* Boston, MA: Allyn and Bacon.

Vygotsky, L. S. (1962). *Thought and language.* Cambridge, MA: MIT Press.

Vygotsky, L. S. (1978). *Mind in society.* Cambridge, MA: Harvard University Press.

Chapter Three

A Whole Language Journey: Are We There Yet?

Dorothy Watson
University of Missouri-Columbia

FIRST STEPS AND FIRST GUIDE

After a day of watching kids and teachers skirmish with flashcards, workbooks, Sullivan Readers, tachistoscopes, SRA kits, phonics drills, reading groups, and each other, Dave Allen and I settled into an inner-Kansas City coffee shop for a rehash of our school visits. It was 1969. Dave was a new University of Missouri-Kansas City faculty member, and I was the director of the Teacher Corps Program. Our conversation that October afternoon, to put it mildly, challenged my thinking and, as we say, changed my life.

Dave Allen was my first whole language guide. Generous to a fault, he (and the 1960s) prepared me for a professional journey that has not come to an end after three decades of exploring, searching for the/a path, getting side-tracked again and again, and learning from both the sure and the wobbly steps taken along the way to a philosophy built on mutually supportive practices, theories, and beliefs.

It did not take long to notice that Dave was not a traditional academic. The Teacher Corps interns and I kept running into him not at the university but at school board sessions, voter registration campaigns, fair housing meetings, and civil rights rallies. Dave loved to talk with students for hours on end about things that were urgent and important in those intense and insecure times. I began to pay attention to their conversations when the interns reported that this man had some "mind-blowing" ideas and "totally heavy" beliefs about schooling in general and reading in particular. Not that I cared to admit it, but I had a gut feeling that our program in reading education was way off the mark despite the hard work of dedicated interns who did every skill and drill exercise in the teacher's manuals and sat up nights constructing even more practice sheets. In truth, we were ready for Dave and his mind-blowing ideas and totally heavy beliefs.

Sometime during our first talk (at which I took three pages of notes that I referred to for months), Dave suggested that I do a couple of things. First, he made me think about kids I had taught for almost a decade in both the inner- and outer-city, kids who were school-advantaged and kids who were school-disadvantaged. Then he told me I desperately (Dave tended to emphasize his points with scary language) needed to study with two people at Wayne State University. One was Brooks Smith, who had a vision about curriculum that included the lives of all learners, and the other was Ken Goodman, whose revolutionary ideas about the reading process, readers, and reading instruction had inspired and shaped Dave's own work.

Once, preparing for a workshop for Vista volunteers and Teacher Corps interns, Dave handed me Ken's article "A Linguistic Study of Cues and Miscues in Reading" (1965). He told me that the report was different from the professional articles I was accustomed to reading: Not only had Ken presented his findings, but he had also pointed out practices in the teaching of reading that his research rendered suspect. In that first publication based on miscue research findings, Ken reported that first-, second-, and third-graders did a better job of reading words when those words were in a meaningful text than when they were on a list with no supporting text. He also said that when a reader regressed it was usually to make a correction and that regressing was a natural part of the reading process. With those two ideas in mind, Dave made me think about the kids we saw day in and day out. My reactions were typical of other teachers when we grasp one of Ken's ideas: "That's true!, He's right," and "I, of course, suspected it all along." Two questions followed: "Why hasn't someone pointed this out before?" and "Why doesn't my curriculum reflect these insights?"

ONCE UPON A JOURNEY IN A VERY SPECIAL PLACE

They forgot to build an ivory tower at Wayne State. Brooks sent us to theaters, churches, museums, movies, and community festivals; Ken sent us out to hear real kids read real stories. In his own way (demonstration), Ken asked us to close our mouths, open our ears, and listen to readers as we had never listened before. What is more, when the kids finished reading, we were not to stick to the routine of asking them to answer our questions; rather, we asked them to talk about what they had constructed from the story. Readers became our informants—not teacher's manuals, not standardized test scores, and not jargon and labels (like, "He's a word-bound, lazy, disabled nonreader").

When I interviewed for an assistantship at the Miscue Center, Ken warned that I might find miscue analysis tedious and boring. Then he showed me what a second-grade reader did with an improbable story about a kitten winning a photography contest and I thought, "This man has just contradicted himself." I think Ken knew that "Kitten Jones" might put readers (and researchers) to sleep, but what kids did with it would never be boring. Although I had taught for years, this was the first time I became completely engrossed in what readers were trying to do as they navigated their way through texts; it was the first time I thought of myself as the learner and the student as the teacher. Suddenly I had more whole language guides—young readers.

After we once put on our "miscue ears" we never ever listened to kids read in the same way again. (I am not sure who coined "miscue ears" and "miscuteers," but I wager it was Ken, Dave, or Dorothy Menosky.) Miscue analysis showed us that we could not attribute all failures to the reader. We learned that kids were sometimes unintentionally misled by the author's language or even by their own knowledge and experiences, and as a result read something unexpected. Kids showed us they could do astonishing things with every cue that language and the context of language had to offer. They showed us that they were smart and could construct meaning when language was whole, and that when it was in bits and pieces they got lost, bored, frustrated, and often did not look smart at all.

The Reading Miscue Center at Wayne State, directed by Ken, was funded first by the U.S. Office of Education Bureau of Research and later by the National Institute of Education. Carolyn Burke served as the first associate director of the miscue research project while focusing on her own study of young readers' uses of grammatical structures (Burke, 1969). Even in the early years of the Center, inquiry into the reading process was centered not only on Ken's work but on, to name a few, Allen's (1969) study of substitution miscues; Page's (1970) look into second-, fourth- and sixth-grade students reading a range of basal reader selections; Gutknecht's (1971) miscue analysis of kids identified as perceptually handicapped; Carlson's (1970) description of fourth-graders reading content materials; Sims' (1972) study of miscues made by youngsters reading Black dialect and Standard English; Martellock's (1971) focus on middle school readers; Menosky's (1971) inquiry into the differences and similarities in miscues that readers made throughout varying portions of text; and Rousch's (1972) investigation into the relationship between the reader's prior knowledge, miscues, silent reading, and retellings. During this time, Smith and Lindberg evaluated Scott, Foresman's Reading Systems (Aaron et al., 1972) through miscue theory in order to determine the suitability of the materials for their intended readers. Although not part of the Miscue Center studies, Yetta Goodman's (1971) investigation of six children as they learned to read across a six-year period contributed to our understanding of the reading process.

My dissertation study (Watson, 1973) combined miscue analysis with an instructional procedure we called strategy lessons and with the use of a controversial artifact not widely accepted in schools at that time—paperback books. I studied the miscues made by kids who were involved in strategy lessons in a school flooded with paperbacks. Yetta helped me with workshops for the teachers, and Ivan Ludington (more later) of Ludington Press in Detroit provided the books. This may have been the first formal study that involved miscue analysis, strategy lessons, and real books as a major part of the curriculum.

Before Ken introduced me to him, all I knew about Ivan Ludington was that he had sponsored Dan Fader's work that resulted in *Hooked on Books* (Fader & McNeil, 1968) and *The Naked Children* (Fader, 1971). I was all set to meet a shrewd businessman who saw the monetary future of paperbacks but knew he needed to partner with people in education like Dan and Ken. I was not prepared for Ludington's astonishing generosity, humanity, and good sense when it came to kids who needed literature in their lives. I do not know how Ken managed it, but before I had time to worry about my dissertation research topic, I was in Ludington's warehouse piling books into grocery carts to be taken to Garden City Elementary School.

Ivan Ludington was not one to give away books and then ignore how they were used; he insisted on meeting with me weekly to hear how the kids liked the books, what the teachers were doing with them (he was death on book reports and "those di-o-gram-uz"), and where the books were placed. He wanted them in the halls, in the gym, and in the principal's and nurse's offices, as well as in the Ludington Reading Room and library. When it came to books and reading, Ludington did not mince words. When I told him that the teachers and I were afraid the kids might make off with those convenient pocket-size books, he said, "So? If they steal them maybe someone at home will read too. Now wouldn't that be dandy if we got a whole nest of birds with one little paperback!" The last time I saw him he wished me well and said he had something important to tell me. I was sure it was that my research would advance literacy immeasurably: "You know, Dorothy, your dissertation is the only hardback book that's ever been in this office!" I apologized, promised never to do it again, and left with an arm load of "too good to miss" *paperbacks*. Ivan Ludington, "bookman," was the first in the meager ranks of publishers and sellers to join us on the whole language journey.

The studies that came out of the Miscue Center during this early period explored inexhaustible components of the reading process and reflected a wide range of interests among the researchers, but one intriguing concept pulled us all together. That enticing word psycholinguistics appeared in the title of almost every dissertation, report, and article, and it made a statement: Here is a new and compelling perspective on reading. Individually, we had no idea where the findings would lead; collectively (as we studied each other's work) we sensed that we were on the creative edge of something significant in literacy education.

The Miscue Center was a thinking place, a talking place, a community founded on professionally important ideas and maintained by the unforgettable times that good friends create. Here I was joined and supported by colleagues and friends along the path leading to whole language.

Like other families, the miscuteers emerged with jokes, stories, and one-liners. We loved to tell about Yetta looking up from a fourth-grader's typescript and asking, "What does a horse do in the past tense?" Or, when she got us all to the window to see the lawn sculpture at the Detroit Museum of Art with, "Wow, have you seen the huge erection on the gallery lawn?" Seldom do any of us talk about the influence of schema and prior knowledge without telling about Peter Rousch's incredulous discovery that there existed in America a red bird called a cardinal. Peter, from Australia where there are no such birds, figured that the bright child who substituted cardinal for canary in a story called "Space Pet" did so because she had in mind an ecclesiastical cardinal clad in a colorful mantel ascending (flying) into heaven (space). We also remember the campus delivery man who managed to outrage us with his racial, cultural, and gender innuendoes, and then dismiss his own behavior with a wink at Peter Rousch (Australian) and Merv Thornton (Canadian) and a confidential stage whisper, "Only in the good ole' U.S.A. can men express themselves!"

Ken's evening classes met from 4:00 to 8:00 and, to put it mildly, they were different in both content and procedure from any I had experienced in my years of theater-style schooling. Each class session started with Ken and students sharing and exploring new information, followed with questions and concerns, then off to dinner in small bunches to dig into topics from every perspective the group members' backgrounds allowed, and finally back to class to share our ideas and to form our next questions. I cannot help but smile when I compare the classes I teach today with those I had with Ken and Brooks. There are the same response cards (now, exit cards and minute memos), the same emphasis on talk (now, say something and interest/action groups), the same questioning (now, inquiry and problem posing), and the same need to nourish the body as well as the mind (as always, food).

My very first study group was SALE (Seminar in the Application of Linguistics in Education). Organized by Yetta and Ken, it was made up of faculty and students from Wayne State and the University of Michigan, as well as public school people, for the purpose of exploring language and its relationship to learning and teaching. Within that group and other Wayne State study groups, there was always someone willing to explore language, learning, and curriculum with you. Remarkably, faculty and students alike considered each other's works to be as important and valuable as any noted theorist or researcher. It was exciting and humbling to have your study talked about at the same meeting in which the ideas of Noam Chomsky, Frank Smith, Michael Halliday, Roger Shuy, and Ron Wardaugh were studied. I think of SALE as the parent of CELT (Center for the Expansion of Language and Thinking), a group of educators from the United States, Canada, Australia, and Venezuela, dedicated to the study and promotion of sociopsycholinguistic endeavors in schools.

Last, but not the least of the experiences that pushed our thinking at Wayne State, were the lunch talks and Miscue Center staff meetings. Those exploratory discussions were as informative and supportive as any professional seminar. (They also were as argumentative, disorderly, and side-splitting as any neighborhood pub gathering.) A typical "discussion" often began with someone writing a miscue on the board and defying the group to figure out the psycholinguistic involvement, as well as the marking and coding. After interminable theories were put forward we came to a hard-fought decision. When someone once suggested that we have a show of hands about the marking of a particularly difficult miscue, Ken crushed the idea with, "Sorry, but we can't vote on reality." Sheepishly, we returned to our "deliberations" and after what seemed hours, agreed on the marking and coding of the troublesome miscue. (Dorothy Menosky then made everyone sign a statement that we would not change our minds. That important document may still exist in the Miscue Center archives.)

TEACHERS AS TEACHERS, GUIDES, AND TRAVELING COMPANIONS

Genuine groups, teams, and partners have always been important in my life. Early on for me, there were Girl Scouts, the School Audubon Society, and the after-school School that at the age of nine I organized and appointed myself Teacher. So when CELT members began talking about teacher support groups, I remembered those glorious experiences and knew that if teachers got together, they would learn as I had from conversations with Dave and from my Audubon bird buddies and the After-school School. It happened. With encouragement from CELT members and on their own initiative, teachers across the country began to talk seriously about what was happening in their classrooms. It was the beginning of a grassroots, pedagogical transformation that spun out some remarkable insights about learners, learning, language, literature, curriculum, and teaching.

Along with hundreds of questions that teachers began to ask about their practices, they opened their basal readers and language arts manuals and asked, "Who are these people who tell us reading is mastering one skill after another? What are those skills anyway? How did they get 'scientifically' arranged in a 'necessary-for-mastery' hierarchy?" When teachers began to doubt the credibility of self-appointed pundits, they asked, "Who can we trust?" Ken urged us to cast our lot with students and with teachers (1971, 1974). Miscue analysis had contributed to teachers placing students at the heart of the curriculum; now teachers were encouraged to place themselves there, too.

Teachers were hungry for conversation. They wanted to talk about their new-found trust in themselves, in their colleagues, and in their students. In order to hear about their own practices and beliefs, teachers began to meet in small groups; TAWL (Teachers Applying (or Attempting) Whole Language) became a reality. As a point of historical interest, the first groups (notice the plural) were formed around 1978 in Tucson with Yetta and Ken as sponsors; at Sonoma State University with Jayne DeLawter as sponsor; in Oneonta, NY with Chalmers Means as sponsor; and in Columbia, MO, with teachers including Kittye Copeland, Sharon Hoge, Pat Jenkins, Jane Decker, and me.

Although I like to, and often do, give Mid-Missouri TAWL credit for starting the first group, in truth the exact beginning date is unclear. The reasons for our fuzzy history are many, but one is that we did not dream that a hand-full of teachers in Missouri, California, New York, and Arizona could possibly make such a deep and profound impression on the shape and dimension of literacy education. Therefore, we did not carefully chronicle our dates, procedures, successes, and failures. We do, however, remember those first meetings. Typically, at early TAWL meetings we shared examples of students' work and then talked about successful teaching strategies. The conversations were about teaching and the artifacts shared were thought to be products of that teaching. Gradually, learning rather than teaching became the focus of TAWL talk. Fresh and exciting learning places were described and defined. Teachers saw a change in their earlier roles of controller, counter, and the one and only source of knowledge. Now they saw their roles as facilitator, coach, one of many resources and researcher. I remember the first time I heard a teacher refer to herself as the learner and to her students as teachers and informants. Instead of someone outside the classroom telling how to teach, educators made pedagogical decisions based on both what they trusted about learning theory and on evidence gained daily from learners. Over time, teachers continued to share generously with each other at TAWL meetings, but it became increasingly evident that what they shared came from students and themselves standing hand-in-hand at the center of the new classroom constructing something that made sense to all its creators.

Classroom teachers became valued resources, first at local TAWL groups, then at small conferences put on by their own group, and finally they were sought after to speak at state, national, and international conferences. They were paid attention to not only by other TAWL members, but by theorists, researchers, parents, and administrators. Several years ago, a young first-grade teacher, a founding member of Mid-Missouri TAWL, told me that her knees almost buckled when she saw Ken Goodman in her audience at a national conference. To add to her distress, he took notes during her presentation. She asked if I thought he was making a grocery list or if she could possibly have said something he valued enough to jot down. I told her he might have been making a grocery list but not to be surprised if some day, at one of Ken's presentations or in an article, she heard or read a reference to her, her students, and her teaching. Despite my warning, that teacher, Kittye Copeland, past-president of NCTE's Whole Language Assembly, a Nila Banton Award winner, current president of the Whole Language Umbrella, and author of numerous articles about whole language, was surprised when it happened. I have learned while on this very long trek called whole language that leaders and followers often do something that is not expected on other journeys—they (students, teachers, theorists, researchers) change roles.

DUMPING THE UPTIGHT MODELS: IN READING, LANGUAGE, AND CURRICULUM

I think it was a calculated choice on Ken's part that the first two questions of the Miscue Taxonomy (Goodman & Burke, 1973) had to do with self-correction and dialect involvement (Does the reader correct the miscue? Is the reader's dialect involved in the miscue?) The *Reading Miscue Inventory: Alternative Procedures* (Goodman, Watson, & Burke, 1987) continues to value that information. These two questions help teachers challenge a model of reading that rewards only immediate and total accuracy and attempts to standardize the language of nonstandardizable kids. The uptight reading model fits with an uptight view of language, and both go hand-in-glove with an uptight concept of curriculum.

Whole language teachers no longer trusted a curriculum presented as a mandate to be rigidly followed. Through inquiry and talk, teachers began to conceptualize curriculum as "everything that genuinely supports learning." Curriculum needed to be flexible, appropriate, and owned by the learners. Teachers searched for the curricular relationships among reading, writing, listening, and speaking; they were concerned about the subject territories that disconnected the knowledge of science, math, and social studies from one another as well as from life and from language. Teachers searched for the curricular connections that led beyond simply meeting objectives, adhering to standards, or gaining competencies. The link to the relationships and connections between all the language arts/acts and the knowledge domains was something that Ken invited us to embrace—a spirit of inquiry. Teachers wrapped up in the life and culture of their classrooms not only pursued their own professional inquiry, but they also invited kids to do the same: to pose and solve problems, to inquire, to research their real questions.

TAWL teachers, through their inquiry, led the way into the study of countless conventional procedures including the use of endless worksheets, blue-bird grouping, traditional spelling programs, single-text sources, drill learning, and formula teaching. As these teachers questioned practices, they also advocated cross-age grouping, talking and writing to learn, literature study, collaborative work, multiple ways of knowing, learner ownership, and communities of scholars. But their particular influence on assessment and evaluation deserves special comment. Unlike conventional procedures, miscue analysis put the learner at the center, focused on the process without neglecting the product, and it informed the student, teacher, and curriculum. Using miscue analysis as a guide, teachers concluded that all evaluation must value language and the learner by maintaining the integrity of both. Teachers told us that evaluation as part of the curriculum must not be competitive; when it was, it destroyed both the spirit of classroom community and learner risk taking. Rather, evaluation needed to be learner-referenced, that is, the only comparisons made should be between what a student does at one time and what that same student does over time. Teachers found continuous self-evaluation to be crucial; in fact, they found that authentic learning could not happen without it. They found that whole language evaluation made everyone involved more, not less, human.

When whole language settled into classrooms, many outsiders began to label and evaluate the phenomenon. To the surprise of many of those outside the whole language community, TAWL teachers were unwilling to relinquish their right to define themselves and describe their own work. Rather, they began to clarify, deepen, and present to all who would listen their concepts of whole language. Early on, for many of us, whole language was defined primarily as a linguistic perspective on literacy. The term reminded us not to disjoin the semantic, syntactic, graphophonic, and pragmatic cues of language when reading. That view continues to be extremely important, especially when we explain what whole language is to novices or detractors. But that perspective was only a beginning. Teachers deepened the concept to include holistic beliefs about all learners (students and teachers), the acts of learning and teaching, a redefinition of what knowledge is, and curriculum. Finally, Carole Edelsky, Patrick Shannon, Bess Altwerger, Barbara Flores, and Frank Smith joined Ken in helping TAWL teachers extend the concept of whole language to include Paulo Freire's (1979) "liberating dream"—to the reality that education is political. These theorists helped teachers proclaim that they teach for all learners inside the classroom and advocate for all learners outside the classroom.

OPENING THE WHOLE LANGUAGE UMBRELLA

A small group of teachers who met informally at NCTE and IRA over a period of two years suggested to Ken that an international group of teachers needed to be formed in order to share ideas and provide support for their work. Inquiry into the political nature of whole language along with increasing politicizing of whole language teachers (in response, in part, to attacks from the Far Right) were additional contributing factors to the founding of an umbrella organization. In summer 1988, 15 educators gathered in Tucson to draft the Whole Language Umbrella (WLU) Constitution that was ratified February 18, 1989, in Winnipeg. I was elected the first president of WLU; because of his contributions and courage, Ken Goodman was named the first WLU past-president.

The elected leaders of this new and spirited group proposed that through networking they would improve learning and teaching at all levels of education in at least four ways: (a) by encouraging the study of whole language philosophy through TAWL, school staff development, and teacher education; (b) by promoting research and critiquing whole language curricula and programs; (c) by publicizing and disseminating whole language information to anyone or any group interested; and (d) by facilitating collaborative whole language work among teachers, researchers, parents, administrators, and teacher educators. To insure that these resolutions had backbone, the WLU constitution stipulated that a goal of the organization was to support and define educators who were unfairly attacked in their attempts to promote whole language philosophy.

The spirit and shape of the WLU Constitution came from whole language teachers across the country, represented by the 15 teachers who met in Tucson and by the first WLU board. The final synthesis and articulation of the constitution was completed under the leadership of Norma Mickelson and Ken.

The members of WLU made it clear that no individual or group should ever be subjected to a loyalty test as a prerequisite for calling themselves whole language teachers or for joining either a TAWL group or WLU. However, the following tenets were considered to be held by whole language educators and are a part of the WLU Constitution. Whole language teachers believe that:

- Language is central to learning;
- Learning is easiest when it is from whole to part, in authentic contexts, and useful;
- Learning is both personal and social, and the most supportive classrooms are learning communities; and
- Learning is joyful and fulfilling.

Further, whole language teachers hold:

- Positive attitudes about all learners, and
- Holistic views of literacy learning and teaching.

Finally, whole language teachers work for the:

- Empowerment of all learners, including students and teachers; and
- Acceptance of whole learners including their languages, cultures, and experiences.

TWO COMMUNITIES OF LEARNERS

A few years ago I left my university classroom to visit the classrooms of educators who were not only good teachers (they walked the walk and talked the talk of whole language), but they understood the scholarship of teaching (they sang the songs and danced the dances of whole language). I stayed a week with each teacher. At the close of the school day, the teacher and I talked through dinner and into the night about the unbelievable number of connections and creations learners made that day. Those inspired and inspiring teachers helped me see the forest as well as the trees, and as I did I came to understand what they referred to as their two communities of learners: their classrooms and their teacher support groups. During my stay, every teacher took me to a TAWL meeting at which the teachers shared, asked their own questions, and explored ideas and artifacts. As a visitor to their whole language classrooms and to their TAWL meetings I sensed commonalties in the two communities. In each setting I saw evidence of commitment and risk taking, flexibility about time, reflection, a spirit of inquiry, changed roles, and scholarship.

Commitment and Risk Taking

It is impossible to create, with youngsters or educators, a community of learners without having genuine commitment on the part of at least one person. Teachers who stick their necks out to make the "liberating dream" come to life must know that they are in a vulnerable position. It is chancy inviting kids or adults into a democratic social order in which they are expected to establish their own boundaries and create their own rules and celebrations. We have not been schooled to collaborate and share; competition is not only expected, but everyone seems to understand it and it is quickly rewarded. We have not been schooled to talk and explore; it is less time consuming and risky to remain silent and do what we are told. We have not been schooled to investigate and learn from our miscues and problems; it is expected that learners get it right as quickly as possible, ignore the difficulty of trying to understand, and forget the pain involved in never getting it. We have not been schooled to develop a spirit of inquiry as we immerse ourselves in phenomena, artifacts, knowledge, and invitations; it is neater and quicker to be told what, when, where, and how to learn.

Taking Time

Developing the philosophy and practices of a support community, whether in the classroom or in the profession, takes the time it takes.

There are classrooms that get at least a toe-hold on their community building during the first few days of school. The members of some TAWL groups begin real talk and sharing from the first meeting. On the other hand, some groups try again and again before meaningful connections are made. If community life is to be genuine we should expect successes and problems. There is no substitute for time to work on solving the problems and on celebrating successes.

Reflection

Members of learning communities contemplate what they have done and what they are doing. Teachers invite students to reflect individually on their learning by encouraging them to write about their understandings and concerns; these reflections show up on exit cards, as minute memos, and in journals and logs. Teachers encourage collective reflection by valuing the thinking that students do together in pairs, small groups, and as a total class. Teachers practice reflection in teacher support groups through evaluation of their mission and their programs. (A tradition of the WLU conferences is that immediately after the very last session, the planners put their heads together for "the melt down"—a collective reflection.)

Spirit of Inquiry

Members of thriving communities do not wait around to do someone else's research; based on real needs and interests, they pose their own inquiry. When teachers ask about curriculum, learning, and teaching, you can be sure important questions are being asked. Whole language teachers have questions in their heads constantly, and it proceeds naturally that their students are encouraged to join them in constructing a curriculum based on student inquiry into life-relevant ideas. One reason whole language classrooms are exciting is that learners are asking immediately significant questions. One reason TAWL groups are at the cutting edge of literacy education is that teachers are asking questions that will have real consequence in their classes.

Changed Roles

In classrooms and in support groups, students and teachers find themselves in roles not always allowed, much less valued, in conventional settings. Foremost, both students and teachers are considered learners; that is a given. Within just one day in a classroom, I have seen teachers learning from students-as-teachers, and students learning from teachers, students learning from other students-as-teachers. TAWL teachers, like their students, are collaborators with their peers, representatives for their group, advocates for nonbiased living and learning, apprentices to and for each other, organizers of suitable activities and rich experiences, and more than likely they are friends.

Scholarship

I am often struck by how hard kids work and by the depth of understanding they achieve when they are digging into some issue or topic that intrigues them. I am also in awe of teachers who devote unbelievable amounts of time in pursuit and presentation of knowledge. Walk into a whole language classroom or a TAWL meeting and you know that intellectually important things are going on. Outsiders may need help in understanding why Johnny spends five minutes gazing out the window or why Jennifer insists on sketching something in the middle of her math paper. Outsiders ask why teachers spend their own money to go to a conference in Phoenix in August and Winnipeg in February, or even why they would give up an evening for a TAWL meeting. The learning achieved through self-disciplined scholarship combined with ownership of both the process and products of learning is reward in and of itself. When students and teachers are encouraged to own and value scholarship, their communities can lighten up on rules and punishment and focus on what they are meant to do—invite and promote learning.

For three decades Ken Goodman has invited teachers, teacher educators, administrators, librarians, authors, and researchers to come together for the purpose of creating a wonder-filled learning place for children. The "coming together" started in the 1960s when Ken asked about the reading process and then when we asked thousands of other questions. That first inquiry and all those following it have kept us, to put it mildly, occupied on our journey. If Dave Allen was still with us he might have remarked that some "mind-blowing, totally heavy" questions have been posed on that journey.

Are we there yet? Well . . . because whole language teachers live their beliefs and constantly carry them in their heads and hearts as they journey, the answer is yes. But . . . because whole language teachers are always asking what's beyond the next curricular bend in the road, the answer is, of course, no.

No matter, we are in unbelievable good company.

REFERENCES

Aaron, I.E., Artley, A.S., Goodman, K.S., Huck, C.S., Jenkins, W.A., Manning, J.C., Monroe, M., Pyle, W.J., Robinson, H.M., Schiller, A., Smith, M.B., Sullivan, L.M., Weintraub, S., & Wepman, J.M. (1972). *Scott, Foresman reading systems*. Glenview, IL: Scott, Foresman.

Allen, P.D. (1969). *A psycholinguistic analysis of the substitution of miscues of selected oral readers in grades two, four, and six and the relationships of these miscues to the reading process: A descriptive study*. Unpublished doctoral dissertation, Wayne State University, Detroit.

Burke, C. (1969). *A psycholinguistic description of grammatical restructuring in the oral reading of a selected group of middle school children*. Unpublished doctoral dissertation, Wayne State University, Detroit.

Carlson, K.L. (1970). *A psycholinguistic description of selected fourth grade children reading a variety of contextual material*. Unpublished doctoral dissertation, Wayne State University, Detroit.

Fader, D., & McNeil, E.B. (1968). *Hooked on books: Program and proof*. New York: Putnam.

Fader, D. (1971). *The naked children*. New York: Macmilan.

Freire, P. (1979). *Pedagogy of the oppressed*. New York: Seabury Press.

Goodman, K.S. (1965). A linguistic study of cues and miscues in reading. *Elementary English Journal, 42*(6), 639–643.

Goodman, K.S. (1971). Children's language and experience: A place to begin. *Coordinating Reading Instruction*. Glenview, IL: Scott, Foresman.

Goodman, K.S. (1974). Effective teachers of reading know language and children. *Elementary English, 51*(6), 823–828. Urbana, IL: NCTE.

Goodman, K.S., & Burke, C. (1973). *Theoretically based studies of patterns of miscues in oral reading performance* (Final Report Project No. 9-0375, Grant No. OEG-O-9-320375-4269), Washington, DC: U.S. Dept. of Health, Education and Welfare.

Goodman, Y.M. (1971). *Longitudinal study of children's oral reading behavior* (U.S.O.E. Final Report). Washington, DC: U.S. Department of Health, Education, and Welfare.

Goodman, Y., Watson, D., & Burke, C. (1987). *Reading miscue inventory: Alternative procedures*. Katonah, NY: Richard Owen Publisher.

Gutknecht, B. (1971). *A psycholinguistic analysis or the oral reading behavior of selected children identified as perceptually handicapped*. Unpublished doctoral dissertation, Wayne State University, Detroit.

Martellock, H. (1971). *A psycholinguistic description of theory and written language of a selected group of middle school children*. Unpublished doctoral dissertation, Wayne State University, Detroit.

Menosky, D.M. (1971). *A psycholinguistic description of oral reading miscues generated during the reading of varying portions of text by selected readers from grades two, four, six, and eight.* Unpublished doctoral dissertation, Wayne State University, Detroit.

Page, W. (1970). *A psycholinguistic description of patterns of miscues generated by a proficient reader in second grade, an average reader in fourth grade, and an average reader in sixth grade encountering basal reader selections ranging from pre-primer to sixth grade.* Unpublished doctoral dissertation, Wayne State University, Detroit.

Rousch, P.D. (1973). *A psycho-linguistic investigation into the relationship between prior conceptual knowledge, oral reading miscues, silent reading, and post-reading performance.* Unpublished doctoral dissertation, Wayne State University, Detroit.

Sims, R. (1972) *A psycholinguistic description of miscues generated by selected young readers during the oral reading of text materials in black dialect and standard English.* Unpublished doctoral dissertation, Wayne State University, Detroit.

Watson, D. (1973). *A psycholinguistic description of the oral reading miscues generated by selected readers prior to and following exposure to a saturated book program.* Unpublished doctoral dissertation, Wayne State University, Detroit.

Chapter Four

Looking at Language in Context: A Common Concern of Whole Language and Systemic Functional Linguistics

Peter H. Fries
Central Michigan University and Hangzhou University

I first met Ken Goodman when he came to the University of Wisconsin to give a lecture on reading. It was in the mid 1960s, and Richard Venezky and I were team teaching a course on linguistics and reading in the Department of Behavioral Disorders (because neither Venezky's department [English] nor my department [Linguistics] would offer the course). Venezky had found out about a researcher who was taking an interesting new approach to the investigation of reading. We therefore arranged for Goodman to give a lecture, sponsored by the Wisconsin Research and Development Center for Cognitive Learning at UW, and announced it campus-wide. An audience of five showed up: Dr. and Mrs. Venezky, Dr. and Mrs. Fries, and one student. So we went up to Venezky's office and had coffee and talked linguistics and reading for several hours. (Times have changed! No, not Goodman, for he still likes to talk about children, reading, education, and language. But these days the times that an audience of only five shows up to listen to what Kenneth Goodman has to say about anything are rare indeed.) I was much taken with his message; it seemed to make sense. As a result, I began to look for other articles he and his associates had written. Indeed, later I attended a number of courses which he or Yetta Goodman taught (it is hard to talk about Ken without talking about Yetta). Much later, I worked with Ken and Yetta on the Commission on the English Language and on the Commission on Reading of the National Council of Teachers of English (this last, during the time when members of the Reading Commission were involved in writing and discussing the "Basal Report"; see Goodman, Shannon, Freeman, & Murphy, 1988). So, many cups of coffee later, the Goodmans and the Frieses still discuss language, children, and education, and it is still as exciting as the first day we met. Anyway, back to the beginning.

FUNCTIONAL LINGUISTS WITH SIMILAR INTERESTS TO GOODMAN'S

In some ways, I had been prepared for Goodman's message by my previous training.[1] As a linguist, I was trained to take language seriously and to treat the language used by any person (including children) as a system. And, as the son of my father, Charles Fries, I was quite familiar with talking about signals of meaning. Most linguists focused their attention on discovering patterns in the language. Charles Fries focused his attention on describing what it was in the language that led listeners/readers to respond to language as they do. In his view:

> [g]rammar aims not at definitions and classifications but at such a description of the formally marked structural units as will make possible a valid prediction of the regular recognition responses that the patterns will elicit in the linguistic community. (1967, p. 668)

Here the goal is not one of classifying items as sentences, nor is it one of describing the patterns in or structures of various units. Rather the goal of linguistics is to predict how speakers and listeners will perceive and interpret what is said to them.[2]

My understanding of the implications of a "signals" approach to the description of language was strengthened and extended by my experience studying acoustic phonetics and experimental phonology with Leigh Lisker, in which very similar questions were asked about the

---

[1]The fact I found that what Goodman was saying resonated with aspects of my previous training should come as no surprise to those who know that Goodman had taken a course with Charles C. Fries and was using aspects of Fries' grammar in his investigation of reading.

[2]For further discussion of this aspect of Charles Fries' approach, see Fries (1983a).

sounds produced in language (see, e.g., Lisker, 1957a, 1957b). Several points impressed me at the time. It was quite obvious that in acoustics at least, listeners needed to know the context in which a given item occurred before one could interpret it. As Lisker (1957b) said "the phonetic evaluation of a segment is not made independently of its neighbors" (p. 267). In other words, the context in which an item occurs constitutes a critical part of the perception and interpretation of that item.

Of course, one factor in relating a segment to its neighbors lies in being aware of which sequences of sounds are possible in a language. Experimental phonologists explicitly discussed the ways in which programming a computer with information on what sequences of sounds are allowed in a language helped it identify those sounds in context. In other words, my experience with acoustic phonetics made it obvious that the predictability of sounds was directly relevant to how accurately they were perceived and that this issue must be explicitly addressed in any discussion of language processing.[3]

Finally, both Fries and Lisker took great pains to emphasize that the perception of language was not simply the perception of unconnected items, with the final perception being the sum of the individual items. Rather a system was involved, and the language was a structure, in which the perception of the whole was more than the perception of the parts. I saw these same sorts of emphases in the message that Goodman was presenting. However, I also saw that Goodman was extending some of the notions. In particular, his notion of predictability extended beyond the sentence to include predictions from the larger context. Again, I had been prepared to consider features above the sentence to be relevant from my training with Fries (who discussed sequence signals—words and phrases that showed how the sentences of a text were related—as part of his theory), and particularly with Kenneth L. Pike (1967), who explicitly viewed language as part of behavior. Goodman, however, was making the predictions from these larger contexts a critical part of his theory.

At the same time that I encountered the work of the Goodmans, I was also following the work of Michael Halliday. In the early 1960s Halliday's published work focused on describing the internal structure of the sentence. However, during the late 1960s and early 1970s he began to focus more explicitly on the relation between language and the culture that language was being used to encode (see, e.g., Halliday,

---

[3]Charles Fries often discussed informally issues of prediction and its relevance to the abilities of non-native speakers to understand lectures and conversations, but these informal discussions were not part of his formal theory.

1973[4]). As with Pike, Halliday's interest in linking language to things outside language arose because of purely linguistic reasons. Both Halliday and Pike objected to the idealization inherent in making the distinction between Saussure's "langue" (the language system) and "parole" (the actual speech produced using the system). Saussure's distinction was later accepted and reworked by Noam Chomsky into the distinction between "competence" and "performance". Chomsky, for example, explicitly assumed a language with no variation. Further, it is quite obvious that Chomsky was not interested in examining actual speech behavior—what he called "performance". A classic statement of this position occurs in Chomsky (1965)

> Linguistic theory is concerned primarily with an ideal speaker-listener, in a completely homogeneous speech-community, who knows its language perfectly and is unaffected by such grammatically irrelevant conditions as memory limitations, distractions, shifts of attention and interest, and errors (random or characteristic) in applying his knowledge of the language in actual performance. (p. 3)

By contrast, Halliday is interested in describing the language as actually used by people in interaction. He has taken as one of his major goals the description of "why texts mean what they do." Because texts are language used by people to interact in actual situations,[5] that goal makes it essential that Halliday consider phenomena that Chomsky categorizes as "performance." However, Halliday believes that part of the account of 'why texts mean what they do' consists in tying the actual texts to what they *could have been*. That is, to describe how a text means what it does, one must link the specific choices that have been made in that particular text to the choices *available in the language as a whole*. A language is seen as a system of interrelated choices that are available to speakers to make in order to convey meaning. In other words, a language is seen as a meaning potential. A text is simply an instance of a set of specific choices that have been made at a given time. Halliday sees no essential gap between the language system as a whole (what Chomsky would call *competence*) and the various instances of the language in use, that is, texts (what Chomsky would include under

[4]At the same time that Halliday was beginning to explore the relation between language and culture, he was also exploring various implications of his view of language for education. For example, he directed the Nuffield project, which resulted in publications such as *Breakthrough to Literacy* (Mackay, Thompson, & Schaub, 1970) and *Language in Use* (Doughty, Pearce, & Thornton, 1972).

[5]A text is the language used in any interaction; thus a text may be a conversation, a poem, an advertisement, or even a text book.

performance). Rather, the two are the same phenomenon looked at from different points of view.

HALLIDAY AND SYSTEMIC FUNCTIONAL GRAMMAR

Because Halliday was interested in describing actual linguistic behavior, he needed to develop a different model for the description of language. The model which resulted was Systemic Functional grammar. Systemic Functional grammar views the language system as a potential of interrelated choices, with each choice having consequences both for the form a unit takes and its interpretation. This may be illustrated by a fragment of the system for describing the grammatical choices available for clauses in English.[6]

The emphasis on choice is obvious in the very shape of Figure 4.1. For example, there is a system called Interpersonal, which contains two options. Clauses may either be Indicative (e.g., *Bill brought Tim a newspaper*) or Imperative (*Bring Tim a newspaper, Bill*). One must choose between having an Indicative clause or an Imperative clause. Each choice point in Figure 4.1 is called a *system*. The Interpersonal system contains only two options, but this is not a requirement to have a system. For example, the system labeled Experiential contains 6 options. Typically, once one has made a choice within one system, that choice will rule out certain further choices and allow others. Thus, if we choose Indicative within the Interpersonal system, we have the further option of choosing Declarative (*Bill brought Tim a newspaper*) or Interrogative (*Did Bill bring Tim a newspaper?*). Braces indicate sets of choices that are simultaneous. That is, given an Indicative clause one must choose either an Interrogative clause or a Declarative clause, as well as either a modal clause or a nonmodal clause. The details of this description are unimportant, but the basic principle is critical to the Systemic view of language. Systemicists view language as a set of choices (represented here as systems) that have consequences both for the meaning of the clause as well as for the grammatical form the clause takes. It is obvious, for example, that the choices represented in Figure 4.1 have consequences for the meaning of the clause. For example, Interrogative clauses (questions) differ in meaning from Indicative clauses

[6]See Matthiessen (1995) for a careful presentation of the systems of the English Clause. Earlier versions of clause systems were presented in Kress (1976) and Fawcett (1980). Eggins (1994) provides an introductory treatment of the relation between systems and structures, and the relation between language and the context of situation.

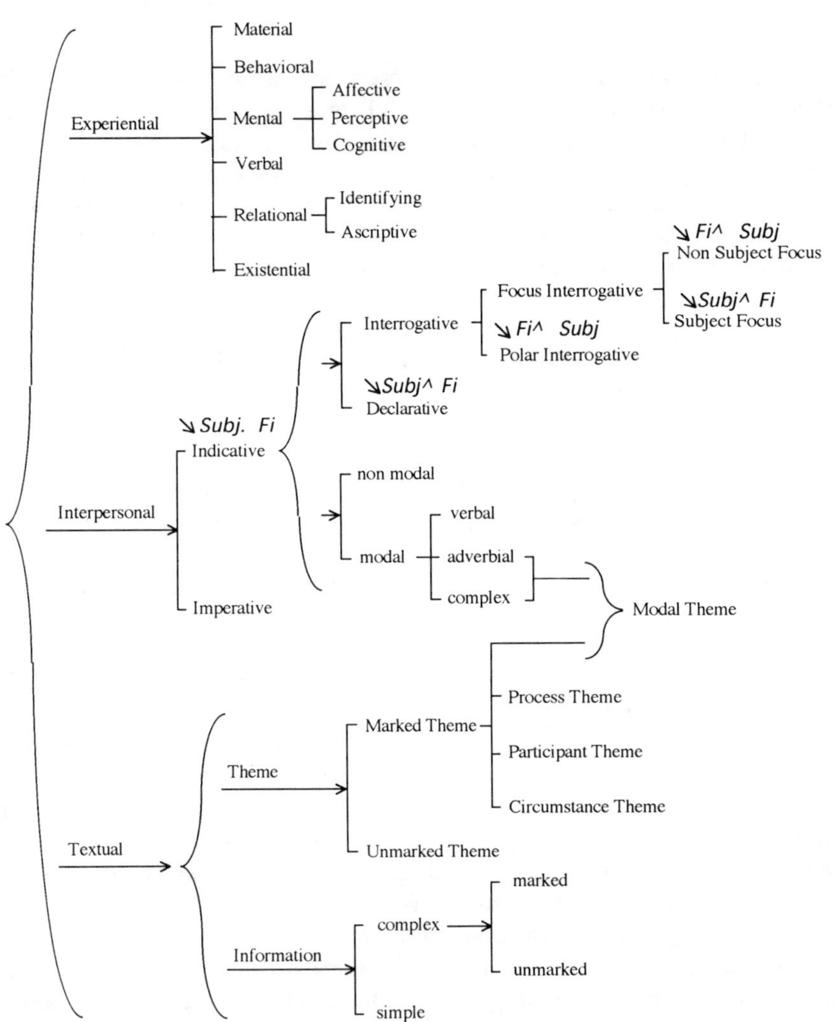

Figure 4.1. Fragment of the grammatical system of the clause

(statements). But further, the choices have consequences for the grammatical form of the clause. The normal order of sentence elements within Indicative clauses is Subject then verb (expressed in Figure 4.1 by an arrow pointing down and to the right followed by *Subj^Fi*), whereas in polar Interrogative clauses (*Did Bill bring Tim a newspaper?*), the normal order is to place part of the verb (the finite portion) before the Subject. In other words, the configuration of choices expressed in a clause determines the grammatical functions it contains and the order in which these functions are found.

Figure 4.1 illustrates one further point: The grammatical systems involved in the description of the clause fall into three major groups. That is, the choices arising out of Experiential rarely make reference to any of the choices arising out of Interpersonal or Textual. (In Figure 4.1 we could say *never make reference to*, but that is an artifact of the small size of the system presented in Figure 4.1.) Similarly, the choices arising out of Interpersonal rarely make reference to choices from either Experiential or Textual, and so on. In Figure 4.1 one system—the system that results in the feature Modal Theme—makes reference both to a choice that derives from Interpersonal and one that derives from Textual. The situation represented in Figure 4.1 is quite typical of the grammar of English. The grammatical choices in the English clause seem to fall into three major groups which are largely, but not totally, independent of one another. Systemicists call these three groups of choices *metafunctions*. As in Figure 4.1, the three metafunctions are the *Experiential* metafunction, the *Interpersonal* metafunction, and the *Textual* metafunction. The metafunctions constitute three general semantic areas in which the grammatical choices in one metafunction are relatively independent of the choices in the other two metafunctions.

Figure 4.2 presents an analysis of a clause in terms of the grammatical functions it contains. Bold type in the example sentence indicates what is often called "sentence accent," so the clause was said with two focuses, one on *other* and the second on *early*. The double slashes indicate the boundaries of the tone patterns. In this case, the sentence was said with two intonation patterns (the specific intonation pattern used is indicated by the numbers at the beginning of each pattern). As might be predicted from Figure 4.1, one set of grammatical functions is not sufficient to describe the clause. Rather, each clause is multiply structured, with four sets of functions. Two sets of functions derive from the textual metafunction, and one set each derives from the other metafunctions. Many of the structures imposed by the metafunctions are similar, but the various metafunctions do not impose identical structures on the clause.

	//4 However,	the **other**	folks	// 1 ʌ would	have gone	home	**early** //
Experiential		Actor		Material Process		Circumstance	Circumstance
Interpersonal	Adjunct	Subject		Finite	Predicator	Adjunct	Adjunct
		Mood			Residue		
Textual							
Thematic structure	Textual Theme	Experiential Theme		Rheme			
	Theme			Rheme			
Information structure	Given	⇐ New	Given	Given		⇐ New	

Figure 4.2. Sample analysis of the structure of a clause

In addition to viewing language as choice, Systemic Functional grammarians take a stratal view of language. They believe that language contains three strata—phonology, lexico-grammar, and semantics—and they link the strata of language with one additional stratum that lies outside grammar—the context of situation. The relation that holds between the strata is *realization*. For example, we cannot say that words are *composed of* sounds (or of graphemes). Certainly there is much more to a word than the way it sounds. However, we cannot perceive a word in a particular context unless it is given some physical manifestation, that is, a sound in phonemes or a shape in graphemes. Only then is it publicly observable by other people. In that sense, the phonology (or graphology, in the case of written language) can be seen to *realize* or *encode* the lexico-grammar. Similarly, meanings cannot be communicated directly through thought; they must be given some sort of wording. (We must use words and grammar to express the meaning.) Again, we can say that the lexico-grammar *realizes* or *encodes* the semantics. And finally, the context of situation—the social interaction—cannot exist apart from the various publicly observable actions that encode it. Of course, many different modalities are used, ranging from physical actions to language. All these modalities combine to *realize* or *encode* the context of situation. However, because language plays a very important role in realizing social interactions, it is reasonable for linguists to focus their major attention on the ways that language realizes the context of situation. Of course, not all of language is equally important in this realization. The semantics—the meanings expressed—plays the most crucial role in the linguistic realization of the context of situation.

LANGUAGE AND SOCIAL INTERACTION

Let me discuss the relation between language and the context of situation in a different way. Systemic grammarians start with the noncontroversial assumption that language works (it conveys meaning) because it encodes the interaction that speakers intend to achieve. This assumption has three implications:

1. The language used in an interaction and the interaction itself are different sorts of things. (The language used in an interaction and the interaction itself have quite different orders of existence.)
2. Given the social interaction which is being achieved, we can predict, within limits, what is likely to be said to achieve that interaction.
3. Given the language of an interaction, we can reconstruct the interaction that is being enacted through that language.

It is important to note that the relation between the language of an interaction and the interaction itself is bi-directional. To paraphrase what was said earlier using more technical language, language works because the social interaction *activates* certain features of language (point 2 above) and also participants in an interaction *construe* the social interaction through the use of language (point 3 above).[7]

---

[7]See Halliday (1978) and Hasan (1981, 1994, 1995) for more extensive presentations of these issues.

LANGUAGE AND CONTEXT OF SITUATION

A focus of much recent work in Systemic Functional grammar has been to articulate the nature of the link between language and the social interaction it realizes. As described earlier, Systemic Functional grammarians achieve this by positing a stratal model of language and social interaction involving three strata within language (phonology, lexico-grammar, and semantics) and one additional stratum that lies outside language (the context of situation). It is the context of situation that determines which meanings are relevant to an interaction and likely to be expressed. This context of situation should not be regarded as a static entity. For example, it is not simply the physical context within which an interaction takes place. Indeed, the physical context within which an interaction takes place is often totally irrelevant to that interaction. It makes no difference to the reader of this book whether I write this chapter on a computer, on a typewriter, or by hand. Nor is it relevant to our interaction how much empty space I happen to have beside me on my desk, or exactly what books are on the shelves around me when I look up from my writing. Rather the context of situation should be regarded as the interactive context. It includes the goals of the participants, their social relations, and those aspects of the physical context that have been constructed through the text as relevant. Many of these factors (most obviously, the goals of the participants) can only be seen through examining the words and actions of the participants. It is this situational (interactive) context that determines which meanings are relevant. If, for example, a mother is feeding a young child, what sorts of meanings are relevant to that interchange? Clearly, one set of meanings relevant to such an interaction concerns whether the child does or does not want more food. The mother is likely to offer food to the child. Sometimes she will do this by saying something such as, "Do you want some more applesauce?", sometimes she will use physical actions (for example, she might take a spoonful of applesauce and put it near the child's mouth). Most typically, she will combine actions with language. Similarly, the child is able to communicate her wishes—again typically through various combinations of actions and language. She can simply turn her head away, or knock the applesauce out of the spoon with her hand, or she can say her approximation of "no." Often children do all of these things together. The meaning of both the mother's actions and language and the child's actions and language derives from the nature of the general interaction taking place at the time. The actions of both participants are interpreted in terms of the other's best guess as to what is taking place. Systemic Functional grammarians talk about this "meaningful" aspect of social interaction by saying that it is a "semiotic." The social interaction defines the relevant meanings. (We can regard a culture as a very complex semiotic or system of meanings which are expressed in various modalities such as actions, visual representations, language, etc.)[8]

GENRE

I should point out here that social interaction is generally repeated again and again and again. Typically we repeatedly engage in the same sorts of interactions with the same people, or the same sorts of interactions with the same sorts of people. Thus, the interactions themselves are routine. How many times has a 1 year old child been fed by her mother? (The routine and predictable nature of these interactions is a critical help to the child learning her first language.) Further, the routine interactions we engage in are typically complex and go through stages. If one goes into a small store to buy a sweater,[9] we can predict the likely course that interaction will take. It is likely that there will be a time in the interaction when the clerk indicates that it is the customer's turn. That is, the clerk will allocate attention to the customer. When that happens the customer will typically indicate some need, and the clerk will offer some product relevant to the need. There may be some negotiation as to the appropriateness of the item offered (Does it fit? Does this color red go with my new slacks? Will it shrink? etc.), and the interchange will typically conclude with some decision.[10] The customer will either decide to purchase the item, or decide not to purchase the item offered. Each of the stages may be achieved by a range of activities. The allocation of attention may be achieved by as simple a tactic as establishing eye contact, or the clerk may ask "Who's next?", or "Can I help you?", or may simply engage the customer in a conversation about the weather. Any of these options will indicate to the customer that the clerk is

[8]It is this meaning-creating aspect of context of situation and the larger cultural environment that led Halliday to title his insightful study of language development *Learning How to Mean* (1975). In his view, language development is not simply learning the forms of language or language structure, but learning the relevant meanings, including relevant interactions, appropriate to a culture.

[9]The scene I am describing here is not the sort of interaction that would take place in a store such as K-Mart or Walmart, but rather a small store that focuses on personal service. Interactions in the K-Mart-sort of store would take a rather different (but again largely predictable) course.

[10]Hasan (Halliday & Hasan, 1989) and Ventola (1987) provide more extensive discussions of the stages of similar interactions.

available to help. By the same token, the customer has many options to indicate a need. She could say, "I'm looking for a red wool sweater" or "Do you carry red wool sweaters?". Again, either of these options indicates a need in the context of this type of interaction. Two points are relevant here: (a) the interaction progresses through time, and thus what occurs at the beginning of the interchange is not appropriate at the end of the interchange; and (b) the stages of the interaction have consequences for the sorts of meanings to be expressed. Of course, rarely do these consequences determine exactly what words will be used, nor even the specific grammar. Rather the stages that an interaction typically goes through enable us to predict roughly what meanings are at risk in the interchange. Thus, if a particular stage in the shopping interaction requires us to express a need, it is most likely that the language used to achieve that stage will identify some class of object (e.g., a sweater). It is also likely to be either a statement about the likes, desires, or needs of the speaker or a question about what the listener has or carries in the store, and so forth.[11] Taking a term from literary analysis we can call the language produced in the sort of structured interaction described here a *genre*.[12]

FIELD, TENOR, AND MODE

As part of the attempt to describe the link between language and the context of situation, Systemic Functional grammarians have tried to describe the social semiotic of social interactions (context of situation) in terms of three variables: Field, Tenor, and Mode. Halliday (Halliday & Hasan, 1989) describes Field, Tenor, and Mode in the following terms:

> 1. The field of discourse refers to what is happening, to the nature of the social interaction that is taking place: what is it that the participants are engaged in, in which the language figures as some essential component?

---

[11]See Fries (1983b) for an illustration of how the context of situation influences the interpretation of what is said in that context.

[12]For more extensive treatments of genres and generic structures see Halliday and Hasan (1989), Hasan (1978, 1984a, 1984b), Martin (1992b, 1993), and Ventola (1987). See Derewianka (1990) for an accessible account directed at teachers in the primary grades. Rothery (1993) and Veel (1994) describe a number of genres relevant to teaching in junior high school and high school. See Fries (1985) for a discussion of how generic structure is encoded on the language of a children's story.

2. The tenor of discourse refers to who is taking part, to the nature of the participants, their statuses and roles: what kinds of role relationship obtain among the participants, including permanent and temporary relationships of one kind or another, both the types of speech role that they are taking on in the dialog and the whole cluster of socially significant relationships in which they are involved?
3. The Mode of discourse refers to what part the language is playing, what it is that the participants are expecting the language to do for them in that situation: the symbolic organization of the text, the status that it has, and its function in the context, including the channel (is it spoken or written or some combination of the two) and also the rhetorical mode, what is being achieved by the text in terms of such categories as persuasive, expository, didactic and the like. (p. 12)

As was pointed out earlier, Field, Tenor, and Mode are not linguistic concepts. Rather they are means of describing the social situation in such a way as to make the link with language most direct. Specifically, a description of a social interaction in terms of Field, Tenor, and Mode should provide an insight into the sorts of meanings which might be used (in other words, the meanings which are "at risk") in a given situation. It should be obvious that not all meanings are equally at risk throughout an interaction. In fact, as described previously, our typical interactions go through several stages.

METAFUNCTIONS: EXPERIENTIAL, INTERPERSONAL, AND TEXTUAL

As illustrated in Figure 4.1, language has three metafunctions: experiential, interpersonal, and textual. Figure 4.1 describes the choices within the experiential metafunction as concerned with the types of processes described in the clause. Does the clause describe an action such as hitting, taking, or doing (a material process)? Or, some sort of cognitive activity such as thinking, believing, disliking, (a mental process)? Or, some sort of relation such as *be* or *seem* (a relational process)? Or another process? Other related questions that would be included in the experiential metafunction are: What participants are involved in the process? (Who did the hitting? Who got hit?) What circumstances obtained for the process? (When and how was the hitting done?) All these meanings concern the real world as apprehended by our experience.

Meanings from the interpersonal metafunction concern the way the speaker is acting on the listeners. What is the speaker doing to her audience through language? For example, every time we make a statement or ask a question we are thereby assigning some sort of role to our audience. It may be the role of someone who will receive the information, or the role of someone who will potentially provide information or do something for the speaker.

Finally, the textual metafunction concerns meanings that make the text "hang together." The meanings of the textual metafunction are ones that enable us to make our language relevant to the context—both the linguistic context and the context of situation. Figure 4.1 shows that two sets of choices are involved in the textual metafunction, the thematic system and the information system. Each of these systems assigns its own structure. (See Figure 4.2 for one example.) The thematic structure of a clause assigns the functions Theme and Rheme. The Theme of a clause expresses the "point of departure" of the message of the clause. It provides a framework in terms of which the remainder of the message is to be interpreted.[13] The information system assigns the status of New and Given to information in the clause. New information is information that is presented as "newsworthy." It is the basic message to which the listener/reader should pay attention. Information which is presented as Given is information that can be reconstructed from the context.[14]

It is claimed that Field tends to be expressed in the experiential metafunction, Tenor in the interpersonal metafunction, and Mode in the textual metafunction.

ANALYSIS OF TEXTS, USING SYSTEMIC FUNCTIONAL GRAMMAR

It was claimed earlier that one reason that language works is that we can reconstruct the context of situation given the language. Let me illustrate that point by looking at some texts. The first group of texts is given in Text 1. (The layout is reproduced as closely as possible.)

---

[13]See Halliday (1967, 1968, 1970, 1994) for a more extensive description of the Theme in clauses. Fries (1981, 1992, 1993) and Martin (1992a) discuss the operation of Thematic choices in texts.

[14]See Halliday (1967, 1968, 1970, 1994) and Martin (1992a) for a more extensive description of information structure.

Text 1: Classified advertisements from a newspaper

1985 FORD RANGER, 4x4, V6, 5 speed, 6" lift, new clutch, $2,000, 517-772-9204

1987 CHEVY Celebrity Classic, loaded, excellent condition, highway miles. 517-772-5827 after 4 p.m.

1987 SUBARU WAGON; 4 wheel drive, runs good, hardly any rust, new brakes, high miles, $2,000 517-772-0603

It is very easy to reconstruct the situation in which these texts occurred. Physically they were found in the classified section of a newspaper, more specifically, in the section of the classified advertisements in which automobiles were offered for sale. Let us reconstruct the interaction that these advertisements encode. The Field of the interaction involves selling. Specifically, each advertisement offers an item for sale and describes that item. No attempt is made to persuade the reader to buy the item in any way other than choosing to mention characteristics that are considered positively valued. The Tenor of the interaction involves language directed at an audience that is not personally known, and so it involves a relatively large social distance. However, the reader does not need to be enticed to read the advertisement. Rather, it is assumed that the reader is in the process of reading the classified advertisements in the newspaper because he or she is already interested. The Mode of the interaction is one in which the advertisement is encountered visually. However, few classified advertisements are visually complex. They primarily use the visual composition/layout (e.g., print colors, sizes of print, or placement on the page) to demarcate the boundaries of the advertisement and separate each advertisement from the surrounding ones. The language constitutes the text. Typically these advertisements contain no pictures.

I have said previously that interactions usually go through stages. The interactions encoded in these texts are no exception. Newspaper classified advertisements for automobiles go through several recognizable stages. First an item is named, typically by identifying the year and the brand and model. Then several relevant attributes are mentioned. A price may be given, as well as a means of contacting the seller.

How does the language construct the interaction? One obvious feature of the language of these advertisements is the absence of complete sentences. The advertisements are to be read as first introducing a referent (the automobile which is for sale), and then listing various relevant attributes of that referent. (Indeed, in most cases, these attributes could be interpreted as Attributes of [implied] relational clauses.) These advertisements are directed at people who already know a great deal about classified advertisements for automobiles. The absence of complete grammatical clauses is part of that direction to a "knowing" audience. In addition, these advertisements often use coded language which must be known if the advertisement is to be understood. What does *loaded* mean in Text 1? Other classified advertisements mention *air, auto* and so on. These are terms that readers who are not familiar with the conventions of classified advertisements for automobiles (for example, non-native speakers) will find unfamiliar and difficult to process.

Text 2 is taken from a different context, a national magazine. Text 2 is the text of the advertisement rewritten with each punctuated sentence given a number and placed on a new line.*

Text 2: Magazine advertisement rewritten

1. THE MOST COSTLY MISTAKES IN BUSINESS.
2. The way most businesses work today simply isn't working.
3. Too much time's wasted calling people who can't be reached.
4. So connections aren't made, and deals fall through.
5. Too much money's spent on overpriced, overnight couriers.
6. That devours your bottom line.
7. And by the time the post office delivers your bid, someone else could have the job.
8. That's why there's MCI Mail.
9. MCI Mail is a new kind of business tool.
10. One that lets you use your personal computer to send and receive information instantly.
11. And inexpensively.
12. So instead of sending out sales information to customers in days, MCI Mail lets you do it now.

---

*Permission to use MCI Mail ad from *Time* (Los Angeles edition, April 18, 1985) granted by MCI Telecommunications Corporation.

13. You can get leads out, now.
14. Send sales updates to all your sales people, instantly.
15. Receive orders the day the deal's signed.
16. And follow up in a flash.
17. All for less than what you're paying for the hassles and headaches tied to the way you usually communicate.
18. Start moving your business ahead now—for less.
19. Call 1-800-MCI-2255.
20. In Washington, D.C., call 833-8484
    [[On coupon]]
21. Now is the time for me to find out about MCI Mail
22. Mail to: MCI Mail, Box 1001, 1900 M Street, N.W., Washington D.C., 20036
    [[Coupon also has lines to fill in reader's name and address]]
23. MCI MAIL
24. NOW IS THE TIME FOR MCI MAIL
25. @ 1985 MCI Communication Corp.
26. MCI Mail* is a registered service mark of MCI Communications Corp.

The advertisement in Text 2 encodes an interaction that differs radically from the interactions encoded in the classified advertisements. Like the advertisements in Text 1, the Field of the advertisement in Text 2 is selling something. However, in this case, the sponsors of the advertisement are selling a service, not an item. In general, companies that buy advertisements in national magazines do not care which instance of their product or service the customer buys. If the advertisement were for Ford automobiles, it would not matter to the company *which* Ford was bought, but simply that the reader bought *some* (new) Ford. (Compare this with the purchaser of a classified advertisement who cares very much that you buy his or her automobile, and not someone else's car—even though that other car may be the same brand and model.) Similarly, the Tenor of the magazine advertisement, the relation between reader and author, is very different from the relation encoded in the newspaper classified advertisements. The magazine advertisement is calculated to entice the reader into reading it. Unlike readers of newspaper classified advertisements, readers of magazines rarely sit down to read the advertisements. Their interest must be captured, and they must be enticed to read the advertisement. Thus, everything in the magazine advertisement is oriented toward that goal. The visual layout is typically striking (i.e., attention getting). Dramatic and interesting pictures are used, and often brilliant colors are used. Print layout and font sizes and types are used to present intriguing messages in quick and snappy ways. Further, there is typically an element of persuasion in magazine advertisements. Magazine ads typically attempt to persuade the reader that the product or service being advertised is desirable. The desirability may result from the inherent attributes of the product or service (as in the case of MCI Mail in Text 2) or may simply be a pleasant association that the writers hope the readers will connect with their product or service (as in many cigarette advertisements). Sometimes these desirable attributes are simply described or alluded to or sometimes they are highlighted by giving the advertisement a problem–solution structure. That is, many advertisements describe a problem which the reader might identify with, and then go on to show how the product or service advertised solves that problem. The Mode is again visual (i.e., the advertisement is encountered visually). However, in the case of magazine advertisements such as that in Text 2, the visual layout (both the pictures and the layout of the print) takes on a very great importance, and often the layout conveys a major portion of the message.

There is an additional difference between the advertisements presented in Texts 1 and 2. The magazine advertisement in Text 2 encodes a complicated Field, Tenor, and Mode. If we look at the Tenor, we see that the actual source of the advertisement is not encoded in the language of the text. That is, it is quite obvious to anyone who knows business practices in our market economy that the company has bought the advertisement in order to bring its name and the name of its product or service to the attention of the reading public. The writer of the advertisement actually is a team of people who have typically put together an advertising campaign for the company. Further, the advertisement has been edited and approved by a large number of people, and often has been tested on readers. In addition, the entire purpose of running the advertisement is one of noticeability and persuasion—the company wishes to bring its name to the attention of the readers and to create a favorable association with the name in the minds of the readers, who will—it is hoped—remember the name when making a purchase. Although the companies producing the advertisement investigate very carefully the demographic characteristics of the users of their products, and the readers of the magazines in which the advertisements are placed, the writers of the ads do not know the readers in any personal way. One might say that the audience is well-defined, but not known.

However, little of this aspect of producing the advertisement is encoded in the language of the ad. Rather, a persona is created through the language of the advertisement. This persona seems to speak to a listener (= the reader) about the company. In most advertisements (as in this one) the exact relation of the persona to the company is left inexplicit. (In some advertisements, the president of the company or some other named member of the company is portrayed as speaking to the reader.) This persona speaks as one who knows the listener/reader and assumes the listener is interested in the message. The language of Text 2 contains a great deal of informal spoken language, including words such as *hassles* and *headaches*. *You* is used to refer to a general antecedent rather than the addressee in sentences such as *That devours your bottom line*, and *One that lets you use your personal computer to send and receive information instantly*. In addition, the advertisement contains many contractions—spellings that are intended to represent the way words are said, not the way they "should" be spelled in formal written English. In other words, the Tenor encoded in the language of this text is one of an informal situation in which people who know each other are talking to one another. The Mode encoded in the language of this advertisement is largely that of the spoken language.

Like the newspaper classified advertisements in Text 1, the magazine advertisement in Text 2 contains many sentence fragments. However, the nature and function of these fragments is quite different in the two advertisements. The newspaper classified advertisements in Text 1 are typical of the sort of sentence fragments one often finds in written lists. These fragments are written to be read. By contrast, most of the sentence fragments found in Text 2 seem to be used for one of two reasons. Some fragments are used to label visual material. Thus the heading of this advertisement (*The most costly mistakes in business*—a noun phrase) labels and gives a value (mistakes) to the three visuals presented in the advertisement just below the heading. However, most of the sentence fragments in Text 2 are used to present the rhythms of the spoken word. Indeed, most often the punctuation in this advertisement seems to be used to show the reader how the text should "sound."

The fact that Text 2 is a persuasive text is made obvious in its structure. This advertisement has a clear Request–Justification–Enablement structure. The Request is made in punctuated sentences 18-20. Punctuated sentences 1-17 provide the Justification for the Request, and the cut-out coupon and the phone numbers provide Enablement. The motivation for the Request takes the form of a suggestion that the customer may have a problem for which MCI mail is the best solution. In other words, the motivation section of this advertisement has a clear Problem–Solution structure, with sentences 1-7 describing the Problem and sentences 8-17 describing the Solution. Two questions guide the discussion of this portion of the advertisement: (a) How do we know that there is a Problem, and what is the exact nature of the Problem? (b) How do we know that a Solution is proposed and that this Solution solves this particular Problem? Let us first look at the Problem.

A cursory examination of the processes in the Problem section indicates that they are almost exclusively actions (or, to put it more technically, they are material processes). The one notable exception is sentence 7 which is a relational process (with the main verb *have*). Clearly the section primarily concerns some kind of doing. However, a second characteristic that appears on cursory examination is the prevalence of negatives. These negatives include the overt grammatical negation of clauses (*isn't working, can't be reached,* and *aren't made*), implied grammatical negations (*too much, someone else*), and lexical negation (*mistakes, waste, overpriced,* and *fall through*). Further, a number of things are happening that should not occur. Deals should not fall through, nor should bottom lines be devoured in the business world. However, it would be wrong to say that the nature of the problem lies in the absence of action. Indeed, a lot of actions occur in this segment as well (*most businesses work, calling people, money's spent, that devours your bottom line,* and *the post office delivers your bid*). Even terms such as *mistake* and *waste* imply action, but action wrongly conceived. A look at the relations that hold between the actions which took place and those which did not is instructive here. Figure 4.3 presents an analysis of the relations between the non-rankshifted clauses of the problem section of the MCI advertisement using Rhetorical Structure Theory (see Mann, Matthiessen & Thompson, 1992; Mann & Thompson, 1987).[15]

As Figure 4.3 shows, the generalization *the way most businesses work today simply isn't working* is supported by three bits of evidence presented in sentences 3-4, 5-6, and 7. These three bits of evidence have a cause-consequence structure. In sentences 3-4 that consequential relation is encoded as a Result with the conjunction *so*. In the case of 5-6, *that* in sentence 6 refers to the action described in the previous punctuated sentence, and as a result of the co-referentiality, it can be seen that sentence 5 causes the action described in sentence 6. In the case of sentence 7, a state (*someone else could have the job*) is declared to occur *by the time* some action occurs. The implication is that a delay in action caused the state (i.e., prevented you from having the job). In each case, the consequence involves some sort of negation or an undesirable result. Thus, the activity in this section of the advertisement is frustrated activity, and hence constitutes a problem. If we look at the causes of the bad consequences, we notice that they all concern wasted time, delays in time, or wasted money.

The Solution section of this advertisement consistently emphasizes meanings related to time and money. From punctuated sentence 10 through to punctuated sentence 17, every punctuated

[15]The analysis represented in Figure 4.3 is based on a draft analysis provided to my by Christian Matthiessen.

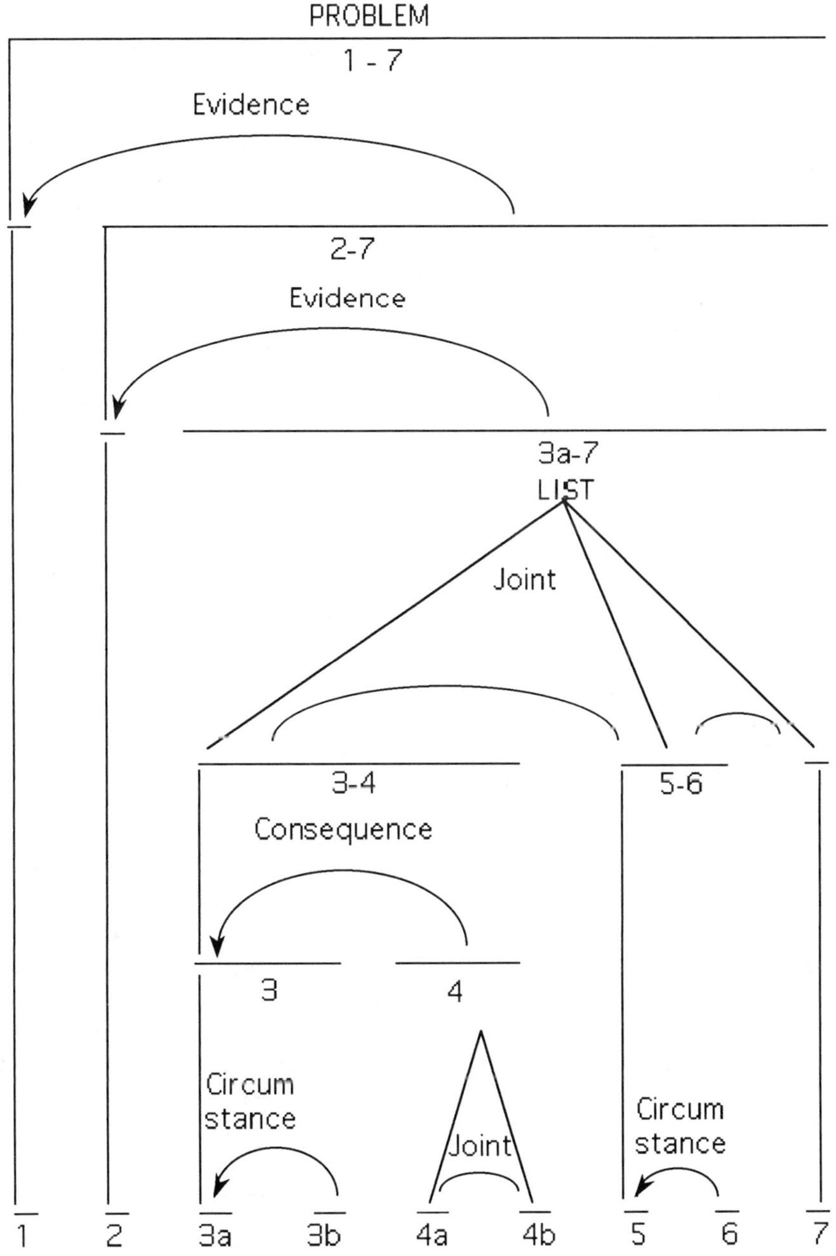

Figure 4.3. RST analysis of sentences 1-7 of MCI mail advertisement

sentence contains at least one reference to time or money. More specifically, the time references refer to immediacy and speed, and the references to money refer to lack of expense. Further, each of these punctuated sentences mentions time or money at the end of the sentence, the place where New information normally occurs if there is no special reason to place it elsewhere. In other words, time and expense are prominent in this section not merely because they are mentioned often in this advertisement, but also because these meanings are given prominent positions within each punctuated sentence. These concepts are regularly being presented as Newsworthy. Notice that many punctuated sentences in the Solution section of the advertisement, are in fact, sentence fragments. However, notice also that these sentence fragments are closely related to their linguistic environment. Sometimes they are Circumstances added on to a previous clause. At other times they are appositives elaborating a nominal group which occurs in a previous clause, or they may be branched clauses elaborating or extending a previous clause. Each of the sentence fragments brings into prominence the end of the previous punctuated sentence, and in this section of the advertisement, the previous punctuated sentence ends with some reference to time or expense. That is, not only does the use of sentence fragments make the ideas expressed in the fragments themselves more prominent, it also makes part of the *preceding* punctuated sentences more prominent. In summary, the effect of this style of punctuation is (a) to make the text read more like spoken language, (b) to create more positions of emphasis, and (c) to increase the independent status of each individual unit of information. The MCI Mail advertisement is typical of many magazine advertisements in its use of punctuation for these purposes.[16] Chunking of information via grammar, punctuation, and the placement of information in the Themes and the ends of the component punctuation units and clauses all play parts in the construction of this kind of advertisement.

To sum up what has been said so far, readers use the language of texts to construct interactions. If the advertisement in Text 2 is perceived as having a Problem–Solution structure, that is the result of the writers using "problem" language and "solution" language within the advertisement. They (both the writers, and later, in a separate act, the readers) construct that structure through the meanings expressed in the text. Now, of course, the meanings make sense because they are referable to some sort of understandable (dare I say predictable?) interaction.

[16]The MCI Mail advertisement discussed here was taken from a group of 63 advertisements found in national magazines which have been studied for the placement of information in the component sentences of the advertisements. Fries (1992, 1993) reported on this study.

However, the texts are not the interactions directly but should be regarded as symptoms of the interaction. Each sort of interaction places values on different sorts of meanings. I have tried to demonstrate this point by discussing two radically different sorts of advertisements. However, it should be obvious that every type of interaction privileges certain meanings (and therefore words and grammar) and makes other meanings less relevant. Thus we cannot evaluate the language of a text without reference to the interaction it encodes. The classified advertisements in Text 1 provide a simple example of this issue. As a composition teacher I have regularly pointed out the sentence fragments my students have used, and I have usually asked students to revise them. I cannot take the position, however, that sentence fragments are in and of themselves bad. Certainly, if we were to attempt to structure a classified advertisement as a well-formed paragraph, beginning with a topic sentence which is then elaborated by several supporting sentences, the advertisements would be *less* effective.[17] (Indeed, such a text would be hardly recognizable as a classified advertisement.) I cannot even say that sentence fragments are inherently bad in formal writing, when sentence fragments can be found in the writing of proficient authors such as Winston Churchill, John Ciardi, Ralph Waldo Emerson, F. O. Matthiesen, and Henry David Thoreau (see Kline & Memering, 1977). Rather, we need to examine each case in its context in terms of the goals of the authors and the effects on readers. We should not view language as a set of rules that *must* inevitably be followed. Rather, language should be seen as a resource for making meanings in contexts and for communicating these meanings to others. Communication involves the creative use of conventional resources in context.

These are the sorts of issues in which the work of Kenneth Goodman resonates with that of the Systemic Functional grammarians.[18] He has regularly insisted on the relevance of the total text to the perception and interpretation of the words and sentences of that text. In his early discussions of reading, he worded those concerns largely by

---

[17]When I discuss the lack of complete sentences in classified advertisements with students, they usually account for this absence by saying that the people who place the advertisements are trying to save money. That may be true because newspapers typically charge for such advertisements by the word, or by the inch. However, I suspect that even people who do not have to worry about the money also write classified advertisements using the same sort of language. They do so because the advertisement is more understandable and easier to read with sentence fragments than it is with full sentences.

[18]In Summer 1994 I was thrilled to learn that Goodman gave a talk in Australia reporting on what Whole Language had learned from Systemic Functional Grammar.

talking about aspects of the "predictability" of the text and its relevance to language processing. His insistence on the relevance of prediction to language was a critical influence in developing linguists' notions of how people perceive language and in bringing predictability into discussions of linguistic theory. As I have shown earlier, Systemic Functional linguists treat the text as the primary unit of linguistic analysis. In their view, texts have structure, and that structure derives from the structure of the interaction encoded by the texts. Just as sentence structure provides a basis for predicting what words will occur and what their grammatical functions will be, the structure of a text can serve as the basis for predicting the meanings encoded by the text and provide a basis for interpreting what is meant in a sentence within that text.

The goal of language education is not simply to teach children more language but to help children cope in a greater range of interactions. To do this, children need to become sensitive to the meanings that are appropriate to various interactions. They need to learn how to mean in these new situations. This task is not simply a cognitive one, in which one learns new concepts. The task is also one that involves language learning; either learning new forms appropriate to the new context, or learning new uses of familiar forms in the new context. That is, one learns not only new ideas but new ways to express these ideas. Underlying this goal is the belief that different interactions place different demands on language.

Clearly, Systemicists are quite comfortable with the idea that different interactive contexts place different demands on language. Indeed one of the major issues within Systemic theory addresses the description of the different demands that are placed on language by different interactions.[19] Goodman has insisted that children extend their language abilities best when they experience authentic texts in real interactions. Perhaps jointly determining what sorts of experiences children need to have in order to attain this goal is one place where Whole Language and Systemic Functional grammar can cooperate effectively.

---

[19]It is well known that the move from elementary school to middle school is particularly difficult for many children. It has often been suggested that one of the causes of this difficulty lies in the fact that children begin to study specific disciplines in early middle school. Often the explanation for the difficulties which is offered is that the children have difficulty gaining control of the new concepts. Another factor that may be relevant to the difficulties of the students is the fact that language is being used in unfamiliar ways in the various disciplines. Halliday and Martin (1993) discuss some of the special features of scientific writing. None of the characteristics they describe (e.g., the use of nominalization) is to be found *only* in scientific writing. However, the frequency of use and the manner of these features in science does seem to be peculiar.

REFERENCES

Chomsky, N. (1965). *Aspects of the theory of syntax.* Cambridge MA: MIT Press.

Derewianka, B. (1990). *Exploring how texts work.* Rozelle, NSW, Australia: Primary English Teaching Association.

Doughty, P., Pearce, J., & Thornton, G. (1972). *Language in use.* London: Edward Arnold.

Eggins, S. (1994). *An introduction to systemic functional linguistics.* London: Pinter.

Fawcett, R. (1980). *Cognitive linguistics and social interaction: Towards an integrated model of a systemic functional grammar and the other components of a communicating mind.* Heidelberg: Julius Groos Verlag.

Fries, C. C. (1967). Structural linguistics. In *Encyclopaedia Britannica.* Chicago: Encyclopaedia Britannica.

Fries, P. H. (1981). On the status of theme in English: Arguments from discourse. *Forum Linguisticum, 6*(1), 1-38. (Reprinted in J. Petöfi & E. Sözer (Eds.), *Micro and macro connexity of texts* (pp. 116-152). Hamburg: Helmut Buske Verlag, 1983).

Fries, P. H. (1983a). C. C. Fries, signals grammar, and the goals of linguistics. In J. Morreall (Ed.), *The ninth LACUS forum 1982* (pp. 146-158). Columbia, SC: Hornbeam.

Fries, P. H. (1983b). Language and interactive behavior: The language of bridge. *Notes on Linguistics, 25,* 17-23.

Fries, P. H. (1985). How does a story mean what it does? A partial answer. In J. Benson and W. Greaves (Eds.), *Systemic perspectives on discourse: Selected theoretical papers from the ninth international systemic workshop* (pp. 295-321). Norwood, NJ: Ablex.

Fries, P. H. (1992). The structuring of written English text. In M. A. K. Halliday and F. C. C. Peng (Eds.), *Current research in functional grammar, discourse, and computational linguistics with a foundation in systemic theory* [Special Issue]. *Language Sciences, 14*(4), 1-28.

Fries, P. H. (1993). Information flow in written advertising. In J. Alatis (Ed.), *Language, communication and social meaning* (pp. 336-352). Washington DC: Georgetown University Press.

Goodman, K. S., Shannon, P., Freeman, Y. S., & Murphy, S. (1988). *Report card on basal readers.* Katonah: Richard Owen Publishers.

Halliday, M. A. K. (1967). Notes on transitivity and theme in English Part I. *Journal of Linguistics, 3*(1), 37–81.

Halliday, M. A. K. (1967). Notes on transitivity and theme in English Part II. *Journal of Linguistics, 3*(2), 199–244.

Halliday, M. A. K. (1967). Notes on transitivity and theme in English Part III. *Journal of Linguistics, 4*(2), 179–215.

Halliday, M. A. K. (1970). Language structure and language function. In J. Lyons (Ed.), *New horizons in linguistics* (pp. 140-164). Harmondsworth, England: Penguin.

Halliday, M. A. K. (1973). *Explorations in the functions of language*. London: Edward Arnold.

Halliday, M. A. K. (1978). *Language as social semiotic: The social interpretation of language and meaning*. London: Edward Arnold.

Halliday, M. A. K. (1994). *An introduction to functional grammar* (2nd ed.). London: Edward Arnold.

Halliday, M. A. K., & Hasan, R. (1989). *Language, context and text*. Oxford: Oxford University Press.

Halliday, M. A. K., & Martin, J. R. (1993). *Writing science: Literacy and discursive power*. London: Falmer.

Hasan, R. (1978). Text in the systemic functional model. In W. Dressler (Ed.), *Current trends in textlinguistics* (pp. 228-246). Berlin and New York: Walter de Gruyter.

Hasan, R. (1981). What's going on, a dynamic view of context in language. In J. E. Copeland & P. Davis (Eds.), *The Seventh LACUS Forum: 1980* (pp. 106-121). Columbia, SC: Hornbeam Press.

Hasan, R. (1984a). The nursery tale as a genre. *Nottingham Linguistic Circular, 13,* 71-102.

Hasan, R. (1984b). The structure of the nursery tale. In L. Coveri (Ed.), *Linguistica testuale* (pp. 96-114). Rome: Bolzoni.

Hasan, R. (1994). Situation and the definition of genre. In A. Grimshaw (Ed.), *What's going on Here? Complementary studies of professional talk* (Vol. 2, Multiple Analysis Project, pp. 127-172). Norwood, NJ: Ablex.

Hasan, R. (1995). The conception of context in text. In P. H. Fries & M. Gregory (Eds.), *Discourse and meaning in society: Functional perspectives* (pp. 183-283). Norwood NJ: Ablex.

Kline, C. R., & Memering, W. D. (1977). Formal fragments: the English minor sentence. *Research in Teaching English, 11,* 97-110.

Kress, G. (Ed.). (1976). *Halliday: System and function in language*. London: Oxford University Press.

Lisker, L. (1957a). Linguistic segments, acoustic segments, and synthetic speech. *Language, 33,* 370-374.

Lisker, L. (1957b). Minimal cues for separating /w, r, l, y/ in intervocalic position. *Word, 13,* 256-267.

Mackay, D., Thompson, B., & Schaub, P. (1970). *Breakthrough to literacy*. London: Longman.

Mann, W. C., Matthiessen, C. M. I. M., & Thompson, S. A. (1992). Rhetorical structure theory and text analysis. In W. C. Mann & S. A. Thompson (Eds.), *Discourse description: Diverse linguistic analyses of a fund-raising text* (pp. 39-78). Amsterdam: John Benjamins.

Mann, W. C., & Thompson, S. A. (1987). *Rhetorical structure theory: A theory of text organization* (Research Report # ISI/RS-87-190). Marina del Rey: University of Southern California, Information Sciences Institute.

Martin, J. R. (1992a). *English text: System and structure.* Amsterdam: Benjamins.

Martin, J. R. (1992b). Genre and literacy—modeling context in educational linguistics. *Annual Review of Applied Linguistics, 13,* 141-172.

Martin, J. R. (1993). A contextual theory of language. In B. Cope and M. Kalantzis (Eds.), *The powers of literacy: A genre approach to teaching writing* (pp. 116-136). London: Falmer.

Matthiessen, C. M. I. M. (1995). *Lexicogrammatical cartography.* Tokyo, Japan: International Language Sciences Publishers.

Pike, K. L. (1967). *Language in relation to a unified theory of human behavior* (2nd ed.). The Hague: Mouton.

Rothery, J. (1993). *Exploring literacy requirements in the junior secondary English syllabus.* Sydney, Australia: Write it Right. Disadvantaged Schools Program, Metropolitan East Region.

Veel, R. (1994). *Exploring literacy in school science.* Sydney, Australia: Write it Right. Disadvantaged Schools Program, Metropolitan East Region.

Ventola, E. (1987). *The structure of social interaction: A systemic approach to the semiotics of service encounters.* London: Pinter.

Chapter Five

The Validity and Reliability of Miscue Analysis

Sharon Murphy
York University

Since Kenneth Goodman first introduced miscue analysis into the educational literature over 25 years ago, a search of the ERIC database reveals that several hundred articles make use of the term. Numerous other books and articles, not indexed by ERIC, also discuss this analytical procedure for assessing reading. In fact, the term *miscue analysis* has become such a part of educational currency that it is often used without reference to its originator. Yet there is a noticeable absence of any broadscale survey of the validity and reliability of the procedure. It seems that the heuristic power of the miscue analysis assessment procedure led researchers to hold of utmost concern its validity and reliability in their own specific context. And, although local validity and reliability are the ultimate concern when using any assessment instrument, the absence of a discussion of validity and reliability issues across studies may create problems for those who are using miscue analysis as a counterpoint to other forms of assessment. This chapter represents an initial attempt to survey some of the literature on miscue analysis with a view to clarifying what sets of procedures can be considered as falling under the category of miscue analysis procedures and the evidentiary arguments that can be used to support claims for the validity and reliability of miscue analysis.

FAMILIES OF MISCUE ANALYSIS PROCEDURES

There are three distinct sets of procedures associated with the term "miscue." The first two share the following similarities: (a) a focus on the multiple cueing systems of language, which include at minimum the graphophonic, syntactic, and semantic systems; and (b) a characterization of the reader as a hypothesizer who uses strategies such as predicting and confirming in the process of reading. The Goodman Taxonomy (see K. Goodman, 1969; Y. Goodman, 1967; Goodman & Burke, 1968, 1973) and a large collection of derivative procedures, among which are the Reading Miscue Inventory (Goodman & Burke, 1972) and alternatives (e.g., Goodman, Watson, & Burke, 1987), share these characteristics. Additionally, both of these procedures are usually accompanied by a post-oral reading measure which takes the format of a retelling of the text read.

The Goodman Taxonomy consists of a series of 18 questions to be asked of each miscue. An example of the kind of question asked is: "*Does the surrounding text (peripheral visual field) influence the miscue?*" If a question in the Goodman Taxonomy is answered affirmatively, there are up to 9 ways in which the miscue can be categorized (with some categories further divided and subdivided). For instance, in the case of the example presented above, there are three possible coding categories: (a) the miscue can be found in the near visual periphery, (b) the miscue can be found in the extended visual periphery, or (c) it is doubtful that the visual periphery was involved in the miscue (Goodman & Burke, 1982/1973). In applying the Goodman Taxonomy, there can be over 100 possible coding categories to consider if each of the coding questions on a single miscue is answered affirmatively. Given this level of detail and analytical technique, it is not surprising to find that Goodman (1976) suggests the Taxonomy be reserved for research involving relatively small numbers of research participants.

For teachers and diagnosticians, Yetta Goodman and Carolyn Burke created the first of many of the derivatives of the Goodman Taxonomy—the Reading Miscue Inventory (RMI) (1972). This procedure, like most subsequent derivatives of the Taxonomy, reduces the number of questions to be asked of each miscue and the number of coding categories used to answer the questions while trying to preserve as much of the reading strategy/cueing system information as possible. Early derivatives of the Goodman Taxonomy focused only on sentences involving miscues. In later derivatives (see, e.g., Procedure IV in Goodman et al., 1987), the focus was broadened to include sentences that were miscue free. Examples of derivatives from the RMI include those of Bean (1979), Cunningham (1984), Siegel (1979), Tortelli (1976), and Pappas, Kiefer, and Levstik (1990).

A third set of procedures uses the term "miscue" but is not considered as part of the family of miscue measures to which the current discussion of validity and reliability applies. This set of procedures is tied to the oral reading assessment techniques prevalent in the 1950s and 1960s. These procedures are often associated with informal reading inventories (sets of passages ranked in order of difficulty followed by comprehension questions). Several contemporary oral reading assessments often conflate some of the marking or coding systems from miscue analysis with the traditional procedures of the informal reading inventories. For instance, a common pattern is to use a marking system highly similar to that used in miscue analysis but to focus on word accuracy (rather than strategy and cue use) in a calculation of the instructional, independent, and frustration levels of the reader. Examples of such an adaptation include Wangberg and Thompson's (1982) procedures.

VALIDITY

In contemporary psychometric theory, a test is not considered valid in and of itself. Rather, test users are obliged to provide the necessary evidence to support the inferences made from the test (American Psychological Association, 1985; Angoff, 1988). These inferences relate to the test's "appropriateness, meaningfulness and usefulness" (APA, p. 9). Even though miscue analysis does not take the form of a standardized test, by virtue of its status as an assessment instrument, it must meet the same validity requirements. Furthermore, because reliability is one aspect of construct validity, and because classic tests and measurement texts claim that reliability is a "necessary, albeit insufficient, condition for validity" (Moss, 1994, p. 6), users of miscue analysis are further obligated to provide evidence of reliability matters as well.

Central to providing the evidentiary bases for the validity of an assessment instrument are arguments that can be martialled to demonstrate that a certain construct is being assessed. In miscue analysis, the construct purported to be assessed is reading. Part of the job of providing evidence for the construct validity of the miscue analysis procedure, then, would be to eliminate any rival hypotheses that would compete with the view that miscue analysis assesses reading.[1]

[1]In traditional psychometric theory, validity and reliability discussions usually refer to a specific instrument. However, because miscue analysis exists in numerous alternate forms, the approach to the validity and reliability discussions taken in this chapter is to delimit the forms of miscue analysis to which the discussion may be applicable and to provide a general discussion of validity and reliability pertaining to those measures.

All other types of evidentiary validity build on construct validity in one way or another. According to Messick (1988), the other types of validity considered in examining a test include: (a) predictive validity—the degree to which performance on this test is predictive of performance on future measures of this construct, (b) concurrent validity—the degree to which performance on this test relates to performance on other measures of the same construct, (c) criterion validity—the degree to which performance on this test relates to some comparable "real" situation in which the construct is brought to bear, and (d) content validity—the degree to which the task is representative of a defined domain of tasks in this area. These types of validity are embedded in the general discussion of the evidential basis for the validity of miscue analysis.

Because miscue analysis falls more into the class of assessments referred to as *performance-based assessments*, there is also an obligation to ensure that two major threats to validity have been avoided: "construct under-representation (which jeopardizes authenticity) and construct-irrelevant variance (which jeopardizes directness)" (Messick, 1994, p. 14). In essence, the questions that must continually be asked are whether the assessment instrument captures enough of the construct to fall within the class of measures that can be said to assess the construct and whether the context of the assessment provides too many other explanations for student performance.

Finally, consequential validity must also be considered. According to Messick (1988), consequential validity is values-based: It is based on "judgmental appraisals of the ends a proposed test use might lead to, that is, of the potential social consequences of proposed use and the actual consequences of the applied testing" (p. 42). Consequential validity calls on test users to make ethical decisions about a test's use in particular circumstances.

To a large extent, evidentiary and consequential validity intertwine. Supportive arguments must clearly be presented in order to determine whether the assessment instrument measures a specific construct. Without such evidence, consequential validity should not be entertained and the assessment instrument should be put aside. Only when substantive evidentiary arguments are positively evaluated, should the instrument's use in particular circumstances be considered.

The evidentiary arguments for miscue analysis can be framed around a series of questions that impinge on how miscue analysis represents the construct of reading. The first issue is its descriptive comprehensiveness of oral reading and retelling. The second is how a measure of oral reading, such as miscue analysis, generalizes to silent reading tasks. The third is whether process measures in miscue analysis are predictive of comprehension. And the last two issues raise questions of how well the reading of a single text generalizes to other texts and across individuals. In essence all of these questions are questions of the depth and breadth of the generalizabilty of miscue analysis.

What Kind of Description of Reading Does Miscue Analysis Provide?

The descriptive point of departure for miscue analysis is that of an oral reading of a text by a reader. Oral reading analysis has a relatively lengthy tradition as a method for assessing the construct of reading. For example, Huey's (1968/1908) turn-of-the-century volume on the psychology of reading reviews the research on the oral reading of words and texts. Similarly, Payne's (1930) article focuses on the classification of word recognition errors derived from children's reading of the Gray Oral Reading Paragraphs. In fact, if the literature in education is any indication, oral reading error analysis has been a highly popular form of reading assessment throughout the first two-thirds of this century (see a review by Weber, 1968).

Although past practice sets some of the groundwork for a concurrent validity argument, it is insufficient for purposes of demonstrating construct validity, particularly if theoretical change is supposed to drive the development of assessment tools. In fact, miscue analysis has come to prominence because it differs from the assessment devices of the past. There are two features of miscue analysis that make it a more veridical descriptive system of reading than past oral reading procedures: One is its marking system and the other is its coding system. The retelling, although an improvement on past "comprehension" gauges, does present some problems.

The marking system. A marking system is used to annotate a text in such a way as to describe the reader's reading whenever it departs from the text. A simple example of an annotation is circling a word that the reader omits. A key facet of any marking system used in oral reading analysis is the recoverability of the reader's reading—that is, the degree to which the oral reading can be reconstructed by using the marking system annotations.

In marking systems used in oral reading assessments developed prior to the mid-1960s, descriptive recoverability of the reading act was not usually the paramount concern of researchers. Instead, reading researchers were often led by a theoretical focus on word accuracy in reading. This theoretical focus meant that reading behaviors such as punctuation omissions or insertions were ignored as was information that could be obtained by examining multiple attempts at a phrase. In essence, reading researchers did not *describe* reading through their annotation system but used a combined descriptive-interpretive marking system. This pattern not only resulted in problems of comparability of studies of oral reading performance as Leu (1982) suggests, but it also meant that a great deal of descriptive detail of reading was lost.

In miscue analysis, the annotation system for marking miscues requires the documentation of as much as possible of the reader's observable responses to the text. For instance, not just the initial or the final attempts at reading a word are documented but all attempts at reading a word. Some intonation features, such as the omission or insertion of punctuation, are noted. Even silence, in the form of pauses of three seconds or greater, is annotated. In this sense, then, the marking system used in miscue analysis provides a fuller description of the oral reading event than descriptive procedures of the past. The fuller description is also revealing of a broader theoretical stance in that Goodman and Goodman (1978) believe that "whatever the readers do is not random but is the result of the reading process, whether used successfully or not " (p. 2-2), whereas theorists of the past assumed that once a word failed to be recognized what followed was of little significance.

Although miscue analysis procedures present a more accurate rendition of the reader's oral reading, annotation systems for prosody and pragmatics are the least developed. For the prosodic cueing system, both the Goodman Taxonomy and the RMI contain annotations for intonation and insertions and omissions of punctuation (print intonational markings). However, in most subsequent derivatives of the Goodman Taxonomy and the RMI, the separate marking system for intonation is not as strongly emphasized.

There are two interrelated explanations for the limitations in the marking system of intonation. First, intonation is difficult to mark as exemplified by difficulties in reaching interrater agreement on intonational features (Goodman, 1971; Hood, 1975-1976). Sophisticated systems of intonational marking (see, e.g., Halliday, 1967) require much training. Furthermore, print is underspecified in terms of intonation. That is, only a handful of features give author-intended intonational cues: (a) lexicogrammatics and semantics—words suggesting *how* something is said (e.g., briskly, lovingly, with a flourish); (b) graphics—underlining, bolding, sizing, italicizing words; and (c) punctuation. Consequently, among readers there can be much more variation in the interpretation of *how* something is said than there is in *what* is said. Second, the role of many of the derivatives of miscue analysis was to provide an accessible and relatively easy-to-use instrument for classroom teachers. To accomplish this goal, marking systems had to remain as simple as possible while retaining a maximum of information. In the derivatives it appears that intonation marking was de-emphasized because research by Goodman and Goodman (1978) indicated "that most intonation miscues involve sentence and intersential syntax" (p. 4-89) and, consequently, were already marked in one way.

As for the pragmatic cueing system, Goodman et al. (1987) draw specific attention to pragmatics, but they do not present a system for annotating the text. This may, in part, reflect the state of the field itself in that pragmatics is "not at present a coherent field of study" (Crystal, 1987, p. 120) rather than any omission on the part of the developers of the procedures. Users of the alternative procedures in Goodman et al. (1987) are reminded to consider the pragmatic constraints of the situation of the reading, the genre and form of the text, and other sociocultural influences. This aspect of miscue analysis could be expanded on to provide a more explicated description of the reading event.

The coding system. The coding system refers to the manner in which the miscue markings are categorized. In older oral reading analysis systems (see, e.g., Gilmore & Gilmore, 1968; Gray, 1921; Greene & Gray, 1946), once reading errors had been marked on the typescript, some kind of count was made of the reading errors according to the different kinds of markings made (i.e., substitutions, omissions, insertions, and sometimes repetitions, dialect forms, and punctuation). Then it was determined (through the use of a formula) whether a passage was at, above, or below a reader's instructional reading level. As for the pedagogical implications of the error analysis, teachers were left with little to draw on in their work with children. As Gray (1921) suggests, errors could be prevented through the use of flash card exercises and, essentially, a variety of other procedures which ultimately admonished children to read more carefully.

In miscue analysis, the *markings* on the typescript are simply the means of recreating the reader's reading. The reader's reading is then categorized, or coded, using the two basic descriptive principles underlying all miscue analysis systems—the reader's utilization of the cueing systems of language and the reader's strategies while reading the text. Each of these basic frameworks was derived from an analysis of language use in reading (Goodman, 1969).

The categorization of the cueing systems into graphophonic, semantic, and syntactic draws on the formal branch of the field of linguistics (Fawcett, 1993) which yielded transformational generative grammar (TGG). This system of analyzing language, developed by Noam Chomsky, provided a linguistic foundation for the idea that a particular meaning can have several forms (see, e.g., K. Goodman, 1982/1967)—thereby allowing for the identification of both semantic and syntactic cueing systems. The use of TGG has meant that miscue analysis has typically focused on the clause as the highest level of analysis. However, research and theorizing by Goodman (see, e.g., K. Goodman, 1983, 1994; Goodman & Bird, 1982; Goodman & Gespass, 1982) draws on systemic functional linguistics (Halliday, 1985; Halliday & Hasan, 1976) and its textual focus. These influences are seen in the revision of questions of the RMI which ask about the acceptability of miscues not only at the sentence level but at the textual level.

The categorization of strategies used by the reader were obtained by observing and categorizing the reader's behavior and by making inferences about what the reader perceived him or herself to be doing (Goodman & Goodman, 1978). The categorization of strategies is at its strongest for "confirming" because readers often manifest some of this strategy overtly through repetition or self-correction. In this sense, then, this category is more "grounded" (Glaser & Strauss, 1967) than that of predicting. Evidence for the predicting strategy, in many respects, is partially grounded in a probability argument. For instance, when a reader miscues, the likelihood of the particular miscue, when contrasted to all the remaining possible letter and word choices, would suggest that chance alone is not driving the reading; rather something is helping to eliminate possibilities. Clay's (1991) findings that 5-year-olds could anticipate the grammatical class of upcoming words in a sentence 79% of the time indicates that prediction is not only nonrandom but it is being driven by specific cues. Research in which miscue analysis is used retrospectively as a means for readers to examine their reading performance (see, e.g., Goodman & Marek, 1995; Raisner, 1977; Worsnop, 1980) provides some additional support for strategy use, although the question can be raised as to whether the description of the strategies that is provided in retrospective miscue analysis leads the reader to see patterns that might not be seen otherwise.

The retelling. The retelling procedures too must be considered both in terms of a method for assessing reading and in terms of the categories used within the method. Requesting that readers "retell" a text is an improvement over other methods associated with oral reading analysis. These other methods often present a list of questions to be asked after the oral reading (see, e.g., Gilmore & Gilmore, 1968). Sometimes, the questions themselves provide cues as to the content of the text. In addition, their sequence can even reconstruct the basic framework of the text (Johnston, 1983). A procedure, such as the retelling, in which the reader provides as much content and structure prior to being questioned could be considered not only as a way to overcome these problems, but as more reflective of the *reader's* construction of the text.

The procedures used to analyze retellings are varied. They include propositional analysis (see, e.g., Feathers, 1985) which draws on the descriptive linguistics tradition (Fawcett, 1993), story schema with its roots in cognitive psychology (see, e.g., Feathers, 1985), cohesion analysis based on the systemic functional school of linguistics (see, e.g., Feathers, 1985) and a system that identifies traditional story constituents, assigns those constituents values, and uses the constituent guide as a mechanism by which to assess comprehension (see, e.g., Goodman & Goodman, 1978). This latter method draws implicitly from basic story grammar research (see, e.g., Mandler & Johnson, 1977). Even though there have been studies that look at the relationship of the existing categories used to code retelling in miscue analysis (see, e.g., Murphy, 1987; Sadoski, 1981), a specific investigation into the categories, their relative weightings, and their applicability to texts of different types has not been undertaken. Consequently, this area remains open to criticism (see, e.g., Groff, 1980) and should be researched further.

Retelling procedures themselves have come under increasing scrutiny as theories of discourse become more refined. In particular, a review by Golden and Pappas (1990) raises several critical issues with respect to the sociolinguistics of retelling events. Golden and Pappas question: (a) how the knowledge of the listener in such events impacts on the degree of explicitness in the language of the reteller, (b) the influence of instructions (e.g., "retell" vs. "recall") on the retelling, (c) the impact of text features such as genre and length, and (d) scoring systems that have an inbuilt bias that meaning resides explicitly in the text. In order to further build on sociolinguistic theory, more attention must be given to the retelling's "context of situation" to enhance validity arguments around it.

Finally, retelling procedures have been evaluated more as memory tasks rather than constructive and interpretive tasks. Authorial wording and phrasing is the barometer against which the retelling is marked. If, however, the retelling is considered in part an interpretive task as per the theories of Rosenblatt (1978) or Fish (1980), then conceivably the retelling could become much more of a dynamic activity in which participants provide evidentiary arguments for their interpretations and reconstructions, and listeners are placed in the position of judging the reasonableness of these interpretations in light of the situation and the text.

To What Extent are the Inferences from Miscue Analysis Generalizable to Silent Reading?

Goodman's (1982/1973) description of miscues as "windows on the reading process" is sometimes interpreted as though miscues describe the whole reading process. In fact, Goodman and Goodman (1978) acknowledge that the full reading process is not revealed through observable behavior. For instance, in their discussion of correction, they note that "all correction is not overt. Readers may correct silently, satisfying themselves with no overt correction" (p. 4-31). Because miscues are gleaned through an oral reading process, the logical question must be raised as to whether inferences made about reading based on oral reading miscues can generalize to silent reading situations (Leu, 1982; Newman, 1978; Weber, 1968).

The oral-silent distinction is more than a physiological one in which the human body's limitations impact the speed of oral reading. The distinction is also psychological in that oral reading situations usually involve audiences toward which readers typically feel a commitment that differs from the commitment they feel toward themselves. The prosodic system as represented in oral language is underrepresented in print. Questions arise as to whether the speed of reading or the nature of an audience impact on prosody and on the reader's understanding of the text. Or, is it the case that oral and silent reading are different processes?

The theoretical extremes of interpretation on this point are:

1. Silent and oral reading are distinctly different processes of reading. It just happens that they share a language in common. The shared language masks what are essentially unique processes.
2. Silent and oral reading are manifestations of the same reading process. It just happens that there are unique physiological and psychological elements governing each.

Researchers use a couple of types of evidence to bolster the generalizability of the process of reading (as revealed by oral miscues) to silent reading. First of all, they correlate miscue analysis patterns with the results of silent reading instruments. Second, they use introspection as a means to study the reading process.

Relationship of miscue scores to silent reading measures. The two most commonly used silent reading measures used in studies of the relationship of miscues to silent reading are cloze tests and standardized reading tests. These types of measures significantly and positively correlate with each other (see, e.g., Carey, 1978; Cunningham & Caplan, 1982). It should be noted, however, that standardized tests, in particular, have come under sharp criticism as to their own validity as measures of reading (see, e.g., Murphy, 1994; Murphy, Shannon, Johnston, & Hansen, 1998). Because standardized tests are still in use and because, historically, tests and measurements specialists build their validity arguments using them, they are used here. However, the generalizability of the evidentiary validity arguments using standardized tests as data should be restricted to comparability with other standardized tests rather than the general process of reading.

The general approach taken to the study of the relationship between miscue analysis and standardized or cloze tests has been to consider either individual miscue coding categories or clusters of miscue categories. Researchers adopt a conceptual approach to this task. For instance, they select the miscue categories involving meaning and correlate them with comprehension.

Page and his colleagues were leaders in exploring the relationships between miscues and both standardized and cloze tests. At the outset, Page concentrated on the relationship of specific miscue categories to test measures. For instance, in Page's (1976) research, semantically and syntactically acceptable miscues were not found to be predictors of cloze comprehension performance. This finding was confirmed for standardized reading tests (Englert & Semmel, 1981; Lindberg, 1987; Murphy, 1987). This general pattern of findings for individual miscue categories makes sense given the fact that cloze items require the reader to draw on syntactic and semantic knowledge simultaneously rather than independently. Similarly, the comprehension portion of standardized tests would also call for integrated use of cues.

After work on individual miscue categories, Page (1977) focused on the combination of miscues known as the "comprehending score"—those miscues that were semantically acceptable or semantically unacceptable but corrected. Page (1977) found a strong linear relationship between the comprehending score and post-oral reading cloze. Page's (1979) later research continued to explore the comprehending score and typically reported combinations that were significant predictors of cloze performance. In a similar vein, Cunningham and Caplan (1982), using the miscue categories of semantic and syntactic acceptability, found that these two categories accounted for 54.87% of the variance in the two cloze studies used in their research. Beebe's (1980) research, which focused only on substitution miscues, also revealed that acceptable and corrected miscues were significant predictors of silent reading comprehension as measured by the comprehension subtest of a standardized reading test.

By 1982, Page's framework for looking at miscues was the altercue index, a matrix which examined semantic acceptability at varying levels of text (e.g., passage, sentence, prior context within a sentence, following context within a sentence) and correction behavior (successful, unsuccessful, not corrected).[2] Using the altercue matrix, Page (1982) found correlations of between .49 and .66 for post-oral reading cloze tests and .57 to .79 for standardized reading comprehension scores. In a later study, Sadoski and Page (1984) found that each of five different types of miscue combination scores were significant predictors of post-oral reading cloze measures, passage-dependent multiple choice measures, and reading comprehension standardized test scores. One study (Murphy, 1987) departs from this general pattern of findings in that the comprehending score was found to have negligible relationships with either the comprehension subtest of a standardized reading comprehension subtest or a standardized cloze test. Murphy's (1987) findings may be the result of the sample (a relatively homogeneous sample of Chapter 1 students, whereas other studies used heterogeneous samples), differences between standardized tests used, sample sizes, and differences in statistical approaches to the data (use of polyserial and polychoric correlations in a causal modeling application).

With a few exceptions, these studies appear to present converging evidence for a significant and positive correlation of the miscue comprehending score with cloze and reading comprehension standardized test measures. The moderate range correlations are appropriate indicators of shared variance given the differences in tasks. Furthermore, the utilization of conceptually logical clusters of miscue scores as significant predictors of silent reading performance on tests gives further support for the generalizability of particular categories of miscue coding to silent reading contexts.

Introspective studies of the reading process. With the exception of studies of textual interpretation and rhetoric, introspective studies of the reading process are not widely reported in the research literature. However, Cowie (1985) conducted such a study of his own silent reading. In that study he collected and classified 52 reading "errors." The classification system he developed for these errors bears a high degree of similarity to the kinds of categories used in miscue analysis. He found miscues that were a result of: (a) expectations—externally generated (text related) or internally generated (reflective of the background knowledge or preoccupation of the reader), (b) spatial

[2]For a detailed discussion of the reliability and validity relating to the work of Page and his colleagues, see Sadoski, Carey, and Page (this volume).

structure—radical errors involving whole phrases or orderings and conservative errors involving word boundaries and locations, (c) acoustic effects—the effects of words that have recently been heard on words that are read, and (d) attention. The similarities reported by Cowie (1985) for his own silent reading lend some support for the kinds of information coded in miscue analysis.

To What Extent are the Inferences from Miscue Analysis Generalizable to Other Reading Texts?

A number of authors (see, e.g., Hittleman, 1973; Kibby, 1979; Wixson, 1979) raise the issue of text effects in miscue analysis. The text has been found to be important in the reading of specific populations such as adults (Norman, Malicky, & Fagan, 1988). This issue of the role of the text requires investigators to take up the question of whether reading is invariant across texts and, if not, whether there are particular textual constraints that create specific boundaries in generalizing from miscue analysis studies of reading.

Pugh and Uljin (1985) present a framework for considering the aspects of texts that can vary. Included in this framework are the following topics:

1. typology (their format and intended function);
2. length;
3. ratio of linguistic to "non-linguistic" information (such as illustrations . . .);
4. linguistic features (register, vocabulary, syntax, etc.);
5. language of text (in relation to language of reader . . .);
6. form of display . . .;
7. authorial intention. (p. 32)

Miscue analysis studies exist across several of these areas. In fact, miscue analysis research has been successful in uncovering the peculiarities of texts.

Length. Research by Menosky (1971) on text length highlights the fact that at about the 250 or 300 word mark, patterns of miscues change. Although there is limited observable evidence for this pattern, it is reasonable to suspect that the greatest degree of uncertainty for readers is as they begin a passage (Smith, 1988). It is at this point that the genre is unspecified, the characters or topics covered are unknown, and the author's writing style is being discovered. Menosky's (1971) research raises questions about the lengths of passages used in informal reading inventories, reading tests, and basal readers.

Ratio of linguistic to nonlinguistic information. Beveridge and Griffiths (1987) examined the impact of illustrations on the reading of "less able readers." They reported that certain aspects of reading performance were better at the lower level of difficulty when pictures were present but better at the higher level of difficulty when pictures were absent. Their criteria for reading performance included word accuracy and grammatical acceptability (word accuracy, in particular, is a departure from miscue analysis with its focus on cues). The absence or presence of illustrations did not appear to influence comprehension. Although this study has mixed results, it indicates that illustrations impact on miscues interactively depending on the reader.

Linguistic features. Goodman and his colleagues have been quite active in studying the role of linguistic attributes in reading. For example, Altwerger and Goodman (1981) studied sentences that generated the highest number of miscues per word to see whether and how linguistic complexity affected miscues. Although moderate, but significant, correlations were found for each text on a measure of linguistic complexity, further analysis of texts revealed that the following features also contributed to miscues:

1. Lack of prior contextual information.
2. Unfamiliar or unusual choice and use of lexical items.
3. Weak sentence structure.
4. Unpredictable but simple structures.
5. Unusual stylized syntax.
6. Complex syntactic structures.
7. Combinations of any of the above. (p. 22)

In a later study, Goodman and Bird (1982) examined the wording of texts and reported the following general findings: (a) word frequency works in relation to language; (b) high frequency words occur in limited numbers and tend to be either function words, "be" forms, or pronouns; (c) context word frequency depends on the content of the text (e.g., in narratives names may recur); and (d) author's style will result in cohesive chains built of pronouns, key content words, and related words which are all semantically related in the story. In addition, studies by Goodman (1983) on the role of determiners as they relate to miscues and studies by Goodman and Gespass (1982) and Freeman (1988) on the role of pronouns as they relate to miscues converge on the importance of the function of the words in the text.

The results from studies of the linguistic features of text are globally manifested in studies of reader performance on primerese texts in contrast to performance on more authentic discourse forms (see, e.g., Sampson, Briggs, & White, 1988; Simons & Ammon, 1989). Hood's (1982) research also underlines text features: She found that student oral reading performances differed when they read two different stories which differed in the use of familiarity of lexical items (as measured by inclusion in the 1,500 most frequently used words) and redundancy. The patterns of miscues she found across the two narrative texts supports the work of Sampson et al. (1988) and Simons and Ammon (1989): Texts with less redundancy and more unfamiliar words resulted in miscues that were more contextually appropriate and involved less meaning loss. The text with high redundancy and more words falling within the familiarity index (typical features of primerese) tended to be read with more omissions and part-word errors but fewer nonsense and no-response errors. In contrast to these studies with their focus on pseudo-narrative texts for young children, Horning (1993) conducted a study focusing on the effects of redundancy in expository adult texts and reported that an increase in the redundancy in such texts resulted in fewer miscues. This conflicting result actually introduces the linguistic category of genre as a variable to be considered.

A fair amount of research has been conducted on the influence of expository texts on the retelling procedure. Raisner (1978) commented that in her study, adults appeared to have difficulty with the recall of expository texts that lack the common macrostructural features associated with the narrative. O'Brien (1988), in a study using expository texts, did not report the typical strong relationship between the comprehending score and comprehension. The use of expository texts in O'Brien's (1988) study may account for the discrepancy in findings between his study and other research examining the relationship between the comprehending score and comprehension (see the earlier section on silent reading). The explanation for these patterns may be found in Horning's (1993) results that suggest that the nature of the redundancy within expository texts may influence comprehension.

Research has also focused on cue and strategy use within genres. Guzzetti's (1984) study indicates that within the expository genre across different content areas readers were consistent in their use of syntactic and semantic cues. However, many more studies have been conducted using narrative texts, and the results are more varied. For example, Hood's (1982) finding that there were differences in miscue patterns across two narratives appears to contradict that of Herman (1985), who found that the general strategies readers appeared to use on a repeated reading of a text were the same even though 80% of the miscues had changed.

Because of such differences, one approach to considering the generalizability of information gleaned from miscue analysis is to limit the generalizability of the results of miscue analysis only to the extent that the other reading materials read are like the material on which miscue analysis was conducted. Indeed, Goodman et al. (1987) take this approach in their discussion of the implementation of reading strategies for the sample case they present.

Miscue analysis has focused attention on textual characteristics in a relatively unprecedented manner. Because of this, miscue analysis has revealed the problems inherent in making broad generalizations across all texts from a reading of a single text with specific features. From the broad perspective of genre, there appear to be differences in the retelling component of miscue analysis procedures. This is likely due to either a greater familiarity with narrative macrostructures or to the specific content loading of the expository texts. Indeed, experimental evidence by Thorndyke (1977) demonstrates that mere exposure to a text of a particular macrostructure positively affected subsequent readings of texts with similar structures. Leslie's (1980) study also demonstrates the specific impact of genres.

However, an additional layer of complexity should be added because it is in many ways irresponsible to consider the issue of text effects without simultaneously considering the background knowledge of the reader in relation to the text read. In fact, to borrow from Fish (1980), there is no text for the reader unless the reader recognizes it as such. This recognition of the reader within miscue analysis leads directly to the next question on background knowledge and individual differences.

To What Extent are the Inferences from Miscue Analysis Generalizable Across Individuals?

Researchers into miscue analysis such as Hood (1978), Hittleman (1973), Taft and Leslie (1985), and Wixson (1979) have brought up the question of how the reader influences miscue analysis. At the heart of the question of the extent to which inferences are generalizable across individuals is a second question of the extent to which individuals are the same. This question has drawn research from several distinct quarters.

Some researchers (e.g., Arellano-Osuna, 1988) have used miscue analysis to assess the impact of the language of the individual on the use of reading strategies and cueing systems when the mother tongue is not English. However, much additional research has been conducted on ESL students and speakers of low status dialects who are reading standard

English texts. In essence, these studies (see, e.g., Goodman & Goodman, 1978; Miramontes, 1990; Mott, 1981; Zhang, 1988) converge on two general conclusions: (a) there are more similarities than differences in the strategies and cue use of these groups when contrasted with the general population, and (b) the differences that occur can often be explained in terms of the interface between the linguistic features of the text and the languages of the reader.

The interface between the specific linguistic features of a speaker and the text is one example of the background knowledge that the reader holds. The influences of background knowledge apply to the content of the text as well (see Johnston, 1984; Langer, 1984). Goodman (1985/1984) too refers explicitly to what the reader brings to the text. Ultimately, a text has no inherent difficulty in and of itself. It only has difficulty in relation to readers.

Readers can be characterized on any number of variables—age, gender, culture, urban/suburban/rural, and so on. Each of these, to some extent, is a pseudovariable for background knowledge. As with other studies, miscue analysis studies have been conducted on the influence of background knowledge. For instance, Sachs (1984) found that engaging in previewing activities prior to reading results in fewer miscues. Guzzetti (1984) reported that being highly interested in the content of the text positively impacts the comprehension demonstrated in the retelling, and Taft and Leslie (1985) reported that background knowledge influences both miscue patterns and the retelling. Norman et al. (1988) reported use of knowledge as one of five factors that explain 73.9% of the variance in adult reading. Goodman and Goodman (1978) found that fourth and sixth grade readers were able to retell more of a story when the story was culturally relevant. Such patterns confirm the research by others who have studied the influence of background knowledge.

In the literature on miscue analysis there is another way in which background knowledge has been studied. In this instance, the background knowledge at stake is the sociopsycholinguistic knowledge required for reading. These studies typically categorize readers as good and poor, or above and below average. The quest of such studies is usually to determine whether such readers use different strategies in reading. This quest is often motivated by a larger theoretical question on the relative use of graphophonic versus semantic and syntactic information. These studies often use commonly held indicators of reading difficulty to select texts. For instance, Pumfrey and Fletcher (1989) reported that on difficult texts, the number of miscues increases for average and above average readers as does their reliance on graphophonic cues. Yet, when reading less difficult text, these groups made better use of all cues than low average readers.

These miscue analysis studies which focus on individual differences (as marked by membership in small collectives) indicate that there may be differences in how some readers interact with texts as compared with other readers. Such a recognition is not problematic nor is it surprising. Because a uniform coding system was applied to oral reading, such patterns are now more than hunches. Linguistic evidence can be used to justify a more complex view of the reading process and of what it means to be an individual reader of an individual text. Such evidence should raise questions of consequential validity for users of miscue analysis. For instance, patterns of miscues or retellings evident on texts that are culturally foreign may be less indicative of a reader's general reading strategies and cue use than texts that are more familiar. Consequently, users of miscue analysis have an ethical obligation to carefully select texts, know the purposes for which texts are being selected, and know the background and interests of the readers for whom they are selecting texts. Even then, users of miscue analysis must always be mindful of how generalizable their findings are to other contexts and situations.

RELIABILITY

Compared to validity, reliability has been a much less contentious issue in the measurement of reading. *Reliability* refers to the consistency of an individual's performance in repeated trials of an activity or when completing alternate forms of an activity (Crocker & Algina, 1986). In assessments using miscue analysis, reliability comes into play in two different ways. First, it must be considered in terms of the consistency of performance of the reader, and second, it must be considered in terms of the consistency of performance of the persons who are coding the miscues.

Test-retest Reliability

Although it has not been presented as such, there has been some research on what amounts to the test-retest reliability of miscue analysis. This type of reliability focuses on the performance of an individual on the same text at two different readings separated by a time interval. Conceptually, research on the effects of background knowledge should indicate that the reading performance at Time 1 may change at Time 2 because the reader would know the general macrostructure of the story and would be able to better anticipate the kinds of language that the author would use in the text. For instance, as already mentioned, Thorndyke's (1977) classic study demonstrates that mere exposure to story structure advantaged story comprehension.

Gonzales and Elijah (1978) used a format for coding errors that was different than miscue analysis; however, their findings inform miscue analysis research. In an immediate rereading task, only 20% of the errors found in the first reading of the text were found in the second reading. New errors appeared in the second reading but the general patterns of these errors were similar to that found in the first reading. In essence, then, these researchers found that it was likely that prior experience with a text influenced the specific type of error made but not the general strategies used by the reader in reading. This pattern gives some support to the theoretically driven expectancy that prior knowledge influences the reading of a text. Herman's (1985) study in which stories were repeatedly read over an interval of several weeks further supports this general trend because the total number of miscues decreased.

These studies question the traditional conception of test-retest reliability. Because each interaction with the text is another opportunity for hypothesis testing for the reader and because the reader's knowledge of the text will have changed by virtue of having read it, the issue of consistency of performance would seem to be somewhat problematic when it comes to the analysis of repeated readings of texts. An alternative conceptualization of reliability is offered by Moss (1994). She proposes a hermeneutic approach to assessment that

> would involve holistic, integrative interpretations of collected performances that seek to understand the whole in light of its parts, that privilege readers [i.e., assessors] who are most knowledgeable about the context in which the assessment occurs, and that ground those interpretations not only in the textual and contextual evidence available, but also in a rational debate among a community of interpreters. (p. 8)

Moss (1994) argues that in such assessment, inconsistencies in performance would be considered puzzles to be solved rather than indicators of invalid assessment practices. Such a conceptualization would seem more appropriate for miscue analysis than traditional conceptualizations. Miscue analysis, in particular, provides support for this reïnterpretation of reliability given Menosky's (1971) and Mott's (1981) findings that the pattern of miscues changes as the reader moves beyond the first portion of the text.

Interrater Reliability

Because the coding procedure used in miscue analysis requires categorization of miscues, it involves interpretive skills. Typically, in such situations, it must be demonstrated that there is sufficient distinctiveness in the categories so that different coders would generate relatively similar results. If statistics in individual miscue studies are considered, interrater agreement is usually quite achievable. For instance, Carnine, Carnine, and Gerstein (1984), D'Angelo and Mahlios (1983), and D'Angelo (1981) achieved interrater agreements above the 90% level, whereas Englert and Semmel (1981), Guzzetti (1984), and O'Brien (1988) achieved interrater agreements at or above 80%. When alpha reliabilities are calculated, with some exceptions, similarly high results have been obtained. For alpha reliabilities, Hood (1975-1976) reported .97 to .99 for the combined stories in her sample and .84 to .94 for contextual appropriateness when multiple judges were used. In a later study, Hood (1982) reported similar alpha reliabilities (.90 to .99) for all scores except contextual appropriateness, which ranged from .59 to .74 depending on the context considered. Taft and Leslie's (1985) study also reports reasonable alpha reliabilities of .87 to .97.

Hood (1975-1976, 1978, 1982) raises several issues with respect to reliability. Although overall interrater reliability is generally quite respectable, interrater reliability on individual coding categories of miscue analysis (as opposed to the miscue analysis procedure as a whole) is not as strong. The area in which agreements are not as strong are those requiring judgments of the meaning of the miscue in relation to the sentence or text. This is an area that Groff (1980) suggests is open to interpretation. Although not all studies report this problem, it may be an area for particular emphasis in in-service on miscue analysis.

Layered on top of the issue of the lower reliability ratings for individual categories is a second issue—that of the generation of a sufficient number of miscues in an individual category—that Hood (1975-1976) refers to in her research. In her discussion, Hood (1975-1976) blurs the distinctions between the marking and coding systems. Consequently, she is sometimes referring to the coding of particular types of marks rather than the act of coding per se. It can be argued that whether a miscue is a substitution, insertion, or reversal is irrelevant in the coding system; rather, what is relevant are the cueing systems and strategies used regardless of categories. Even if it was considered appropriate to code particular types of markings, the dilemma is this: because reading is a highly interactive process and miscue analysis merely documents that process, it can often be the case that particular types of miscues occur infrequently. When this occurs, interrater agreement can be dramatically affected (e.g., if there are only two miscues requiring a particular coding and there is one disagreement, then interrater agreement is 50%, whereas if there are 25 miscues requiring the same coding and there is one disagreement, then there is 96% agreement). The solution to the dilemma seems to be to preserve the distinction between marking and coding. For research purposes, broad scale studies of particular markings may be of interest (e.g., Goodman & Gollasch, 1980), and in such cases interrater reliabilities are easily calculated across samples of texts.

The difficulties or perceived difficulties in learning miscue analysis have led to the creation of alternate systems (e.g., Cunningham, 1984). In addition, Davey and Theofield (1983) have undertaken a study of the effectiveness of training on teachers' perceptions of reading, their accuracy in generating descriptions of reading behavior, and their judgments of teacher strengths. Although this was not a reliability study, it did demonstrate that teachers could make significant gains in all areas if given education on miscue analysis.

Within miscue studies, three researchers single out the retelling in terms of interrater agreement. Guzzetti (1984) reports an 82% interrater agreement rate, Miramontes (1990) reports .89 interrater reliability, and Beebe (1980) a correlation of 0.99 which yielded an alpha reliability of 0.756. These ranges appear adequate; however, further studies in this area are warranted.

CONCLUSION

This review suggests that there are multiple converging pieces of evidence that can be used to argue for the validity of miscue analysis. Miscue analysis has advanced oral reading analysis by separating the description of a reading from the coding of a reading. Even though miscue analysis is an orally based procedure, it correlates significantly and positively with silent measures of reading. Clusters of miscue categories (which focus on meaning) correlate well with comprehension measures. Miscue analysis reveals both textual and individual reader differences. These patterns should be expected given current theoretical knowledge about reading; indeed, it would be problematic if such patterns did not emerge. Even though there are compelling evidentiary arguments to bolster miscue analysis, a number of areas are in need of improvement. Of particular note are the development of coding procedures for pragmatics and refinements in the retelling procedures.

Despite these problems, miscue analysis appears to be a tool sensitive to many of the subtleties of reading. As such, it can be a powerful instrument. Consequently, the demand that users of miscue analysis be sensitive to the consequences of its use is all the more imperative. It does not present a highly scripted administrative guide nor does it present norming tables for consultation. Instead, it demands that the administrator/interpreter of the procedure be both knowledgeable and reasoned in his or her approach to reading and the reader. If such a criterion is met, then miscue analysis, unlike standardized testing, should reveal much more than it conceals. Furthermore, as witnessed by research on readers with low status dialects or who speak English as a second language, the revelations should provide explanations for performance that maintain an ethic of responsibility to the reader as a learner.

REFERENCES

Altwerger, B., & Goodman, K. S. (1981). *Studying text difficulty through miscue analysis* (Occasional Paper No. 3). Program in Language and Literacy, Arizona Center for Research and Development, College of Education, University of Arizona.

American Psychological Association, AERA, & National Council on Measurement in Education. (1985). *Standards for educational and psychological testing*. Washington, DC: American Psychological Association.

Angoff, W. H. (1988). Validity: An evolving concept. In H. Wainer & H. I. Braun (Eds.), *Test validity* (pp. 19-32). Hillsdale, NJ: Erlbaum.

Arellano-Osuna, A. E. (1988). Oral reading miscues of fourth grade Venezuelan children from five dialect regions. *Dissertation Abstracts International, 49,* 1104-1.

Bean, T. W. (1979). The miscue mini-form: Refining the informal reading inventory. *Reading World, 18*(2), 400-405.

Beebe, M. (1980). The effect of different types of substitution miscues on reading. *Reading Research Quarterly, 15*(3), 324-336.

Beveridge, M., & Griffiths, V. (1987). The effect of pictures on the reading processes of less able readers: A miscue analysis approach. *Journal of Research in Reading, 10*(1), 29-42.

Carey, R. F. (1978). *A psycholinguistic analysis of the effects of semantic acceptability of oral reading miscues on reading comprehension.* Unpublished doctoral dissertation, University of Connecticut, Storrs.

Carnine, L., Carnine, D., & Gerstein, R. (1984). Analysis of oral reading errors made by economically disadvantaged students taught with a synthetic-phonics approach. *Reading Research Quarterly, 19*(3), 343-356.

Clay, M. M. (1991). *Becoming literate: The construction of inner control.* Portsmouth, NH: Heinemann.

Cowie, R. (1985). Reading errors as clues to the nature of reading. In A. L. Ellis (Ed.), *Progress in the psychology of language* (pp. 73-107). Hillsdale, NJ: Erlbaum.

Crocker, L., & Algina, J. (1986). *Introduction to classical and modern test theory*. New York: Holt, Rinehart, and Winston.

Crystal, D. (1987). *The Cambridge encyclopedia of language*. Cambridge: Cambridge University Press.

Cunningham, J. W. (1984). A simplified miscue analysis for classroom and clinic. *Reading Horizons, 24*(2), 83–89.

Cunningham, J. W., & Caplan, R. M. (1982). Investigating the concurrent validity of miscue analysis as a measure of silent reading processes. *Reading World, 21*(4), 299-310.

D'Angelo, K. (1981). Correction behavior of good and poor readers. *Reading World, 21*(2), 123-129.

D'Angelo, K., & Mahlios, M. (1983). Insertion and omission miscues of good and poor readers. *Reading Teacher, 36*(8), 778-782.

Davey, B., & Theofield, M. (1983). An investigation of miscue analysis training for teachers. *Reading Improvement, 20*(2), 105-110.

Englert, C. S., & Semmel, M. I. (1981). The relationship of oral reading substitution miscues to comprehension. *Reading Teacher, 35*, 273-280.

Fawcett, R. (1993). Lecture given at the Pre-Conference Institute of the International Systemic Functional Linguistics Workshop. Vancouver, Canada.

Feathers, K.M. (1985). The semantic features of text: Their interaction and influence on comprehending. *Dissertation Abstracts International, 46*, 937A.

Fish, S. (1980). *Is there a text in this class? The authority of interpretive communities*. Cambridge: Harvard University Press.

Freeman, D. E. (1988). Assignment of pronoun reference: Evidence that young readers control cohesion. *Linguistics and Education, 1*, 153-176.

Gilmore, J. V., & Gilmore, E. C. (1968). *Gilmore Oral Reading Test: Manual of directions*. New York: Harcourt Brace Jovanovich.

Glaser, B. G., & Strauss, A. L. (1967). *The discovery of grounded theory: Strategies for qualitative research*. New York: Aldine de Gruyter.

Golden, J. M., & Pappas, C. C. (1990). A sociolinguistic perspective on retelling procedures in research on children's cognitive processing of written text. *Linguistics and Education, 2*, 21-41.

Gonzales, P. C., & Elijah, D. (1978). Stability of error patterns on the informal reading inventory. *Reading Improvement, 15*(4), 279-288.

Goodman, K. (1969). Analysis of oral reading miscues: Applied psycholinguistics. *Reading Research Quarterly, 5*, 9-30.

Goodman, K. S. (1976). Miscue analysis: Theory and reality in reading. In J. E. Merritt (Ed.), *New horizons in reading* (pp. 15–26) Newark, DE: International Reading Association.

Goodman, K. S. (1982). Reading: A psycholinguistic guessing game. In F. V. Gollasch (Ed.), *Language and literacy—The selected writings of Kenneth S. Goodman* (pp. 33-43). Boston: Routledge & Kegan Paul. (Original work published 1967)

Goodman, K. S. (1982). Miscues: Windows on the reading process. In F. V. Gollasch (Ed.), *Language and literacy. The selected writings of Kenneth S. Goodman. Volume 1: Process, theory, research* (pp. 93-101). Boston: Routledge, Kegan & Paul. (Original work published 1973)

Goodman, K. S. (1983). *Text features as they relate to miscues: Determiners* (Occasional Paper No. 8). Program in Language and Literacy, Arizona Center for Research and Development, College of Education, University of Arizona.

Goodman, K. S. (1985). Unity in reading. In H. Singer & R. B. Ruddell (Eds.), *Theoretical models and processes of reading* (pp. 813-840). Newark, DE: International Reading Association. (Original work published 1984)

Goodman, K. S. (1994). Reading, writing, and written texts: A transactional sociopsycho-linguistic view. In R.B. Ruddell, M.R. Ruddell, & H. Singer (Eds.), *Theoretical models and processes of reading* (pp. 1093-1130). Newark, DE: International Reading Association.

Goodman, K. S., & Bird, L. B. (1982). *On the wording of texts: A study of intra-text word frequency* (Occasional Paper No. 6). Program in Language and Literacy, Arizona Center for Research and Development, College of Education, University of Arizona.

Goodman, K. S., & Burke, C. (1968). *Study of children's behavior while reading orally. Report of Project No. 5425.* Washington, DC: U.S. Dept. of Health, Education and Welfare.

Goodman, K. S., & Burke, C. (1973). *Theoretically based studies of patterns of miscues in oral reading performance* (Final report of project 920.9-0375, Grant No. OEG-0-9370375-4269). Washington, DC: U.S. Dept. of Health, Education and Welfare.

Goodman, K. S., & Burke, C. L. (1982). The Goodman taxonomy of reading miscues. In F. V. Gollasch (Ed.), *Language and literacy: The selected writings of Kenneth S. Goodman* (pp. 215-302). Boston: Routledge & Kegan Paul. (Original work published 1973)

Goodman, K. S., & Gespass, S. (1982). *Text features as they relate to miscues: Pronouns* (Occasional Paper No. 8). Program in Language and Literacy, Arizona Center for Research and Development, College of Education, University of Arizona.

Goodman, K. S., & Gollasch, F. V. (1980). Word omissions: Deliberate and non-deliberate. *Reading Research Quarterly, 16*, 6-31.

Goodman, K. S., & Goodman, Y. M. (1978). *Reading of American children whose language is a stable rural dialect of English or a language other than English* (National Institute of Education contract NIE-C-00-3-0087).

Washington, DC: U.S. Department of Health, Education, and Welfare.

Goodman, Y. M. (1967). *A psycholinguistic description of observed oral reading phenomena in selected beginning readers.* Unpublished doctoral dissertation, Wayne State University, Detroit.

Goodman, Y. M. (1971). *Longitudinal study of children's oral reading behavior* (Final report. Contract No. OEG 5-9-325062-0046). Washington, DC: U.S. Office of Education.

Goodman, Y. M., & Burke, C. L. (1972). *Reading miscue inventory manual: Procedure for diagnosis and evaluation.* New York: Richard C. Owen Publishers.

Goodman, Y.M., & Marek, A. (1995). *Retrospective miscue analysis: Revaluing readers and reading.* New York: Richard C. Owen Publishers.

Goodman, Y. M., Watson, D., & Burke, C. (1987). *Reading miscue inventory: Alternate procedures.* New York: Richard C. Owen Publishers.

Gray, W. S. (1921). Diagnostic and remedial steps in reading. *Journal of Educational Research, 4*(1), 1-15.

Greene, H. A., & Gray, W. S. (1946). The measurement of understanding in the language arts. In N. B. Henry (Ed.), *The measurement of understanding. The forty-fifth yearbook of the National Society for the Study of Education* (pp. 175-200). Chicago: University of Chicago Press.

Groff, P. (1980). A critique of an oral reading miscue analysis. *Reading World, 19*(3), 254-264.

Guzzetti, B. J. (1984). The reading process in content fields: A psycholinguistic investigation. *American Educational Research Journal, 21*(3), 659-668.

Halliday, M. A. K. (1967). *Intonation and grammar in British English.* The Hague: Mouton.

Halliday, M. A. K. (1985). *An introduction to functional grammar.* London: Edward Arnold.

Halliday, M. A. K., & Hasan, R. (1976). *Cohesion in English.* London: Longman.

Herman, P. A. (1985). The effect of repeated readings on reading rate, speech pauses, and word recognition accuracy. *Reading Research Quarterly, 20*(5), 553-565.

Hittleman, D. R. (1973). Seeking a psycholinguistic definition of readability. *Reading Teacher, 26,* 783-789.

Hood, J. (1975-1976). Qualitative analysis of oral reading errors: The inter-judge reliability of scores. *Reading Research Quarterly, 11*(4), 577-598.

Hood, J. (1978). Is miscue analysis practical for teachers? *Reading Teacher, 32,* 260-266.

Hood, J. (1982). The relationship of selected text variables to miscue scores of second graders. *Journal of Reading Behavior, 14*(2), 141-158.

Horning, A. S. (1993). *The psycholinguistics of readable writing: A multidisciplinary exploration*. Norwood, NJ: Ablex.

Huey, E. B. (1968). *The psychology and pedagogy of reading with a review of the history of reading and writing and of methods, texts, and hygiene in reading* Cambridge, MA: The MIT Press. (Original work published 1908)

Johnston, P. H. (1983). *Reading comprehension assessment: A cognitive basis.* Newark, DE: International Reading Association.

Johnston, P. H. (1984). Prior knowledge and reading comprehension. *Reading Research Quarterly, 19,* 219-239.

Kibby, M. W. (1979). Passage readability affects the oral reading strategies of disabled readers. *Reading Teacher, 32,* 390-396.

Langer, J. A. (1984). Examining background knowledge and text comprehension. *Reading Research Quarterly, 19*(4), 468-481.

Leslie, L. (1980). The use of graphic and contextual information by average and below-average readers. *Journal of Reading Behavior, 12*(2), 139-149.

Leu, D. J. (1982). Oral reading error analysis; A critical review of research and application. *Reading Research Quarterly, 17*(3), 420-437.

Lindberg, S. A. (1987). *The relationship between product and in-process assessments of reading of third-grade students.* Unpublished doctoral dissertation, University of Southern California.

Mandler, J. M., & Johnson, N. S. (1977). Remembrance of things parsed. *Cognitive Psychology, 9,* 111-151.

Menosky, D. (1971). *A psycholinguistic description of oral reading miscues generated during the reading of varying portions of text by selected readers from grades two, four, six and eight.* Unpublished doctoral dissertation: Wayne State University, Detroit, MI.

Messick, S. (1988). The once and future issues of validity: Assessing the meaning and consequences of measurement. In H. Wainer & H. I. Braun (Eds.), *Test validity* (pp. 33-45). Hillsdale, NJ: Erlbaum.

Messick, S. (1994). The interplay of evidence and consequences in the validation of performance assessments. *Educational Researcher, 23*(2), 13-23.

Miramontes, O. B. (1990). A comparative study of English oral reading skills in differently schooled groups of Hispanic students. *Journal of Reading Behavior, 22*(4), 373-394.

Moss, P. A. (1994). Can there be validity without reliability? *Educational Researcher, 23*(2), 5-12.

Mott, B. W. (1981). A miscue analysis of German speakers reading in German and English. In S. Hudelson (Ed.), *Learning to read in different languages* (pp. 54-68). Washington, DC: Center for Applied Linguistics.

Murphy, S. M. (1987). *The application of causal modeling to the Goodman model of reading*. Unpublished doctoral dissertation, University of Arizona, Tucson.

Murphy, S. (1994). "No one ever grew taller by being measured": Some educational measurement lessons for Canadians. In L. Erwin & D. MacLennan (Eds.), *Sociology of education in Canada: Critical perspectives on theory, research and practice* (pp. 238-252). Toronto: Copp Clark Longman.

Murphy, S., Shannon, P., Johnston, P., & Hansen, J. (1998). *Fragile evidence: A critique of reading assessment*. Mahwah, NJ: Erlbaum.

Newman, H. (1978). Oral reading miscue analysis is good but not complete. *Reading Teacher, 31*(8), 883-886.

Norman, C. A., Malicky, G., & Fagan, W. T. (1988). The reading processes of adults in literacy programs. *Adult Literacy and Basic Education, 12*(1), 14-26.

O'Brien, D. G. (1988). The relation between oral reading miscue patterns and comprehension: A test of the relative explanatory power of psycholinguistic and interactive views of reading. *Journal of Psycholinguistic Research, 17*(5), 379-401.

Page, W. D. (1976). Pseudocues, supercues and comprehension. *Reading World, 15*(4), 232-238.

Page, W. D. (1977). Comprehending and cloze performance. *Reading World, 17*(1), 17-22.

Page, W. D. (1979). Oral reading error correction behavior and cloze performance. *Reading World, 19*(2), 168-178.

Page, W. D. (1982). *The altercue comprehension technique*. Storrs: The University of Connecticut Cooperative Corporation.

Pappas, C. C., Kiefer, B. Z., & Levstik, L. S. (1990). *An integrated language perspective in the elementary school: Theory into action*. New York: Longman.

Payne, C. S. (1930). The classification of errors in oral reading. *Elementary School Journal, 31*(2), 142-146.

Pugh, A. K., & Ulijn, J. M. (1985). Realistic reading tasks in research in reading. *I.T.L. Review of Applied Linguistics, 69*, 29-41.

Pumfrey, P. D., & Fletcher, J. (1989). Differences in reading strategies among 7 to 8 year old children. *Journal of Research in Reading, 12*(2), 114-130.

Raisner, B. (1977). *Reading strategies employed by non-proficient adult college students as observed through miscue analysis.* Unpublished doctoral dissertation, Hofstra University, Hempstead, NY.

Raisner, B. (1978). Adult reading strategies: Do they differ from the strategies of children? *Reading World, 18*(1), 37-47.

Rosenblatt, L. M. (1978). *The reader, the text, the poem: The transactional theory of the literary work.* Carbondale: Southern Illinois University Press.

Sachs, A. (1984). The effects of previewing activities on oral reading miscues. *Reading and Special Education, 5*(3), 45-49.

Sadoski, M. C. (1981). *The relationships between student retellings and selected comprehension measures.* Unpublished doctoral dissertation, University of Connecticut, Storrs.

Sadoski, M., & Page, W. D. (1984). Miscue combination scores and reading comprehension: Analysis and comparison. *Reading World, 23,* 43-53.

Sampson, M. R., Briggs, L. D., & White, J. H. (1988). Student authorship and reading: The joy of literacy. *Reading Improvement, 25*(1), 82-84.

Siegel, F. (1979). Adapted miscue analysis. *Reading World, 19*(1), 36-43.

Simons, H. D., & Ammon, P. (1989). Child knowledge and primerese text: Mismatches and miscues. *Research in the Teaching of English, 23*(4), 380-398.

Smith, F. (1988). *Understanding reading: A psycholinguistic analysis of reading and learning to read* (4th ed.). Hillsdale, NJ: Erlbaum.

Taft, M. L., & Leslie, L. (1985). The effects of prior knowledge and oral reading accuracy on miscues and comprehension. *Journal of Reading Behavior, 17*(2), 163-179.

Thorndyke, P. W. (1977). Cognitive structures in comprehension and memory of narrative discourse. *Cognitive Psychology, 9,* 77-110.

Tortelli, J. P. (1976). Simplified psycholinguistic diagnosis. *Reading Teacher, 29*(7), 637-639.

Wangberg, E. G., & Thompson, B. (1982). Miscue and cognitive development patterns of differentially skilled readers. *Reading Improvement, 19*(2), 98-103.

Weber, R. (1968). The study of oral reading errors: A survey of the literature. *Reading Research Quarterly, 4*(1), 96-119.

Wixson, K. L. (1979). Miscue analysis: A critical review. *Journal of Reading Behavior, 11*(2), 163-175.

Worsnop, C. M. (1980). *A procedure for using the technique of the Reading Miscue Inventory as a remedial teaching tool with adolescents* (ERIC Document Reproduction Number ED 324 644)

Zhang, J. (1988). Reading miscues and 9 adult Chinese learners of English. *Journal of Reading, 32*(1), 34-41.

Chapter Six

Empirical Evidence for the Validity and Reliability of Miscue Analysis as a Measure of Reading Comprehension

Mark Sadoski
Texas A&M University

Robert F. Carey
Rhode Island College

William D. Page†
University of Connecticut

This chapter deals with empirical evidence for the validity and reliability of miscue analysis, and particularly scoring systems derived from miscue analysis, as indicators or measures of reading comprehension. Although a miscue analysis is not a test, nor should miscues by any means be equated with test items, the approach to validity and reliability assumed here is that of "classical" measurement theory: to treat miscues as responses indicative of the workings of a psychological construct, subject to the same professional standards of validation as other psychological tests and measures.

†Deceased in 1984. William D. Page was the inspiration and impetus for much of the research reported here and is included honorifically. Any errors or omissions are the sole responsibility of the other authors.

Standards for such validation were originally suggested by a joint committee of the American Psychological Association (APA), the American Educational Research Association (AERA), and the National Council on Measurements in Education (NCME) (APA, 1966; updated by AERA, APA, & NCME, 1985). Three types of validity are identified: content, criterion-related, and construct. Seminal explication of these ideas is often attributed to Cronbach (1971). We have employed Cronbach's recent discussion of these three types of validity, plus a fourth type which has since been suggested: validity as persuasive argument (Cronbach, 1984). We have also drawn on a parallel discussion by Nunnally (1978) which discusses content validity, criterion-related validity, construct validity, and validity as circumstantial evidence for the usefulness of a new measurement method. Similarly, we look at miscue reliability from a "classical" perspective, investigating possible sources of error such as rater variability in the findings of miscue research.

A comprehensive review of the literature investigating the validity and reliability of miscue analysis is presented elsewhere in this volume (see Murphy). This chapter offers additional insights and focuses in detail on validity and reliability evidence as derived from three miscue databases collected by the authors between 1978 and 1985.

MISCUES AND ALTERCUES

The Altercue Matrix

The specific approach to miscue analysis used here is to employ the concept of an "altercue continuum" (Page, 1978). The term "altercue" is used as a substitute for "miscue" simply to denote the fact that miscues are not all erroneous, as the prefix "mis" implies, but can alternately be indicators of very successful reading, very unsuccessful reading, or some degree of reading in between. The altercue continuum conceptualization posits that because all frequency counts of miscues or altercues can be statistically described in relation to other measures of reading comprehension, all miscues can be categorized as strong positive predictors, strong negative predictors, or weak predictors of other measures of reading comprehension. Strong positive predictors have been termed *supercues* (for superreading), strong negative predictors have been termed *pseudocues* (for pseudoreading), and weak or nonsignificant predictors have been termed *entropicues* (to indicate entropy) (Page, 1978).

Operational definitions for supercues, pseudocues, and entropicues were empirically established by Carey (1978). Using the altercue continuum as a basis, an Altercue Matrix was constructed in which miscues were classified according to their degree of semantic acceptability and the type of correction behavior demonstrated by the reader. Both the semantic acceptability and correction behavior associated with miscues have been shown in previous research to be major characteristics of miscues that are theoretically and empirically related to reading comprehension (e.g., Clay, 1969; Goodman & Burke, 1973).

The Altercue Matrix uses five degrees of semantic acceptability and four categories of correction behavior drawn from the Goodman Taxonomy of Oral Reading Miscues (Goodman, 1969). In the Altercue Matrix, all miscues are categorized as being semantically acceptable either: (a) within the entire passage being read, (b) within the sentence in which the miscue occurs but not the entire passage, (c) with what precedes the miscue in the sentence but not with what follows it in the sentence, (d) with what follows the miscue in the sentence but not with what precedes it in the sentence, or (e) completely semantically unacceptable. In the Altercue Matrix all miscues are also categorized according to the correction behavior elicited: (a) successfully corrected, (b) a partially successful correction attempt, (c) an unsuccessful correction attempt, or (d) no correction attempt. This dual classification system results in a 5x4 matrix that defines 20 possible miscue types. The Altercue Matrix with miscue types M1 to M20 is exhibited in Figure 6.1.

Semantic Acceptability	**Correction Behavior**			
	Successful	Partially Successful	Unsuccessful	No Attempt
In Total Passage	M1	M2	M3	M4
In Sentence Only	M5	M6	M7	M8
With Prior Sentence Context	M9	M10	M11	M12
With Following Sentence Context	M13	M14	M15	M16
Unacceptable	M17	M18	M19	M20

Figure 6.1. The Altercue Matrix (from Carey, 1978)

Using multiple regression techniques, Carey (1978) determined that miscues 1, 4, and 9 could be classified as supercues, the strongest positive predictors of other measures of reading comprehension; that miscue 20 could be classified as a pseudocue, the strongest negative predictor of other measures of reading comprehension; and that the remaining miscue types could be classified as entropicues, or weaker, nonsignificant predictors of other measures of reading comprehension.

Miscue Combination Scores

A small variety of miscue combination scores have been formulated with the goal of reducing a reader's miscue performance to a numerical score. Several of these scoring systems have been empirically tested. These include the Comprehending Score, the Comprehension Process Score, the Altercue Index, the Extended Altercue Index, and the Additive Index. The formulation and empirical base for each of these is briefly discussed in turn.

The Comprehending Score. This was developed by Goodman and Burke (1973) and Rousch (1976). This score is obtained by adding the percent of miscues that are fully semantically acceptable to the percent of miscues that are not semantically acceptable but are successfully corrected. Using the Altercue Matrix (Figure 6.1) this score would be calculated by adding the respective percentages of miscues 1, 2, 3, 4, 5, 9, 13, and 17 (see Figure 6.2). The Comprehending Score has been demonstrated to have significant positive relationships to various other reading comprehension measures in Goodman and Burke (1973), Sadoski and Page (1984), and Sadoski and Lee (1986).

The Comprehension Process Score. This score was developed by Sadoski (1980, 1985a) and is the ratio of the percentage of miscues that are significant positive predictors of comprehension (supercues) to the total percentage of miscues that are both significant positive predictors and significant negative predictors of comprehension (supercues and pseudocues). A formula for computing this score is given in Figure 6.2. The Comprehension Process Score has been demonstrated to have significant positive relationships to various other reading comprehension measures in Sadoski (1981), Sadoski, Page, and Carey (1981), and Sadoski and Lee (1986).

The Altercue Index. This score was developed by Page (1982). It is computed by adding the percentage of the three strongest supercues—1, 4, and 9—to the percentage of the three strongest pseudocues—20, 8, and 12. (See Figure 6.2). The Altercue Index has been demonstrated to have significant positive relationships to various other reading comprehension measures in Sadoski and Page (1984) and Sadoski and Lee (1986).

The Extended Altercue Index. This score was developed by Page (1982) and is similar to the Altercue Index except that still more of the less strong supercues and pseudocues are included in the computation. (See Figure 6.2). This score has also been demonstrated to have significant positive relationships to various other reading comprehension measures in Sadoski and Page (1984) and Sadoski and Lee (1986).

The Additive Index. This score was developed by Page (1982). In this score, the percents of all miscues that are positive correlates of reading comprehension are added and the percents of all miscues that are negative correlates of reading comprehension are then subtracted to produce a score (See Figure 6.2). This score has also been demonstrated to have significant positive relationships to various other reading comprehension measures in Sadoski and Page (1984) and Sadoski and Lee (1986).

Comprehending Score = M1 + M2 + M3 + M4 + M5 + M9 + M13 + M17

Comprehension Process Score = $\frac{M1 + M4 + M9}{100 - (100 - (M1 + M4 + M9 + M20))} \times 100$

Altercue Index = M1 + M4 + M9 - M8 - M12 - M20

Extended Altercue Index = M1 + M3 + M4 + M9 - M6 - M8 - M12 - M15 - M17 - M20

Additive Index = M1 + M2 + M3 + M4 + M5 + M7 + M9 + M13 + M14 - M8 - M10 - M11 - M12 - M15 - M16 - M17 - M18 - M19 - M20

Figure 6.2. Miscue Combination Score Formulas (from Sadoski & Page, 1984)*

*All formulas use percentage of miscue types

Validation Data Base

The five foregoing miscue combination scores are used here in an effort to circumspectly investigate the empirical validity of miscue analysis as a measure of reading comprehension. The data for this investigation are aggregated from Carey (1978) and Sadoski (1981, 1985b). Carey's (1978) data included 100 subjects from a suburban Rhode Island school randomly selected from grades 6, 7, 8, and 9 who orally read a story appropriate to the age group. Sadoski's (1981) data included 48 subjects comprising the entire fifth grade of a suburban Connecticut school who orally read another story appropriate to the age group. Sadoski's (1985b) data included 26 subjects comprising the entire third and fourth grades of a suburban Texas school who orally read another story appropriate to the age group. All 174 students were administered a miscue analysis on their oral reading and, in addition, were given a standardized reading comprehension test appropriate to their grade level (either the California Achievement Test or the Metropolitan Achievement Test), and a 50 item post-oral-reading cloze text constructed from a passage taken from the story read orally for the miscue analysis.

The miscue analyses were administered in accordance with procedures in Goodman and Burke (1972). Each of the first 25 miscues for each subject was subsequently classified in the Altercue Matrix (Figure 6.1). The standardized tests were administered using their respective standard procedures, and the post oral-reading cloze tests were administered in accordance with procedures validated by Bormuth (1975) and Page (1975). Additional reading comprehension measures available in Sadoski's (1981) data included story retellings done according to the format described in Goodman and Burke (1972). Evidence for the reliability and validity of this data was demonstrated in Sadoski (1981). Another measure, a 9-item passage-dependent multiple-choice test, was also employed in Sadoski's (1981) data. This test was constructed in accordance with guidelines for passage dependency in Hanna and Oaster (1978-1979); reliability and validity were demonstrated in Sadoski (1981). The foregoing data were drawn on and analyzed here to address validity and reliability issues. We now consider those issues, providing empirical demonstrations as called for.

CONTENT VALIDITY

The basic question in the content validation of miscues might be phrased: Is the "content" of miscues representative of the "content" of reading comprehension? That is, are deviations from the expected response to a text useful in determining that a reader is processing a text with comprehension?

"Error" analysis has enjoyed a long and fruitful history for researchers in psychology, language, and learning. Piaget's early interest in mental development was propelled by his work in standardizing intelligence tests in Alfred Binet's laboratory. Piaget became absorbed in children's incorrect answers and began to explore the processes by which children arrived at their responses. These insights led to much of his qualitative theorizing about intellectual growth (Ginsburg & Opper, 1979). In psychoanalysis, Freud described how a reading error may anticipate something that is becoming conscious in the person who makes the error (Freud, 1901/1960). Such errors, colloquially known as "Freudian slips," are seen to be the external manifestation of underlying thoughts. Bettleheim and Zelan (1981) carried these Freudian insights into investigations of children's oral reading. Thorndike (1917) published a very influential study of mistakes in paragraph reading and determined that errors could be seen as more potent or less potent. Bartlett (1932) studied deviations in subjects' memory of unfamiliar stories that they had read and found these deviations to be useful in understanding how people comprehend, remember, and recall stories. This research has been influential in the development of modern schema theory, which is very much concerned with meaningful variations and deviations from texts (e.g., Steffenson, Joag-Dev, & Anderson, 1979). Error analysis has also characterized much research in composition (Kroll & Schafer, 1978), ESL (Richards, 1974), and mathematics learning (Ashlock, 1994).

In keeping with this tradition, Goodman (1977) described miscues as "windows on the reading process" through which the nature of the underlying process could be studied. Besides deriving from a fruitful tradition of error analysis, miscues have a substantial theoretical base in linguistics, cognitive psychology, and psycholinguistics. The original Goodman Taxonomy of Oral Reading Miscues (Goodman, 1969) was substantially linked to the transformational-generative grammar of Chomsky (1957). The history of this and other developments in linguistics that contributed to the development of miscue analysis is recounted in Allen (1976).

In psychology, theories of cognition as typified by Neisser (1967, 1977) hold that in perception and cognition we constantly use anticipation and prediction based on past experiences to shape our perception of new experiences and guide our search of available information in constructing meaning and knowledge. The use of psychological prediction and the linguistic transformation of deep structures to surface structures are central precepts in the "psycholinguistic guessing game" theory and model of reading on which miscue analysis is based (Goodman, 1967). Similar models of the reading process have also been put forward by other psycholinguists (Ruddell, 1969; Smith, 1988).

Because the research tradition and theoretical bases of miscue analysis are firmly founded in related modern sciences, miscue analysis can be seen to explore the same "content" as that studied in accepted research paradigms in related fields of knowledge. There is also theoretical support that miscues are evidence of mental processes important to reading. These findings confer a substantial degree of content validity on miscue analysis as an indicator of the process of reading comprehension.

CRITERION-RELATED VALIDITY

Criterion-related validity is determined by a measure's ability to predict; that is, its degree of correspondence with outcomes on other measures of the same construct or another suitable criterion variable. A technique often used in establishing this type of validity is the correlation of the measure in question with accepted measures of the same construct or other theoretically related external criteria.

One consideration with this type of validation is the nature of the criteria. Because no single criterion exists in reading comprehension measurement that is irrefutable, multiple criteria are in order. In the data set employed for this study, two commonly accepted criteria were used with all subjects, and two other validated criteria were used with subgroups. The two primary criteria were widely accepted standardized reading comprehension tests and cloze tests; the other measures were retellings and a passage-dependent multiple choice test. This array of measures substantially satisfies the need for multiple criteria.

A second consideration with this type of validation is the degree of correspondence sought between the measures. Extreme correspondence between miscues and the common criterion measures used here is unlikely, in that miscues are an oral reading measure taken from a reading in progress (i.e., a process measure), whereas the other measures are from silent reading or derived after the reading is completed (i.e., product measures). The impact of the text mutilation and clerical tasks in the cloze test, and the demonstrated effects of memory and prior knowledge on standardized reading test performance (Johnston, 1984), also mediate against very high correlations. Sadoski and Page (1984) suggest that an oral reading process measure might be expected to account for roughly half the variance in a post-reading criterion such as a standardized test. Similarly, miscue scores might account for roughly half the variance in a cloze task involving the silent reading of mutilated text with attendant clerical responsibilities. These variance estimates are seen as rational, "ballpark" estimates only. Applying these estimates as criteria for validity would call for correlation coefficients approaching .70.

In order to assess the criterion-related validity of miscues in the form of various miscue combination scores, the database for this study was analyzed using both simple and partial correlation. Because the database involved students from grades 3-9 reading three stories of differing difficulty, grade level was held constant through partialing to neutralize the effects that passage difficulty may have had on processing (cf. Blaxall & Willows, 1984; Leu, 1982; Wixson, 1979), or that developmental changes in the quality of miscues might account for (Christie, 1981). Standardized test scores were converted to z scores for comparability. The zero-order and first-order partial correlations for the set of miscue combination scores are given in Table 6.1.

Observing the partial correlations, all coefficients are .60 or higher, with the exception of the coefficients for the Comprehending Score. The highest partial correlation coefficient, found between the Comprehension Process Score and the standardized reading comprehension test, is $r = .66$, $p < .0001$. This is nearly as high as most standardized reading tests correlate with each other.

Subsets of this database analyzed elsewhere provide further criterion-related validity estimates. Sadoski (1981) found Comprehension Process Scores correlated with retelling total scores at $r = .62$, $p < .001$, using 48 fifth graders. Lower, but statistically significant correlations were also found between the Comprehending Score and retelling scores in Goodman and Burke (1973) and Goodman and Goodman (1978).

Using 48 fifth graders, Sadoski and Page (1984) found the following correlations between passage-dependent multiple choice test scores and the various miscue combination scores: Comprehending Score: $r = .32$, $p < .01$; Comprehension Process Score: $r = .37$, $p < .005$; Altercue Index: $r = .33$, $p < .01$; Extended Altercue Index: $r = .33$, $p < .01$; Additive Index: $r = .34$, $p < .009$. These correlations are distinctly lower, quite probably due to a ceiling effect in the passage-dependent multiple choice test data that restricted the range of variation (Sadoski, 1981). However, the pattern of performance of the miscue scores is much the same as with the standardized test and cloze variables; the Comprehending Score exhibits the lowest correlation coefficient, and the Comprehension Process Score exhibits the highest correlation coefficient.

In summary, all the miscue combination scores correlate in a generally expected manner with other reading measures of accepted

Table 6.1. Zero–Order (*r*) and Partial Correlations Controlling for Grade Level (*rp*) Between Miscue Combination Scores and Criterion Variables (N = 174).*

	Comprehending Score		Comprehension Process Score		Altercue Index		Extended Altercue Index		Additive Index	
	r	*rp*	*r*	*rp*	*r*	*rp*	*r*	*rp*	*r*	*rp*
Standardized Reading Comprehension Test	.56	.55	.67	.66	.61	.60	.62	.61	.61	.60
Cloze Test	.56	.57	.58	.61	.60	.61	.64	.64	.61	.62

*All correlations are significant at $p < .0001$ or beyond.

validation. This holds true using a large sample of socially and geographically diverse students drawn from primary grades through high school reading several different stories and employing analytical methods that control for certain sources of extraneous variance. This evidence confers a substantial degree of criterion-related validity on miscue analysis scoring as a measure of reading comprehension.

CONSTRUCT VALIDITY

The term "construct" in construct validity derives from the word "construe": A construct is a way of constructing, organizing, and explaining what has been observed. Construct validity deals with the identification of a measure with the construct it supposedly reflects, and not other constructs. Essentially, construct validity looks at the relative degree of the "purity" of a measure in what it claims to measure. The process of construct validation is ongoing, fluid, and subject to theory (Cronbach, 1984).

In using numerical scores, the technique of factor analysis is very useful in a "classical" psychometric demonstration of construct validity (Crocker & Algina, 1986; Cronbach, 1984; Nunnally, 1978). Essentially, factor analysis statistically reveals dimensions of correlated variables which can be thought of as unitary attributes, that is, constructs. The construct validity of a given measure can then be inferred from the extent to which it correlates with, or loads on, the factor or factors in question. Factor analysis is empirically very useful in determining the internal structure of a set of variables thought to measure a construct.

Although there is no given size to such a set of variables, factor analysis must be substantially multivariate for useful interpretations to emerge. Data from Sadoski (1981) were selected for factor analysis because five accepted measures of reading comprehension were available for each subject. These measures included Comprehension Process Scores, post-oral-reading cloze test scores, retelling total scores, passage-dependent multiple choice test scores, and standardized reading comprehension test scores. Following Nunnally's (1978) recommendation for factor analyses using smaller numbers of variables, a principal-factor method was employed using communalities in the leading diagonal, with iterations. Using the standard eigenvalue criterion of 1.00, a single factor was extracted that accounted for 63.0% of the total variance. This factor is exhibited in Table 6.2. Loadings of the five variables on the factor are all very substantial, with the highest loadings being associated with the standardized reading comprehension

Table 6.2. Factor Analysis of Five Reading Comprehension Variables (N = 48).

Variable	Factor I
Standardized Reading Comprehension Test	.90
Comprehension Process Score	.80
Post Oral-Reading Cloze Test	.77
Retelling Total Score	.68
Passage-Dependent Multiple-Choice Test	.50

% of Total Variance = 63%

test and the Comprehension Process Score, respectively. As the Comprehension Process Score behaves in a manner similar to other miscue combination scores in the partial correlations (see Table 6.1), it might be seen as representative of these scores as a group. To the extent that the single factor in this analysis can be seen to signify the construct "reading comprehension," the Comprehension Process Score, and by inference the other miscue combination scores, are highly representative of this construct. These findings are consonant with more complex factor-analytic studies using still more variables in Sadoski (1983, 1985b).

Although the logic of factor analysis offers compelling evidence for the construct validity of miscue analysis, perhaps a more prudent approach would be to treat factorial validity as a necessary but not sufficient condition for construct validity. Another approach to construct validity is to establish both convergence and discriminability (Campbell & Fiske, 1959; Crocker & Algina, 1986). Convergence can be demonstrated when different methods of measurement converge on the same construct, as in factor analysis. Discriminability, however, comes from determining what the measure in question can be discriminated from, that is, what it is not correlated with or what it is negatively correlated with.

Evidence for discriminability is available from earlier miscue studies and in Sadoski's (1981, 1985b) data in the form of miscues per hundred words (MPHW) for the subjects' oral readings. Goodman and Burke (1973) and Goodman and Goodman (1978) have determined that an inverse relationship exists between the quantity of miscues and the ability of the reader to retain meaning or quality in reading. A negative correlation of $r = -.67$ was found between Comprehending Scores and MPHW in a total population of 94 students from second, fourth, sixth, eighth, and tenth grades (Goodman & Burke, 1973). Negative correlations ranging from r = -.32 to r = -.60 were found between Comprehending Scores and MPHW in populations of second, fourth, and sixth grade students selected on the basis of geographic, cultural, and dialect diversity (Goodman & Goodman, 1978). Similar findings are found in Sadoski (1981) in which MPHW for entire stories are negatively correlated with Comprehension Process Scores, r= -.61, in 48 fifth graders; and in Sadoski's (1985b) data in which a negative partial correlation of r= -.58, controlling for grade level, is found in 26 third and fourth graders. These findings further support the contentions of Goodman and Burke (1973) and Goodman and Goodman (1978) and adhere to the traditional notion in reading diagnosis that excessive deviations from the expected response to the text are indicative of material that is confusing, incomprehensible, or too difficult for the reader (Betts, 1957). These findings indicate that miscue analysis scoring is useful in discriminating readings in which a high degree of comprehension likely exists from those in which it likely does not; that is, students who have higher miscue scores are finding the passage more comprehensible and are making fewer overall miscues. This confers some measure of discriminant validity on miscue scoring.

Another type of evidence for the construct validity of miscue analysis and miscue scores can be found in the degree to which reader background knowledge effects miscues. Numerous studies have demonstrated the general effect of background knowledge on reading comprehension (Spiro, Bruce, & Brewer, 1980). If miscues can be considered true indicators of comprehension, then readers' prior knowledge of the content of passages being read should have effects on miscue performance.

Rousch (1972) qualitatively analyzed the types of miscues made by children who had either high or low prior knowledge of a science passage, and found that the high prior knowledge group made more miscues that were syntactically and semantically acceptable and corrected miscues that changed meaning more often than the low prior knowledge group. Taft and Leslie (1985) extended this knowledge by investigating the effect of high and low background knowledge on miscue quality and other reading comprehension measures while controlling for oral reading accuracy (95-99% accuracy vs. 90-94% accuracy). Results indicated that regardless of reading accuracy, children with high prior knowledge made significantly more semantically acceptable miscues and relied less on graphic cues by making significantly fewer miscues that were graphically similar to the words in print. The children with high prior knowledge also correctly answered significantly more comprehension questions of three types: textually explicit, textually implicit, and scriptally implicit. These findings suggest that miscue qualities are functionally related to reader knowledge independent of oral reading accuracy rates. Similar findings were reported by Malik (1990), who found that miscue semantic and syntactic acceptability with the prior context of the sentence was greater for culturally familiar text than for culturally unfamiliar text in EFL readers. These readers also comprehended the culturally familiar text better as determined by retelling scores. This evidence also suggests the construct validity of miscue analysis.

A final type of evidence for the construct validity of miscue scores might be found in the extent to which these scores are sensitive to treatment or instruction. An ample literature is available to demonstrate that instruction affects characteristic patterns of miscues (Wixson, 1979). For example, the tendency of heavy emphasis on phonics in early reading instruction to produce readers whose miscues are graphophonically similar to the text but lack semantic acceptability and contextual appropriateness has been demonstrated by Elder (1971) in Scotland; Barr (1972), DeLawter (1975), Norton (1976), and Carnine, Carnine, and Gersten (1984) in the United States; and Board (1982) in Canada. Research by Hoffman, O'Neal, Kastler, Clements, Segel, & Nash (1984) and Chinn, Waggoner, Anderson, Schommer, and Wilkinson (1993) found that characteristics of teacher feedback to miscues influenced the characteristics of those miscues. The finding that miscue processes seem to be to some degree affected by instructional treatment adds an additional note of construct validity to these measures.

VALIDITY AS PERSUASIVE ARGUMENT

Although the logical intricacies of construct validity pose a formidable argument for validation, the bottom line in validation is the collective judgment of a forum of critical users (Cronbach, 1984). Measures finally become valid if they are persuasive enough to become accepted as useful in the field they claim to serve. Nunnally (1978) states:

> Although there is nothing wrong with the logical analysis that was presented [factor analysis], one could rightly argue that all this fuss and bother about construct validity really boils down to something rather homespun—namely, *circumstantial evidence* for the usefulness of a new measurement method. New measurement methods, like most new ways of doing things, should not be trusted until they have proved themselves in many applications. If over the course of numerous investigations a measuring instrument produces interesting findings and tends to fit the construct name applied to the instrument, then

> investigators are encouraged to continue using the instrument in research and to use the name to refer to the instrument. . . . From the standpoint of the work-a-day world of the behavioral scientist, essentially this is what construct validity is about. (p. 109)

In order to determine the general degree of acceptance that miscue analysis has received, a literature search was undertaken. The ERIC database was computer scanned for all documents abstracted in *Resources in Education*, and for journal articles abstracted in *Current Index to Journals in Education*, in which the word "miscue" appeared in the title or in which the author(s) identified "miscue" as an ERIC descriptor for the piece. This search provision was used to place the decision on the authors of the articles themselves as to whether the piece was significantly related to miscue analysis. This search, therefore, did not include studies in which miscue analysis may have been used but was not considered to be a major thrust of the study. Excluded also from the search were doctoral dissertation abstracts (only full dissertations refereed and accepted into ERIC) and miscue bibliographies. The remaining entries included a number of federally funded study reports; journal articles from the United States, Great Britain, Australia, and China; studies using miscue analysis with varied populations including various age and dialect groups, bilinguals, delinquents, emotionally disturbed, learning disabled, mentally retarded, deaf, blind, and learners with various cognitive styles; miscue relationships to writing; and critiques and rebuttals of miscue theory and/or procedures. Many, if not most, of these studies were conducted by researchers other than the originators of miscue analysis, including several of the federally funded research projects. Many of these studies used selected categories of miscues to describe the performance of readers or the reactions of teachers to readers' miscues.

This literature search revealed that on average, about 14 miscue studies per year were added to the ERIC database between 1970 and 1993. Studies in which miscue analysis was noted as a major thrust seem to have enjoyed an initial surge of interest with the introduction of the miscue analysis procedures in the early 1970s, and have since found an equilibrium of use. This suggests that miscue analysis has become an accepted tool. These findings suggest a substantial degree of acceptance of miscue analysis among researchers and practitioners.

RELIABILITY

Reliability is usually seen as a prerequisite to, or companion of, validity; that is, reliability is seen as a necessary but not sufficient condition for validity. Unreliable measurements put limits on validity; they are unpredictable and cannot be depended on to serve their purpose in a consistently interpretable way (Crocker & Algina, 1986; Cronbach, 1984; Nunnally, 1978). Reliability estimates relative to subjective scoring have been approached in two ways: intrarater reliability (the same rater rescoring the same data at separate points in time) or interrater reliability (different raters independently scoring the same data). Reliability is often approximated by simply finding the correlation coefficient between the different sets of scores in these two cases. A more sophisticated assessment of reliability is to use reliability coefficients which are derived from broad theories of measurement error. Nunnally (1978) suggests that reliability coefficient alpha (Cronbach's alpha) be applied to all new measurement methods.

Hood (1975-1976) determined alpha reliability coefficients for miscues classified in a similar manner used to determined the miscue combination scores described here. In Hood's study, five trained raters classified all the miscues of 45 students reading two stories each as: (a) contextually appropriate in the passage as a whole, (b) contextually appropriate in the sentence only, (c) contextually appropriate with the previous context in the sentence, or (d) not contextually appropriate. Miscues were also classified as either corrected or not corrected. The following alpha reliability coefficients were reported for the categories of contextual appropriateness (i.e., semantic acceptability): passage = .95, sentence only = .84, prior context in sentence = .88, not appropriate = .93. The alpha reliability for the correction judgment was .98 overall, and ranged from a low of .84 to a high of .94 for proportion of corrections rated within the four categories of contextual appropriateness.

Carey (1978), using three independent raters, demonstrated an interrater correlation coefficient of $r = .96$ for the categorization of miscues into the Altercue Matrix (Figure 6.1). Sadoski (1981) demonstrated the following intrarater correlation coefficient for the altercue categories used in the Comprehension Process Score: supercues $r = .97$, pseudocues $r = .91$, entropicues $r = .91$, Comprehension Process Scores $r = .96$.

Other researchers have also demonstrated high reliability using categorizations similar to those used here. Carnine, Carnine, and Gersten (1984), using Goodman's Taxonomy of miscues, reported an average interrater agreement of 93% in classifying semantic and syntactic acceptability with the prior portion of the sentence, following portion of the sentence, or total sentence, and whether or not the miscue was self-corrected, among other categories. Christie (1981) similarly reports interrater agreement of at least 90% on semantic acceptability/unacceptability and corrected/uncorrected classifications.

CONCLUSION

The issues of validity and reliability surrounding the use of miscue analysis as a reading comprehension scoring technique have been addressed in this chapter, but by no means exhaustively. Empirical evidence for the validity of miscue combination scores has been presented according to established professional standards, drawing on a substantial population of students from upper primary to secondary grades in different geographic locations reading different texts. Evidence for the reliability of miscue scoring in this fashion has also been presented from various sources. Validity, however, is relative and perhaps never completely achieved. As Kerlinger (1973) pointed out, the idea of validity is heavily philosophical, inquiring into the reality, nature, and meaning of the properties being measured. We also acknowledge that there are other validity issues not addressed here, such as the practical and ethical consequences of the use of an assessment device (see Moss, 1992, for a review). It is perhaps most appropriate to view this chapter as an incremental contribution toward the validation of certain miscue analysis procedures, with much left unsaid, and more work to be done.

Nor have we discussed the limitations of the use of miscue analysis or miscue combination scores. None of these techniques is powerful enough to be the sole basis for decisions that affect the academic destinies of children. Miscue combination scores have noteworthy limitations on their clinical use and on their use in research (cf. Sadoski, 1985a; Sadoski & Page, 1984). Our purpose here has not been the circumspect examination of all related issues, but an examination of the basic viability of the use of miscue analysis as an indicator of reading comprehension consistent with established professional standards for the measurement of such constructs. We hope that this chapter serves to stimulate continued exploration of these issues.

REFERENCES

Allen, P.D. (1976). The miscue research studies. In P.D. Allen & D.J. Watson (Eds.), *Findings of research in miscue analysis: Classroom implications* (pp. 1-9). Urbana, IL: ERIC, National Council of Teachers of English.

American Educational Research Association, American Psychological Association, & National Council on Measurement in Education (1985). *Standards for educational and psychological testing*. Washington DC: American Educational Research Association.

American Psychological Association (1966). *Standards for educational psychological tests*. Washington DC: American Psychological Association.

Ashlock, R. (1994). *Error patterns in computation* (6th ed.). Columbus, OH: Merrill.

Barr, R.C. (1972). The influence of instructional conditions on word recognition errors. *Reading Research Quarterly, 7*, 509-529.

Bartlett, F.C. (1932). *Remembering*. Cambridge: Cambridge University Press.

Bettleheim, B., & Zelan, K. (1981). *On learning to read: The child's fascination with meaning*. New York: Alfred A. Knopf.

Betts, E.A. (1957). *Foundations of reading instruction*. New York: American Book.

Blaxall J., & Willows, D. E. (1984). Reading ability and text difficulty as influences on second graders' oral reading errors. *Journal of Educational Psychology, 76*, 330-341.

Board, P.E. (1982). *Toward a theory of instructional influence: Aspects of the instructional environment and their influence on children's acquisition of reading*. Unpublished doctoral dissertation, University of Toronto.

Bormuth, J.R. (1975). Literacy in the classroom. In W.D. Page (Ed.), *Help for the reading teacher: New directions in research* (pp. 60-90). Urbana, IL: ERIC/CRCS, National Council of Teachers of English.

Campbell, D. T., & Fiske, D. W. (1959). Convergent and discriminant validity in the multitrait-multimethod matrix. *Psychological Bulletin, 56*, 81-105.

Carey, R.F. (1978). *A psycholinguistic analysis of the effects of the semantic acceptability of oral reading miscues on reading comprehension*. Unpublished doctoral dissertation, University of Connecticut, Storrs.

Carnine, L., Carnine, D., & Gersten, R. (1984). Analysis of oral reading errors made by economically disadvantaged students taught with a synthetic-phonics approach. *Reading Research Quarterly, 19*, 343-356.

Chinn, C. A., Waggoner, M. A., Anderson, R. C., Schommer, M., & Wilkinson, I. A. G. (1993). Situated actions during reading lessons: A microanalysis of oral reading error episodes. *American Educational Research Journal, 30,* 361-392.

Chomsky, N. (1957). *Syntactic structures.* The Hague: Mouton.

Christie, J.F. (1981). The effects of grade level and reading ability on children's miscue patterns. *The Journal of Educational Research, 74,* 419-423.

Clay, M. M. (1969). Reading errors and self-correction behavior. British *Journal of Educational Psychology, 39,* 47-56.

Crocker, L., & Algina, J. (1986). *Introduction to classical and modern test theory.* New York: Holt, Rinehart, & Winston.

Cronbach, L. (1971). Test validation. in R. Thorndike (Ed.), *Educational measurement* (2nd ed., pp. 443-507). Washington, DC: American Council on Education.

Cronbach, L. (1984). *Essentials of psychological testing* (4th ed.). New York: Harper & Row.

DeLawter, J.A. (1975). Three miscue patterns: The relationship of beginning reading instruction and miscue patterns. In W.D. Page (Ed.), *Help for the reading teacher: New directions in research* (pp. 42-51). Urbana, IL: ERIC/CRCS, National Council of Teachers of English.

Elder, R.D. (1971). Oral reading achievement of Scottish and American children. *Elementary School Journal, 71,* 216-230.

Freud, S. (1960). The psychopathology of everyday life. In J. Strachey (Ed.), *The standard edition of the complete psychological works of Sigmund Freud, Vol. VI.* London: Hogarth Press. (Original work published in 1901)

Ginsburg, H., & Opper, S. (1979). *Piaget's theory of intellectual development* (2nd ed.). Englewood Cliffs, NJ: Prentice-Hall.

Goodman, K. S. (1967). Reading: A psycholinguistic guessing game. *Journal of the Reading Specialist, 4,* 126-135.

Goodman, K.S. (1969). Analysis of oral reading miscues: Applied psycholinguistics. *Reading Research Quarterly, 5,* 9-30.

Goodman, K.S. (1977). Miscues: Windows on the reading process. In K.S. Goodman (Ed.), *Miscue analysis: Applications to reading instruction* (pp. 3-14). Urbana, IL: ERIC, National Council of Teachers of English.

Goodman, K.S., & Burke, C.L. (1973). *Theoretically based studies of patterns of miscues in oral reading performance* (U.S.O.E. Project No. OEG-0-9-32-375-4269). Washington, DC: U.S. Department of Health, Education and Welfare.

Goodman, K.S., & Goodman, Y.M. (1978). *Reading of American children whose language is a stable rural dialect of English or a language other than English.* National Institute of Education Project No. NIE-C-00-3-0087. Washington, DC: U.S. Department of Health, Education and Welfare.

Goodman, Y.M., & Burke, C.L. (1972). *Reading miscue inventory: Manual.* New York: Macmillan.

Hanna, G.S., & Oaster, T.R. (1978-1979). Toward a unified theory of context dependence. *Reading Research Quarterly, 14,* 226-243.

Hoffman, J.V., O'Neal, S.F., Kastler, L.A., Clements, R.O., Segel, K.W., & Nash, M.F. (1984). Guided oral reading and miscue focused verbal feedback in second-grade classrooms. *Reading Research Quarterly, 19,* 367-384.

Hood, J. (1975-1976). Qualitative analysis of oral reading errors: The inter-judge reliability of scores. *Reading Research Quarterly, 9,* 577-598.

Johnston, P. (1984). Prior knowledge and reading comprehension test bias. *Reading Research Quarterly, 19,* 219-239.

Kerlinger, F. (1973). *Foundations of behavioral research* (2nd ed.). New York: Holt, Rinehart & Winston.

Kroll, B.M., & Schafer, J.C. (1978). Error analysis and the teaching of composition. *College Composition and Communication, 24,* 242-248.

Leu, D.J. (1982). Oral reading error analysis: A critical review of research and application. *Reading Research Quarterly, 17,* 420-437.

Malik, A. A. (1990). A psycholinguistic analysis of the reading behavior of EFL-proficient readers using culturally familiar and culturally nonfamiliar expository texts. *American Educational Research Journal, 27,* 205-223.

Moss, P. A. (1992). Shifting conceptions of validity in educational measurement: Implications for performance assessment. *Review of Educational Research, 62,* 229-258.

Neisser, U. (1967). *Cognitive psychology.* New York: Appleton.

Neisser, U. (1977). *Cognition and reality.* San Francisco: Freeman.

Norton, D. (1976). *A comparison of the oral reading errors of high and low ability first and third graders taught by two approaches—synthetic phonic and analytic-eclectic.* Unpublished doctoral dissertation, University of Wisconsin, Madison.

Nunnally, J. (1978). *Psychometric theory* (2nd ed.). New York: McGraw-Hill.

Page, W.D. (1975). The post oral-reading cloze test: New link between oral reading and comprehension. *Journal of Reading Behavior, 7,* 383-389.

Page, W.D. (1978). *The altercue continuum: Theoretical considerations.* (ERIC Document Reproduction Service #ED 155 677).

Page, W.D. (1982). *The altercue comprehension technique.* Storrs, CT: The University of Connecticut Cooperative Corporation.

Richards, J.C. (Ed.). (1974). *Error analysis: Perspectives on second language acquisition.* London: Longman.

Rousch, P. (1972). *A psycholinguistic investigation into the relationship between prior conceptual knowledge, and oral reading miscues, silent reading, and post-reading performance.* Unpublished doctoral dissertation, Wayne State University, Detroit.

Rousch, P. (1976). Testing. In P.D. Allen & D. Watson (Eds.), *Findings of research in miscue analysis: Classroom implications* (pp. 132-136). Urbana, IL: ERIC/CRCS, National Council of Teachers of English.

Ruddell, R.B. (1969). Psycholinguistic implications for a systems of communication model. In K.S. Goodman & J. T. Fleming (Eds.), *Psycholinguistics and the teaching of reading* (pp. 61-78). Newark: DE: International Reading Association.

Sadoski, M.C. (1980). A unitive psycholinguistic comprehension measure: The comprehension process score. In W.D. Page & J.A. Meagher (Eds.), *Language centered reading instruction* (pp. 86-90). Storrs: University of Connecticut Reading-Language Arts Center.

Sadoski, M. C. (1981). *The relationships between student retellings and selected comprehension measures.* Unpublished doctoral dissertation, University of Connecticut, Storrs.

Sadoski, M. (1983). An exploratory study of the relationships between reported imagery and the comprehension and recall of a story. *Reading Research Quarterly, 19,* 110-123.

Sadoski, M.C. (1985a). Comprehension process score. In W.T. Fagan, C.R. Cooper, & J.M. Jensen (Eds.), *Measures for research and evaluation in the English language arts* (Vol 2, pp. 103-105). Urbana, IL: National Council of Teachers of English.

Sadoski, M. (1985b). The natural use of imagery in story comprehension and recall: Replication and extension. *Reading Research Quarterly, 20,* 658-667.

Sadoski, M., & Lee, S. (1986). Reading comprehension and miscue combination scores: Further analysis and comparison. *Reading Research and Instruction, 25,* 160-167.

Sadoski, M., & Page W.D. (1984). Miscue combination scores and reading comprehension: Analysis and comparison. *Reading World, 24,* 43-53.

Sadoski, M.C., Page, W.D., & Carey, R.F. (1981). Empirical testing of a new miscue sorting technique. *New England Reading Association Journal, 16,* 41- 47.

Smith, F. (1988). *Understanding reading* (4th ed.). Hillsdale, NJ: Erlbaum

Spiro, R. J., Bruce, B. C., & Brewer, W. F. (1980). *Theoretical issues in reading comprehension.* Hillsdale, NJ: Erlbaum.

Steffensen, M., Joag-Dev, C., & Anderson, R. (1979). A cross-cultural perspective on reading comprehension. *Reading Research Quarterly, 15,* 10-29.

Taft, M. L., & Leslie, L. (1985). The effects of prior knowledge and oral reading accuracy on miscues and comprehension. *Journal of Reading Behavior, 17,* 163-179.

Thorndike, E.L. (1917). Reading as reasoning: A study of mistakes in paragraph reading. *Journal of Educational Psychology, 8,* 323-332. (Reprinted in *Reading Research Quarterly, 6,* 425-434.)

Wixson, K. L. (1979). Miscue analysis: A critical review. *Journal of Reading Behavior, 11,* 163-175.

Chapter Seven

Reading Reading Miscue Research

David Bloome
Vanderbilt University

David Landis
University of Northern Iowa

John Villemaire
Landmark College & University of Massachusetts-Amherst

The term "miscue" was first used in an article published by Kenneth Goodman in 1965 (Brown, Marek, & Goodman, 1994). Goodman used the concept of miscue, instead of error, to focus attention on the strategies a reader was using rather than on what the reader did not do. Although seemingly a subtle distinction, the focus on reader strategies (miscues) rather than on reader mistakes (errors) marked a shift in the study of reading, and ultimately, a shift in reading assessment. Since the first use of "miscue" in 1965, miscue analysis has been employed in hundreds of studies, educational papers, and a plethora of reading assessment tools and tests.

In this chapter, we examine the use of miscue analysis in reading research. We have two purposes: (a) we discuss how the concept of miscue has been used to define and understand reading and reading instruction, and (b) we reconceptualize miscue in order to provide additional insights into the nature of reading. In order to address our purposes, we have given miscue research two "readings." Our review has included 295 articles, book chapters, papers, and technical reports located in a computerized search of ERIC and Psychological Abstracts, conducted in October 1994, using the words "miscue," and "miscue analysis."[1] Because the purpose of the review was to understand the scope and diversity of miscue analysis research, theoretically and empirically, no criteria were used to cull lower quality studies from higher quality ones or to distinguish works of research from other types of articles and manuscripts[2] (hereafter articles refer to papers, articles, book chapters, and other manuscripts).

Table 7.1 shows the articles placed in 14 groups.[3] The 14 groups are a combination of procedure groups (research design) and topic groups. There were three procedure groups: comparison studies (a category that was divided into two subgroups: comparisons between groups of readers and comparisons based on individual differences and reader factors), studies about reading research, and bibliographic reviews of miscue studies. There were 11 topic groups: dialect studies, ESL/EFL second language and bilingual education studies, studies of curricular and instructional factors, studies of reading-writing connections, studies of teacher response to student reading, studies of the reading process and development of theoretical models of reading, studies of diagnostic procedures, studies of text factors, discussions about the usefulness of miscue analysis, discussions about classroom use of miscue analysis, and discussions about how to do miscue analysis. Each article was placed into a group based on what appeared to us to be its main focus. If an article did not fit into a group, a new group was created until all of the articles were placed in a group. Because of space limitations we have not referenced in the bibliography all of the articles we reviewed. However, the source of each article is listed in Table 7.1 and articles may be tracked through ERIC or one of the several bibliographies of miscue research that are fully referenced in our bibliography.

---

[1]We have not included dissertation studies, papers not available through ERIC, illegible documents, books, some chapters in edited anthologies, materials not available in English, and a small number of articles not available in local libraries or through interlibrary loan. Brown, Marek, and Goodman (1994) provide a more extensive miscue bibliography.

[2]We have included "nonresearch" articles because these articles occasionally raise new theoretical insights.

[3]Most of the articles could have been placed in more than one category; however, based on what we considered to be the primary content or emphasis of the article we placed the articles in one group.

Table 7.1. Select Studies Employing the Concept of Reading Miscues.

Bibliographies and Reviews Full bibliographic information is provided in the references list for each item listed in this this section	Brown, Joel, Marek, Ann, & Goodman, Kenneth. (1994). *Program in Language and Literacy Occasional Paper No. 16*, University of Arizona. Donald, D. R. (1980). *Journal of Research in Reading.* Goodman, Kenneth. (Ed.). (1973). ERIC ED080973. Goodman, Kenneth, & Goodman, Yetta. (1980). *Linguistics, Psycholinguistics, and the Teaching of Reading: Annotated Bibliography (3rd ed.).* Graham, Steve, & Hudson, Floyd. (1978). ERIC ED159604. Marek, Ann, & others. (1985). ERIC ED275998. Page, William. (1973). ERIC ED083545. Rupley, William. (1977). *Reading Teacher.* Shuman, R. Baird. (1984). *Illinois Schools Journal.* Theofield, Mary. (1978). ERIC ED169476.
About Reading Research	Goodman, Kenneth. (1979). *Language Arts* Goodman, Kenneth. (1976). *Language and Literacy: The Selected Writings of K. Goodman.* Simons, Herbert, & Chambers, Richard. (1979). ERIC ED192287, ED192286, ED192285, ED192284, ED192283, ED192282.
Reading Process and Theoretical Models of Reading	Allen, JoBeth. (1983). ERIC ED240518. Allington, Richard, & Strange, Michael. (1977). ERIC ED136248. Beebe, Mona. (1980). *Reading Research Quarterly.* Burke, Elizabeth. (1976). *Educational Review.* Cambourne, Brian. (1976-77). *Reading Research Quarterly.* Campbell, Robin. (1987). *Journal of Research in Reading.* Danks, Joseph, & Fears, Ramona. (1976). ERIC ED155644. Englert, Carol, & Semmel, Melvyn. (1981). *Reading Teacher.* Freeman, David. (1986). ERIC 280012. Goodman, Kenneth. (1976-77). *Reading Research Quarterly.* Goodman, Kenneth. (1975). *Research in the Teaching of English.* Goodman, Kenneth. (1967). *The Journal of the Reading Specialist.* Goodman, Kenneth, & Burke, Carolyn. (1973). ERIC ED079708. Goodman, Kenneth, & Burke, Carolyn. (1973). ERIC ED021698. Goodman, Kenneth, & Goodman, Yetta. (1981). *New York University Education Quarterly.* Goodman, Kenneth, & Goodman, Yetta. (1978). ERIC ED173754. Goodman, Kenneth, & Goodman, Yetta. (1977). *Harvard Educational Review.* Goodman, Yetta. (1982). *Theory into Practice.* Hutson, Barbara, & Niles, Jerome. (1973). ERIC ED094324. Miller, Bonnie. (1977). ERIC ED177598. Miller, John, & Isakson, Richard. (1976). ERIC ED123591. Mosenthal, Peter. (1976). *Reading Research Quarterly.* Mosenthal, Peter. (1976-77). *Reading Research Quarterly*

Table 7.1.Select Studies Employing the Concept of Reading Miscues (con't).

	Newman, Harold. (1978). *Reading Teacher.* Nicholson, Tom, & others. (1979). *Journal of Reading Behavior.* O'Brien, David. (1988). *Journal of Psycholinguistic Research.* Otto, Jean. (1978). ERIC ED165106. Page, William. (1976). ERIC ED155644. Page, William. (1974). *Reading World.* Research Report. (1985). *Australian Journal of Reading.* Ulasevich, Alec, & others. (1991). *Language and Communication.* Thomas, Sharon. (1980). ERIC ED203283. Watson, Dorothy, & Stansell, John. (1980). *Reading Psychology.* Wixson, Karen. (1979). *Journal of Reading Behavior.*
Comparison Studies Part 1: Good vs. Poor Readers, Novice vs. Mature Readers, Remedial / LD vs. NonRemedial / Non-LD Readers	Adams, Arlene. (1986). ERIC ED311630. Bean, Thomas. (1978). *Reading World.* Bromley, Karen, & Mahlios, Marc. (1985). *Educational and Psychological Research.* Cambourne, Brian, & Rousch, Peter. (1982). *Topics in Learning and Learning Disabilities.* Chang, Ji-Mei, & others. (1992). *Journal of Chinese Linguistics.* Christie, James. (1981). *Journal of Educational Research.* D'Angelo, Karen. (1981). *Reading World.* D'Angelo, Karen, & Mahlios, Marc. (1983). *Reading Teacher.* Fleisher, Barbara. (1988). *Reading Research and Instruction.* Harding, Leonora. (1984). *Journal of Research in Reading.* Hittleman, Daniel, & Robinson, H. Alan. (1975). *Journal of Reading Behavior.* Hood, Joyce. (1982). *Journal of Reading Behavior.* Johns, Jerry. (1974). *Education.* Kolczynski, Richard. (1978). ERIC ED214107. Leslie, Lauren. (1980). *Journal of Reading Behavior.* Leslie, Lauren, & Pacl, Penne. (1976). ERIC ED137760. Levy, Rochelle. (1977). *Graduate Research in Education and Related Disciplines.* Miramontes, Ofelia. (1987). *Journal of Learning Disabilities.* Mudd, Norma. (1987). *Educational Research.* Norman, Charles A., & others. (1988). *Adult Literacy and Basic Education.* Pany, Darlene, McCoy, Kathleen, & Peters, Ellen. (1981). *Journal of Reading Behavior.* Patberg, Judythe, Dewitz, Peter, & Samuels, Jay. (1981). *Journal of Reading Behavior.* Pumfrey, Peter D., & Fletcher, J. (1989). *Journal of Research in Reading.* Research Report: *Patterns of Comprehension in Third Grade. (1985). Australian Journal of Reading.*

Table 7.1.Select Studies Employing the Concept of Reading Miscues (con't).

	Page, William. (1974). *Reading World.* Rupley, William H., & Longnion, Bonnie. (1990). ERIC ED332162. Smith, Mabel. (1978). ERIC ED162280. Wangberg, Elaine, & Thompson, Bruce. (1980). ERIC ED193603. Willich, Yve, Prior, Margot, Cumming, Geoff, & Spanos, Tom. (1988). *British Journal of Educational Psychology.*
Comparison Studies Part 2 Individual Reader Differences and Other Factors	Adams, Arlene. (1991). *Remedial and Special Education.* Blumenthal, Susan. (1980). *Journal of Learning Disabilities.* Butler, Lester. (1974). ERIC ED094325. Chinn, Clark A., & others. (1993). *American Educational Research Journal.* Christiansen, Janet. (1980). ERIC ED200915. Chung, In-ho. (1993). *Japanese Journal of Special Education.* De Santi, R. J. (1979). *Educational Gerontology.* Boraks, Nancy, & Schumacher, Sally. (1981). ERIC ED219552. Ewoldt, Carolyn. (1978). *American Annuals of the Deaf.* Ewoldt, Carolyn. (1981). *Reading Research Quarterly.* Feldman, David. (1981). ERIC ED206147. Goodman, Yetta. (1971). ERIC ED 058008. Goodman, Kenneth, & Gollasch, Frederick. (1980). *Reading Research Quarterly.* Hood, Joyce, & Kendell, Janet. (1974). ERIC ED092880. Hood, Joyce, & Kendall, Janet. (1975). *Journal of Reading Behavior.* Keith, Claire, & others. (1981). *Reading Improvement.* Ney, James. (1980). ERIC ED194886. Raisner, Barbara. (1978). *Reading World.* Rigg, Pat, & Kazemek, Francis E. (1990) *Adult Literacy and Basic Education.* Rupley, William H., & Longnion, Bonnie. (1990). ERIC ED332162. Sahu, Shantilata, & Pattnaik, Susmita. (1987). *Psycho-lingua.* Scott, Edward, & others. (1980). ERIC ED200914. Shapiro, John, & Riley, James. (1989). *Clearing-House.* Taft, Marylynn, and Leslie, Lauren. (1985). *Journal of Reading Behavior.* Tchaconas, Terry, & Spiridakis, John. (1988). ERIC ED295497. Vipond, Douglas, Hunt, Russell, & Wheeler, Lynwood. (1987). *Reading Research and Instruction.* Wangberg, Elaine, & Thompson, Bruce. (1982). *Reading Improvement.* Whaley, Jill, & Kibby, Michael. (1980). *Journal of Educational Research.*
Studies of Dialect and Reading	Bean, Thomas. (1976). ERIC ED137770. Bousquet, Robert. (1978). ERIC ED181446. Burke, Suzanne, & others. (1980). ERIC ED185543. Burke, Suzanne, Pflaum, Susanna, & Knafle, June. (1982). *Journal of Learning Disabilities.*

Table 7.1. Select Studies Employing the Concept of Reading Miscues (con't).

	Eberwein, Lowell. (1982). *Reading World.* Goodman, Kenneth, & Buck, Catherine. (1973). *Reading Teacher.* Goodman, Kenneth, & Gespass, Suzanne. (1983). ERIC ED297259. Goodman, Kenneth, & Goodman, Yetta. (1978). ERIC ED173754. Granger, Robert, & Ramig, Christopher. (1978). ERIC ED153197. Rigg, Pat. (1978). *Language Arts.* Taylor, Janet. (1983). *Journal of Educational Psychology.*
Studies of ESL, EFL, Bilingual Readers and Education, and Second Language Learning	Allen, Edward. (1977). *Foreign Language Annals.* Coll, Julia & Osuna, Adelina. (1990). *Hispania.* Deyes, Tony. (1987). *Reading in a Foreign Language.* Ellis, Rod. (1980). *Reading.* Garcia, Ricardo. (1977). ERIC ED145449. Hodes, Phyllis. (1977). ERIC ED137731. Malik, Ali. (1990). *American Educational Research Journal.* Miramontes, Ofelia. (1990). *Journal of Reading Behavior.* Rodriguez-Brown, Flora, & Yirchott, Lynne. (1980). ERIC ED192273. Shannon, Albert. (1983). *Reading Improvement.* Tchaconas, Terry, & Spiridakis, John. (1988). ERIC ED295497. Tyler, Andrea, & Bro, John. (1993). *Studies in Second Language Acquisition.* Williamson, Leon, & Young, Freda. (1976). ERIC ED130252. Zhang, Jian. (1988). *Journal of Reading.*
Studies of Curricular and Instructional Factors	Angeletti, Sara. (1990). ERIC ED321231. Biskin, Donald, Hoskisson, Kenneth, & Modlin, Marjorie. (1976). *Elementary School Journal.* Bock, Joan. (1989). ERIC ED318988. Dank, Marion. (1977). *Reading Improvement.* Denner, Peter, & others. (1988). ERIC ED301855. Hoffman, James V., & others. (1984). *Reading Research Quarterly.* Kozleski, Elizabeth. (1989). *Reading Improvement.* Love, Fannye. (1981). *Reading Improvement.* Mitchell, Katherine. (1978). ERIC ED182716. Ng, Seok. (1980). ERIC ED205901. Norton, Donna, & Hubert, Patty. (1977). ERIC ED145393. Pollock, John, & Brown, Garth. (1980). ERIC ED198500. Ramig, Christopher, & Hall, Mary Anne. (1980). *Reading World.* Recht, Donna. (1976). *Reading Teacher.* Sachs, Arlene. (1984). *Remedial and Special Education.* Shanklin, Nancy. (1990). *Journal of Reading, Writing, & Learning Disabilities International.* Saulawa, Danjuma. (1992). ERIC ED354482. Stansell, John. (1981). *English Education.* Stansell, John. (1978). *Reading World.*

Table 7.1. Select Studies Employing the Concept of Reading Miscues (con't).

Studies of Teacher Response to Student Reading	Campbell, Robin. (1990). *Reading.*
	Cunningham, Patricia. (1977). *Reading Research Quarterly.*
	Geissal, Mary Ann, & Knafle, June. (1978). ERIC ED165105.
	Hoffman, James, & Kugle, Cherry. (1981). ERIC ED203304.
	Hoffman, James. (1982). ERIC ED227455.
	Hoffman, James. (1981). ERIC ED200946.
	Hoffman, James. (1980). ERIC ED189541.
	Hoffman, James. (1979). *Reading World.*
	Hoffman, James, & Baker, Christopher. (1981). *Reading Teacher.*
	Hoffman, James, & Clements, Richard. (1984). *Elementary School Journal.*
	Hoffman, James, & others. (1981). ERIC ED200900.
	Jongsma, Eugene, (1978). *Reading World.*
	Knafle, June, & Geissal, Mary Ann. (1979). ERIC ED182741.
	Lass, Bonnie. (1984). *Reading World.*
	McNaughton, Stuart. (1981). *Journal of Reading Behavior.*
	Meyer, Linda. (1986). *Elementary School Journal.*
	Mudre, Lynda, & McCormick, Sandra. (1989). *Reading Research Quarterly.*
	Shanklin, Nancy. (1990). *Journal of Reading, Writing and Learning Disabilities International.*
	Singh, Judy. (1989). *Journal of Reading.*
	Spiegel, Dixie Lee, & Rogers, Carol. (1980). *Journal of Educational Research.*
	Terry, Pamela. (1982). ERIC ED219894.
	Terry, Pamela, & Cohen, Darla. (1977). ERIC ED141766.
Reading-Writing Connections	Greene, Brenda. (1989). ERIC ED305665.
	Greene, Brenda. (1989). ERIC ED305619.
	Horning, Alice S. (1989). *Journal of Basic Writing.*
	Ney, James. (1975). ERIC ED161009.
	Ney, James. (1977). ERIC ED161077.
	Ney, James, & Leyba, Rachel. (1975). ERIC ED161078.
Text Factors	Adams, Arlene. (1988). ERIC ED320113.
	Altwerger, Bess, & Goodman, Kenneth. (1981). ERIC ED209657.
	Ammon, Paul, & others. (1990). ERIC ED334542.
	Anderson, Jonathan. (1982). ERIC ED222885.
	Beveridge, M., & Griffiths, V. (1987). *Journal of Research in Reading.*
	Bristow, Page, & Leslie, Lauren. (1988). *Reading Research Quarterly.*
	Christie, James, & Alonso, Patricia. (1980). *Educational Research Quarterly.*
	Gonzales, Phillip, & Elijah, David. (1978). *Reading Improvement.*
	Goodman, Kenneth. (1983). ERIC ED297260.
	Goodman, Kenneth, & Gespass, Suzanne. (1983). ERIC ED297259.
	Gourley, Judith. (1984). *Journal of Reading Behavior.*

Table 7.1.Select Studies Employing the Concept of Reading Miscues (con't).

	Guzzetti, Barbara J. (1984). *American Educational Research Journal.* Henshaw (1992). *Educational Research.* Hittleman, Daniel, & Robinson, H. Alan. (1973). ERIC ED075794. Hocevar, Susan, & Hocevar, Dennis. (1978). *Journal of Reading Behavior.* Hood, Joyce. (1982). *Journal of Reading Behavior.* Leslie, Lauren, & Osol, Pat. (1978). *Journal of Reading Behavior.* MacMullin, M. Roderick. (1980). ERIC ED191002. Mazurkiewicz, Albert, & Kleederman, Frances. (1978). ERIC ED167958. Nicholson, Tom, & others. (1979). *Journal of Reading Behavior.* Nicholson, Tom, & others. (1988). *Reading Teacher.* Oyetunde, Timothy O., & Umolu, Joanne J. (1989). *Reading.* Sampson, Michael, & others. (1988). *Reading Improvement.* Simons, Herbert, & Ammon, Paul. (1988). *National Reading Conference Yearbook.* Simons, Herbert D., & Ammon, Paul. (1989). *Research in the Teaching of English.* Smith, Judith, & Elkins, John. (1985). *Reading Psychology.* Stansell, John, & others. (1977). ERIC ED151791. Swarts, Heidi, & others (1980). ERIC ED192344. Thomas, Sharon. (1980). ERIC ED203283. Williamson, Leon, & others (1980). ERIC ED195966.
Studies of Diagnostic Procedures	Anderson, Jonathan. (1980). ERIC ED198516. Bristow, Page, & Leslie, Lauren. (1988). *Reading Research Quarterly.* Burke, Suzanne, & others. (1980). ERIC ED185543. Cunningham, James, & Caplan, Robert. (1982). *Reading World.* D'Angelo, Karen. (1980). ERIC ED190982. D'Angelo, Karen, & Wilson, Robert. (1979). *Reading Teacher.* Donald, D. R. (1979). *Reading.* Ewoldt, Carolyn. (1982). *Volta Review.* Garcia, Georgia. (1992). ERIC ED348665. Henk, William. (1993). *Reading and Writing Quarterly.* Hood, Joyce. (1976). *Reading Research Quarterly.* Johns, Jerry L., & Magliari, Anne Marie. (1989). *Reading Improvement.* Hutson, Barbara, & Niles, Jerome. (1981). *Reading Improvement.* Keefe, Donald. (1993). *Reading and Writing Quarterly.* King, Martha. (1977). *Theory Into Practice.* Kuhns, Carolyn, Morre, David, & Moore, Sharon. (1986). *Reading Research and Instruction.* Lamberg, Walter. (1975). ERIC ED128767. Lipson, Marjorie. (1982). ERIC ED230915. MacLean, Margaret. (1979). ERIC ED184103. Norton, Marian, & Falk, Ian. (1992). *International Journal of Disability, Development, and Education.*

Table 7.1. Select Studies Employing the Concept of Reading Miscues (con't).

	Page, William. (1976). *Reading World.* Page, William. (1977). *Reading World.* Page, William. (1979). ERIC ED181406. Parker, Richard, Hasbrouck, Jan, & Tindal, Gerald. (1992). *Journal of Special Education.* Paterra, Mary. (1976), ERIC ED133706. Potter, Frank. (1980). *Journal of Research in Reading.* Sadoski, Mark. (1982). ERIC ED214127. Sadoski, Mark, & Lee, Sharon. (1986). *Reading Research and Instruction.* Sadoski, Mark, & Page, William D. (1984). *Reading World.* Shearer, Arleen. (1979). ERIC ED255870. Upshur, John. (1972). ERIC ED061805. Williamson, Leon, & Young, Freda. (1974). *Journal of Reading Behavior.*
Discussions About the Usefulness of Miscue Analysis	Brown, Virginia. (1975). *Journal of Learning Disabilities.* Biggs, Shirley, & Scales, Albert. (1977). ERIC ED142982. Feeley, Joan. (1979). *Reading Improvement.* Goodman, Yetta. (1974). *English Journal.* Groff, Patrick. (1980). *Reading World.* Nieratka, Ernest. (1973). ERIC ED215301. O'Brien, David. (1981). *Reading Teacher.* Parker, Richard, & others. (1992). *Journal of Special Education.* Viera, Diana. (1986). *Journal of Reading, Writing and Learning Disabilities International.*
Discussions About the Classroom Use of Miscue Analysis	Baghban, Marcia. (1981). ERIC ED206411. Bean, Thomas. (1979). *Reading World.* Crawford, Leslie. (1982). ERIC ED217373. Damron, Shayla. (1977). ERIC ED210128. D'Angelo, Karen. (1982). *Reading Teacher.* Daniels, Harry. (1988). *British Journal of Special Education.* Dempsey, Jane. (1975). ERIC ED117682. Fernandez, Evelyn, & Baker, Susan. (1993). ERIC ED364079. Flynt, E. Sutton, & Cooter, Robert B., Jr. (1993). ERIC ED363853. Green, Frank. (1986). *Reading Teacher.* Griffin, Margaret, & Jongsma, Kathleen. (1980). ERIC ED190984. Harp, Bill. (1988). *Reading Teacher.* Henrichs, Margaret. (1981). ERIC ED207034. Hoffman, James, & Baker, Christopher. (1980). ERIC ED188160. Hoge, Sharon. (1983). *Journal of Reading.* Hood, Joyce. (1978). *Reading Teacher.* Johns, Jerry. (1975). *Language Arts.* Kamil, Michael, & Pearson, P. David. (1978). *Reading Improvement.* Maring, Gerald. (1978). *Reading Teacher.* Matz, Karl. (1990). ERIC ED323492. Scales, Alice. (1980). *The Reading Instruction Journal.*

Table 7.1. Select Studies Employing the Concept of Reading Miscues (con't).

	Shafer, Robert. (1977). *English Quarterly.*
	Siegel, Florence. (1979). *Reading World.*
	Taylor, Barbara, & Nosbush, Linda. (1983). *Reading Teacher.*
	Watson, Dorothy. (1978). *English Education.*
	Wheldall, Kevin, Merrett, Frank, & Colmar, Susan. (1987). *Support for Learning.*
	Winser, Bill. (1988). *Australian Journal of Reading.*
	Woodley, John. (1988). ERIC ED296309.
	Wuthrick, Marjorie. (1990). *Ohio Reading Teacher.*
Discussions About How to Do Miscue Analysis	Cohn, Marvin, & D'Alessandro, Cynthia. (1978). *Reading Teacher.*
	Cunningham, Patricia. (1977). *Reading Teacher.*
	Davey, Beth, & Theofield, Mary. (1983). *Reading Improvement.*
	Goodman, Yetta M., & others. (1987). *Reading Improvement.*
	Graham, Steve, & Miller, Lamoine. (1979). *Diagnostique.*
	Kaufman, Maurice. (1976). *Reading World.*
	Miller, John. (1973). *Reading Improvement.*
	Miller, Wilma H. (1993). ERIC ED361662.
	Rhodes, Lynn K., & Shanklin, Nancy L. (1990). *Reading Teacher.*
	Tortelli, James. (1976). *Reading Teacher.*
	Vinegrad, M. D. (1988). *Reading.*
	Watson, Dorothy, & others. (1979). ERIC ED182724.
	Zutell, Jerome. (1977). *Theory Into Practice.*

Our approach to constructing a review of the studies has been to give the research two "readings." We first "read" the research focusing on the underlying theoretical constructs, that is, on how researchers were building knowledge about reading, readers, and instruction through miscue analysis. This first reading takes up the larger share of this chapter because we frame past and current miscue analysis research in a manner that provides a rationale for the second "reading." The second reading is a revisionist reading. The reading is derived from discussions of language by Kristeva (e.g., 1977/1980, 1986), Volosinov (1929/1973), and Bakhtin (1935/1981, 1953/1986), among others. One issue among the many they raise is that language is always social and historical. The importance of this second reading is that it connects miscue analysis with reading as a set of social events and social practices. Other "readings" are, of course, possible. Space limitations require us to limit our discussion in this chapter to only two "readings."

READING #1: UNDERLYING THEORETICAL CONSTRUCTS AND BUILDING KNOWLEDGE ABOUT READING AND READERS THROUGH MISCUE ANALYSIS

The concept of reading miscue refers not only to unexpected responses but to a set of interpretive constructs suggested by Goodman (1967, 1973, 1975; Goodman & Burke, 1973; Goodman & Goodman, 1977) about the nature of reading.[4] Goodman (1967) described the theoretical basis for miscue analysis based on a definition of reading as part of a communicative process with meaning at the center.

> Reading is a selective process. It involves partial use of available, minimal language cues selected from perceptual input on the basis of the reader's expectations. As this partial information is processed, tentative decisions are made to be confirmed, rejected, or refined as reading progresses. More simply stated, reading is a psycholinguistic guessing game. It involves an interaction between thought and language. (pp. 33-34)

This view expressed by Goodman can be viewed against the corpus of articles and theories about reading produced in the 1960s and 1970s and against common sense views of reading. "[The common sense view is that] reading is a precise process. It involves exact, detailed, sequential perception, and identification of letters, words, spelling patterns, and large language units" (Goodman, 1967, p. 33). There were relatively few reading researchers or educators at the time who defined reading in terms of meaning, comprehension, communication, or language. Rather, the dominant view and impetus for research was grounded in theories of perception (see Pearson & Stephens, 1994). In the United States there was limited discussion in educational research—and even in psychological research—about the relationship of thought and language, with most of that discussion occurring in what was then the emerging field of psycholinguistics.

A "reading" of the miscue analysis research shows that the use of miscue analysis in many of the studies reflects two different general models. The first, shown in Figure 7.1, focuses on reading conditions and miscues. A particular reading condition (e.g., text difficulty) is assumed to be related to a pattern of miscues, and based on the pattern of miscues, inferences are made about the reading process and about readers. We call this model, "Reading Conditions and Miscues" (see Figure 7.1).

---

[4]In some studies of reading and in some education textbooks, the term *reading miscue* was borrowed without the interpretive constructs Goodman presented or with a different set of interpretive constructs.

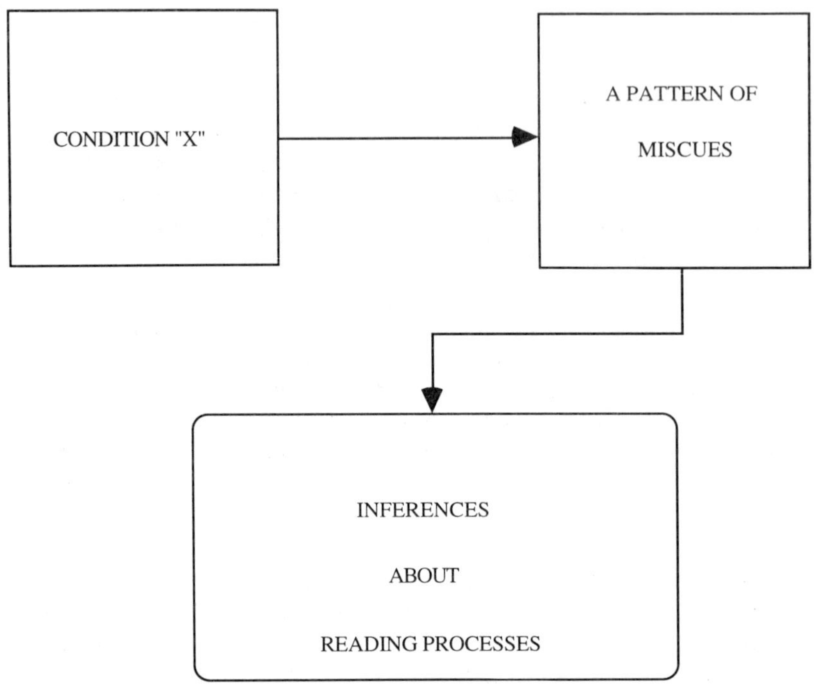

Figure 7.1. Reading conditions and miscues

There are many variations of the model shown in Figure 7.1. In some studies, no special manipulation or selection of conditions was apparent. Rather, at-hand conditions and miscues were examined for insights about the reading process (e.g., Chinn, Waggoner, Anderson, Schommer, & Wilkinson, 1993). In other studies, conditions were manipulated. Manipulations included distortions of a text (e.g., Shearer, 1979; Swarts et al., 1980) and the type and language of a text (e.g., Anderson, 1982; Damron, 1977), among others. The manipulation of conditions also included purposeful selection of subjects. Selections differentiated subjects by age (e.g., Adams, 1991), level of cognitive development (e.g., Christie, 1981; Feeley, 1979; Ney, 1980), degree of impulsivity (e.g., Butler, 1974; Hood & Kendall, 1975; Ulasevich, Leaton, Kramer, Hiecke, & O'Connell, 1991), geographical location (e.g., Shanklin, 1990; Rigg & Kazemek, 1990), and distinguished Standard English speakers from non-Standard English speakers and native English speakers from nonnative speakers (e.g., Dank, 1977; Tyler & Bro, 1992), among many others.

The Comparison Studies can be viewed as an attempt to control the influence of confounding factors by attempting to limit differences in patterns of miscues to a single dimension. Differences in patterns of miscues are assumed to be a consequence of differences in the readers because the other factors are assumed constant or similar. In Comparison Studies, in order to gain insight about the condition being studied (e.g., learning disabilities), the relationship between other conditions (e.g., the text), a pattern of miscues, and the reading process is viewed as stable. That is, a particular condition or a particular combination of conditions will yield a stable, reliable pattern of miscues.

Such an assumption implies that the reading process itself is stable and monolithic. An assumption of stability may also be a part of a view of reading that assumes that there are different ways of reading for different purposes or conditions. Rather than viewing reading as stable and monolithic *across* purposes and conditions, reading is viewed as stable and monolithic *within* a given purpose and set of conditions. Nonetheless, stability and a monolithic nature are underlying assumptions about the reading process. As discussed later, there are views of reading that do not assume stability or a monolithic nature either within or across purposes and conditions.

There have also been a series of articles based on a different underlying theoretical model as shown in Figure 7.2. Figure 7.2 shows a general model of inquiry in which the nature of reading is taken as a given and inferences are then made about reading instruction, evaluation, and other educational practices. We call this model, "Reading Instruction and The Nature of Reading." One purpose of studies and articles employing the model in Figure 7.2 is to identify and promote reading instruction, curriculum, and evaluation processes consistent with findings about reading as a psycholinguistic guessing game (cf., Goodman, 1967, 1979).

Among the studies that employ the model in Figure 7.2 are studies of teachers' responses to student reading miscues. One direction taken by these studies has been to examine teachers' responses as indicative of their theoretical stance to reading as a condition that, in turn, influences patterns of students' miscues (e.g., Knafle & Geissal, 1979; Lass, 1984). Other studies have examined how various curricular and instructional conditions (e.g., Campbell, 1990; Mitchell, 1978), text factors (e.g., Simons & Ammon, 1989), the language of basal textbooks, and classroom uses of miscue analysis promote or hinder students' engagement in the reading process (defined similarly to the model of the reading process outlined by Goodman, 1967).

There are studies employing miscue analysis that find fault with Goodman's model of the reading process and with related curricular and

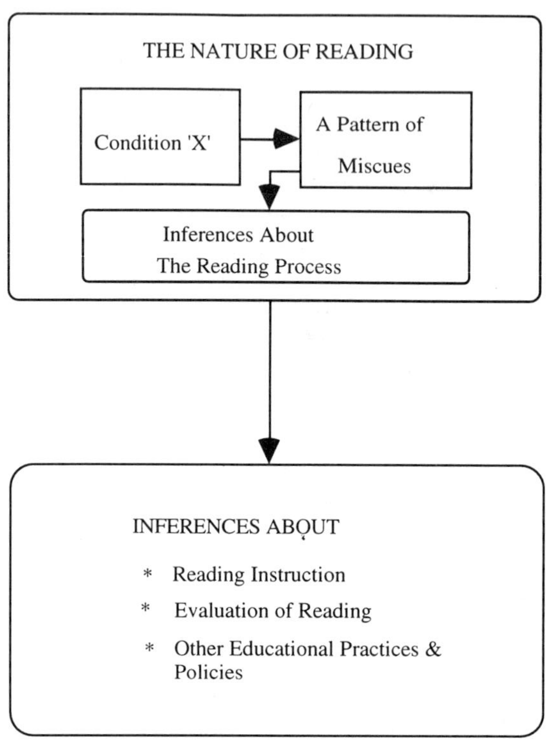

Figure 7.2. Reading instruction and the nature of reading

instructional directions, as well as with miscue analysis itself (e.g. Allington & Strange, 1977; Dank, 1977; Groff, 1980; Wixson, 1979). These studies have primarily employed manipulation of text factors, comparisons of learning disabled versus nonlearning disabled readers, and poor versus good readers, among other comparisons, and comparisons of various diagnostic procedures with miscue analysis. Differences in findings have led to debates about the rigor, validity, and interpretation of research both supporting and critiquing the theoretical principles and models of reading that are the foundations for miscue analysis. Critiques of miscue research disagree with the nature of the insights made about reading.[5] For example, Wixson (1979) has suggested that oral reading and silent reading are different processes, therefore miscue analysis cannot be used to diagnose silent reading. It is not our

[5]We have not reviewed any studies that dismiss miscue analysis completely.

intent to review those debates here. Rather, what we want to point out is that the studies that find fault are also grounded in the models of research shown in Figures 7.1 and 7.2. That is, they either infer that patterns of miscues within a particular set of conditions do or do not yield insights about the reading process (Model 1), or they hold *the* reading process as a theoretical constant to make inferences about the efficacy of various curricular, instructional, and diagnostic procedures (Model 2).

Models 1 and 2 are particular ways of building knowledge about reading; that is, they represent particular modes of reasoning about reading (or, perhaps more accurately, they represent particular kinds of arguments about how the nature of reading might be known). Models 1 and 2 build knowledge about reading based on a deductive model of reasoning. Deduction applies an overarching rule to a particular case. With regard to Models 1 and 2, sets of conditions are assumed to be related to reading in a principled way (this is the rule), and then the assumption is applied to a specific case (e.g., a pattern of miscues). As a result, inferences are made about the reading process (Model 1) or about reading instruction (Model 2).

In addition to deductive reasoning, there are at least two other modes of reasoning: inductive and abductive (analogical) reasoning. Inductive reasoning begins with the specific case and then considers the result, followed by a general rule. For example, a pattern of miscues (the specific case) suggests inferences about the nature of the reading process (the result), which may suggest a general rule about how various conditions affect reading processes (the general rule).

Abductive reasoning begins by considering how the nature of a phenomenon (like reading) is analogous to, or different from, other phenomena. For example, a pattern of miscues observed in a particular condition is understood as analogous to, or different from, other patterns of miscues observed in other conditions. Rather than consider the various patterns of miscues as building general rules about reading or being explained by general rules about reading, knowledge about the reading process is derived from the relationships of various patterns of miscues to each other. For example, the miscues observed in multiple readings (perhaps by different readers) through abductive reasoning might be considered similar. As such, these multiple readings might be considered to constitute similar types of reading. Dissimilar patterns of miscues across multiple readings might be considered different types of reading.

As a mode of reasoning, deductive arguments do not easily facilitate the generation of alternative and new explanations or understandings of reading. Inductive and abductive arguments highlight alternative and new explanations. Although Goodman's original research in which the concept of miscue was developed appears to have been grounded in inductive reasoning, much of the subsequent research employing the concept of miscue (both in Model 1 and Model 2) appears to have been grounded in deductive reasoning. Little research employing the concept of miscue seems to involve abductive reasoning.

READING #2: READING MISCUE RESEARCH—UNDERLYING CONSTRUCTS

One consequence of European literary and linguistic theory building (e.g., Bakhtin, 1981, 1986; Kristeva, 1980, 1986; Volosinov, 1929/1973) and of work in the United States in sociolinguistics (e.g., Bauman & Sherzer, 1989; Bloome & Green, 1984; Gumperz, 1982; Heath, 1983; Hymes, 1974) has been to make definitions of language and reading problematic. It has recently been argued widely that there is no single definition of language and that language cannot be simply defined as communication (Kristeva, 1980). Reading has also become a problematic term. It is not just a recognition that variation in background knowledge results in differences in what is comprehended, but that what constitutes reading itself is a social and cultural process (e.g., Heath, 1983; Street, 1984). The definition of reading can no longer be taken for granted, and defining reading is often seen as an act of struggle and conflict between various cultural ideologies (Brodkey, 1987; Street 1993). Such a perspective on reading suggests that reading cannot be considered a stable or monolithic phenomenon, either across or within contexts.

In addition to understanding language and reading as having multiple and evolving definitions, Kristeva's work (1980) has raised another set of issues important to consider. She points out that language is the tool we use to explore language and that this presents problems—inherent and unresolvable problems—for the language researcher. Because the meaning of any bit of language depends on the cultural ideology in which it is framed, understanding language requires explicating its cultural and social frame; but in explicating a frame one uses language which is itself located within a cultural ideology. As a result, the process of language inquiry can be seen as recursive, reflective, dialectic, and inherently tentative. One way to interpret this view of language inquiry is as another mode of building knowledge.

The theoretical work of European linguists and literary scholars, American sociolinguists, and Kristeva's work, has implications for how Goodman's (1967) article, "Reading As a Psycholinguistic Guessing Game," might be understood. In brief, these implications are to raise questions about the interpretive processes involved in miscue research and about the definitions of language, reading, and thought employed.

Returning to consider Figures 7.1 and 7.2, each involves an interpretation, what might be called a "reading." Thus, the titles of both figures (Figure 7.1—Reading Conditions and Miscues; Figure 7.2—Reading Instruction and The Nature of Reading) may be read with the word "reading" treated as a verb rather than as an adjective (cf. Bloome & Solsken, 1992). As a verb, *reading* refers not only to actions that readers take with written language, but it also refers to the act of invoking and constructing an interpretive framework which itself reflects underlying cultural definitions, including definitions of reading, thought, and language. In brief, to paraphrase Goodman, understanding the reading of reading miscues, the reading of reading miscue research, and even the reading of Goodman's 1967 article, requires that we look beyond the eye and the text. But whereas the 1967 article directed attention beyond the eye to the mind, now we must look beyond the individual—to the situation, and to the cultural, social, and political dynamics in which the situation is embedded, remembering that reading is a site of contesting cultural ideologies.

In the 1967 article and later in a 1979 article, Goodman foreshadows an understanding of reading as a verb, an action located at the site of conflict of multiple definitions of language, reading, and thought. Goodman (1979) writes:

> The theory of the reading process I developed is still best summed up in the statement "Reading is a Psycholinguistic Guessing Game" (Goodman 1967). I reached the conclusion that tentative information processing, guessing on the basis of minimal actual information, is the primary characteristic of reading. The reader interacts with an author through a text to construct meaning. That means that there is an interaction between thought and language, hence a psycholinguistic process is in operation. Most recently, I've realized that the *tentativeness* of the information processing is even more significant than I had thought earlier . . . At the core of the theory I have developed is the view that language processes must be studied in the context of their use. (pp. 341-342; emphasis in original)

"Tentativeness" in reading is not treated as a negative or a disability but as an enabling factor that allows increasingly sophisticated understandings of written language. And, if research can itself be defined as a kind of reading, then tentativeness in research—tentativeness in definitions of reading, language, and thought—ought to be seen as an enabling factor, too. Of all the words, phrases, and ideas in Goodman's (1967) article that have or might have impacted the field of reading research and how knowledge is derived, *tentativeness* has perhaps been the most overlooked. Perhaps in re-reading the 1967 article and in reading reading miscue research we need to pay more attention to tentativeness and indeed to be more tentative in reading.

REFERENCES

Adams, A. (1991). The oral reading errors of readers with learning disabilities: Variations produced within the instructional and frustrational ranges. *Remedial and Special Education, 12*(1), 48-55.

Allington, R. L., & Strange, M. (1977). *Effects of grapheme substitutions in connected text upon reading behaviors.* ED136248.

Anderson, J. (1982). *The measurement of the perception of cohesion: A second language example.* ED 222885.

Bakhtin, M. (1981). *Discourse in the novel.* In M. Holquist (Ed.), *The dialogic imagination* (pp. 259-422). (C. Emerson & M. Holquist, Trans.). Austin: University of Texas Press. (Original work published in 1935)

Bakhtin, Mikhail. (1986). The problem of speech genres. In C. Emerson & M. Holquist (Eds.), *Speech genres & other late essays* (pp. 60-102). (V.W. McGee, Trans.). Austin: University of Texas Press. (Original work published in 1953)

Bauman, R., & Sherzer, J. (Eds.). (1989). *Explorations in the ethnography of speaking* (2nd ed.). New York: Cambridge University Press.

Bloome, D., & Green, J. (1984). Directions in the sociolinguistic study of reading. In P. D. Pearson, R. Barr, M. L. Kamil, & P. Mosenthal (Eds.), *Handbook of reading research* (pp. 395-422). New York: Longman.

Bloome, D., & Solsken, J. (1992). *Reading as a verb.* Paper presented at the Annual Meeting of the American Anthropological Association, Phoenix, AZ.

Brodkey, L. (1987). *Academic writing as social practice.* Philadelphia: Temple University Press.

Brown, J., Marek, A., & Goodman, K. (1994). *Annotated chronological miscue analysis bibliography.* Program in Language and Literacy Occasional Paper No. 16. University of Arizona, Tucson.

Butler, L. (1974). *A psycholinguistic analysis of the oral reading behavior of selected impulsive and reflective second grade boys.* ED 094325.

Campbell, R. (1990). Reading and the national curriculum: Responding to miscues. *Reading, 24*(3), 133-138.

Chinn, C. A., Waggoner, M. A., Anderson, R. C., Schommer, M., & Wilkinson, I. A. G. (1993). Situated actions during reading lessons: A microanalysis of oral reading error episodes. *American Educational Research Journal, 30*(2), 361-392.

Christie, J. (1981). The effects of grade level and reading ability on children's miscue patterns. *Journal of Educational Research, 74*(6), 419-423.

Damron, S. (1977). *A bidialectical approach: Strategies for assimilating the mainstream dialect into the non-mainstream southern mountain dialect.* ED 210128.

Dank, M. (1977). What effect do reading programs have on the oral reading behavior of children. *Reading Improvement, 14*(2), 66-69.

Donald, D. R. (1980). Analysis of Children's Oral Reading Errors: A Current Perspective. *Journal of Research in Reading, 3*(2), 106-114.

Feeley, J. (1979). Adding the reading miscue inventory to the reading case study. *Reading Improvement, 16*, 75-81.

Goodman, K. (1967). Reading: A psycholinguistic guessing game. *The Journal of the Reading Specialist, 6*(4), 126-135 (Reprinted in F. Gollasch (Ed.). (1982). *Language and literacy; The selected writings of Kenneth Goodman, vol. 1.* Boston: Routledge & Kegan Paul).

Goodman, K. (Ed.). (1973). *Miscue analysis: Applications to reading instruction.* Urbana, IL: ERIC Clearinghouse on Reading and Communication Skills.

Goodman, K. (1975). Influences of the visual peripheral field in reading. *Research in the Teaching of English, 9*(2), 210-222.

Goodman, K. (1979). The know-more and the know-nothing movements in reading. *Language Arts, 55*(8), 657-663. (reprinted in F. Gollasch (Ed.). (1982). *Language and literacy: The selected writings of Kenneth Goodman, vol. 2.* Boston: Routledge & Kegan Paul).

Goodman, K., & Burke, C. (1973). *Theoretically based studies of patterns of miscues in oral reading performance.* Final Report. Washington, DC: Bureau of Research, Office of Education.

Goodman, K., & Goodman, Y. (1977). Learning about psycholinguistic processes by analyzing oral reading. *Harvard Educational Review, 47*(3), 317-333.

Goodman, K., & Goodman, Y. (1980). *Linguistics, psycholinguistics, and the teaching of reading: Annotated bibliography* (3rd ed.) ED 190994.

Graham, S., & Hudson, F. (1978). *Oral reading miscues or errors: A bibliography of research.* ED159604.

Groff, P. (1980). A critique of an oral reading miscue analysis. *Reading World, 19*(3), 254-264.

Gumperz, J. J. (1982). *Discourse strategies.* New York: Cambridge University Press.

Heath, Shirley Brice. (1983). *Ways with words.* New York: Cambridge University Press.

Hood, J., & Kendall, J. (1975). A qualitative analysis of oral reading errors of reflective and impulsive second graders: A follow-up study. *Journal of Reading Behavior, 7*(3), 269-281.

Hymes, D. (1974). *Foundations in sociolinguistics: An ethnographic approach.* Philadelphia: University of Pennsylvania Press.

Knafle, J. D., & Geissal, M. (1979). *Variations in attitudes towards children's oral reading errors.* ED 182741.

Kristeva, J. (1980). *Desire in language: A semiotic approach to literature and art* (T. Gora, A. Jardine, & L.S. Roudiez, Trans.). New York: Columbia University Press. (Original work published 1977)

Kristeva, J. (1986). Word, dialogue, and novel. In T. Moi (Ed.), *The Kristeva reader* (pp. 34-61). Oxford: Basil Blackwell.

Lass, B. (1984). Do teachers individualize their responses to reading miscues?: A study of feedback during oral reading. *Reading World, 23*(3), 242-254.

Marek, A., & others. (1985). *Annotated Miscue Analysis Bibliography.* Program in Language and Literacy Occasional Paper No. 16. University of Arizona. ED275998

Mitchell, K. A. (1978). *Patterns of teacher-student responses to oral reading errors as related to teachers' previous training in different theoretical frameworks.* ED182716.

Ney, J. W. (1980). *Cognitive styles and miscue analysis of reading and writing.* ED 194886.

Page, W. (1973). *Concise miscue bibliography.* ED083545

Pearson, P. D., & Stephens, D. (1994). Learning about literacy: A 30-year journey. In R. Ruddell, M. R. Ruddell, & H. Singer (Eds.), *Theoretical models and processes of reading* (4th ed., pp. 22-44). Newark, DE: International Reading Association.

Rigg, P., & Kazemek, F. E. (1990). Four inmates read. *Adult Literacy and Basic Education, 14*(1), 28-44.

Rupley, W. (1977). Miscue analysis research. *Reading Teacher, 30*(5), 580-583.

Shanklin, N. L. (1990). Improving the comprehension of at-risk readers: An ethnographic study of four Chapter I teachers, grades 4-6. *Journal of Reading, Writing, and Learning Disabilities International, 6*(2), 137-148.

Shearer, A. P. (1979). *A psycholinguistic comparison using cloze and oral miscue analysis of good and poor readers.* ED 255870.

Shuman, R. B. (1984). How classroom teachers can use the research in miscue analysis. *Illinois Schools Journal, 64,* 1-4, 18-26.

Simons, H. D., & Ammon, P. (1989). Child knowledge and primerese text: Mismatches and miscues. *Research in the Teaching of English, 23*(4), 380-398.

Street, B. V. (1984). *Literacy in theory and practice.* New York: Cambridge University Press.

Street, B. V. (1993). Introduction: The new literacy studies. In B. V. Street (Ed.), *Cross-cultural approaches to literacy*. New York: Cambridge University Press.

Swarts, H., & others. (1980). *How headings in documents can mislead readers*. ED 192344.

Theofield, M. (1978). *Oral reading: A toll for student assessment and teacher training*. ED169476.

Tyler, A., & Bro, J. (1992). Discourse structure in nonnative english discourse: The effect of ordering and interpretive cues on perceptions of comprehensibility. *Studies in Second Language Acquisition, 14*(1), 71-86.

Ulasevich, A., Leaton, B., Kramer, D., Hiecke, A. E., & O'Connell, D. C. (1991). American and Japanese subjects' reports of pause occurrences and duration. *Language and Communication, 11*(4), 299-307

Volosinov, V.I. (1973). *Marxism and the philosophy of language* (I. Matejka & I. Titunik, Trans.). Cambridge, MA: Harvard University Press. (Original work published 1929)

Wixson, K. (1979). Miscue analysis: A critical review. *Journal of Reading Behavior, 11*(2), 163-175

CONNECTIONS

Chapter Eight

Ideology and the Teaching of Phonics: An Australian Experience

Brian Cambourne
University of Wollongong

In a recent publication Vellutino (1991) makes the claim that whole-language teachers do not believe in teaching letter-sound correspondences to young learner-readers. Among other things he states that whole language advocates believe "words are never to be presented out of context, fluency in identifying words out of context is not a legitimate objective, and analysis of a word's internal structure ('sounding words out') is to be assiduously avoided" (p. 437). In another part of the same article he claims that "[whole-language advocates] contend that the skill [of recognizing and using letter-sound correspondences] need not be taught directly" (p. 437).

Vellutino's claims are representative of many that have appeared in recent publications on reading acquisition. Typically such articles set up an adversarial dichotomy between something called a *code-oriented approach* and a *meaning-oriented approach* (often putting the word "versus" between them) and proceed to argue in an either-or way. In such articles whole language is directly equated with the meaning-oriented approach. The writers of these articles then seek to justify their claims by citing research findings that support their particular point of view. Usually such articles advocate a set of pedagogical practices that purport to be the best way (often the only way!) of promoting effective reading acquisition.

Vellutino's claims about what whole language teachers are supposed to believe and do with respect to phonics do not match my experiences. Between 1985 and 1994, I spent hundreds of hours in classrooms that were described by the teachers who ran them as holistic or whole language in orientation. I documented what happened in literacy sessions in these classrooms by taking field notes, by capturing the ongoing stream of classroom behavior on video-and audiotape, by constant debriefing of teachers and children, and by collecting the written products that both teachers and children produced. The data I collected are rich, deep, and authentic. They do not reflect Vellutino's claims at all.

For example, the following is one of dozens of cameos of classroom behavior relating to phonics teaching that are at variance with his claims. I have constructed it from field notes, videotapes, and teacher interview notes.

Background to Cameo:
The excerpt below is from a grade 1 classroom. It has been taken from the field notes and audio/video records from a typical morning in the first week of April, the ninth week of the first term of the new school year. On the previous day the teacher had conducted a shared book session with the whole class, using an enlarged book in that an illustrated version of "The Little Red Hen" had been retold. On this morning the teacher had planned to demonstrate how a primitive "literary sociogram" is developed by jointly constructing one based on the characters in the story. After about five minutes the chart had a circle in the middle with "Little Red Hen" written within it, and there were lines radiating out connecting to circles that contained the names of the other characters—dog, cat, pig, cow. The teacher pointed to the circle containing "dog" and asked:

T: What was the dog like? What's a word that we could write on the line next to dog that would describe the dog?

Class response: Lazy.

T: How do you spell lazy? Help me.

Class response: L—, A—, Z (Letter names. Teacher writes each letter as they call it out.)[1]

At this point there was a lack of response. The class was obviously stuck for the next letter?

T: What letter or letters carry the "ee" sound?

Chris: (very definitely) It's "Y" (letter name).

T: How do you know?

---

[1]It is important to note that Australian children refer to the letter "Z" as "zed" not "zee."

Chris: I think I've seen it. It's "Y" on the end of "lady" and "baby".
T: That's very interesting Chris. Could it be anything else?
Chris: (Again with firm conviction) Yes, "E". (letter name)
T: Why?
Chris: Because it's "E" in "he", "she" and "we".
T: Could it be anything else?
Chris: It could be double "e" (i.e., "ee").
T: Could it? How do you know?
Chris: Cause I saw it in "meet" and "sleep" and it's on that chart over there, in "feet".
T: So, Chris knows three different sets of letters that can carry the "ee" sound, "Y", "E" and double "EE" . . . (voice trailing off)
Chris: I know some others, like "EA" in "eat" and "meat" and "EI" cause that's how my friend Leif writes his name.

Could we claim that this self-confessed whole language teacher does not believe in teaching letter-sound correspondences? Is this a teacher who believes that "analysis" of a word's internal structure ('sounding words out') is to be assiduously avoided"? Is this an example of a whole language advocate who contends "that the skill [of recognizing and using letter-sound correspondences] need not be taught directly"? Her behavior in this short segment belies Vellutino's claims about what whole language teachers believe and do. She is not an isolated example. There are many teachers in Australia who would classify themselves as whole language advocates who do similar things every day.

How can such discrepancies be explained? Usually in academic debates of this kind, one side tries to discredit the other by impugning the integrity, intelligence, or the methodological competence of their opponents. This is difficult to do in Vellutino's case. He is an established researcher with an outstanding reputation in the field. Even if he were not, I can see little value in adopting the traditional adversarial tactic of trying to discredit his work. Not only are such tactics unproductive, they are drearily predictive and conceptually shallow. They are drearily predictive in the sense that the protagonists on each side selectively interpret (and often distort) the message that they are trying to debunk, and in the process generate misinformation that only serves to confuse teachers. They are conceptually shallow because they ignore a deeper, very important philosophical issue. Freire (1970) recognized this deeper philosophical issue nearly 20 years ago when he wrote, "All educational practice implies a theoretical stance on the educator's part. This stance in turn implies—sometimes more sometimes less explicitly—an interpretation of man (sic) and the world" (p. 205).

Freire's use of the word "interpretation" is crucial. I interpret him to mean that both theoretical stances and the educational practices through that they are realized are inevitably linked to and controlled by the values, beliefs, attitudes, assumptions, understandings, knowledge, past learning, and other personal subjective experiences that everyone is heir to. As such it is essentially a constructivist view of the world. For purposes of this chapter I define the aggregation and intersection of such beliefs, values, assumptions, understandings, knowledge, past learning, and other personal subjective experiences as an *ideology*.

In this chapter I argue that the kinds of debates that writers like Vellutino initiate are basically ideological in nature. The practices that advocates of the so-called code-emphasis approach to reading acquisition recommend certainly imply a theoretical stance which, in turn, carries with it an interpretation of man and the world. So does what has become known as whole language or holistic teaching. I also argue that what happens in literacy classrooms is dependent on what those who actually do the teaching believe, value, assume, and know about literacy and literacy education. I use three questions modified from Luke's (1988) work to frame these ideologies:

- What is effective literate behavior?
- How is such effective literate behavior best acquired?
- What should such effective literate behavior be used for once acquisition is completed?

Figure 8.1 captures this aggregation.

In what follows I explore the relationship between ideology and literacy instruction through two classroom cameos. The classroom examples I have chosen to explore focus specifically on the teaching of letter-sound correspondences to emergent readers, an area typically referred to as the teaching of phonics. Next I argue that much of what has become known as the phonics debate is really more an issue about ideology than an issue about that research method is the more rigorous, or that theoretical orientation is the more robust and/or valid. Finally, I suggest that much of the debate and argument that occurs with respect to literacy education beyond the phonics issue is underpinned by an ideological stratum that is ignored as if it does not exist. I finally suggest that if would be more fruitful and productive if the antagonists in any adversarial debate made their ideologies explicit and showed how these ideologies are reflected in the practices and theories they advocate.

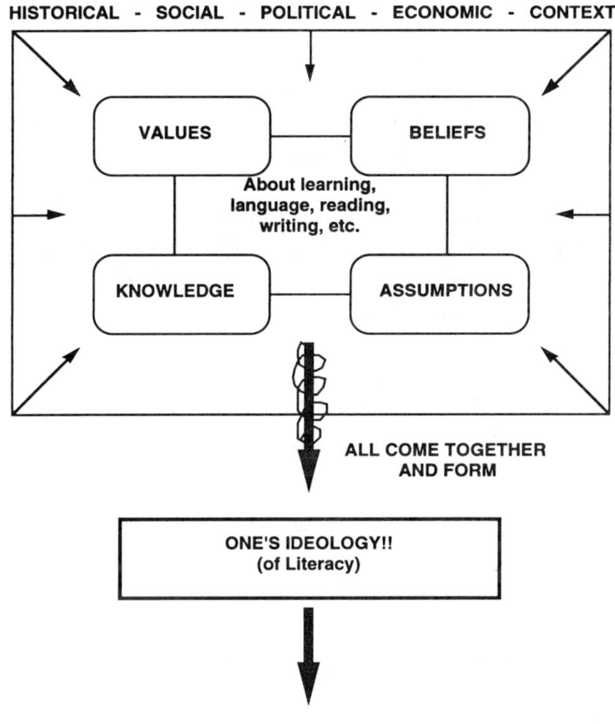

Figure 8.1. An organizational map of one's ideology

THE RELATIONSHIP BETWEEN IDEOLOGY AND CLASSROOM PRACTICE

Cameo #1

Let us go back in time, some 35 years ago, to a one-teacher school of 42 pupils, nestled on the mouth of the Shoalhaven River, on the lower third of the eastern seaboard of the Australian continent. A young male teacher in his third year[2] of teaching is about to begin teaching lower division (Grades K-2). Upper division (Grades 3-6) is engaged in working from their graded arithmetic textbooks. On the wall there is a timetable that lists the various lessons that are planned each day. Most of them are of between 15 and 30 minutes duration and have various

[2]This cameo has been reconstructed from the memory and records of the author.

labels such as Number Drill, Reading Comprehension, Spelling, and Mechanical Arithmetic.

The lower division timetable indicates that it is time for the lesson called Phonic Drill. The official planning book (called a "Program" in Australia) would indicate that he was supposed to be teaching the letters "m" and "n" during this particular week. His daily preparation book (called a "Day Book" in Australia) would show that today included an introduction to the letter "m." There were a number of charts (purchased from commercial publishers) hanging around the room that had letters and pictures associated with those letters on them. The lesson he gave proceeded something like this:

All eyes on me.
(points to preselected letter on chart)
This letter's name is "M" (em)
Say it after me.
(M)
The sound it makes is "mmm".
Say it after me.
(mmm)
Say its name again.
(M)
What sound does it make?
(mm)
Everybody say it.
(mmm)
Say this after me. "Em says mm."
(em says mm)
Again.
(em says mm)
All the boys say it.
(em says mm)
All the girls say it.
(em says mm)
Very good girls. Boys, see if you can say it as well as the girls.
(em says mmmmm)
All together.
(em says mmm)
Who can think of a word that begins with mm?
(Mummy)
Another?
(mouse)
Another?
(am)
No Bobby, "am" begins with an "a" sound. You're not listening carefully.
(continues "think of a word" for 5 minutes)
Now let's look at our stencil. Join up the letters to the pictures that start with the

mm sound. Watch me as I do the first one for you. This is a picture of a marrow, mmm for marrow. I know it looks like a watermelon Bobby, but it's a marrow. Now you do the rest and if you finish quickly don't talk. I want you to colour in the stencil beautifully.
(5 minutes pass)
Let's correct it.
(corrects en masse)
Let's practice the sound we learned last week.
(points to other letters on chart)
Sit up straight; it's time for the next lesson.
Melissa, will you give out these comprehension stencils.

Cameo #2

This cameo comes from a Grade 1 classroom from that I collected data last year. The teacher had a timetable with the entry "Language" from 9:00 a.m.-11:00 a.m. each day of the week. Her usual practice was to begin her language session with the children sitting around her in what she called a whole-class focus position. Usually she read aloud from a book. On this particular day it was an enlarged book that had not previously been read to the class. It could just as easily have been an old favorite that the class was revisiting. It could also have been a normal-sized book. Because the focus of these examples is the teaching of phonics, I have extrapolated from my field notes those parts of the two-hour session that obviously dealt with phonics instruction. I have had to condense two hours (some 23 pages of closely written field notes) to a few short paragraphs. What follows is an edited version of my field notes for that particular day.

She begins with what she calls a Shared Book Lesson. With respect to phonics, in the next 10 minutes she deals with five different initial letter names and sounds. One of these is the "CH" digraph. As well, during this segment she demonstrates phonemic segmentation as a strategy when blocked on three occasions. She invites predictions of letter-sound relationships using masks to cover words on five occasions, and she invites the children help her compile a list of words that rhyme in the story she's reading. She writes these on the chalkboard and they study the graphic similarities. She finds those that look alike and draws attention to the notion of graphic rhyming: that is, some words in this book not only sound alike (rhyme) but the parts that sound alike sometimes look alike.

Next, she begins a segment that involves collaborative analysis of word structure. The children stay in the whole-class focus position. She directs their attention to a large book labeled Demonstration Book. She opens it to a fresh page and picks up a fat, felt pen. She explains that in the past when she "demonstrated" or "showed things to them," she usually put it up on a chart, but because "we'll soon run out of space, I've started to put them in this book now, that you can use to help you with writing."

She then writes "ch" in the middle of the top of the blank page and begins immersing them in knowledge and information associated with the "ch" sound. She uses a range of techniques to do this: for example, "Can we find any words around the room, or think of any in our head, that have a "ch" sound in it. It can be at the beginning, or the end, or in the middle. Remember in the story I just read we looked at some letters that carried the "ch" sound didn't we?"

Then she invites contributions and uses each contribution to elaborate, expand, explain, demonstrate, praise, and make connections. For example, one contribution was "chook" (local colloquialism for "chicken"). She accepted this contribution and said, "Yes, chook, that starts with a 'ch' sound doesn't it? I'll make a column here for words that start with this sound. Watch me while I write the two letters that usually carry this sound, 'c' (letter name) and 'h' (letter name). First a 'c' and then an 'h.' Then there's the sound 'oo.' That letters carry that sound? Rhymes with 'book', and 'look.' Yes, Renee, double 'o' sometimes carries the 'oo' sound. Now watch how I write it, 'd-o-u-b-l-e o,' (stretching the spelling of the word out to coincide with the writing), and now a 'k' sound, that can be carried by a 'c' or a 'ck' or just a 'k'. That do you think it might be? Yes Frank, like the end of your name, a 'k'".

She then switches the focus to words that end in the "ch" sound. She creates a second column on the page, and again she uses each response to elaborate, expand, make connections, and praise.

The contributions come thick and fast. The kids seem to be using two strategies to generate them:

1. Scrounging from wall print.
2. Pulling words that they already know from their heads.

She also gets some plausible exceptions that don't fit the general case, for example:

1. "Christine"—from a child who scrounged and responded to the visual display only.

2. "Picture"—that clearly has the "ch" sound in it when these children say it, and one of the children's surnames "Lucci" (pronounced "Luchie").

She handles these by making more connections for the learners. She creates two other columns on the page she is using, and writes "picture" and "Lucci" in one and explains that there are other combinations of letters that can carry the "ch" sound. She then writes "Christin"' in the other and states that there are also some words that begin with "ch" (letter names) that don't carry the "ch" sound. She doesn't dwell on either case, except to say, "We'll try to fill up these columns during the year. See if we can find anymore 'ch' (letter names) words like these two."

She finishes this segment with a choral reading, follow-the-pointer, follow-the-leader, demonstration of reading the words they'd generated. This choral reading emphasizes syllabification, particularly with respect to the "ch" sound. The majority of kids respond by joining in. While they're doing this, some spillover from other sessions comes through—one of the girls comments that "if you changed the 'c' to 's' in 'ch', and added an 'e' the word should be 'she'."

A segment that she calls "joint construction of a written text" now begins. During the previous two weeks she had been reading to the class from some enlarged books about Prehistoric Animals. She had been careful while reading these books to continually draw attention to the way that scientific text (actually report genre) was structured and set out on the page. They'd also spent some time discussing why what they called information books were set out the way that they were, and what purposes such books served. They'd made some simple comparisons between the structure and purposes of fairy tales that they'd been reading and information texts. Today she helps them construct on the chalkboard a similarly structured report on one of the Australian animals they'd seen at a recent class excursion to a nature park. She reminds them of the visit, gives them a purpose and audience ("We want to summarize what we found about these animals for our 'buddy' class"), and then begins to demonstrate how she might compose a report on the kangaroo. She does most of the talking, pretending to be thinking out loud, judiciously asking a question now and then and including children's contributions in the developing text. She uses the information texts they'd been reading as a model to refer to. As well, many of her think-alouds are almost incidental repetitions of the phonics concepts she'd just been dealing with. After about 10 minutes of this joint construction she announces, "It's writing time now. You might like to begin working on a report of one of the animals we saw at the park last week, or you can work on any other piece of writing you like."

The children then began the individual writing segment, working individually at constructing a text. During this segment she hits base with at least two thirds of them and discusses and generally supports their writing. On many occasions she asks the learner to make explicit the phonic knowledge or processes he or she is drawing on to write.

After 20 minutes a new segment begins. The teacher takes them on a print walk around the room reading the wall charts. She invites them to read the words on different charts and to "find words within words."

Frank, a slow starter, points to the word "this" on one of the charts. He says, "If you take the 't' off 'this' you get 'his'." She praises him and asks for others. Frank's contribution is picked up by many of the others and they try to outdo his effort. Renee, a high flyer, points to the word "don't" on an adjacent chart and says, "If you take away the 't' on the end, and that thing that looks like a comma, and then turn the 'n' upside down, and then change the 'd' on the front to a 'y', it becomes 'you'." Not to be outdone, Amy points to the word "like" on the same chart and says, "If you take off the 'l' at the front and move the 'k' up to take its place and then put a 't' where the 'k' used to be you get 'kite'."

The sustained reading segment now begins as the children select books to read from. They continue this until break time.

WHAT IDEOLOGIES DO THESE EXAMPLES REFLECT?

As explained earlier, the framework that I used to tap into the ideologies of literacy education that these two teachers held was based on these teachers' beliefs, values, and so on, concerning these three domains:

- the nature of effective literate behavior;
- how such effective literate behavior is best acquired; and
- what such effective literate behavior should be used for once acquisition is completed.

Let us take each of these examples and try to tease out the relevant ideological aspects of each.

CAMEO #1: TEACHING PHONICS IN THE 1950S

Thirty-five years ago this young male teacher would have been hard pressed to make explicit why he taught phonics the way he did. It would have meant being able to take what is essentially tacit knowledge and turn it into propositional form. This kind of reflective behavior was not part of the teaching culture in that he found himself at that time. It is possible, however, to identify a multiplicity of related beliefs, values, assumptions, and knowledge (i.e., an ideology) that motivated what he did.

First, he would have had knowledge of the major functions that literacy served in that era. In the late 1950s the emphasis was on functional literacy. This emphasis could be directly traced to the fact that during World War II the U.S. army had found high rates of something called *functional illiteracy* in its recruits. As was the practice with most other things American, Australians automatically assumed the same findings could be applied to them. We assumed that we probably also had many school graduates who were functionally illiterate. Furthermore, this young teacher would have been taught in training college that universal functional literacy was an essential condition for true participatory democracy. He would have also accepted that there was a general agreement among the business community that economic progress was somehow tied to a functionally literate workforce. Thus, his ideology motivated him to ensure that as many of his pupils as possible acquired functional literacy (enough "to get by on"). This was, in turn, linked to specific views he held regarding the purposes that reading and writing might ultimately serve in his pupils' lives. To this end he considered reading predominantly as a skill that enabled one to get information from books and/or as means of escape through fantasy. Somewhere in his teacher training course he was also probably told that great literature could serve as a humanizing medium. Writing, he believed, was essentially for the utilitarian purpose of communicating information (writing letters of thanks, applying for jobs, being called on to write reports appropriate to certain occupations, for displaying learning at examination time) or for the purpose of developing something called creativity and/or imagination.

Second, he had very strong beliefs about the nature of reading and the role that phonic knowledge played in the reading process. He had been taught that reading was an extremely complex process, the key to that was the decoding of letters and letter combinations to sound. Linked to this was the belief that because one learns best by first learning the bits and working up to the whole, learners need lots of practice in getting the little bits right before moving on to the bigger bits.

Third, all of these beliefs were linked to some very strongly held beliefs about learning that were held by the majority of teachers when he first began teaching in the mid-1950s. These beliefs were enshrined in the curriculum documents and policy guides of the time. They were also emphasized throughout the two-year training course he had just completed. These beliefs were:

- learning is essentially habit formation
- complex habits like reading are best learned if they are broken down into sequences of smaller, less complex, simpler habits and presented to learners in graded sequences of increasing complexity
- habits are best formed by associating a desired response with the appropriate stimulus
- strong association leads to strong habits
- associative strength is a function of frequency of pairing S-R, or "practice makes perfect"
- inappropriate responses (i.e., approximations) are incipient bad habits and must be extinguished before they firm up and become fixed
- learners are too immature and/or underdeveloped to make decisions about their learning, so the process must be directed and totally controlled by the teacher

Finally, he had very thin knowledge about language per se. He had been taught in college that there was research that showed a statistical relationship between tests of reading and tests of vocabulary. That was about it. In his mind poor language was equated with poor speech and bad grammar and needed to be eradicated. He had no insights into the ways language was structured, how it functioned, or the role it played in learning.

The ideology that the sum total of these beliefs, values, assumptions, and knowledge reflect is very evident in the phonics lesson described earlier. He decided what phonic knowledge would be learned, when it would be learned, and how it would be learned. There were no degrees of freedom in terms of learner response. He stripped the phonemic system away from the other language systems with that it interacts in the real world of reading and writing and directly taught it as a system in its own right. He isolated the processes involved in letter-sound recognition and use from the functions that they typically serve (reading and writing). This ideology was not restricted to the teaching of phonics. It pervaded everything he did in every part of the literacy curriculum that he taught: spelling, handwriting, vocabulary, grammar, punctuation, composition, and reading comprehension. It also pervaded the way he taught other curriculum areas.

CAMEO #2: TEACHING PHONICS IN THE 1990S

The behavior of the teacher in the 1990 example reflects a quite different ideology. An analysis of the many debriefing interviews I have conducted gives the following account of her ideology of literacy.

At the core of her ideology is the notion of social, intellectual, economic, and political empowerment. She has a passionate belief that society as a whole can only benefit from having as many powerful thinkers, learners, knowers, and understanders as possible. This is accompanied by a strong concern for equity, especially with respect to those she considers to be underprivileged. She believes that the economically, socially, and politically underprivileged in our community can be empowered if they are powerful thinkers and learners.

Just as the 1950s teachers' "participate in democracy/be employable" motive for teaching reading was influenced by a complex network of values, beliefs, understandings, and assumptions about reading, writing, learning, and language, so her "empowerment" motive was also connected to and influenced by a network.

Her network of beliefs, values, understandings, and assumptions about reading, writing, learning, and language seemed to be more tightly and coherently organized than that of the 1950s teachers. My data indicate that she believed that the empowerment that she valued could be made possible by control of those forms of language that enabled people to think, know, learn, and understand in certain domains of knowledge. For example, learning, thinking, knowing, and understanding like a scientist, mathematician, lawyer, and so forth, required control of the forms of discourse that these different kinds of knowing and thinking typically used. For her, reading and writing functioned primarily as technologies for getting control of those written forms of discourse that enabled certain kinds of thinking and learning to be controlled. This meant that learners needed to be taught how to use reading and writing as a means of getting control of language, not merely as a means of transmitting or acquiring information.

These beliefs and values were embedded in and connected to a view of learning that was quite different from the habit-formation view of learning that the young male teacher of the 1950s held. She based what she did in her classroom on a model of learning that characterized the complex kind of learning that regularly occurred outside classrooms and exemplified by the conditions that accompany the acquisition of spoken language. Some writers in the field have called this view of learning "acquisition learning" (Holdaway, 1990), others have called it "natural learning" (Cambourne, 1988). Essentially, it refers to the kind of learning that typically takes place outside of the formal school setting. It is exemplified by all the kinds of culturally based learning to which members of any culture are heir; for example, learning how to hunt like the rest of the tribe, learning to play the complex games that are part of any culture, and so on. A good exemplar is learning how to talk as described by Cambourne (1988).

Whereas in the 1950s he saw both written and oral language as sets of skills to be acquired for purposes of gaining and/or transmitting information, she sees language as a precious ore that can be mined (through reading, listening, and exploring texts) and subsequently turned into a range of valuable cognitive artifacts (learnings, understandings) by writing and social interaction.

The phonics lesson described earlier reflects this ideology in practice. Whereas the teacher of the 1950s taught phonics for the purposes of helping learners decode words they wished to read, the teacher of the 1990s taught phonics because she believed that learners needed phonic information to begin constructing written text. She further believed that as they attempted to construct written text using their underdeveloped and incomplete knowledge of the way letter-sound correspondences can be used, they were forced to explore the phonemic structure of words in ways that led to a deep and intensive knowledge of letters and sounds. The knowledge gained from this exploration in turn spilled over into their reading behavior, that in turn fed back into their developing writing power, that in turn spilled back into their reading behavior, and so on. She calls this process *generative learning*.

In the previous session she also implements the theory of learning that she holds. She immerses, demonstrates, and provides opportunity for the learners to take various degrees of control of what, when, and how they learn. She repeats and recycles the same information and skills (through different media), and she encourages and invites discussion and talk, through sharing and collaborative ventures. She provides scaffolds when necessary. She is also honest about letter-sound correspondences. (She does not pretend that the phonemic system is regular.) She chooses metaphors carefully. (Letters carry sounds, they do not say or make them.) She helps the learners make the graphophonic connections that they need to make. She demonstrates phonic knowledge in ways that makes it possible for learners to see how the phonemic system fits in with other systems of language in order to make meaning. I would also argue that her students are developing a set of analytic and metalinguistic skills and knowledge about the graphophonic system and how it works that will enable them to grow as readers and writers. Figure 8.2 compares the various facets of each of these teachers' ideologies.

So what does all this mean? There are at least three conclusions that I think should be drawn.

First, it means that Freire was on the right track. There is an important relationship between world view (i.e., ideology) and pedagogical practice (including aims, outcomes, etc.).

Second, it suggests that debate that merely cites different research results to support a position (as does Vellutino) without also making explicit the ideology that underpins that position is not very helpful.

Third, it means that although teachers, theorists, and researchers can often appear to have the same desired outcomes (e.g., highly literate students), if these outcomes are mediated through different ideologies, they end up being very different for the learners involved. This state of affairs was illustrated by the phonics cameos presented earlier. Both teachers would agree that children in grade one need a thorough grounding in letter-sound knowledge and relationships (i.e., phonics). However, because each was motivated by different ideologies, what they actually did in order to achieve their desired outcomes was very different, and as a consequence, the outcomes themselves were very different. It seems that even when dealing with something as focused as phonics teaching, when one begins to explore the ideological dimension one inevitably ends up exploring world views. We cannot seem to escape it.

FACET OF IDEOLOGY	1950s TEACHER	1990s TEACHER
Desired literacy	▪functional literacy	▪productive, critical, literacy ▪control of language for increased ability to think, learn, know, understand
Motive, rationale for teaching literacy	▪functional literacy necessary for participatory democracy ▪functionally literate workforce is necessary for successful	▪empowerment in society through being a powerful knower, thinker, learner ▪control of language leads to power in learning, etc.
Role reading plays in students' lives	▪acquisition of information ▪escape through literature ▪humanizing through literature	▪as for 1950s PLUS ▪technology for getting control of language
Role writing plays in students' lives	▪communication and transmission of information	▪as for 1950s PLUS ▪a technology for getting control of language
View of learning	▪hierarchical, skills-based, fragmented, lock-step, habit formation	▪natural, acquisition, holistic
Language information knowledge	▪language as oral speech only	▪language as a unified multilayered series of systems that interact to produce meaning
Motive for teaching phonic relationships	▪reading is decoding to sound; learners need to have automatic control of letter-sound relations in order to "hear" words inside head prior to comprehension ▪learning is most effective if worked up from parts to whole	▪learners need phonic knowledge in order to write in the process of composing written messages ▪learners explore the phonemic structure of written language; this spills over into reading, which in turn spills back into writing, and so on

Figure 8.2. A comparison of ideologies

CONCLUDING STATEMENT

I am beginning to believe that most of the academic arguments that I become involved in, or that I see and hear happening around me, are essentially ideological in nature. I have always assumed that ultimately those of us who engage in debate and argument (often heated) about literacy have the same long-term goal in mind, namely, the best possible literacy education for the current generation (and future generations?) of school children. This usually involves arguing about what counts as legitimate knowledge and practice in literacy education. This is in turn inextricably linked to why we think literacy is important in our culture, that in turn presupposes that we have beliefs (often implicit) about the social and cultural purposes that literacy should serve in our society and the uses to that it can be put. This is what I see as the ideological dimension.

Often we gloss over or ignore the ideological dimensions of what we are presenting, as if there is no underlying stratum of strongly held beliefs, values, assumptions, and knowledge about what "good literacy" is, what should count as effective literacy behavior, how this kind of behavior should be taught in schools, and why we should be teaching whatever good literacy is.

Writers like Vellutino certainly make no attempt to make their ideologies explicit. Why? Are they consciously aware of what ideologies about "good reading" they hold? About the purposes that reading should serve in our culture? Can they make them explicit? Can they justify why phonics should be taught the way they advocate in ways that are congruent with this ideology?

Vellutino's interpretation "man (sic) and the world" can be inferred from those things he advocates and those he debunks in his article. His representation of whole language is a king of ideological Rorschach test, similar to that of many who view literacy through the same set of ideological lenses. Essentially his view is a functionalist one, similar to the 1950s teacher described earlier, with a seductive and very appealing pragmatic emphasis on preparing learners for successful entry to the workforce. Knoblauch and Bannon (1993) have offered this critique of the functionalist view:

> The functionalist argument has a more hidden advantage [as well], at least from the standpoint of those whose literacy is more than minimal; it safeguards the socioeconomic status quo . . . In short, the tendency of a functionalist perspective is to accept a given social order. (p. 18)

What is the long-term effect of teaching phonics and indeed literacy from the functionalist perspective that lies at the core of Vellutino's argument? I would argue that although it may certainly produce technically competent readers and writers who have skills that are appropriate for specific contexts of use, it is doubtful that it will produce readers and writers who are equipped to produce a better society by questioning those who wield power. As Knoblauch and Bannon (1993) assert, "The soldier will know how to repair an MX missile by reading the field manual but will not question the use of such weapons because of her reading of antimilitarist philosophers" (p. 18).

The fact that writers like Vellutino either will not or cannot make their ideologies explicit and justify them in terms that go beyond research findings and methods concerns me. If they cannot, it suggests that they are operating at a superficial pragmatic level that scares me given the sociopolitical context in that we live. If they will not, then it also scares me. What kind of society and power structures are they (surreptitiously) trying to set up and maintain?

Perhaps this is why academics who have significant ideological differences about reading typically seek to reject their opponents' points of view by seeking to discredit or find fault with their research methodologies and findings. I believe it would be more productive to get our ideologies out in the open and discuss them. In fact I would argue that it should be incumbent on all who decide to debate and argue about things like the ways that phonics (or spelling, or reading, or genre, etc.) should or should not be taught make their ideologies of literacy explicit before beginning to argue.

I suspect that many debates would be a lot more enlightening if this were an agreed upon prerequisite.

REFERENCES

Cambourne, B. L. (1988) *The whole story. Natural learning and the acquisition of literacy.* Auckland: Ashton-Scholastic

Freire, P. (1970). The adult literacy process as cultural action for freedom. *Harvard Educational Review, 40,* 205.

Holdaway, D. (1990) The social dynamics of acquisition learning. In J. Howell, A. McNamara, & J. Clough (Eds.), *Selected papers from the 15th Australian reading association national conference* (pp. 124-135). Canberra, ACT: Australian Reading Association.

Knoblauch, C. H., & Bannon, L. (1993). *Critical teaching and the idea of literacy.* Portsmouth, NH: Boynton-Cook.

Luke, A. (1988). *Literacy, textbooks and ideology: Postwar literacy instruction and the mythology of Dick and Jane.* Bristol, PA: Taylor & Francis.

Vellutino, F. R. (1991). Introduction to three studies on reading acquisition: Convergent findings on theoretical foundations of code-oriented versus whole-language Approaches to reading instruction. *Journal of Educational Psychology, 83*(4), 437-443.

Chapter Nine

Growing Up Whole Language

Debra Goodman
Detroit Public Schools

In 1967, when Ken Goodman wrote "Reading: A Psycholinguistic Guessing Game," I was 12 years old. He was 39. Now I am 39, and I have just completed 15 years of teaching in the Detroit Public Schools. Throughout the last year, as the deadline for this chapter loomed and passed, I have been trying to compose a piece that can begin to describe how the man who cooked me breakfast every morning of my childhood influenced my own learning and teaching.

Once, in my early 20s, I rushed home from a conference to tell my dad how excited I was to meet Noam Chomsky in person. He told me that I had already met Noam Chomsky when I was 10. "Remember that summer we stayed at the dorm in Cornell? I cooked breakfast for Noam Chomsky. We all had breakfast together." Later, as a master's student, I quoted Frank Smith in one of my classes. "Where did Frank Smith say that?" the professor asked, concerned that he had missed something. "Um," I said, a little embarrassed, "He said it at a party."

Social occasions, particularly those involving food, have played a large role in my own professional development. Orchestrated by my mother, but with my father as chef, someone was always coming to dinner or breakfast. I have a feeling most of the contributors to this book have eaten my father's sukiyaki or his huevos rancheros. The menu, the guests, and the conversation were culturally diverse. My understandings of teaching and learning were constructed within these social/language events.

For this reason I have always valued the social nature of learning for my students, myself, and my colleagues. At the end of her fifth-grade year in my classroom, Cassie reflected in detail on her growth in understanding new concepts and strategies for social science, language arts, and research. But she finished her self-evaluation by saying that the most important thing about the year was her friends because "without friends nothing else matters." Like me, Cassie placed a higher value on the social structures that support content and process learning in my classroom.

My goals as a teacher, which I shared with Cassie and her classmates, included content, process, and social elements. I tried to create the social community of learners that I grew up with. That social community was as important for me as it was for my students. For the past 10 years my social community has centered around my professional friendship with Toby Kahn Curry. We met when I was a substitute teacher assigned to assist Toby in taking her 65 eighth graders on a field trip to the library. I was in awe of her ease with middle schoolers, and she was thirsty for my ideas about language teaching. Since then, she has been my life-line in the Detroit Schools.

I went on to a Chapter One position, and Toby came down for lunches during which we collaborated on ideas for integrated curriculum in our classrooms. We were lucky enough to work with David Bloome and gain ethnographic perspectives for our classroom observations. As teacher/researchers we learned, with David, how all children take on the underlying social agenda of school classrooms. Access to literacy, we discovered, means more than filling the room with books and immersing children in literacy experiences. The social layer of teaching and learning took on heightened importance as we considered that schooling may be different for each child.

It was Toby's idea that we should get together with other teachers to write a proposal for a whole language magnet school. "I'll help write it," I told Toby, "but it will never happen." Two years and several setbacks later, Toby and I were conducting staff development sessions for our new school, the Dewey Center for Urban Education. As Toby and I spent large amounts of time working and planning together it became harder, but more important, to just get together and be friends. We learned to schedule lunch dates for rejuvenation. Even on our 20-minute lunch period at Burton International School, we dashed off every Friday to a local greasy spoon.

These weekly lunch dates were essential because, to paraphrase Cassie, what good is all the best theory and practice if there is no one to get the joke, appreciate the peak moments, and understand completely when things are not going well? In my last few years of teaching at the Dewey Center, I was privileged to eat lunch each day with teachers who were seriously exploring teaching and learning and wanted to exchange ideas. As we shared sandwiches, language stories, popcorn, and writing samples, we shared our appreciation for each other as teachers and researchers. I felt treasured and valued.

My teaching certainly didn't start out that way.

In the Spring of 1978, a (very young) substitute teacher sat having a reading conference with a second grader. The door opened and the principal slid into the room like a knife. He took in the noisy scene. Some children sat in one corner reading picture books while others listened to tapes. Some children were in the "post office" area writing notes, while others were illustrating a class publication. There was lots of talking and movement.

In one corner, four boys sat in a small cluster laughing and fooling around. The principal's casual glance immediately took focus.

I finished the conference and walked over, my heart pounding.

"What are those boys doing over there?", he asked.

I tried to appear calm as my thoughts raced. I'd been in the room three weeks. On my first day the parapro had told me that the boys would be repeating second grade. Their fate had been decided in September. Now I was held accountable.

"Well," I tried, "They're supposed to be . . ."

"What were you doing over there with that girl?" The principal had not really expected an answer.

"We were having a reading conference."

"A reading conference?", the principal said, "Aren't you using the Ginn readers?"

"Yes I am," I said, "but half of the students have finished the second grade reader already, and I thought. .. "

"I'll send Mrs. Jones in to explain to you how to organize the reading lessons," the principal said.

I said nothing. I was very interested in keeping my job.

"There have been complaints that your room is too noisy. You can't allow the students to disturb other classes."

I looked at the bathroom doors connecting to the next room. Several times each day our class was treated to the sound of kids being spanked by the teacher whom we were "disturbing."

The principal left. He had been there 10 minutes. The children stared at me, their eyes wide with concern. It was April. I was their third teacher that year. They wrote love notes on tiny scraps of paper and left them in my mailbox.

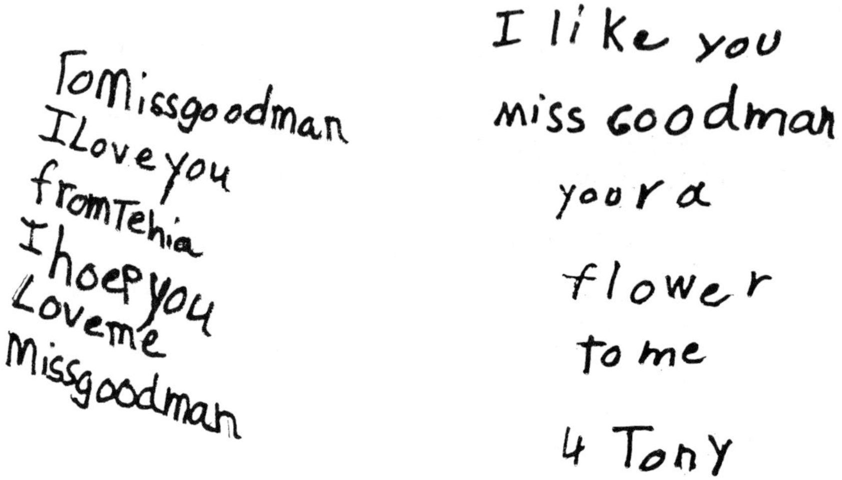

To miss goodman
I Love you
from Tehia
I hoep you
Love me
Miss goodman

I like you
miss Goodman
your a
flower
to me
4 Tony

Figure 9.1.

The children didn't know that in one week I was eligible for a raise to the rate of a first year teacher. I spent three days cooperating with Mrs. Jones. Mrs. Jones wondered why I hadn't been giving the DORT (objective reference tests). Although I knew that subs weren't supposed to do DORT, I rushed to catch the children up. I tried not to think of the more pleasant reading conferences as I read off nonsense syllables for the children to mark with an X on their grid-like sheets.

My eyes anxiously roved the little reading group clusters, willing them to be quiet in case the principal returned. "1A- tid, cross out tid. 1-B, pid, cross out pid. 1-C trid, cross out trid." Suddenly Jimmy jumped up out of his seat, "Bingo!"

He looked at me, urging me to share the joke. I smiled and continued to hurry through the DORT tests. The children left love letters in my mailbox.

The next morning the principal called me into his office. "I'm replacing you with Miss Smith," he said "I'm sure you'll agree that you're an inexperienced teacher." He sat behind his desk, never glancing up from his paperwork.

It was at that point that I was ready to fight back. "I'm a beginning teacher," I said, "but I have a great deal of experience. . ."

"But you're not sure how to teach reading," the principal said.

"Actually, I have a very strong background in reading. I was using an individualized reading approach. I wasn't told I had to teach reading in a certain way. If you had told me. . ."

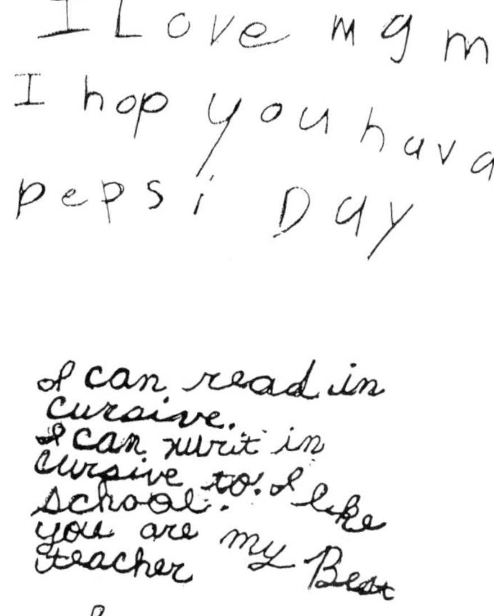

Figure 9.2.

"Well, I never imagined that you would teach reading like that." The principal looked up at me for the first time. "I've never even heard of individualized reading."

"I never imagined teaching reading any other way." I told him in complete honesty, "Jeanette Veatch wrote about individualized reading in the 1940s. This is how our university professors suggested we teach reading."

The principal got just a little defensive. "I'm sure there are a lot of principals who have never heard of individualized reading."

"Unfortunately, I'm sure you're right."

I stood and watched him for a long minute as he began to shuffle busily through the papers on the wooden desk. "Individualization is a luxury we can not afford in the Detroit Public Schools," he said finally.

If this were a Hollywood movie (Miracle Worker Part II, the Detroit years) the teacher's passionate arguments would convince the principal to give her another chance. In two weeks her career would be saved, and the four boys would be reading Shakespeare. Unfortunately, this was not a movie. This was my life. And this was only the first in a series of similar encounters with principals, supervisors, and other teachers. My knowledge and experience (and phone calls home) provided strength and determination, but they certainly didn't make public school teaching easy.

I entered teaching just as we had started talking about whole language, and I knew what kind of teacher I wanted to be. As a pre-student teacher in Vera Milz's first/second grade classroom, I had watched how she quietly supported young readers and writers. One day I taught the kids a song where we made up verses as we went along, but Vera was in the back of the group writing the verses down. She invited children to come over and work on the class composition and before I knew it I was putting together a publication.

I know a teacher named Miss Milz
Hey Lolly, lolly lo
She teaches up in Bloomfield Hills

I learned from Vera how to stretch and extend every literacy learning opportunity. My college supervisor, Jane Romatowski, who had worked with my parents, organized and supported wonderful student teaching experiences for me. I student taught with Laura Nebel and Mary Lou Hess in a team-taught open classroom in Dearborn. What impressed me, in that time when individualization sometimes meant that each child worked in a carrel alone, was the growth the children made that year, not just as individuals but as members of a community. This was because of Laura and Mary Lou's infinite patience and understanding and the value they placed on pairing kids into teams and groups for collaborative and socially supported learning.

One child, Mariama, was born in Lebanon and had lived in Northern Africa, but had never gone to school. The school was over 50% Arab-American, but Mariama appeared different from her Lebanese classmates. She approached school like a 4-year-old with great enthusiasm for new things and huge tantrums when she was disappointed. The Arab-American children who translated for the new immigrants told us that Mariama didn't make much sense in Arabic. She required constant attention, and I spent many hours with Mariama until Laura was able to match her up with Denise who had a big and generous heart and took Mariama under her wing.

Mariama was very bright and eager to learn. One day she was called out of the room for testing, and she was disgusted by the waste of her time. "We didn't do no work. Just check this, check that!" When we sat in the circle and talked things over, Mariama soon began to wave her hands for her turn to speak. And there was great celebration on the day that she was able to say something related to the discussion. Mariama hated to sit next to boys, and Laura tolerated this until one day when there was only one empty seat. Anticipating a furor, Laura took Mariama around the room to show her how many girls were sitting next to boys and then plunked her into the empty seat.

When I came to the author's conference in the Spring, Mariama had written a book about a boy and a girl who were friends. We had worked with the parents in conferences facilitated by a district bilingual specialist who was fluent in Arabic, partly because Mariama was being beaten at home for her behavior. It was discouraging to hear, the following year, that Mariama had returned to Northern Africa with her family. "You can't let it break your heart," Laura said "You just have to give them the best year you can."

Although I never set out to rock the boat, my "open classroom" or "language experience approach" became a target for attack. It was the "back to the basics" era, and even Laura and Mary Lou were suddenly told they had to use certain textbooks and methods. Many of the teachers of my generation left teaching during those years of so-called teacher surplus, discouraged by the hard work, the focus on behavioral objectives, the lack of support, and the constant layoffs. I stayed for the love letters, I guess. And because I was born and raised to teach.

It's hard to boil down a lifetime of mealtime conversations and social interactions to some key factors or memories that might have compelled me to want to be a teacher even when it meant fighting tooth and nail for my place in a classroom. My dad says that we ate breakfast together every day because he and my mom often taught evening classes. But I mostly remember the dinners extended by hours of conversation until every morsel of food had been eaten. When the Reading Miscue Center was opened in the Park Shelton Hotel in Detroit, there were also daily pot-luck lunches. And, when NCTE met during the Thanksgiving holiday, my sisters and I ate Thanksgiving dinner in cities around the United States, celebrating the holiday as we chewed over the latest bit of research or classroom practice.

When I consider myself as a teacher, I already see a number of qualities in that young teacher in the story that continue to be important to me today:

- a belief in myself and my ideas
- a respect for other human beings and a belief in civil rights
- an appreciation of language and learning
- an understanding of grassroots movements for change
- a respect for teachers and teaching (as an exalted profession!)
- a view of teachers as researchers

- an understanding of the power of story, parable and metaphor in expressing and coming to know complex ideas

My mother tells a story about the day when I was about four and she was reading me a book called *The Wonderful Story of How You Were Born*. When she got to the last line, "And then you were born," I looked up at her and said, "And weren't you proud!" I think it meant a lot to my mother, who was never complimented and always compared unfavorably to her older sister, that I already knew she was proud of me.

My father tells of me, again at four, wandering off at the beach. After almost an hour of frantic searching, he came upon me observing a family picnic and listening to their radio. "Didn't you know you were lost?", he asked me. "Yes," I said. "But I knew you would find me." For my father, who hadn't experienced a dad who was loving and attentive, that sort of confidence was startling.

Of course it was their loving and accepting responses to my language and learning that were the basis of my own confidence and pride. But I also knew, because of mealtime stories, that they had the same confidence and respect for all learners. This faith in myself and other young people prompted me to start a block club day camp when I was 16. I had training sessions for my 11-15-year-old staff and I told them, "If you give a child a rule, always explain it. If you can't explain it, it's probably not a very good rule."

It is important to me that my pride and self-confidence were never diminished because I was female. It never occurred to me that a girl shouldn't do anything that a boy would do. In 1967 my friend Llenda and I were 12-year old radical feminists. We wrote to 40 congressmen and senators asking to become the first female pages. In 1969 we went to the first women's teach-in at Wayne State University. But we couldn't really understand the movement's focus on getting women out of the "kitchen" and into the workforce. Llenda's parents were both educators. All the mothers that we knew worked outside of the home in the integrated community where we grew up. What kind of liberation movement was this? And what about the women who made their living working in homes? As I watched my father cooking breakfast or tending his garden while my mother worked on her doctoral dissertation, I was of the naive opinion that women's liberation is simply a personal decision to act liberated.

My parents, their colleagues, and students shared (and argued over) language stories and were eager for our insider's view of schooling. I was the subject of quite a few doctoral studies. One student insisted that I name the *one* most influential person in my life, and my mom still feels upset that I picked my dad. I think I chose my dad because I was, at 12, in love with ideas and excited by parables, wit, and satire. When I brought my father an idea, he would ask me a question or tell me a story.

One day I told my father that I had decided I was a pacifist. I had even stopped hitting boys "just for fun" because I realized I was taking advantage of the sexist notion that they were not supposed to hit me back. My decision was also painstaking because I was also a revolutionary and in those stormy days in the late 1960s, we thought the revolution was coming any time. My friend Llenda and I read widely, from Shakespeare to Tolkien and from Karl Marx to Malcolm X. We wore buttons that said, "Freedom by any means necessary," and we joined our hero, Angela Davis, and gave our lives to the struggle. But I reconciled my pacifist and revolutionary perspectives by considering Thoreau's perspective that only those who oppose the violence of slavery have a right to oppose the violence against slavery.

At any rate, my own life was very precious to me, and I imagined other people felt the same way. I figured that, even during the revolution, someone would have to teach the children. When I reported all this to my father he asked, "What if your own life was threatened?" After considering, I told him I would not return violence with violence. He then asked, "What if it was a member of your family or a close friend who was threatened?"

In this conversation and countless others, my ideas were taken seriously. The questions helped me to interrogate and refine my own thinking. In the Miscue Center in Detroit, ideas were not simply hatched in my father's mind. I saw them born in conversation and debate, as well as in stories and jokes and pot-luck lunches. There was actually a bulletin board "model of the reading process" to provide hours of thought and discussion. But there was also a large tangle of audiotape hanging from the conference room door labeled "complex miscue." A sign in the bathroom read "research lavatory." And certain researchers were fond of collecting food miscues or sex miscues. Like the time one boy read "testicles" for "typical" throughout an entire story. Or the day Dorothy Watson was leaning a little too close to the computer keyboard and accidentally brushed her breast against it. The machine typed out "unrecognizable command." "That," said Margaret Lindberg as she passed by, "is the difference between man and computer."

As I watched my parents learn with their students, I realized that the child readers were the ultimate teachers. I carried this into my classroom, taking my own students seriously as learners and as teachers. Cassie and her classmates, my first group of fifth graders, taught me that fun and play and friendship make learning rich and long-lasting. It was

Cassie who suggested that we could have a "play town," which helped me to develop a meaningful committee structure where the children could organize and run the classroom.

I knew how to sing and play with little kids, but fifth graders were such capable learners and wanted so much to be "grown" that it was sometimes hard to remember they were children. I had watched these "cool" kids get into the dirt and play in the sandbox. But it took Cassie's prompting to make me consider that Vygotsky's notion of play is as true for big kids as for little kids. As we "played town" the kids were a head taller than themselves (Vygotsky, 1978), taking on roles that they had never considered.

I watched the girls snuggle during quiet reading, while the boys could only tackle and wrestle. I brought my own love of folk dancing into the school, and we were able to hold hands and run and laugh together even if we were boys, and even if we could not speak English. I brought my guitar and we sang our way through history. I knew Pete Seeger and Holly Near and discovered Fred Small, a social studies teacher's dream come true. I even grew brave enough to sing Fred Small's *The Hug* (1994). The boys crawled under the table, but they knew we cared about each other.

In our classroom we cared about each other. We laughed and danced and sang and cried together. Once Cassie jumped up and shouted across the room at her best friend, "I love you Rebecca!" Merna described sustained silent reading as "a reading massage." Richard brought souvenirs from Sea World; Amy shared her gymnastics wins; Camille said "Can we talk?" and then proceeded to describe how it felt to be skinny when boys only go for girls who are built. Timothy discussed his painful unrequited love. Betty Ann confided that she cut her leg by sleeping in a bed with broken glass. Rena sang us a song from Ghana in her home language. And David sat with tears streaming down his face because Sadako had died in Hiroshima more than 40 years before.

Cassie and her classmates (my first group of fifth graders) are now first-year university students. As a first-year doctoral student I found them on e-mail, and they write to me about the wonderful far-ranging conversations they have about what and how they are learning. Julia writes that it is truly amazing to hear the things they talk about. As I attend the 4-hour marathons that sometimes pass as graduate classes, I can't help but think we might learn more at the university if we spent a little time singing together, dancing together, or eating together.

In recent years, members of the whole language community have begun to have a more broad-based discussion of some of the social and cultural issues that I have always seen as having birthed miscue analysis. In other words, whole language teachers seem to be becoming more political. This may be because teachers who never considered themselves politically active have found themselves under attack for apparently apolitical acts such as sustained silent reading or journal writing.

Of course, as soon as you make school personally and socially relevant, you get into touchy and controversial areas. Although teaching in urban settings involves struggle and hardship, there are benefits to teaching in a primarily African American, pro-union town. When I was a high school student in Detroit, during the time of the "generation gap," Detroit teenagers did not consider our parents "the establishment." While Detroit teens were part of the protests against the Vietnam War and the struggles for racial equality of the late 1960s, our parents shared stories of their own freedom fighting during the 1940s and 1950s.

As a teacher in the Detroit Public Schools, my colleagues and I produced publications and elaborate stage productions written by the children at the end of each school year. The children read their own poetry, recited Langston Hughes, sang union songs, performed Utopia Town raps, acted out scenes from historic fiction novels, performed folk dances, and shared family histories and brief reports. The parents were thrilled. "If they learned even half of what we heard tonight," one parent told me, "We'd be ecstatic." For parents, social and personal milestones were treasured as much as content learning. Michael could not believe that his shy daughter Kate sang a solo in a women's rights song. All of us rejoiced when Yanfang, who had arrived from China in September, read a poem about her grandfather for the first time.

> He is a Dragon who came to help us all.
> He is the longest river in the world
> and with the sweetest water.
> He is a chair that is made by gold
> and everybody wanted to sit on it.
> He is an old man
> with a snow white beard
> and looking very interesting.
> He's my Grandpa, the one I love best.
> And the one who'd dead,
> but still alive in my heart
> Yanfang

These sociocultural family learning events had far reaching results that I had not anticipated. They established a reputation for me as a teacher. After my first performance, the principal nodded and said "good job" (a very high compliment). But he saw how impressed the parents were, which gave me a kind of hands-off status as "good teacher." Parents looked forward to having children in my room. Fourth graders, who were invited to all expositions and dress rehearsals, came to my room with well-formed expectations. For example, Billy Jo felt free (on the second day of school) to talk to the class about having cerebral palsy and how she felt when she was teased because of her differences.

Differences among children have always been accepted, acknowledged, and celebrated in my family. I don't really remember my father working on the "Psycholinguistic Guessing Game" (K. Goodman, 1967), but I do remember my mother's work on "The Culture of the Culturally Deprived" (Y. Goodman, 1971). She investigated this topic by going out to school playgrounds and collecting play party games and rhymes. She believed that these "children's games" demonstrated how smart kids were and how much they knew.

At dinner one day, my mother told us about her first time out to collect some rhymes. She had been told of a version of *Hush, Little Baby.* She tried to get the kids to sign it by starting them off, "Hush Little Baby...." For some reason, it wasn't going very well. Further conversations brought out the whole rhyme. It starts, "Hambone, Hambone, have you heard? Papa's going to buy you a mockingbird." And it ends, "If that baseball suit don't fit, papa's going to say, 'Aw shoot, I quit.'"

From stories like this one I learned about kids being language experts. I learned about language change and language variations. I learned that grown-up researchers can make mistakes, particularly if they impose their own cultural assumptions on their subjects. I learned about racist labels, like culturally deprived, that destroy children's lives. I learned the power of singing a song.

Soon my sisters and I started collecting play party songs. Sometime around 1967, an article in the local newspaper was written that described my sisters and I as "guinea pigs" in my parent's work. But I think of us as participant-observers rather than objects of study.

Hey Debi
Who's calling my name?
Hey Debi
I'm playing a game.
You're wanted on the telephone.
If it ain't my baby, tell them I ain't home.
It's the city. Listen to the tickin' of the clock—tick tock
Listen to the tickin' of the clock.
Saying A-B-C-D-E-F-G
Saying H-I-J-K-L-M-N-O-P
Saying MMM daddy MMMM daddy MMMM daddy MMMM

Apples on the table, peaches on the floor
Step back baby—I don't want you no more.
To the front, to the back, to the side by side
She went away to college. She went away to school.
And when she got back she was an educated fool.

Besides collecting the rhymes, my sisters and I "presented" them at conferences and workshops. This was the first "formal" study in my own life-long involvement in research and presentation. I spent my high school and college vacations working as a research assistant in the Reading Miscue Research Center at Wayne State University where language was the center of discussion. My sisters and I learned miscue analysis in pieces. First we copied computer codes (in the old days when computer information had to be fed by coding sheets). Then we transcribed retellings, went on to serve as first reader for transcribing miscues, and finally were allowed to code miscues—one question at a time.

As we listened to children read, we learned to value the social and cultural influences on readings and story interpretation. We were valued for our own expertise and knowledge of the youth language of our times and of the African American language spoken by our Detroit classmates. Miscues involving a child's home language are considered high-level miscues. Pat Rigg called my sister Karen "golden ears" because of the way she could tune in to variations in language.

I saw research potential everywhere. I was in Vera Milz's classroom the year she collected her children's writing samples, and I served as second reader for her dissertation (Milz, 1983). Then, when I was student teaching in Dearborn, we had a snow day. Laura Nebel took the children outside in small groups for science activities in the snow. At that time, the children were ability grouped for language arts mini-lessons. I noticed that the higher ability readers all had boots and mittens, while the lower ability readers tended not to have boots and mittens. Of course, many of the "lower ability readers" were newly arrived from the Middle East and just learning English. This research finding, which we called the "boots and reading" theory, seemed an ironic twist on the statistical studies that were popular at the time which "measured" how specific variables affected reading achievement. All we had to do was buy kids boots and mittens and their reading achievement would improve, right?

Even in my 3-week second-grade teaching job I discovered the self-fulfilling nature of spelling instruction by administering a pretest each week. Although three-fourths of the students scored 90-100% by the end of the week, I discovered that the top scoring students actually could spell most of the words at the beginning of the week. At most, each student was "learning to spell" two to three words a week.

I have also borrowed research ideas for evaluation and assessment. When I was a Chapter One teacher I used miscue analysis to describe readers and provide holistic goals for each child. I have used a written version of the Burke Interview of the Reading Process to learn about my fifth graders as readers and writers. Last year I interviewed 20 kindergarten students in order to explore student and teacher progress in our whole language school. This is the beginning of my doctoral thesis work—and I have continued to observe and interview these children in first and second grade.

An inquiry-research perspective on my teaching has not only influenced my own teaching but has had a great impact on my colleagues and the parents of my students. One year I worked with Brea, who had failed the Ginn Level 10 reading test twice, even after going through the skillpack and workbook an extra time. I asked her to read some of the test items and concluded that she was having difficulty with the basic concepts and ideas in the text and could not really understand the test questions. So I told her teacher to send her down to my room every day during the basal reading period.

Brea read to herself every day. Once a week we had a conference. After about a month, she passed the Ginn Level 10 end-of-level reading test. Toby Curry was fond of repeating this story, proving the wide-ranging results of "just reading," and it soon became a legend in our school. In the same direct and sincere manner that always earned Toby invitations to serve on local committees and councils, she began to openly advocate for holistic education. She would joke that the basal reader was just the right size to prop up the windows in her classroom. When the Houghton Mifflin consultant came around to see how we were doing, Toby explained that we had an integrated language arts and social studies program and were not using Houghton Mifflin. The consultant and her supervisors agreed that we had an "enriched program" and didn't have to use the basal.

Later we met David Schaafsma who helped us to explain the power of stories in transforming childrens' and teachers' lives (Schaafsma, 1994). But we had already witnessed this in these oral retellings of our own kidwatching. When research becomes a social story in the lives of researchers, the ideas and processes can be very powerful. The day we met David, Toby and I had been invited to the University of Michigan to talk to some professors and doctoral students about holding a writing project in Detroit. We were a little wary of this meeting. Although we had enjoyed the teaching-learning community of my parents and David Bloome, we had also experienced the "rape and pillage" mentality of some university types who had come into school settings for their own purposes and never considered the purposes of students and teachers. We were amazed when Jay Robinson and Patty Stock asked for our ideas and insights before sharing their own thoughts and potential plans.

The writing project that grew out of that meeting came as close to an ideal teaching-learning community as I can imagine. Children, classroom teachers, pre-service teachers, college professors, and doctoral students all came together with the idea of investigating and writing about the local community. Parents, community members, and local artists and writers all served as "guest experts" for our study. Students and staff planned learning experiences and daily agendas together and were both involved in publication standards and ongoing evaluation of the project. We had access to, and support of, university and school district resources.

The staff met each afternoon to collaboratively plan and reflect. The collaborative staff structure (no one was "in charge") was sometimes frustrating, but it forced us to confront issues directly and try to work them out. Discussion of children, language, and writing always had case study as its focus; we were talking about real learners, not those hypothetical "my students can't . . ." statements I often hear at staff meetings and conferences.

There was Jerry, whose fifth-grade teacher was a teacher in the summer project. She described him as a nonreader and nonachiever. I wrote with him one day and noticed a creative spark and a real knack for storytelling. Other staff members began to tell different stories about Jerry. Jerry's teacher started telling different stories about Jerry. And Jerry left the project with different stories about himself and stories he had written to share with others.

Of course, students are always present in schools, but during the summer project, staff and students met as a whole group and then grouped themselves in various combinations for different learning experiences. Toby and I began to talk about the transition in our school as a process of "changing the story." I do not want to imply that teachers can come into schools like saviors and transform kids' lives. I do believe that when we invite children to write, talk, think, and make choices, we are inviting children to tell the stories of their lives. And their lives are not neatly separated into content, process, and social categories.

The Real Me
by Billie Jo
(Original version shown as Figure 9.3)

When I was born, I was dead because I got stabbed in my mommy's stomach. Outside of my house, my dad and another man were fighting. My mommy jumped in it. The man stabbed her in the stomach and it went in my leg. That's why I don't walk the same as other people.

But I'm doing okay. I like to cook. I like to play games and puzzles, school and writing. I like some sports like basketball, hockey, baseball and football. I like dancing a lot. The especially thing in my life is my club house.

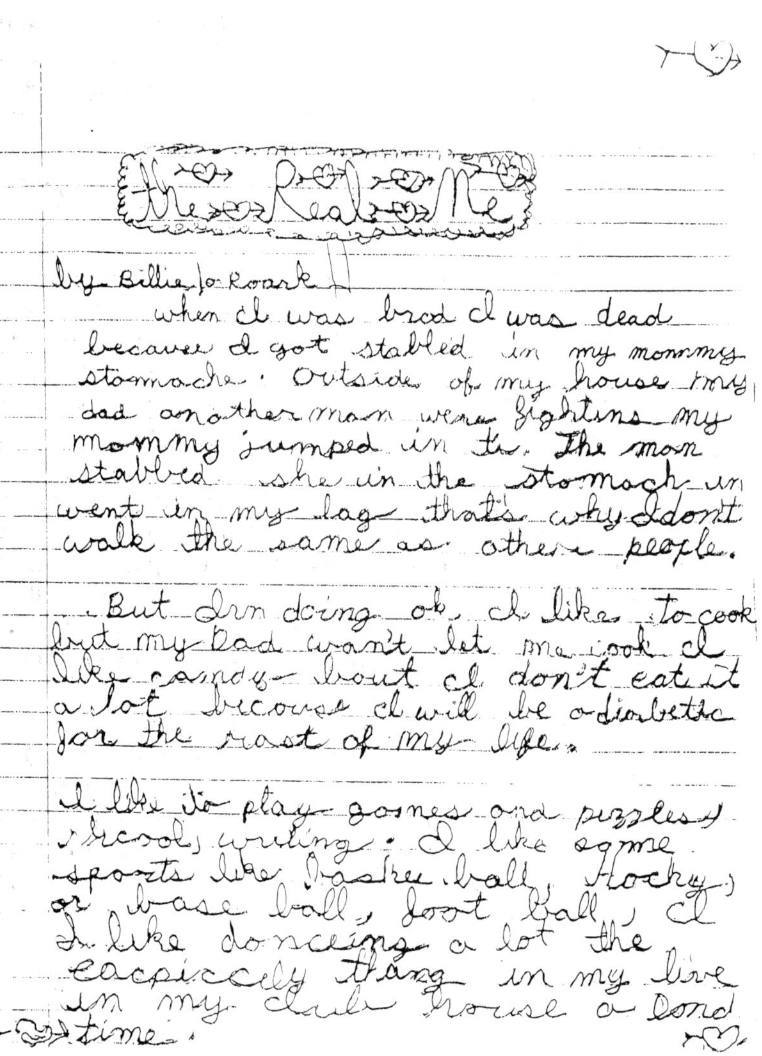

The Real Me

by Billie Jo Roark

when I was brod I was dead
because I got stabled in my mommys
stomache. Outside of my house my
dad another man were fightins my
mommy jumped in to. The man
stabbed she in the stomach in
went in my lag that's why I don't
walk the same as other people.

But Im doing ok. I like to cook
but my Dad won't let me cook I
like candy but I don't eat it
a lot because I will be a diabetic
for the rast of my life.

I like to play games and puzzles,
school, writing. I like some
sports like basket ball, Hocky,
or base ball, foot ball, I
I like dancing a lot the
eacpiccaly thang in my live
in my club house a lond
time.

Figure 9.3

As children share the stories of their lives within communities of learners, they begin to describe and understand their own stories in new ways. I have watched my father invite teachers, as well as learners, to seek new understandings in the stories they tell about their classroom. Denny Taylor has recently described portfolios as "autobiographical and biographical literacy profiles" in which we collect data that advocates for children as learners (Taylor, 1993). In the same way, the whole language community provides advocacy for teachers as learners, thinkers, and writers.

Because my dad was a movement person, he never believed much in talking to himself. As a speaker and writer he has always used a language and style that was meant to be understood. My father's own learning was in conversation—conversation with his family, his friends, his colleagues, his students, and my sisters and I. When he quotes me he's not just bragging; his ideas and my teaching—my ideas and his teaching—have become a transactive process.

Our conversations about learning and teaching began when I was very small. When my sisters and I reported that our friends got paid for report card grades, he told us, "Okay, I'll give you a dollar for each E (failing), 50 cents for every D, and a quarter for every C." He saved a lot of money this way, although I got my share of Cs in handwriting and spelling. My father also wrote notes to my teacher asking for more information than the letter grade on the report card.

Through these transactions, I understood that learning is more important than schooling, although I took on an irreverent view of schooling that got me into trouble sometimes. I considered myself a writer, so I didn't worry very much about my own poor handwriting and spelling. "When I publish my first book," I told my teachers, "My editors will take care of it." By upper elementary I conducted language studies, searching for cases in oral and written language that defied the grammar rules in our English books. I argued that well-known authors started sentences with "and." I argued that milk could be a "count noun" as in "I'll take two milks."

I also enjoyed wandering the exhibit halls at NCTE and IRA conferences, picking fights with the publishers' reps. I was certainly aware of the psycholinguistic guessing game because I remember explaining to a speed-reading machine salesman that he was ignoring the use of peripheral vision, re-reading, and reading ahead. This unfortunate salesman told me that John Kennedy had taken speed-reading classes and "even your father could probably improve his reading speed with this machine."

In junior high I wrote essays on true and false tests in social studies, explaining to my teacher that "I understand you think this is true, but I think it's false for this reason." My teacher, unimpressed by my reasoning and understandings, marked my answers wrong. About this time my parents, who had always been staunch advocates in my schooling, told me I was old enough to "fight my own battles."

Because of dinner conversations, after dinner renditions of old protest songs, and family attendance at marches and rallies, I seldom took these battles personally. Even in junior high school, I placed them in a larger political context. Outside of school we were marching against the war, reading *Soul on Ice*, petitioning to free Angela Davis, and canvassing for precinct delegates supporting Eugene McCarthy. Inside school we were filibustering our social studies class on the racist and stereotypical text of our class textbook, marching against the dress code, and petitioning for elective classes.

Besides thinking about the issues that prompted political battles, I thought a lot about the process of political struggles. When I watched friends respond to racism and classism, I realized that they often felt defeated if they saw themselves as victims in a single situation. However, if they felt connected to a political group or social community, they saw themselves as resistors against an oppressive system. The same autobiographical story might portray a lone victim or a freedom fighter.

As a teenager discovering my own intelligence, I saw struggle as its sharpening stone. I even wrote a story about a world where human beings had solved all their problems. In this world of peace and harmony, intelligence became unnecessary and began to disappear. For a brief time, it worried me that improving the human condition would be the end of learning until I decided that there would always be new problems to face.

Although I saw progressive education and progressive politics as connected, it surprised me that other people did not always make these connections. Progressive educators on the one hand were, and are, often reluctant to discuss politics. This may be a remnant of the red-baiting of Joe McCarthy, which drove radical teachers of the 1950s out of schools or underground. Left-wing political circles advocated changing the textbooks and changing the content rather than changing the way schools and learners were organized.

It is strange and frightening to note that the McCarthy era of the 1950s, like the religious right movement of the 1990s, pushed progressives to hide their own political beliefs as teachers. The ultra-conservatives who attack teachers have certainly been open about their own political agenda where schools are concerned. I knew, ironically, that my father went on to get a doctorate partially because he was blacklisted as a radical in the 1950s and not allowed to teach in the state of California. But this irony was not discussed openly because of the impact it had and could have had on our family's livelihood and welfare.

I'm not sure if I drew connections as a teenager across areas all of my life: between my parent's "hidden" politics, the struggle of the Black Power Movement of the 1960s, Watson's struggles with the computer, my own struggles with social studies, the struggle to Free Angela Davis (who, by the way, lost all her doctoral research when she was arrested), and a child's struggle with the printed word. But I know these issues tempered me to see life constructed and reconstructed by complex systems of meaning that include political, social and cultural strata, as well as meaning, function, and form.

I came to teaching as a beginner, but with a lot of experience and knowledge (just as our young beginners come to reading and writing). From the beginning I chose to suffer, struggle, and fight to teach. Following my substitute teaching fiasco, I did get a Chapter One teaching job with a principal who called me "the miracle worker." But after one good year the Chapter One supervisor walked in and suddenly I was facing 17 counts of unsatisfactory teaching. ("It's not 'cost-effective' to have 6-7 kids in a group instead of 12-15.")

"You can't be a rebel in Detroit," the principal advised me. "You can be a maverick, but you can't be a rebel." But mavericks tend to be loners, with little impact on the world, although it may leave them alone. With my movement background, I became a subversive.

I learned to write extremely detailed lesson plans and document every smidgen of learning that went on in my classroom (including any possible relationship to state objectives). I used my knowledge to explain what I was doing in an authoritative way. "That child isn't at the alphabetic stage yet," I would say, "So phonics is meaningless to him at this point." Later, when I taught fifth grade, I kept basal readers and social studies textbooks under the children's desks in case the principal walked in. "If you're not prepared for quiet reading," I would threaten, "You'll have to read your textbook."

I tried very hard to comply with direct orders from administrators. But when I tried traditional teaching, everything went wrong. I would forget to remind kids to put their names on the papers. I would have too few ditto sheets to go around. My ditto sheets always came out smeared, and the kids could not read them. I was a mediocre teacher of skills. My cooperation did not gain me any advantage. In one position where I willingly "taught the basal," I was told that first graders were not mature enough to walk to the library corner or sharpen their own pencils. Journals were also not appropriate as they "taught bad habits."

I asked myself, "Why be attacked as a mediocre skills teacher when I could be attacked as a good whole language teacher?" By the time

I began my seventh year of teaching in my eighth position, I taught each year as if it were my last. I have applied the same fatalistic attitude to my graduate classes, telling myself I would be happy to get a "B." I never did get a B but, with this perspective, I took control of my own teaching and learning. My struggle was possible because I saw myself as part of a movement of teachers fighting for the rights of learners. In those early years, I actually anticipated being fired and entering into a modern version of the Scopes Monkey Trial with the focal issue being the right of teachers to use their best knowledge of how kids learn. Recent legislation defining research and reading have brought this possibility back to life.

The kids always kept me focused. When I came into Chapter One my faith in "the language experience approach" was shaken by Morris, who refused to say anything. His first book, *The Sad Story,* about being brought to school by the police, was dragged out of him by provoking him to correct my own inaccurate retelling of the incident. During one difficult time, Janella left a note in my box saying, "I hope you not in no trouble." There was Samira, who wrote suicide notes in her journal. And Robert who told us at magic circle about having to call the police himself to protect his mother from his own father. Every day I thought of Laura telling me, "You've just got to give them your best."

It was difficult to give kids my best when I was busy trying to comply with mandates, write detailed lesson plans, administer required tests, and fight for the space to teach. I tried to keep focused on my own inquiry questions and keep children and learning at my heart. It is not "What score did Morris get on the CAT test?"; it is "What can I do to get Morris to look up from the floor?" It is not, "What grade did Samira get on her English test?"; it is "Why is Samira so unhappy?" It is, "How can I establish a classroom that will support Robert when the times get rough?" "What books will really excite kids who choose not to read?" "How can I provide holistic math experiences in authentic contexts?" And, "What do I say to Regina who walks home on harsh and violent streets (while I drive my car to my clean, friendly neighborhood) and tells me her mom told her to smack anybody who messes with her?"

Sometimes I wonder what my 15 years of teaching would have been like with supportive administrators, no standardized testing, time for planning, schedules designed for children, system-wide respect for students and teachers, decent class size, new furniture, budgets for books and materials, and clean bathrooms with toilet paper. Or pick any three from the above menu. It often seems like I spent more time resisting than teaching.

But perhaps resistance sharpened my intelligence as it heightened my connection and concern with important social and political issues. In the past year, as a doctoral student, I have returned to the Dewey Center for several days each month to observe some first and second graders as they learn to read and write. One of the teachers, Susan Austin, attended a course I taught at Wayne State University five years ago. The other teacher, Mary Jo Regnier, came to the workshop that Toby and I conducted in preparation for starting the Dewey Center. I participated with teachers and students as they established learning communities in these classrooms.

As I did every school day for 15 years, I have driven to Dewey past the gun shops, boarded buildings, homeless people sweeping the streets around the rescue missions, and prostitutes looking for a little extra money. I have listened to National Public Radio reports on drugs, gangs, lack of jobs, and lack of health care. My stomach has twisted as I heard exposes and sound bites in which complex human issues were boiled down into a simple package with one person or group (often a teacher) to be blamed. Someone should do something, I would think.

At lunch time, and at the end of the day, Mary Jo and Susan were eager to talk with me. They were glad to hear, as they struggled with the logistics of working with almost 30 children, that I observed a lot of reading and writing during each visit. It was good to be able to tell them that the children felt confident with reading and writing. It's amazing how easy it sounds to become a reader and writer in these rooms:

"My teacher reads to me and then I read to myself."

"The second graders help us."

But there were also things I noticed as a researcher that are hard to spot from the teacher's chair. How Marvin suffers when he has to wait for his turn to speak. How Ashley is so quiet that no one notices she is there. I also talked over these issues with Susan and Mary Jo. Mary Jo talked about learning to be a whole language teacher as a process of "being less and less a teacher." I watched as the roles of teacher and learner blurred, with students setting their own learning agendas and proposing and conducting class discussions.

The role of researcher and learner got blurry as well when the kids got very interested in my field notes. The first was LaShay, a second grader. Mary Jo was concerned because LaShay showed little interest in reading and writing. But she attached herself to me during each visit and watched all my activities. One day she got a piece of paper and began writing strings of letters, numbers, and sketches that looked very much like my field notes.

I wondered what would happen if I asked the children to help me with my research project, and so I invited them to take field notes and, being a good whole language teacher, I even made up a form for that purpose. In June, on my last visit with the kids, I found two field notes written by Brian—a boy who came into the classroom just a few months before.

On May 25, Brian wrote, "I made a writeing club." This was important to him "becuse I never had a club" (See Figure 9.4). On June 9, Brian wrote, "I font a friend." This was important because "I never had a friend that nice. She is very nice and she is not mean" (See Figure 9.5).

Like Brian, I started out as a learner/researcher/teacher when I was still very young. Like Brian, I am still learning. We have both learned that reading and writing come pretty naturally when you have the reason and the desire, but it also helps if you start a club. And we have learned how important it is to have good friends.

Brian's field notes may appear to be a simplified way to describe learning, but they place literacy learning into a context of the complex relationships between friends and within communities. Brian and his classmates have helped me remember that if we are going to change the world, the breakfast table or the classroom mailbox just may be the best place to start.

Room 117 - Field Notes Date

Something important happened today:

Tell what happened: Draw a picture:

I made a writeing club

Why is this important to you?

becuse I never had a club

Name of researher Brian

Figure 9.4

Figure 9.5

REFERENCES

Goodman, K. (1967). Reading: A psycholinguistic guessing game. *Journal of the Reading Specialist, 6*(4), 126-135.

Goodman, Y. (1971). The culture of the culturally deprived. *Elementary School Journal, 71*(7), 377-383.

Milz, V. (1983). *A psycholinguistic description of the development of writing in selected first grade students*. Unpublished doctoral dissertation, University of Arizona, Tucson.

Schaafsma, D. (1994). *Eating on the street*. Pittsburgh: University of Pittsburgh Press.

Small, F. (1994). The hug. In *Promises worth keeping, The songs of Fred Small* (Vol. 2, pp. 106-107). Cambridge, MA: Yellow Moon Press.

Taylor, D. (1993). Teaching without testing. In *From the child's point of view*. Portsmouth, NH: Heinemann.

Vygotsky, L. S. (1978). *Mind in society*. Cambridge, MA: Harvard University Press.

Chapter Ten

Learning Professional Change

Lois Bridges
Palo Alto, CA

What is learning? How does it occur? Most teachers ask themselves these questions many times during their teaching lives. And the answers they choose seldom remain unaltered as they learn to change professionally. Learning professional change is indeed a complex and, to me, a fascinating process. In this chapter I consider how it occurs, how to support it, some of its drawbacks (change can be painful and provocative), and its great benefits—all of which I attempt to illustrate with reference to the theoretical literature and to my personal experience.

As Smith (1981) reminds us, we are born to learn. We cannot stop learning. Indeed, if we are conscious and most of our faculties engaged, then we are learning something. But thoughtful, deliberate learning when we are controlling, monitoring, and reflecting on our thoughts and actions is not as easy. Indeed, Dewey suggests that it is not simple experience per se that results in learning so much as it is reflection on experience.

So what is learning and how does it occur? For decades educators thought the answer lay in the laboratories of behavioral psychologists. Teachers were taught to control their students' learning in much the same way psychologists controlled their laboratory experiments: break learning into a hierarchy of discrete steps, teach the steps in a precise manner, reward correct answers, punish wrong answers, test the steps, and move on to the next learning sequence.

Gradually over the past three decades, researchers and theorists from multiple disciplines and perspectives—cognitive psychology, developmental psychology, anthropology, linguistics, and education—have painted a very different picture of learning. Learning occurs from the inside out, not the outside in. Learning cannot be controlled by an outside agent; learners control their own learning. This new understanding of learning, widely known as *generative-constructivist learning theory*, can be simply stated as six overarching principles (Cambourne, 1988; Goodman, Smith, Meredith, & Goodman, 1987; Holdaway, 1979; Weaver, 1990):

- Learners learn what matters to them.
  The most significant learning—and often the most effortless—arises from that which sparks the interest and meets the needs of the learner. Learners must have some choice about what and how they will learn.
- Learners construct meaning for themselves.
  Learning is constructed by the learner, not imposed from without. Learners learn best when they are actively engaged in planning, monitoring, and controlling their own learning to meet their own needs and interests.
- Learners thrive in a safe, supportive environment.
  Learners must be confident that they can take the risks necessary for learning; that they can explore and experiment unhindered by a fear of failing or negative judgment.
- Learners explore their learning over time.
  Learners need time for rough draft thinking, communicating, and reflecting. Learners explore, refine, and elaborate their meaning over multiple drafts.
- Learners learn from collaboration with others.
  Learners often learn best when they are not isolated from others but are part of a community of learners that invites dialogue and collaboration.
- Learners never stop learning.
  One line of inquiry leads to another. The measure of true learning is not recall of old material, but new questions that address new possibilities, leading the learner into new realms of exploration.

These principles are not limited to the classrooms of young children; indeed, they apply equally to all learners, young and old alike, students and teachers. The need for autonomy in the learning process is just as necessary for first grade teachers as it is for their six-year-old students.

Historically, autonomy is not something that has been encouraged or even valued in the teaching profession (Apple, 1986). Teaching has been widely regarded as "women's work." Thus, teachers have long endured a lack of respect, low salaries, and the outside control and interference of district administrators, state legislators, and others who have little to do with the actual life of classrooms. Decisions about curriculum and instructional practices are left to outside experts. Teachers are told what to teach and how to teach it. Apple (1986) and Shannon (1990) argue that teachers have been "deskilled," stripped through textbooks and packaged curriculum of the real art of teaching: "setting relevant curriculum goals, establishing content, designing lessons and instructional strategies that are responsive to students, and individualizing instruction based on an intimate knowledge of students' desires and needs" (Apple, 1991, p. 416). Thus, teachers are denied the most critical (and rewarding) aspect of teaching.

It is not surprising, then, that the same control that governs the lives of teachers inside their classrooms also characterizes the so-called "teacher training" typical of institutions of teacher credentialing or district inservice programs. Often what is taught has little real bearing on the classroom. Veteran and student teachers alike receive few tools to understand what their students are doing. Furthermore, they are not shown how they can rely on their own professional planning and evaluation to support their students. Rather than helping teachers understand human development and use their expertise to plan instruction and build curriculum, teacher training often centers on the latest instructional program and how to use it—a newly adopted basal reading program, science kit, or the like. Teachers are handed curriculum guides and mandated textbooks. Their professional decision making is often limited to designing a weekly schedule that will accommodate all the demands of a district and state-controlled curriculum. "In one way or another, educational decisions are made from the top down and the outside in, and teachers carry out the educational programs designed for them by others" (Bullock, 1987, p. 22).

That is something I did not know when I was working on my teaching credential in the early 1970s at the University of California at Riverside. I spent hours carefully designing my own lessons and projects. One of my most ambitious efforts was a several month long study of Riverside's local history. My fourth grade students and I went on walking tours of the school neighborhood noting the local history reflected in street and building names. We invited prominent Riverside citizens in for interviews and pored over such primary sources as old newspapers, letters, and legal documents that we found in the downtown library. I was exhilarated. The children were enthusiastic. But my master teacher cautioned me: "You can't create curriculum yourself. You have to learn how to use a textbook."

I managed to complete my teacher credential with honors; yet, I was woefully ill-prepared to meet the tremendous professional demands of public school teaching. That became evident as I entered my first classroom.

NEW TEACHER

Two days before a new school year was to start, I was hired for my first teaching position, a first grade at Running Springs Elementary. Running Springs, CA, is little more than a village ski resort perched on the "Rim-of-the-World," a granite ridge that soars to 6,000 feet in the San Bernardino Mountains of Southern California. Twice a week, the children were released early from school for an afternoon of skiing. The principal told me I should feel very proud of myself. They had received more than 900 applications for the job. He expressed satisfaction with my records and with his observations of my teaching. "And," he added, "you can ski."

The skiing and beautiful mountain setting notwithstanding, Running Springs Elementary was a traditional school. The mostly young and athletic staff fully embraced the prevailing behavioral learning theory of the 1970s. The mimeograph machine was in continual use. Favorite worksheets were posted on the teachers' room bulletin board which served as an informal ditto exchange.

I remember well the experience of entering my first classroom. It was large and bright with a row of windows that opened onto a rocky incline and sparse, pine forest. Six listening booths lined one wall; textbooks and basals, another. I opened a tall, grey, metal cabinet and found myself staring at stacks of unused worksheets and boxes of blackline masters. What do first graders learn? The alphabet? Letter sounds? Syllabication? Did the metal cabinet really contain the answer?

The veteran first grade teacher in the classroom next to mine stopped by and explained that all Running Springs first graders followed a comprehensive phonics program. The children spent 20 minutes daily in the listening booths to learn their letter sounds beginning with the consonants, initial and final, the vowels, short and long, and everything else in between—blends, digraphs, and diphthongs. I nodded agreeably, too embarrassed to admit to her that I had never heard of phonics. What was it?

After she left, I sat in a listening booth and put on the earphones. Listening to one lesson, I attempted to complete the accompanying worksheet. It was overwhelming. I had always been a voracious reader. Reading was as easy and natural as breathing. Never had I dreamed that learning to read was so complicated and required so many separate skills. What was I going to do with the 27 first graders who would soon enter my classroom?

I found myself thinking about my own schooling. What had I liked? What had stirred my interest? The answer was immediate. I had loved to read and write. Surely my first graders would, too. We would read literature from our school and district libraries, and they could write their own stories. Fortunately, no one had told me that first graders could not write. In the early 1970s, real writing was reserved for the latter grades. Children had to master the mysteries of conventional spelling, punctuation, and handwriting before they were allowed to compose. I knew my first graders could not spell conventionally. But they could write words the way they sounded. After all, they could tell stories—and that is what really mattered.

In my own classroom with the door shut I enjoyed every minute of teaching. I witnessed the joy of young authorship and saw my students developing awareness of the way letters and sounds work together as they used them to tell stories about their lives, real or imagined. But when the door opened, I saw the first graders from other classrooms running down the hallway carrying bundles of vocabulary cards to practice at home with mom or dad. I saw blue lettered mimeographed spelling lists. I saw basal readers and basal workbooks and basal worksheets. Some of my students' parents saw them, too, and wondered why their kids were not receiving the same. And what about the stories they were writing with all the misspellings?

Oddly enough, in spite of my anxiety and concern that my unusual literacy instruction might harm the children, I knew what we were doing was right. I began to realize that on some level, kids did need to know about the components that make up language, but they learned all about words and letters and sounds through their own writing. And in this way they controlled the process. It seemed to me the real phonics drill occurred not in the listening booth, but as they worked to figure out a spelling of a word they wanted to use in a story. I was able to explain to concerned parents that reading and writing went together. They were mutually supportive processes. And, perhaps, because their children were fast becoming both readers and writers, and because they loved the student-authored books their children brought home, the parents believed me.

But the other first grade teachers talked. What would happen next year when my students entered second grade? How could they compete with kids who knew their way around a basal reader and workbook? During the day, my children convinced me we were on the right track, but, often at night, inside my mountain cabin, I agonized over not using the contents of the metal cabinet.

During the last week of school, I took down the phonics workbooks which had remained unopened on top of the metal cabinet, blew the dust off them, and handed them to my kids. "Yippee!" they shouted. "Real work!" Within the week, they had completed the first and final consonants, the long and short vowels, and everything in between. They knew their letters and sounds.

Still, doubts persisted and followed me to other schools as I worked with new classes of first grade students. It was hard. The children were the only support I found for reading real books and writing real stories. All the professional books my colleagues lent me and all the workshops I attended extolled the importance of phonics drill and a carefully planned scope and sequence of skills for young readers.

Thus, traditional authority oppressed me until, in summer 1978, I enrolled in a graduate language arts course at the University of California at Berkeley taught by Marilyn Hanf Buckley. In the remaining three days of the class, students were required to present their chosen research projects. I listened politely to all. Then a woman with a cascade of orange curls stepped up to the podium. As she explained her overheads, I felt a growing sense of excitement. Her research project was about something called miscue analysis, a research/assessment tool developed by someone named Kenneth Goodman. It was the first time I had ever encountered a theory that seemed to substantiate the instructional practices I had developed, largely out of intuition, in my first grade classroom. These were practices that were often at odds with the skill-driven reading instruction that dominated the classrooms of my colleagues. My Berkeley peer's presentation was inspiring. More importantly, it was liberating. It marked the beginning of my release from the years of anxiety I had experienced as a teacher who did not follow the skill and drill regimen.

ON THE RESERVATION

One month later, Kenneth Goodman became more than just a name to me. I saw him sitting directly in front of me eating Trish Johnson's green, pistachio nut jello salad. We were enjoying a welcome-back-to-school potluck on the Tohono O'odham Reservation 75 miles southeast of Tucson, AZ. I had just accepted a first grade teaching position at Sells Elementary School on the Reservation. Ken, and his wife, Professor Yetta Goodman, had been hired by the district to provide a year's worth of inservice. After lunch, Ken addressed the school faculty; and, once again, I discovered in his ideas the theoretical support I so needed to justify my refusal to use the basal, assign phonics worksheets, or drill my students on vocabulary flashcards.

Ken's research confirmed for me that reading is not "getting the words." It is a problem-solving process. Readers use their own language, experiences, and understandings of the world to interpret the author's language and thoughts. Readers construct meaning from text. The active, problem-solving nature of reading is reflected in readers' miscues (actual observed responses in oral reading that do not match the expected responses to the text). Ken analyzed readers' miscues from multiple perspectives revealing the linguistic and cognitive strategies readers were using to interpret the text. Miscues were "windows on the reading process," revealing the readers' attempts to build meaning from print (Goodman, 1973, p. 3).

In my new teaching position on the Tohono O'odham Reservation, I had the opportunity to work directly with Ken and Yetta. Once a month they visited my classroom, and I also participated in their workshops on the reading process. Their workshops were unlike any inservices or teacher education courses I had previously attended. Ken and Yetta did not stand at a podium and talk at us, telling us what and how to teach. They presented compelling audiotapes and written transcripts of real kids in real classrooms reading real books and invited us to explore what these young readers were doing. We listened as the readers made their way through the text and miscued—skipping, changing, and reversing the words. Instead of counting the errors, the Goodmans asked us to consider the quality of the miscues and their effect on meaning. We began to ask questions and explore issues we had never considered before: Was the meaning acceptable after the miscue? Did the reader correct the miscue if it was not? If a word was substituted for another word, was it the same part of speech? Was the reader's dialect involved?

After just one workshop I returned to my classroom and sat transfixed as one child after another read aloud to me. When they stumbled over the words I no longer cringed but listened intently to the effect the miscues had on meaning. Sure enough. My most proficient readers often miscued as they flew over the text but caught themselves if the miscue interfered with the meaning. I was ecstatic. Finally, after watching class after class of first graders become readers without really understanding how it happened, I now understood that reading was language. The mistakes young readers made were not random but revealed their understanding of reading, language and the strategies they could use to make sense of print. Furthermore, miscues revealed readers' strengths as well as their needs. With this insight, for the first time as a first grade teacher, I could deliberately plan thoughtful instruction that would build on my young readers' strengths and nudge them into new developmental realms. My intuition had served me well over the years. But how much better, how freeing, to understand what I was doing and why. Now I could use my understanding to teach, and I could explain my instructional decisions to others.

The Goodmans showed me how to ask questions, observe my students, and find my own answers. "Everything we know we learned from kids," they insisted (Goodman, 1973, p. 3). Their research showed teachers how they, too, could learn from kids. I became my own best authority. I observed my students as they lived and learned in our classroom. I then used my observations and new understanding of language and learning to make informed decisions about instruction and curriculum. I became, for the first time, a professionally informed decision maker. I could ignore the scope and sequence charts in my teacher manuals. Indeed, I could ignore the manuals. Finally, I was liberated from the instructional technology in the metal cabinet!

Besides helping me discover the specific, concrete information I had longed for to support my intuitive instructional practices, the Goodmans provided me with something less tangible but equally important—self-respect. At that time, I was the wife of a theoretical geochemist, a post-doctoral fellow at the University of Arizona. When we attended university functions, his colleagues would inevitably ask me about my work. I would answer that I was an educator and quickly change the subject. As much as I loved teaching, I had absorbed the societal view of elementary school teachers. Teaching young children was women's work, of little value or importance, requiring minimal intellectual creativity.

It was startling, then, to realize that Ken and Yetta were spending time in my classroom, not to teach me, but to learn with me. They asked *me* questions. They were genuinely interested in everything I did and wanted to understand the thinking behind my instructional decisions. Through my interactions with the Goodmans, I began to think of myself as a professional educator. I embraced, for the first time, my own professional life and learning.

The culmination of this professional birth occurred during an end-of-the-year final meeting with Ken and Yetta in the multipurpose room. We had finished our potluck luncheon and had placed metal folding chairs in a large circle around Ken and Yetta. At their invitation, one by one, we went around the circle, sharing something that we had learned as teachers, or something that we had experienced with our students of which we were especially proud. I shared my student-authored books. My heart raced. My hands trembled as I held up the books and explained my first grade writing program. It was the first time as a teacher that I had been asked to explain what I was doing—and why—in such a way that other teachers might learn from my example. Ken and Yetta helped me feel that the work I was doing was making a difference for children and was worth sharing with other educators.

That year, under the Goodmans' tutelage, the Sells Elementary School faculty grew as a professional community. We came to view each other not as competitors for limited instructional materials but as colleagues from whom we could learn. It was another first. I had never experienced a sense of collegiality with the teachers with whom I worked. Indeed, in the past, isolated in my own classroom, I could go days without even seeing some of my colleagues. Now, I found myself seeking them out—to discuss, debate, and question the instructional course I was taking as an individual teacher as well as the course we were following as a school. We were not fully aware of the transformation we experienced that year as a faculty, but in retrospect I can see that our talk in the teachers' room shifted from complaining about "off-task" kids to sharing the wonderful logic of invented spellings, favorite miscues, or breakthroughs in classroom organization that enabled us to create learner-centered curriculums.

GRADUATE SCHOOL

In 1979, a fortuitous chain of events led me from an elementary classroom to the University of Arizona, where I began five years of graduate study with the Goodmans. My first emotion, besides the pure delight of sharing a real lunch hour with colleagues without a single time-out to deal with a needy child, was anger. As I began a deeper exploration of the sociopsycholinguistic theory underlying Ken's work, I felt outraged. This critically important information about language and learning had been known for years, but, to my knowledge, had not been available to those who needed it most—classroom teachers. The pangs of self-doubt that had plagued me throughout my teaching career were completely unnecessary. Yet not one professional book I had read, workshop I had attended, nor class in which I had participated (with the exception of the Berkeley class) had apprised me of Ken's work. At that time the educational establishment was mired in behavioral psychology. Ken's work, which overturned behavioral thinking, was slow to filter into the professional arenas in which classroom teachers participated. Sensitive, scientific research that questioned the comfortable, controlled status quo had no place in the "make and take," instructional, cookie-cutter teacher workshops of the 1970s.

Ken's sociopsycholinguistic analysis of reading miscues demonstrated that language is not a set of tinker toys that can be disassembled and reassembled on dittos. Language is an infinitely complex and subtle system for sharing and creating meanings within a common community. When it is whole, it breathes, alive with potential to shape and change. In pieces, its meaning—and potential to create—is shattered. The doors of the metal cabinet in my classroom had rightfully remained sealed.

Building on the work of linguist Michael Halliday (1975), Ken also showed us that language is learned as language is used. The notes that had circulated around my classroom, the stories that were lovingly illustrated, the lists, cartoons, directions, instructions, scripts, signs, warnings, recipes, scientific observations, and game rules were real language in use. Children were learning what language is and how language works as they used it to accomplish their own purposes.

I learned something else I had never considered. Teaching is a political act. Ultimately, my decision to ignore the contents of the metal cabinet was a political, albeit unconscious, political act. As a classroom teacher, I thought of politics as a drama enacted on the evening news, far removed from the life I shared with my students. However, I came to understand that literacy is as much about politics and power as about poetry and pedagogy. Mastery learning, packaged curriculum, and standardized tests numb, deny, and too often silence those they are meant to educate. Ken's research has revolutionized our understanding of written language; what it is, how it develops, and how we use it to shape and create our worlds. But his research has also revolutionized our understanding of language and literacy as tools that broaden the boundaries of our human experience. Reading, writing, and literacy can create—or conquer—a critical, compassionate citizenry. What is taught and how it is taught is of the utmost significance. Teachers are deskilled, depowered, and often depressed after years of pushing atomistic knowledge and skills that do nothing to intellectually invigorate or inspire. A skill-driven curriculum results in intellectual pabulum that fails to nourish the curious, questioning, challenging minds needed for an informed democracy. Ken's work encourages professional and pedagogical liberation from an instructional technology that subjugates as it simplifies.

I also discovered my professional mission. I would share with teachers the research and knowledge that would enable them to throw off the shackles of textbooks and standardized tests; that would enable them to listen to and learn from their own voices as well as those of their students. Ken taught me that the potential for transformative social-political change lies in the daily interactions between teachers and students. It was an understanding that changed my life. Naively, I thought all I had to do was inform other teachers of this research and knowledge and it would transform their lives as well. But I would soon discover that not all teachers were eager to embrace my message.

BISBEE, ARIZONA

It was August, 1979. Ken and I were on Highway 92 driving to Bisbee, AZ, an old mining town on the southern border of Arizona, just 10 miles north of Mexico. The Bisbee School District had asked Ken to begin a year-long program of professional development with the elementary faculty. Ken was scheduled to give an hour long introductory talk to the teachers. He invited me to go along.

Bisbee had been a booming metropolis around the turn of the century. Copper was king and Bisbee's red rock hills hid rich veins of the golden metal. As the mines began to fail, so too did the town's economy. Miners left, businesses folded, and abandoned homes and shops deteriorated. Those who remained found other ways to make a living. But, in general, the area was poor and economically depressed.

Ken and I found Bisbee Elementary School, a stately, stone building built in the 1920s with a wide porch that ran the length of the school. We entered and walked into a district meeting already in progress. Teachers were being apprised of new textbooks, new busing schedules, new state-required forms, and the dozens of other demands that absorb teachers' time and energy each new school year. Without pausing to give teachers a break, the district official briefly introduced Ken and handed him the microphone.

Even as a new, enthusiastic graduate student, it did not take me long to figure out that no one knew who Ken Goodman was, nor did anyone particularly care. Ken gave his usual enlightened presentation, but I seemed to be the only one in the audience who was inspired. Everyone else, it seemed, was anxious to be on their way to deal with the new books, schedules, and forms.

On the drive home, Ken asked me whether I would like to be involved in the professional development effort at Bisbee. The cool reception he had received at the school had left me with a stomach ache.

But I wanted to try to make a difference for teachers. Here was a real chance. I agreed to help.

My stomach ache that afternoon was only the first of many I was to suffer as part of my work in Bisbee. Joining me in the effort were two other University of Arizona graduate students, Barbara Flores and Myna Matlin. We drove the 90 miles from Tucson to Bisbee once a month. Each time, as the miles dropped away bringing us closer to Bisbee, my stomach would begin to hurt. And I knew why. Bisbee teachers had not asked for our help. They did not want our help. We had been brought in by one district official who knew the Goodmans' work and thought it was just what Bisbee teachers needed.

The teachers thought differently and let us know in no uncertain terms every time we set foot in their classrooms. According to plan, we visited their classrooms once a month, spending two to three days in town so that we could see every teacher. We also gave after-school workshops on developmental literacy and miscue analysis. For the most part, the teachers were uniformly grim-faced every time we appeared on campus. They went about their business, administering spelling tests, assigning workbook pages, and, in general, doing the exact opposite of everything we suggested.

You cannot mandate change. The district administrator who had brought us in was enthusiastic and well-meaning, eager to help Bisbee teachers and students. But these were veteran teachers who had spent years creating instructional programs that now ran like well-oiled machinery. They had no desire to change. One teacher proudly showed me a file box in which she stored packets of dittos—one packet for every day of the school year. "Curriculum-in-a-box," I remember thinking to myself. It made little difference to her who sat in her classroom. Every child regardless of interest, experience, or cultural and language background, was handed the same packets of dittos.

Bisbee taught me two valuable lessons: Learners learn what matters to them, and learners construct meaning for themselves. I felt as though I had discovered the truth and it had liberated me from the metal cabinet. All I had to do was to pass that truth on to other teachers and it would set them free as well. My experience at Bisbee taught me otherwise. It was our agenda for change, not the teachers'. We were answering our questions, not theirs.

We left Bisbee feeling as though we had failed. But Bisbee ultimately taught me a third lesson: Learners explore their learning *over time*. Two years after we had left Bisbee, feeling as though we really had not made a difference for anyone there, we held one of the first whole language conferences at the University of Arizona. Barbara Flores and I were chatting with the other attendees in the auditorium waiting for the next speaker. Suddenly, I heard Barbara shout and laugh and turned to see her locked in the embrace of one of the most disinterested Bisbee teachers with whom we had worked. Another Bisbee teacher was waiting her turn for a hug. What were they doing at a whole language conference? They were grinning ear to ear as they admitted (as we had guessed) that they had hated our monthly visits. Working with us forced them to examine some of their long held and deeply cherished beliefs about learning and teaching. Teachers were supposed to stand up in front of the classroom and teach and students were supposed to sit in their seats and learn. These teachers hated our visits because they found it painful and disturbing to question themselves and their instructional practices. But we had planted a seed. They asked questions of themselves, observed their students, found answers, and with time that seed grew and blossomed into a full-fledged learner-centered program. It takes time to discover your own questions and to learn from them.

FAIR OAKS SCHOOL

In Fall 1982 my family and I moved to the San Francisco Bay Area. Considering myself a veteran of professional development efforts after my work at Bisbee and several other school districts, I did not hesitate for a moment when I was invited, in 1986, to serve as a literacy consultant at Fair Oaks School in Redwood City, CA. Housed in a salmon-colored, stucco building, surrounded by an asphalt yard, Fairs Oaks is wedged in the south end of a barrio, between dilapidated apartment buildings whose balconies are draped with laundry hung out to dry, and Raychem, a huge industrial complex.

Fair Oaks had a very different sociopolitical climate from Bisbee. The teachers had worked with a variety of leading experts in the field including Yetta Goodman and Carole Edelsky. They had given up Saturdays to learn about miscue analysis and the reading process, and they had given up basal readers in favor of classroom libraries and literature studies. I could not wait to get started.

Ever-mindful of my experience in Bisbee, I did not impose an agenda of change at Fair Oaks but rather invited each teacher to set his or her own goals. "How can I help you? What are your needs?", I would ask. I asked each teacher to identify a goal or goals that we could work on together. It seemed to work best when teachers identified one specific goal such as launching a writers' workshop or designing their curriculum around themes. Not only did teachers need to own their professional goals, but they also had to define how they wanted to achieve those goals. Once they identified a goal, my next question would be, "How can I help you achieve it?"

Although Fair Oaks teachers were clear about what they wanted to achieve in the way of professional change, the Fair Oaks administration was not. For every step we advanced, underlying strife created by a suspicious principal dragged us two steps back. Fair Oaks taught me the importance of community, open dialogue, and a strong leader. Learners learn best in a safe, supportive community that invites dialogue, collaboration, and risk taking. Teachers need to meet, discuss, and debate with their colleagues without fear of negative judgment or evaluation. The Fair Oaks community was undermined by a controlling and distrustful principal. I left after two years of weekly professional development visits. A core group of teachers persevered and became recognized experts in their own right (Bridges Bird, 1989; Heath & Mangiola, 1993). But it was not until the district hired a new, visionary principal who reestablished Fair Oaks as a community of learners that the school was able to strike out in directions that reflected its true potential.

THE GALEF INSTITUTE

Today I work for the Galef Institute, a nonprofit educational organization based in Los Angeles, CA, that targets inner-city teachers and kids. Many of the teachers with whom we work are bound to textbooks, skill programs, and packaged curriculum. Helping them push out the dehumanizing instructional technology and enliven and enlarge their classrooms with the bright voices and experiences of their children takes time and patience, action and reflection, commitment and caring.

Learners Learn in a Community of Learners

My professional development focus at the Galef Institute has been authentic assessment. Together with 25 teachers, kindergarten through middle school, we have been exploring new ways of evaluating students' learning and development. Our time together in the Galef Assessment Project has been limited. Last year we met for a whole school day, once a month, over the course of the school year. In addition, we spent five days during the summer engaged in an in-depth study of multiple assessment tools. Although we had little time to actually meet together, my Fair Oaks experience had taught me the inherent value of community in the learning process. Accordingly, we began our work in the Assessment Project by simply getting to know each other. Our first official meeting was spent sharing the books that had most influenced us as human beings and as teachers. We talked about the books that we carried in our hearts—and why. By sharing our transformative experiences with a range of books, both fiction and nonfiction, adult and children's literature, we took the critical first steps toward the bonds of intimacy that support and enable the risk taking necessary for learning. We laughed a lot and even shed a tear or two as our personal literary lives unfolded in our community sharing of memorable books. We discovered that we had a lot in common and a lot that we wanted to learn from each other.

I began to understand more clearly than ever that teachers are more likely to successfully rethink and change their practice when they are part of a supportive group of educators who are working to adopt new practices and roles. Furthermore, reform works best when it has widespread support. Teachers need to be part of a larger learning community. Our group of 25 teachers represented 14 different school sites. Each building principal supported the teacher-participant by paying for a substitute teacher, enabling the teacher to attend our sessions. What is more, whenever possible, principals, district curriculum directors, and an assistant superintendent sat in on our sessions. Teachers knew that their commitment to professional growth was appreciated and supported. Successful change does not occur in a void. Freire (1985) and Giroux (1988) remind us that the changes a single educator makes always evolve within a greater social, political, and cultural context. Although Fair Oaks teachers made changes in their classrooms without support from the principal, the change was limited.

Our first day of sharing in the Assessment Project ended with a new sense of community. From Ken I had learned that interpersonal relationships—a sense of caring and sharing—is not peripheral to effective learning: It is basic. "Community in itself, is more important to learning than any method or technique" (Peterson, 1991, p. 2). Together, the teachers in the Assessment Project and I were going to embark on an exciting two-year learning adventure. We were eager to begin.

Learners Learn What Matters to Them

Just as the Goodmans had helped me discover my own questions in their workshops and to trust my own ideas, so we began with the teachers' own questions about assessment. It is simply true that it is easier to learn about those things that you are interested in and care about. When the professional development focus shifts from controlling what teachers will do to helping teachers transform themselves, then teachers must set their own agendas and choose their own paths of inquiry. With ownership comes commitment and levels of productive engagement rarely achieved with assigned projects.

Working in groups of three, teachers brainstormed a list of issues related to assessment that they wanted to investigate. Following the phases of a theme cycle (Edelsky, Altwerger, & Flores, 1991), we combined our lists and next brainstormed everything we already knew about the issues, as well as everything we did not know. In this way, we were able to establish our knowledge base and to identify a dozen focus questions that would guide our inquiry.

Learners Construct Meaning for Themselves.

The theme cycle enabled us to identify a genuine inquiry project. As the teacher-leader, I resisted the temptation to take control and outline exactly how we would spend each meeting. Instead, together we created a list of inquiry questions that would guide our exploration of a wide range of issues related to authentic assessment. Each teacher-participant agreed to explore a variety of resources to find answers. Accordingly, we next discussed how we might find answers and identified four major informational sources:

Professional literature. We agreed to read journal articles and books and to reflect and respond to our readings in interactive journals. As the group leader, I read each teacher's journal and responded in writing to each entry. We also spent a portion of our monthly group meetings in literature circles, sharing our journals with each other, and extending and refining our understanding of what we were reading.

The educational community. The teachers in the Galef Assessment Project agreed that yet another informational source was a wide community of educators, specifically teachers and researchers in and outside of our group, who had implemented or developed assessment instruments such as the *California Learning Record* (Barr, 1994), (an extension of the British *Primary Language Record* [Barr, Ellis, Hester, & Thomas, 1988]). We understood that these experts could provide us with firsthand accounts of what had worked, and what had not.

As the teacher-leader of the group, I would often launch a discussion with a mini-presentation. I explained, for example, such assessment instruments as learning logs and teacher-student interviews. I also gave an all-day workshop on miscue analysis. But as a community of learners, we were each called on to share our own professional expertise. Almost every teacher in our project, at one time or another, presented to the group. Several teachers took the lead for an entire day. Two shared invaluable information about how they were using portfolios with their students. Another led us through the intricacies of the new California Learning Assessment System (CLAS), the performance-based test that replaced the more traditional achievement tests.[1]

Classroom research. Most of our inquiry work centered on classroom research. Each teacher committed to choosing and trying out a range of authentic assessment instruments such as learning logs, students' self-reflections, teacher-student interviews, parent-student-teacher conferences, anecdotal record-keeping, and miscue analysis. Teachers were free to choose their own assessment instruments; furthermore, they outlined their own research projects and established their own timetables for change. Together as a group we committed to completing *Learning Records* on three students. The *Record* requires teachers to engage in rigorous observations of specific literate behaviors and understandings related to language and literacy development. As teachers observe their students in authentic learning experiences, they discover the complexities that govern and guide cognitive and linguistic development. Time was set aside at each meeting for sharing the results of our research. The focus, always, was *what had we learned*? What had worked? What had not worked as well? Why? How might we revise our strategies to be more successful?

My work with Ken had taught me that the answers to my questions about teaching, learning, curriculum, and evaluation did not lie in a metal cabinet or even in his inspiring graduate courses. The real answers could only be found in my own classroom. Using my theoretical understanding of language and learning, I could engage in sensitive observations of my students and discover everything I needed to know to provide the instruction that would make a difference for them. As Bissex (1987) has written, "Everything that happens in a classroom can be seen as data to be understood rather than causes for blaming or congratulating ourselves or our students" (p. 4). When the classroom is viewed as a laboratory for learning—for both the teacher and students—then we can become what Bissex defines as a teacher researcher: "an observer, questioner, learner, and more complete teacher" (p. 4).

Assessment Project participant Nan Mohr, a fifth-grade teacher at Emma Shuey School in Rosemead, CA, explains how her commitment to classroom research helped her:

---

[1]The CLAS was opposed from many quarters and, eventually, in the midst of a heated political debate, Governor Pete Wilson threw it out.

> I became more conscious of the kidwatching I was doing and came to trust my intuitive responses to my students. I relaxed somewhat as I gained confidence from my research and the group mentoring. I also learned that constructivist theory and authentic assessment are valid. I found support for them in my own classroom. My students grew in self-reflection and responsibility, also.

Learners Explore Their Learning Over Time

All of us in the Assessment Project were especially intrigued with the possibilities of portfolio keeping; however, following the lead of Graves and Sunstein (1992), we recognized that we should try creating our own before introducing them to our students. Over the course of the year, we began to build our own portfolios focusing on the overarching question, "What does this tell me about myself as a learner?" We began each monthly meeting by sharing the newest entry to our portfolios. We explained to our colleagues why we had chosen the entry and how it related to our personal learning odysseys. The experience not only helped us discover and appreciate the possibilities of portfolio keeping, but it also pushed us into self-reflection and evaluation. Reflecting on ourselves as learners led us to a sensitive, thoughtful analysis of human learning in general, and, more specifically, of our students as learners. And ultimately, it forced us to consider how our current instructional practices aligned—or did not align—with what we understood about learning.

Self-evaluation is a critical part of all classroom transactions. Indeed, as the two Bisbee teachers had discovered, there is no way to separate teacher self-reflection and evaluation from the dynamics of successful teaching, learning, and curriculum. Each teacher-participant engaged in continual self-evaluation through our interactive dialogue journals, small group discussions, and sharing of research findings. In addition, each participant was asked to complete a final self-evaluation at the year's end. Nancy Gates, a sixth-grade teacher at Savanah School in Rosemead, CA, testified to the value of self-reflection:

> Of all the workshops I have been involved in this past year, our Assessment Project has driven me to delve deep inside myself more than any other. Self-reflection is like taking time to smell the flowers or listen to the songs of birds. Too often I run pell mell from one project to the next without thinking about what has been accomplished. It's sad when I do this because I really miss out on what builds the inner spirit and feeds the imagination.

Learners Never Stop Learning

Real learning is generative. One question leads to another. The first year of the Assessment Project ended, but the need for answers did not. As some questions were answered, others arose. We were not in the business of learning a finite set of facts and figures or acquiring teaching tips and techniques. Our focus, initially, was authentic assessment, but, ultimately, we found ourselves addressing the broader, more profound issue of learning. What is learning? How does it unfold in classrooms? What can we do as teachers to support it? Our thoughtful contemplation of these questions helped us consider ourselves as lifelong learners. At the same time, we discussed and debated how best to inspire our students as learners.

What Was Learned

Teacher research, unlike the make-and-take workshops of the 1970s that I had suffered through, is liberating. When teachers ask their own questions about learning and teaching, observe their own students, document their findings, and draw conclusions, they are transformed as teachers and, often, as human beings. The changes in the teachers with whom I worked in the Assessment Project paralleled the changes I experienced as I learned with Ken:

- they grew in their understanding of theory and were able to explain constructivist learning theory with examples from their own classrooms;
- they were able to use their new understandings to plan sensitive instruction and stimulating curriculum; they also understood how to monitor and document their students' development;
- they became more critical readers of research and published materials; they were less susceptible to the packaged programs and various educational fads that seem to appear daily in teachers' boxes;
- they became professional resources for their colleagues at their school sites and in the wider professional community; several of our Project participants presented at county and state conferences, and all agreed to serve as teacher mentors in their own districts;
- and less tangible, but all-important, they grew in self-confidence and feelings of self-esteem; they emerged as more competent, more self-assured professionals who felt connected to a professional community.

Ken and Yetta have fostered the professional birth of thousands of educators worldwide. The Whole Language Umbrella, an organization inspired in large part by the Goodmans' work, serves as an international community of professional teachers. Most of the professional sessions at the annual Umbrella Conference are organized and conducted by teachers. Ken Goodman (1991) stated, "whole language means coming of age as a profession" for teachers (p. 4). The Goodmans' open respect and admiration for teachers have helped us all believe in ourselves as professionals and learn with and from our colleagues. It has liberated us from overstuffed metal cabinets everywhere. Today, we rely, instead, on our own philosophies, scientific understandings, and classroom research to make the countless professional decisions necessary to help our students learn as much as they can. As Bullock (1987) has written, "doing classroom research changes teachers and the teaching profession from the inside out, from the bottom up, through changes in teachers themselves. And therein lies its power" (p. 27). After all, as human beings, teachers, too, are creative, capable learners. When we possess the power to change and control our learning lives, there is little we cannot do.

REFERENCES

Apple, M. (1986). *Teachers and texts: The political economy of class and gender relations in education.* Boston: Routledge & Kegan Paul.

Apple, M. (1991). Teachers, politics, and whole language instruction. In K. Goodman, L. Bridges Bird, & Y. Goodman (Eds.), *The whole language catalog.* New York: Macmillan/McGraw Hill.

Barr, M., Ellis, S., Hester, H., and Thomas, A. (1988). *The primary language record.* Portsmouth, NH: Heinemann.

Barr, M. (1994). *The California learning record.* Sacramento, CA: California State Department of Education.

Bissex, G. (1987). What is a teacher-researcher. In G. Bissex & R. Bullock (Eds.), *Seeing for ourselves: Case-study research by teachers of writing.* Portsmouth, NH: Heinemann.

Bridges Bird, L. (Ed.). (1989). *The Fair Oaks story: Becoming a whole language school.* Katonah, NY: Richard C. Owen.

Bullock, R. (1987). A quiet revolution: The power of teacher research. In G. Bissex and R. Bullock (Eds.), *Seeing For ourselves: Case-study research by teachers of writing.* Portsmouth, NH: Heinemann.

Cambourne, B. (1988). *The whole story: Natural learning and the acquisition of literacy in the classroom.* Auckland, New Zealand: Scholastic.

Edelsky, C., Altwerger, B., and Flores, B. (1991). *Whole language: What's the difference?* Portsmouth, NH: Heinemann.

Freire, P. (1985). *The politics of education.* South Hadley, MA: Bergin & Harvey.

Giroux, H. (1988). *Teachers as intellectuals.* South Hadley, MA: Bergin & Harvey.

Goodman, K. (1973). Miscues: Windows on the reading process. In K. Goodman (Ed.), *Miscue analysis: Applications to reading instruction* (pp. 3-14). Urbana, IL: National Council Teachers of English.

Goodman, K. (1991). What is whole language? In K. Goodman, L. Bridges Bird, & Y. Goodman, (Eds.), *The whole language catalog.* New York: Macmillan/McGraw Hill.

Goodman, K., Smith, E. B., Meredith, R., and Goodman, Y. (1987). *Language and thinking in schools* (3rd ed.). Katonah, NY: Richard C. Owen.

Graves, D., & Sunstein, B. (1992). *Portfolio portraits.* Portsmouth, NH: Heinemann.

Halliday, M. A. K. (1975). *Learning how to mean: Explorations in the development of language.* London: Edward Arnold.

Heath, S., & Mangiola, L. (1993). *Children of promise.* Berkeley, CA, and Pittsburgh, PA: Center for the Study of Writing.

Holdaway, D. (1979). *The foundations of literacy.* Sydney, Australia: Ashton, Scholastic.

Peterson, R. (1991). *Life in a crowded place: Making a learning community.* Portsmouth, NH: Heinemann.

Shannon, P. (1990). *The struggle to continue: Progressive reading instruction in the United States.* Portsmouth, NH: Heinemann.

Smith, F. (1981). Demonstrations, engagement and Sensitivity. *Language Arts, 58,* 103-112.

Weaver, C. (1990). *Understanding whole language: From principles to practice.* Portsmouth, NH: Heinemann.

Chapter Eleven

Reading as a Psycholinguistic Guessing Game: A Teacher Development Strategy

Jan Turbill
University of Wollongong, Australia

This chapter focuses on the story of how one person's thinking evolved over the past 20 years with respect to staff development or, preferably, teacher learning. Other chapters in this book refer to the key contributions that Ken Goodman's work has made to the reading world. It is my contention that there is another dimension to Goodman's reading research that forced educators to examine not only the reading process and how it was best taught and learned in classrooms, but how this information was best taught to and learned by those who were to be the teachers of reading. The concept that reading was "a psycholinguistic guessing game" (K. Goodman, 1967) was not an easy one to tell teachers about. It seemed that the most appropriate way to get the message across to teachers was for them to focus on their own reading process and experience what they as proficient readers did as they read. However, reading was something that most teachers did very easily without being conscious of the many decisions they made, the strategies they used, or the background skills and knowledge they needed to have and use as they made meaning from print. Moreover, the very notion that meaning was not locked into the text on the page was a major shift in thinking for most teachers.

Thus, no longer was it adequate to simply transmit knowledge about reading to teachers by telling through the usual sit-up-shut-up-lecture format. If teachers were to gain a deep understanding of the reading process and how reading worked, they needed to understand reading from an inside view; they needed to both feel and experience the highly invisible processes they used. They needed to become aware of the miscues they made as readers and why they made them. They needed to make explicit the reading strategies they knew and used. They needed to make visible what is usually invisible. Finally, they needed to consider the implications of these new insights gained from an inside view with respect to their own teaching of reading. Thus, Goodman found it necessary to forge new ways of presenting his emerging concepts and understandings about reading by developing activities that forced his learners to gain an inside view of reading. Such activities were indeed windows into their own reading process. Such activities led those educators who participated in them to see quite literally the key concepts that Goodman's research with children had highlighted. Few could deny what they saw. Thus, such activities were powerful learning experiences in their own right. As a staff developer, it was this dimension with which I became involved. It was the beginning of my paradigm shift in what constitutes staff development or what I would now prefer to call "teacher learning."

At the time that all this was happening in Australia I was certainly not as consciously aware of what was going on as I am in hindsight. In retrospect it seems obvious now why I began to make the changes I did in the staff development work with which I was daily involved. At the time, however, it was not that obvious. It was a trial-and-error process. It was a time to reflect on the "miscues" that we were making, what these were telling us about teacher learning, and what these were telling us for future instruction.

Furthermore, it can be argued that this early work of Goodman in reading and reading instruction was the beginning of a new paradigm in literacy education—a paradigm soon to be known as whole language.

A NEW PARADIGM IN LITERACY EDUCATION

Whole language or holistic learning is a view of learning and language development that is quite different from traditionally accepted views of learning and language development. As such it can be likened to a paradigm in that it represents "the thoughts, perceptions and values that form a particular vision of reality, a vision that is the basis of the way a society organises itself" (Capra, 1988, p. 11).

The movement to a whole language paradigm can be viewed as a "paradigm shift" (Kuhn, 1970) in learning and the teaching of language and literacy, a shift that is as significant to the educational world as the Einsteinian relativity paradigm was to the scientific world (Covey, 1989). Capra (1982) defines a paradigm shift as "a profound change in the thoughts, perceptions and values that form a particular vision of reality, a vision that is the basis of the way a society organises itself" (p. 22).

Although whole language has been perceived to be the answer to our literacy problems by some and a laissez-faire move to mediocrity by others, it represents a profound change in the thinking, perceptions, and values that form a particular vision of reality of what literacy is and the role that literacy plays in learning. It can be argued that the whole language paradigm, if adopted as the paradigm which underpins the literacy curriculum in our schools, will provide learning cultures that are highly conducive to producing literate students; students who think critically, problem solve, exercise judgments, and learn new skills and knowledge which will be durable throughout a lifetime. These are learning cultures in which empowered teachers are creating empowered learners (Cambourne, 1991; Turbill, 1991).

THE CHALLENGE OF STAFF DEVELOPMENT

The challenge to those involved in the staff development of teachers is to create learning programs and learning cultures that not only set out to teach the concepts inherent in this paradigm called whole language, but also to support teachers as learners as they move through such a paradigm shift.

In what follows I have outlined the development of a personal theory of staff development which has attempted to do this. It is a theory that evolved over time and now forms the basis of a staff development program, *Frameworks* (Turbill, Butler, & Cambourne, 1991). Inherent in this personal story are the many presuppositions which I hold about learning, language, teacher learning and the role that language plays in learning.

A PERSONAL THEORY OF STAFF DEVELOPMENT AND TEACHERS' LEARNING

Background Information

My interest in the professional development of teachers began some 16 years ago during my employment in the New South Wales Department of Education, a very large, monolithic, centralized bureaucracy which employed some 45,000 teachers across the range of Kindergarten–Grade 12. The Department of Education was subdivided into 10 regions across the state of New South Wales, each with approximately 220 schools.

In 1976, I was invited by the central administration of the St. George Region in which I taught to leave the classroom and, drawing on my skills as a successful teacher of 12 years, to work with other teachers to support them in their attempts to put into practice the new centrally written curriculum guide on language education. This document, commonly known as *1974 Primary Language Document,*[1] was the first of a series of documents written by teachers recruited from their classrooms into the central office. Their brief was to review the current research and writings in language and literacy education, analyze and synthesize this thinking, and write it into a curriculum statement for teachers. The philosophy underpinning the 1974 Language Document was holistic in its intent, child-centered, and experientially based. It drew greatly on the work of the British Bullock Report (Department of Education and Science, 1975).

Other documents followed. In 1978, the Reading K-12 Policy Statement was released based on the research of psycholinguists such as Ken Goodman, Yetta Goodman, Carolyn Burke, Virginia Woodward, Frank Smith, Peter Rousch, and Brian Cambourne. In 1985, Writing K-12 was released. This document drew on the work of Donald Graves, Brian Cambourne, R. D. Walshe, James Britton, and the St. George Writing Project (Turbill, 1982).

During these years my role and responsibility was mainly to help teachers, and school staffs as a whole to implement the philosophy of these documents into school-based curriculum and classroom practice which reflected the needs of the students in their particular schools.

Another responsibility that increased in importance over the years was to represent the teachers and schools in my region in the interactive development of curricula in reading and writing. This meant regular workshops in which staff developers from the 10 regions met with central office curriculum developers to consider the needs of the students and teachers in the regions as well as the current research and thinking in the field. The outcomes of these workshops were to be documents that reflected the best of current theory and classroom practice and the particular needs of students in New South Wales schools, namely, Reading K-12 and Writing K-12 mentioned earlier. Because of the interaction between central office and regions in the development of these documents, Reading K-12 and Writing K-12 each took approximately five years to develop and publish.

---

[1]For teachers of Kindergarten-Grade 6.

Thus, my role over this period was not only to be a staff developer but also a curriculum developer. My perception of my role was to act as translator of theory into practice, to act as a clearinghouse for new ideas and resources; and to respond to the needs of the schools in light of the current curriculum documents. I saw myself more as a specialist in the language education field rather than an expert; however, I realized that many teachers in the schools perceived me to be the expert.

My Role in Schools as a Staff Developer

During the nine years I was employed as a staff developer I spent much of the time in schools, mostly in classrooms working alongside teachers. These teachers invited me into their classrooms to work with students, to demonstrate new activities, to observe them in action, and to generally help them reflect on their classroom practice and how they might change this practice. My personal theory of staff development which emerged over those nine years went through several interesting changes or phases, culminating in a staff development model that was used as the basic model for the design of *Frameworks*.

Phase One: Practice. During the first years my focus, as a staff developer, was on practice. I brought along ideas and the latest resources to show teachers. I demonstrated new practices for them to emulate. The expectation was that the teacher would take these new practices and adopt them into his or her classroom. My role was to transmit the knowledge.

My staff development model could be summarized as:[2]

By 1977 I began to realize that just giving teachers a shopping bag of new tricks may satisfy them for the short term, but it did not seem to result in any long-term change in their teaching practice.

---

[2]As this section takes the form of a personal account, it was decided not to label the models drawn throughout as figures, except in one instance in which I reference a model published elsewhere.

Phase Two: Theory into Practice. With the release of Reading K-12 in 1978, those of us in staff development began to consider ways of helping teachers make the links between the theory or philosophy espoused in the document and how this theory could be implemented in the classroom. It was at this point that we were greatly influenced by the reading theory and workshops which many of our Australian colleagues brought back from their work with Ken Goodman. And so I entered the theory-into-practice phase.

As the perceived specialist and authority in the field, I conducted many workshops which engaged teachers in considering how they went about reading and in linking the principles which came together from these workshops with the theory that the document was espousing. These workshops were mostly held during 1-day inservice courses with little or no follow-up for the teachers. They were workshops that required the participants to examine their own reading process and the strategies they used for reading. But just how teachers incorporated the theory-into-practice workshops in their classroom practice was left to them.

My staff development model now could be summarized as:

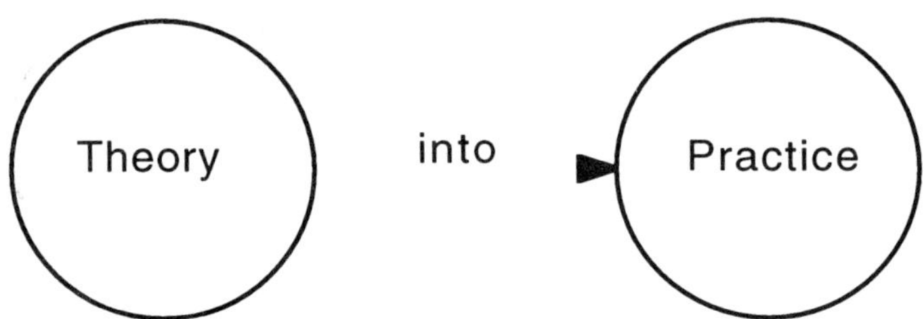

It was a one-sided model. I saw my responsibility as helping teachers understand how the current theory in literacy education, and reading in particular, should be reflected in their teaching practice. It was my belief that having given teachers the information on the theory into practice, they were responsible for implementing this in their classrooms. After all, it was my belief at this point that I was the "thinker." It was my role to take the theory and help teachers understand it. Teachers were the "doers"; the practitioners. It was their role to take what they had learned and "do it"; to turn it into classroom practices.

Phase Three: Theory's Impact on Teachers' Beliefs and Practice. The period of the late 1970s and early 1980s was another time of change. As funds in Department of Education staff development budgets were cut, staff developers across the 10 regions began to question their effectiveness over the years and how they could be more effective with less finances. It was during this period that action research surfaced as a valuable professional and staff development model. I had also begun to realize that working with teachers in their own classrooms and within the school itself over a period of time seemed to bring about more effective change.

And so I moved into the third phase of my development as a staff developer. I began to design school and class activities with teachers in which, together, we examined their classroom practice, their personal beliefs, and the theory which was presented in the curriculum documents that were still mandated as guides for what was to occur in classrooms. This model meant I would work with teachers as a group and also within their classrooms.

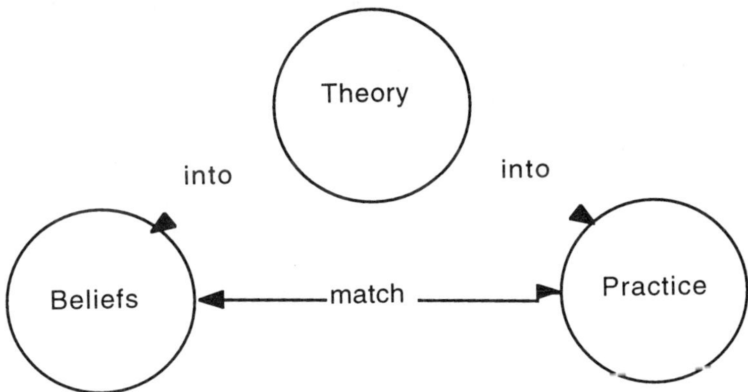

This model depicts my belief that I needed to help teachers examine their beliefs and practices in light of the current theory espoused in the curriculum. They did this through workshop activities in which they were asked to reflect on their own beliefs and processes. My personal theory, at this point, assumed that changes in teachers' beliefs and practices would occur as a result of this involvement, interaction, and reflection. All this had to be guided by the curriculum policy (the theory) mandated by the Department of Education, which was still seen to be the main source of change. However, there was a changing focus on the role of the teacher vis-a-vis the staff developer. I was now viewing teachers as learners as well as thinkers. I was learning from them and with them in their classrooms. Teachers were also beginning to view themselves as more than doers. They wanted to be more responsible for the teaching and learning decisions made in their own classrooms. And they were being expected to take such responsibility, particularly at a the whole school level. School-based curriculum development was a requirement of the system at this point in time.

There continued to be a strong focus on theory into practice. However, my role was beginning to change. I began to operate more as a process consultant, someone who set up the processes for the learning of the mandated theory within the context of the school.

An evident result at the school level was the significant interaction among the teachers during these meetings. This interaction continued long after I left the context. I could see that change was occurring at the classroom level because teachers were changing their beliefs and thinking about how children learned and they were articulating these changing beliefs. Teachers were growing more confident about the teaching practice they chose to implement. The congruence between their beliefs and their practice appeared to be greater than was evident in previous years.

However, there were still too many teachers with whom I worked who appeared to know what they were supposed to think and do but did not do it; that is, they seemed to be able to articulate the theory and principles espoused in the current curriculum documents in discussion with their peers and in the rationale which prefaced their classroom programs, but this apparent knowledge did not show itself in their classroom practice. Change here seemed very superficial and occurred mainly in the adoption of some new teaching approaches and organizational procedures. Scratch the surface of these teachers and their classroom practice and there was little evidence of change. Innovations seemed to have a very short life and disappeared once the key mover in the school (myself or a key member of staff) left, or time passed.

Phase Four: An Interactive Model. In 1981 it was my responsibility as a curriculum consultant to initiate, maintain, and monitor a curriculum innovation in three schools in the K-3 grades (Turbill, 1982). The foci of this project were, "How do young children learn to write?" and "How can teachers support this learning?" The methodology used in the project was based on action research as outlined by Kemmis and McTaggert (1982).

I now had the opportunity of not only observing young children learning to write in natural settings but teachers as they struggled with learning new theories about young children learning to write (Goodman ,1984; Graves, 1983). They were also learning from the observations of what their young children were doing as a result of their changed teaching practice. It was an exciting period for all of us—teachers, children, and myself. We were very much a community of learners, (Barth, 1990). Together we formulated theory and curriculum about young children's literacy development. This work found its way into the Writing K-12 Document (1988) and two books (Turbill, 1982, 1983).

During this same year I went through the process of being a learner-writer. I attended a 1-week Writing Workshop in which I and the others in the group went through the process of writing "a piece with which I was personally satisfied." Each morning we wrote, shared with peers, learned about leads and editing, and gained other insights into the writing process. In the afternoon we reflected on the processes that we were experiencing and considered the implications for the teaching of writing.

This experience gave me insights into how I learned and went about the process of writing. This experience was not unlike those that I had when we were first introduced to Goodman's research on reading and the reading process. These insights reinforced that which I already believed about teacher learning and staff development, namely, that teachers need to experience the processes of learning that they expect their students to go through. Although we had begun to carry out workshops in the reading area that required teachers to examine their own reading process, we had not spent time taking the next step of considering the implications for the classroom. My beliefs were not only being reinforced but also were expanding.

Those of us involved in the Writing Project began to realize that we, the community of learners, were all in a position to influence and teach each other. We were in a position to create our own personal theories, which in turn could influence others' theories. Collaboration, reflection, and peer teaching were powerful staff development tools for us. Such collaboration saw us trying to solve our own problems, having been forced to reflect on what we were doing in the classroom and why we were doing it. It meant we needed to read and reflect on what others were doing in the area. It was indeed an empowering process for us.

And so, from all of these experiences, a new theory about staff development was beginning to emerge for me. It could be summarized as:

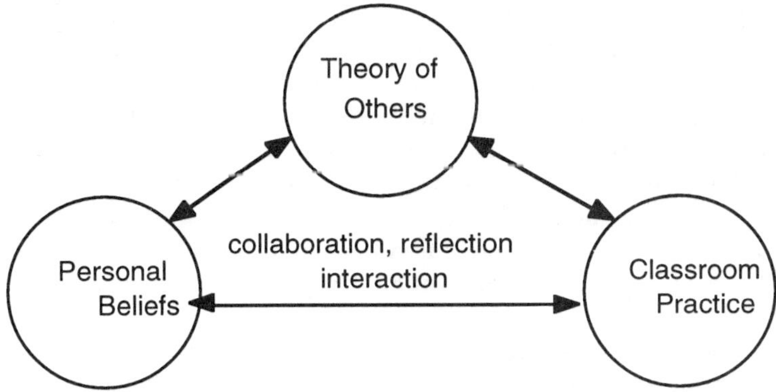

I now began to believe that teachers needed to understand their own language and learning processes (reading, writing, talking, listening, spelling) in order to be aware of their own beliefs about language and learning. They also needed to be aware of and understand the theories that others (including their peers) espoused about language and learning. Finally, they needed to be aware not only of the many classroom practices which they could use in their classrooms, but also understand how these practices could reflect their own beliefs about language and learning. I was becoming increasingly more aware of how these three areas supported and fed off each other. I still felt the most powerful influence was the theory of others; that is, the theory that was espoused in the curriculum documents that the teachers were required to implement. It was also my belief that these documents were a culmination of the latest academic theories of others.

Phase Five: The Role of Language in Teacher Learning: Facilitating Staff Development. A critical factor in my emerging theory was the realization of the role that language played in teachers' learning. It became evident to me that I made decisions about how I could best facilitate the learning of teachers by listening to the language they used in their daily teaching.

In order for me to support teachers it was necessary for me to evaluate their needs. Therefore, I had to make various judgments about the teachers' beliefs, practices, and areas of strengths, and then determine the places where I could step in and make suggestions for classroom practice. In order to make these decisions, I found I had to listen carefully to what the teacher said to me; that is, the language the teacher used. This included what assistance the teacher asked for (the teacher's perceived needs) and what the teacher chatted to me about (the teacher's implicit beliefs about language and learning).

I only became fully aware of how I operated when I was put into the position of supporting new staff developers and forced to make my processes explicit for others. The region in which I worked decided to adopt a buddy system to support newly appointed staff developers. My buddy, a young male mathematics consultant, accompanied me for the first three weeks of his employment. One hot day in February, as we were driving back to the office after spending a morning in a school in several classrooms, he asked me, "How do you make the decision about what is the best thing to suggest to a particular teacher? How do you do that?" Those simple questions initiated my reflection and research into this area.

My colleague's questions forced me to reflect and make explicit what I had been doing implicitly since my involvement in the St. George

Writing Project. I was forced to make explicit the tacit knowledge that I was constantly gathering and drawing on to make evaluative judgments about teachers' degrees of implementation of the philosophy that underpinned the curriculum documents that guided language education in the NSW Department of Education.

My reflection highlighted the fact that I drew very strongly on the language each teacher used in dealing with the students in his or her care. This language was used in the classroom, in the playground, and often in discussion with me about the students. This language—what the teacher said and how the teacher said it—seemed to tell me more about the needs of the teacher in the process of implementing holistic child-centered philosophy in his or her language and literacy curriculum.

Another source of information I identified through my reflections was the language the students used in talking with me and with their teacher. I found I made judgments about "where the teacher was at" through interviewing students and asking questions such as, "Why are you doing this activity?" "What do you do in reading in your classroom?" "What do you do in spelling?" And then when I worked with the students I considered their responses, that is, how they responded to the discourse I used with them. This included how they coped with responding to my questioning techniques, how confident they were to respond to my questions, and how willing they were to take risks with their responses and to have a go at the activities I was introducing to them. And finally, I drew on the language that was displayed around the room and the language the students were asked to read and write—how this displayed language was used by the teacher, and how the language produced by the students was used by the teacher.

"But what does this language tell you?", my buddy probed further. It was then I realized that I had developed a working hypothesis that had emerged from the classroom data I had tacitly gathered and that was constantly being grounded in the classroom data. A grounded theory had emerged for me. It went something like this: A teacher's beliefs about language and literacy learning are reflected in the language that he or she uses in the practice of the classroom.

For me, the implications of this theory were that if I were to help teachers change their practice, which is what they asked me to do, I needed to also help them change their beliefs. In changing their beliefs they would begin to change the language they used in their teaching, particularly the language used to establish the ethos of the classroom. Teachers would begin to ask different types of questions and thus provide different responses to children. The indicators of this change process for me were embedded in the language the teachers used. But what exactly these indicators were and how they operated I could not clearly identify. I did, however, realize that I knew it was important and that I needed to research the area, both in the classroom and through the literature.

It was at this time that I changed my context; I became a lecturer in Language Education at a university. Within this context I was expected to carry out research. I also continued to work in the field of staff development in various ways, all of which had impact on my thinking about teacher learning. And so my personal theory began to change again.

I became involved with two major research projects. One was an evaluation of a curriculum staff development program and the other a classroom ethnography. The university received a large grant to evaluate the impact that a staff development course, the Early Literacy Inservice Course (ELIC), had as an agent of teacher change. Headed by Dr. Brian Cambourne, a group of five carried out a "responsive evaluation" (Guba & Lincoln, 1981) over a 2-year period to evaluate the impact of ELIC.

I also set up a research project using microethnography as the methodology to examine the language teachers use to teach literacy. Using a small radio microphone, I collected the language of literacy episodes used by teachers who espoused whole language philosophy. Data were also collected from the classrooms of six of the teachers in the ELIC study. These teachers were at various stages of development in their thinking about implementing whole language philosophy in their classrooms. Several could be considered traditional in their teaching approaches, following a fragmentationist subskill methodology.

The majority of data, however, were collected on a weekly basis from a kindergarten classroom in which two teachers were team teaching 54 children. This research followed certain procedures over a school year. I would arrive at the school each Wednesday morning. I would talk to the teachers about the week gone by, the plan of the day to come, individual children, and literacy, learning theory, and practice. One of the teachers was "wired up" before the children entered the room, and the language used from that point until the morning break two hours later was audiotaped. I took field notes of what was going on, noting the behaviors of the students as well as the teachers' practices. I focused on specific students each week. These students changed from week to week, although sometimes I stayed with the same child for several weeks. Each week I also took copies of the teachers' day plan and curriculum, students' work samples, and other artifacts emanating from the morning's teaching. I returned the following week with the transcript of the previous week's lesson and my field notes. These were left with the teachers to be discussed during the following week. And so the cycle continued.

Over the year the data revealed that:

- the language that teachers use in their classroom practice is a reflection of the beliefs—the paradigm—they hold about learning and language development
- the differences in the language are clearly reflected in the tenor of the language, the type of questions asked,and the responses teachers make
- there is a greater use of inclusive language rather than exclusive language in classrooms where teachers hold holistic beliefs about language and learning
- questions are used to help students make connections rather than to test their knowledge
- questions are also used to force students to reflect, to think, to problem solve
- teachers use metacognitive language to reflect and make explicit the purposes of the learning as well as the strategies used in learning.

Three major categories of language use emerged. These categories were evident in the classrooms of traditional class teachers (TTs) and of those who espoused whole language philosophy (WLTs). What differed was the way the language was structured (Turbill, 1987).

The first category can be described as the language of teaching, demonstration, and intervention. All teachers use language to teach. It was the type of language used by the two groups that differed. WLTs used language to demonstrate and explain literacy knowledge to the children. For example, they explained the surface features of the language:

> This letter is a "c" and this one an "h." When they are together, like they are in this word, they create the sound "ch."

They also explained the processes of learning to the children:

> When I come to a word like this one (points to "cow") I can try and work it out by looking at the first letter, "c," looking at the picture, remember what the story is about and then guess it, "cow." If I still can't work it out, it doesn't matter—can read ahead and see if that will help me work it out.

WLTs also tended to explain the purpose of what was about to be discussed and why it was important for the children to learn it. This type of language use was rarely used by TTs.

Both groups of teachers asked many questions of the children. However, the types of questions and the purpose of the questioning differed. WLTs tended to ask questions to help children make connections in their literacy learning, whereas TTs' questions were more in the domain of recitation (Brown, 1991; Cazden, 1988) and testing.

WLTs did ask questions that fit within the recitation format, for example:

> Who can remember the next one? Shaun?
> Yes, two big crayfish.

The function of the question in this context (shared book experience with a big book) was not as much to test the child but to check his understanding, to focus all children's attention, to encourage Shaun to predict using his background knowledge, and to use the picture as a clue. More importantly, WLTs asked other types of questions that forced the children to reflect on their own learning and the strategies they used to learn. Questions such as these encouraged students to think, reflect, and problem solve:

> How did you work out how to spell that word?
> Where did you get that idea to write about?
> Why do you think that?
> What does that word say? Tell the children how you worked that out?

Most of the TTs' questions tended to follow the recitation format: Who knows what that word says?

> Robert?
> No. Gary?
> No. Look, everyone, it starts with—?
> Yes, Sarah. A "c." So the word, Sarah, is?
> Yes, good.

The second category of language use to emerge was that of control and organization. Both groups of teachers used language of control and organization, particularly at the beginning of a school year.

However, what was clearly evident was that WLTs began to use less language of control and organization as the year progressed because the children were aware of the rules of operation (the structures and processes) and what was expected of them. Because WLTs spent more time explaining to their children the purpose of the lesson events and what was expected of them, and because there was a high degree of predictability in the daily lesson plans, there was less ambiguity for the children. Thus, it seemed there was less need to control and organize them. In contrast, TTs' use of language of control continued throughout the year and, in fact often increased in lessons in which the teacher was transmitting new information.

The third major category of language use to emerge was language of response. Because teachers used questioning for different purposes, the language they used to respond to the students also differed. Both groups used language to respond to students in an evaluative sense; however, TTs' responses tended to evaluate the child's response as right or wrong and then to move on to another child.

> No, Steve, that's not quite right. Sarah ...?
> Yes, good girl.

WLTs also evaluated the children's responses but tended to follow them up if they were not on course. WLTs' responses tended to follow this format:

evaluate	No, that's not "cow"; that's a good thought, but you are not quite right. . .
demonstrate again	Have another look. The word begins with a "c" and this is a picture of a "cow."
extend the demonstration	Yes, this word says "cow." But look, this word here also starts with a "c' but the picture is of a "cat." So what must this word be?
try a new demonstration	We saw that word in another book yesterday. Let me show you. Look, here it is. "Cow." Now look at the word here. They look the same. So this word must also be "cow."
celebrate	Aren't you clever, Shaun, for using the picture to help you work out that word.

WHAT DID ALL THIS MEAN FOR STAFF DEVELOPMENT?

I was beginning to understand that there was a high degree of congruence between the beliefs that teachers held about language development and learning and their classroom practices (Cambourne, 1991; Cho, 1990). Furthermore, it seemed that these beliefs were realized into classroom practice *through* the language the teachers used as they related to their students, interacted with them, and demonstrated that which was to be learned. Not only was this language a major source of content information for the young learners but it was also the shaper of the classroom ethos and culture; a culture in which certain conditions could be clearly identified. These were conditions that enhance "natural learning" (Cambourne, 1988; Holdaway, 1979) and encourage young learners to think, reflect, problem solve, and be active learners (Brown, 1991; Cambourne, 1991). It was a climate that actively encouraged social interaction (Turbill, 1987).

Some questions now began to emerge. If the classroom discourse that the teacher uses is so powerful in creating the classroom ethos and curriculum, if this language is a reflection of the teachers' beliefs, and if teaching practice is a realization of teachers' beliefs through their language, what can we learn from this for teachers' learning and staff development? Do we try to change teachers' beliefs and will this lead to a change in language? Should we try to change teachers' practice and hope that this will, in turn, change the language they use which, in turn, will impact the beliefs they hold?

The Evaluation of the Early Literacy Inservice Course (ELIC) (Cambourne, Turbill, Keeble, Ferguson, & Colvin, 1988) sheds some light here. ELIC was a staff development course run by a highly trained tutor over a 10-week period. The underlying philosophy was based on developmental learning' (Holdaway, 1979) and holistic language learning. Teachers were asked through various workshops and activities to focus on their students as learners. These reflections, plus what they were given to read about children's learning, formed the basis of the content of the course. A range of new teaching strategies was introduced through the course, and the teachers were asked to try these and reflect on how they worked in their classrooms. The ELIC tutor worked in classrooms with the teachers, sharing their concerns and often demonstrating new teaching strategies for them. Overall, ELIC was a highly successful agent of change of teachers' beliefs about language and learning.

Two years after their involvement in the course, the evaluation found that those teachers who had little understanding of holistic philosophy when they began the course, focused on using the new strategies in their classrooms. Reflecting on these strategies with their colleagues in sharing sessions in the course and in informal situations after the course seemed to help these teachers begin to articulate their beliefs about language and learning. As time went on, they developed a more coherent and cohesive belief system which was more clearly reflected in their teaching practice.

Those teachers who had already begun to embrace the principles of whole language philosophy found that ELIC helped them to consolidate and enhance their emerging belief systems. These people moved well beyond the content within the course by seeking further input from other courses, professional articles, and conferences. They became very confident about what they were doing and could justify clearly why they were doing it.

The study found that there were many factors involved in initiating and supporting this change process. These included:

- the course was conducted over time
- support was given by a tutor during the period of implementation
- support and guidance were given by the leaders in the school
- teachers had the opportunity to reflect and share with peers
- teachers had the opportunity to collaborate with the tutor and other teachers over time
- a network for continued sharing was established

Fullan (1991) clearly demonstrates that teacher change is not an isolated process. It is certainly not a linear cause-and-effect process. There are many interacting variables which need to be considered and these variables are highly integrated. Thus it seemed that a successful staff development aimed at helping teachers make the paradigm shift to holistic learning and thinking needed to challenge teachers' thinking and practice at many levels. And the way for teachers to get control of a certain classroom discourse was to be immersed in it and to have opportunities to use it. As Halliday (1980) has so often stated in his lectures and writings, "We learn language, we learn through language and we learn about language simultaneously as we use language" (p. 1).

It seemed to me, therefore, that teachers needed to hear the language of a holistic view of learning; to experience (to feel) this view of learning in practice; to examine their own beliefs and theories about learning and language development; to be made aware of the theories that others in the field have put forward, including their peers; to see how this theory lends itself to classroom practice; and to have opportunities to try things in their classrooms and reflect on them and what they mean. All this needs to occur in a nonthreatening and supportive learning environment, an environment in which a "community of learners" can grow (Barth, 1990). Processes that Fullan (1990) alludes to such as collaboration, reflection, action research, and trying new techniques, need to play equally major roles.

By 1988 my personal theory of staff development had emerged into the following model.

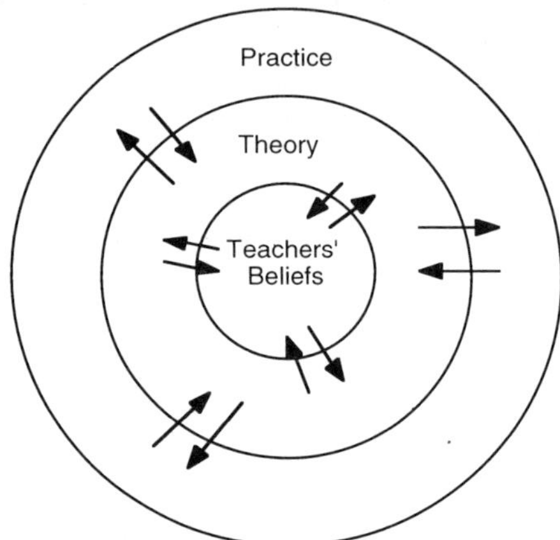

This model formed the basis for the design of a staff development program developed by Brian Cambourne and myself called the Secondary Literacy Inservice Course (Cambourne & Turbill, 1989). SLIC was a spaced learning program conducted over six weeks by a coordinator who needed no specific training.

SLIC emphasized that the focus of teacher learning was the teachers' own beliefs and understandings of how learning, writing, and reading worked, what language was, and the role it played in learning. In order for teachers to learn new things they needed to become aware of the theory of others and how this theory of others was implemented in the classroom. They needed opportunities to share this information and to try things in their classroom; but ultimately it was how this new information impacted on their own personal beliefs and understandings that created teacher change or teacher learning. Processes such as collaboration with peers, reflective thinking, support over the time that implementation was occurring, and a supportive learning environment, were all necessary variables in creating a community of learners; a community in which learners felt comfortable to take risks and share their newly forming beliefs. The dynamo that powered these processes and the learning which occurred was language. This model placed the focus on the inside circle, the core. It is an inside-out process.

Figure 11.1 is an overview of how these processes operated in SLIC and indicates the role that language played in these processes.

During this same period Cambourne and I were developing a research methodology, which we referred to as Teacher as Co-Researcher (TACOR), into an approach for staff development (Cambourne & Turbill, 1991).

While carrying out our research work with class teachers and their students we began to realize that both parties (whether it be academic and teacher or academic and child) had expertise to offer and share with each other. There were times, for example, when I looked to my co-researcher teacher for the expert knowledge, and there were times when she looked to me for expertise. There were more times, however, when we both struggled over a problem trying to make sense of our data. This understanding that the role of expert/novice oscillated between us, and, in fact, eventually did not exist at all, forced us to make explicit this relationship which we called *co-researching*. Together, the teacher and I researched questions and problems from our different perspectives in the setting; together, we solved the research questions; together we learned. It was this type of relationship that I had established with the 27 teachers involved in the St. George Writing

Figure 11.1. Overview of SLIC Process (Cambourne & Turbill, 1989, p. 6)

Project in 1982. However, it was not until Cambourne and I undertook this joint project that we began to formalize the process as a valuable methodology in qualitative research projects. What also became blatantly clear was that this process served as a powerful form of professional development for all those involved: academics, teachers, and students (Barton, 1992; Cambourne & Turbill, 1991).

We argued that traditional staff development programs—the 1- or 2-day inservice inputs; summer workshops; make-and-take workshops; long-term, spaced-learning lecture/workshops; onsite, ongoing, peer coaching; mentoring by a more experienced peer; or the clinical-supervision-by-a-senior-peer model—all have at least one thing in common. There is an acknowledged and accepted difference in status between those who teach in these programs and those who are supposed to learn from them. Those who teach are automatically accorded the status of expert, whereas those who learn are automatically accorded the status of novice (Cambourne & Turbill, 1991). We further argued that once a staff development enterprise establishes the expert-novice dichotomy, it becomes locked into a certain model of learning based on the premise that learning is essentially a process of transmitting information and/or skills from an expert to a novice. The expert therefore has the responsibility for ensuring that learning will occur.

The concept of co-researching as a methodology for staff development is a form of collaborative educational inquiry. As such it involves both parties (or all parties) working together in ways that encourage a merging of roles and responsibilities. This merging of roles and responsibilities requires equal status between the parties. All involved are acknowledged as having different kinds of expertise, all of which are valued and necessary.

The challenge I began to wrestle with was how the TACOR model could be incorporated into my staff development model. In addition, there was a problem which was causing me concern. Whole language was becoming a set of orthodoxies due to some dreadful misunderstandings and lack of information. Whole language was beginning to sweep through schools in both the United States and Australia. It was a strong grass roots movement in the United States and teachers were seeking support. From my work with teachers in the United States and Australia it was also obvious that orthodoxies were beginning to appear. Teachers were taking on board the theory of others in the sense that they could articulate these theories. However, as in past experiences mentioned earlier in this chapter, they did not seem to be making these theories their own.

They were adopting classroom practices that they either saw other teachers trying or read about in the many books and articles written by teachers for teachers. But many of them were not taking such practice and going beyond the adopting phase. They were not adapting these activities to suit their situations and the needs of their children. Teachers did not seem to have enough confidence in what they believed to take risks and create new strategies in order to best teach what it was they wanted to teach. Although they seemed to be able to articulate their beliefs about whole language philosophy, they were not allowing these beliefs to orchestrate their practice. They were not operating from the inside-out. Teachers, it seemed, wanted to turn whole language into a set of do's and don'ts. Too many teachers were still perceiving themselves as the doers of someone else's thinking.

How could teachers empower their young learners to think critically, be analytical, problem solve, and make decisions which were appropriate for the situation when they themselves did not appear to be empowered. They were not able to think critically, be analytical, problem solve, and make decisions which were appropriate for the situation. Staff development about whole language not only needed to teach a content which was about the empowering of young learners, it also needed to empower its own learners in the process.

It seemed that the three-circle model needed another layer and a slightly different focus. And so a fourth layer, implications for *my* classroom, was added. The focus of the model shifted from the professional development of teachers, generally, to the professional development of individual teachers, incorporating the notion of empowering teachers so they could empower their student learners. Thus, I found I was beginning to talk about teacher learning using the four circles as a model, as well as the design of a staff development program for groups of teachers. These four circles represented four domains of knowledge which were both interactive and integrative.

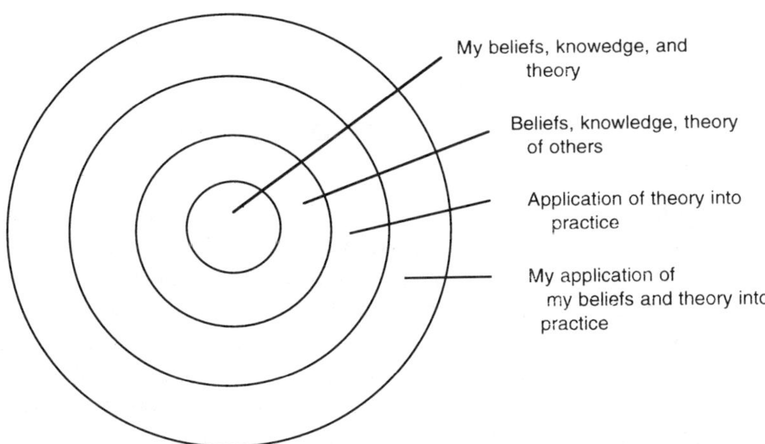

It was this model that was used as a basis for the design of *Frameworks*. In general terms the model operates this way: The inner core represents the basic beliefs and knowledge a learner (any learner) already holds about that which is to be learned. The next layer represents the knowledge and beliefs held by others about that which is to be learned. The third layer is the application of these beliefs and knowledge of that which is to be learned by those who have learned it. The last layer represents the learner's attempts to apply that which is to be learned or is being learned in his or her own context. It is a model which operates from the inside-out and then moves from the outside-in. It is both interactive and integrative. The model helped me to begin to understand the difference between a disempowered learner and an empowered learner, whether the learner be a child or teacher.

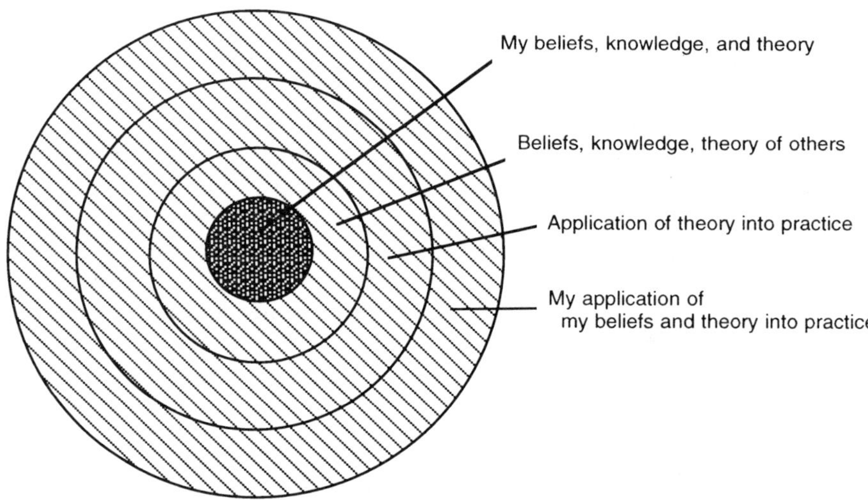

THE DISEMPOWERED LEARNER

The disempowered learner's inner core of beliefs and knowledge about that which is to be learned are messy, unclear, lacking in cohesion, and certainly more subconscious than conscious. The learner may refer to this inner core as gut feelings and intuitions. Whatever the name given to such knowledge and beliefs, they are not valued by the learner as being important, and certainly not valued by those people in the learner's learning environment. They are usually dismissed, in the case of the teacher, as being too subjective when important decisions are to be made about learning experiences for students.

Disempowered learners rely strongly on the theory of others and how that theory is implemented into practice by others. Thus, the how-to manuals that come with various curriculum programs in reading, writing, science, and so on, become the basis for their teaching. They tend to follow these manuals to the letter, not believing they have the knowledge or the power to challenge the authors' instructions and adapt them to suit the needs of individual students.

Thus, the disempowered learner does not operate in the fourth layer. He or she takes on board the practice of others and tries to implement this practice as either shown or written. If things do not work well, the learner blames him- or herself or, in the case of the teacher, often blames the student for not understanding. There is no room for problem solving, analytical thinking, and decision making because the disempowered learner does not value his or her beliefs and knowledge in such a way that any type of critical reflection about what others say and do can occur. Because these teachers think that what others, that is, the experts, say and do is the truth and there is a right and a wrong way to go about teaching, orthodoxies occur. A disempowered teacher/learner, therefore, is in no position to begin the process of empowering student learners. This teacher is a do-er of others' thinking. This teacher is not a thinker.

Basal reading programs have supported, if not created, thousands of disempowered teachers in classrooms. The testing procedures built into these programs operate only to reinforce the need for the disempowered teacher to adhere to the strict, linear, lock-step teaching procedures set out in many of these programs. The programs may have been written with the intention to support teachers and their students' learning but, in fact, the opposite is seen to occur (Goodman, Shannon, Freeman, & Murphy, 1988; Shannon, 1989). Much of Ken Goodman's latter work has been directed at exposing those who have worked so hard to control teachers in this way. It is my belief that the first step in moving these teachers to become empowered learners and teachers is to help them begin to value their beliefs, their gut feelings and intuitions, and to value their inner core.

THE EMPOWERED LEARNER

The empowered learner is aware of the beliefs and understandings he or she has in a particular field of knowledge, in this case, literacy learning. Empowered learners can clearly articulate these beliefs, and they value them highly to the point of almost appearing arrogant. This inner core of beliefs and knowledge is constantly being drawn on and used to think

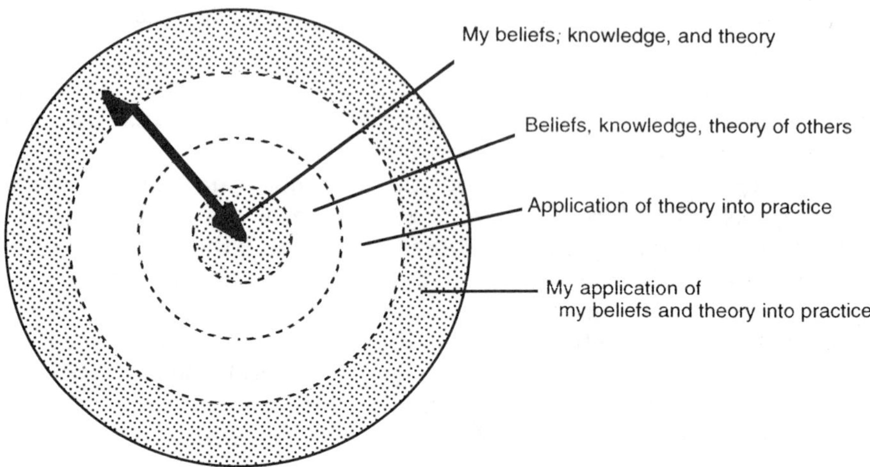

critically about, analyze, and make judgments about the theory of others being presented to them. The new theories and new knowledge often create "intellectual unrest" (Cambourne, 1988). This unrest is often uncomfortable for the learner because the new knowledge is challenging the very core of the learner—his or her existing beliefs and knowledge. The learner moves to lessen the degree of unrest by considering the information in light of his or her existing beliefs and knowledge and the application of such knowledge in his or her own context.

This interaction does not only operate between the inner core and the second layer. The learner also considers how this new knowledge is applied in practice. What do others do with the new knowledge and beliefs? What can I do with it? How can I use this new knowledge in my context? These are important considerations which the learner puts into play.

The process of interaction which comes into play across the four circles can be likened to what happens in cells in an organism. The movement of ionic particles in solutions across cells through the semi-permeable membranes is a constant dynamic process. When the pressure (turgor pressure) builds up in one cell it becomes "uncomfortable" for the cell. Movement of the solution needs to occur to decrease the turgor pressure in the cell wall. The fluid moves in a direction in which there is less pressure, thus moving toward a greater degree of congruence. In this movement to and fro, the cell moves the ions which need to be moved from one cell to another through the semi-permeable membrane (Gruelach, 1973).

This analogy helps to describe how the learner takes what he or she needs from the theory of others and the implications for practice, tries these in his or her contexts, analyses what goes on in light of the knowledge and beliefs already held in the inner core, and makes judgments about what to use from what is seen and heard as part of the inner core of beliefs and the outer layer of practices. In this sense, the learner is constantly moving toward a high degree of congruence between the beliefs that she or he holds about language and learning and the practices that occur in his or her classroom.

The empowered teacher will critically examine programs such as basal reading and after analyzing (testing) the apparent philosophy of the basal program against his or her beliefs about language and literacy learning and considering the needs of the learners in his or her care, will make decisions about the appropriateness of such materials for the learners in his or her classroom. This problem-solving process occurs because the empowered teacher not only is aware of his or her beliefs and knowledge and can clearly articulate them, but because he or she also values them highly (Cho, 1990). The empowered teacher is thus in a position to empower student learners.

Frameworks was designed with this model clearly in mind by its three authors—Turbill, Butler, and Cambourne (1991). The model is set out in the beginning session accompanied by a clear explanation of how the design and the delivery of the program underpins it. The model has since been used by teachers when planning learning experiences in their classrooms. Cambourne and I also use the model to design our Master's classes.

CONCLUDING REMARKS

In relating my story of how my paradigm about teacher learning and staff development changed and evolved over the years to the present model I hold about teacher learning and staff development, I hope that other staff developers will find it useful. Many will identify with it, and it may begin for them the process of making explicit their current beliefs about teacher learning and staff development. This story was not written as a form of navel gazing but in an attempt to make explicit my beliefs and assumptions about teacher learning and staff development. I found the process of starting at the beginning and seeing where I had come from and what had influenced my thinking very informative and empowering in itself. It is a process I highly recommend to all those who work in the field of learning, be it children's learning or teacher learning.

Educators are in the business of educating but to be successful at it we all need to examine our own belief system and understand why we do what we do. Once we can do this we are in a far more empowered position to carry out the tasks we are expected to do.

As mentioned in the beginning of this chapter, I contend that we are experiencing a paradigm shift in literacy education. Key indicators in this paradigm shift for me are evidenced in the change from:

- teachers as doers to teachers as thinkers
- teacher-centered classrooms to child-centered classrooms in which teachers realize they must understand not only what they are doing but also why they do it
- teachers-as-testers to teachers-as-observers, data collectors, researchers, and participants who understand that they need to participate in their students' learning and gather information about their students and their own classroom practices so that they can adequately respond to the needs of their students by developing relevant and authentic learning experiences

The curious thing about paradigms and paradigm shifts is that they are made both collectively and singularly at the same time. And always, there are those at the cutting edge, challenging the existing paradigm and nudging it toward change.

REFERENCES

Barth, R. (1990). *Improving schools from within*. San Francisco: Jossey-Bass.

Barton, B. (1992). *An evaluation of "teacher-as-co-researcher" as a methodology for staff development*. Unpublished master of Education thesis, University of Wollongong, Australia.

Brown, R.G. (1991). *Schools of thought: How the politics of schools shape the thinking in the classroom*. San Francisco: Jossey Bass.

Cambourne, B. (1988). *The whole story: Natural learning and the acquisition of literacy*. Auckland, New Zealand: Ashton Scholastic.

Cambourne, B. (1991). *Ideology and the literacy curriculum: The teaching of phonics*. Paper presented at the Australian Reading Conference, Adelaide.

Cambourne, B., & Turbill, J. (1989). *Secondary literacy inservice course: Coordinator's manual*. Canberra, Australia: Curriculum Development Corporation.

Cambourne, B., & Turbill, J. (1991). Teacher-as-co-researcher: How an approach to research became the methodology for staff development. In J. Turbill, A. Butler, & B. Cambourne, *Frameworks: Theory of others*. Stanley, NY: Wayne Finger-Lakes Board of Cooperative Educational Services.

Cambourne, B., Turbill, J., Keeble, P., Ferguson, B., & Colvin, R. (1988). *The report on the Evaluation of the early literacy inservice course (ELIC)*. Wollongong, NSW, Australia: University of Wollongong.

Capra, F. (1982). *The turning point*. London: Fontana Paperbacks.

Capra, F. (1988). *Uncommon wisdom*. New York: Bantam Books.

Cazden, C. (1988). *Classroom discourse:The language of teaching and learning*. Portsmouth, NH: Heinemann.

Cho, H.Y. (1990). *An examination of the relationship between teachers' beliefs in ESL education and their teaching and assessment practices in their classrooms*. Unpublished master of Education thesis, University of Wollongong, Australia.

Covey, S. (1989). *The 7 habits of highly effective people*. New York: Fireside, Simon and Schuster.

Department of Education and Science. (1975). *A language for life*. Report of the Committee of Inquiry for the Department of Education and Science under the Chairmanship of Sir Alan Bullock. London: Her Majesty's Stationary Office.

Fullan, M. (1990). Staff development, innovation, and institutional development. In B. Joyce, (Ed) *Changing school culture through staff development* (pp. 3-25). 1990 Yearbook of the Association for Supervision and Curriculum Development, Alexandria, Virginia.

Fullan, M. (1991). *The new meaning of educational change* (2nd ed.) New York: Teachers College Press.

Goodman, K. (1967). Reading: A psycholinguistic guessing game. The *Journal of the Reading Specialist*, 6(4), 126-135.

Goodman, K., Shannon, P., Freeman, Y., & Murphy, S. (1988). *Report card on basal readers*. New York: Richard C. Owen Publishers.

Goodman, Y. (1984). The development of initial literacy. In H. Goelman, A. Oberg, & F. Smith (Eds.), *Awakening to literacy* (pp. 102-109). Portsmouth, NH: Heinemann.

Graves, D. (1983). *Writing: Teachers and children at work*. Exeter, NH: Heinemann.

Gruelach, V. (1973). *Plant function and structure*. New York: Macmillan.

Guba, E., & Lincoln Y. (1981). *Effective evaluation: Improving the usefulness of evaluation results through responsive and naturalistic approaches*. San Francisco: Jossey Bass.

Halliday, M.A.K. (1980). *Three aspects of children's language development: Learning language, learning through language, learning about language.*

Paper presented in Master Education Course, Sydney University, Australia.

Holdaway, D. (1979). *The foundations of literacy*. Sydney: Ashton Scholastic.

Kemmis, S., & McTaggert, R. (1982). *The action research planner*. Geelong, Victoria, Australia: Deakin University Press.

Kuhn, T. (1970). *The structure of scientific revolutions* (2nd ed.). Chicago: University of Chicago Press.

Shannon, P. (1989). *Broken promises*. New York: Bergin and Garvey.

Turbill, J. (Ed.). (1982). *No better way to teach writing*. Rozelle, Australia: Primary English Teaching Association.

Turbill, J. (1983). *Now, we want to write!* Rozelle, Australia: Primary English Teaching Association.

Turbill, J. (1987). *The language teachers use to teach literacy in whole language classrooms*. Unpublished paper presented at the Post Graduate Colloquium, University of Wollongong, Australia.

Turbill, J. (1991). *Teachers as learners: Let's practise what we preach*. Unpublished keynote address presented at the Australian Reading Association Conference, Adelaide.

Turbill, J., Butler, A., & Cambourne, B. (1991). *Frameworks: A whole language staff development program 3-8*. Stanley, NY: Wayne Finger Lakes Board of Cooperative Services.

Chapter Twelve

The Influence of Miscue Analysis on Australian Teachers' Views of Reading

Patricia C. Long
The University of Melbourne

The purpose of this chapter is to provide some indication of developments in instruction and evaluation of children's reading in my home state of Victoria, and to report briefly on the work I have done in attempting to make miscue analysis and Ken Goodman's model of the reading process more accessible to teachers.

The 1960s and 1970s saw considerable expansion in Australian education. Postwar immigration and the baby boom filled schools to bursting and caused a serious teacher shortage. New teachers' colleges and universities were founded, and their younger, less traditionally minded staff brought fresh influences to teacher training. Teachers were also imported from the United Kingdom and the United States, and local educators were encouraged to seek experience abroad.

There was much interest in developing more student-centered approaches to reading and writing. Educational materials flowed in from Canada and the United States, but these presented problems of cultural match and cost. Happily, local writers and artists collaborated with publishers to develop materials based on Australian children's language and interests such as the *Mt. Gravatt Readers* (Thompson, 1978) for young children. The *Trend Series* paperbacks (Bird, Scanlon, Falk, &

Hart, 1968) with catchy titles like "Hey! That's My Bike!" and "Coffee at Charlie's" provided upbeat, easy-to-read books for older children who shied away from conventional school readers.

Individualized reading and creative writing programs also challenged the traditional basal reader approaches. There was a drive to publish children's writing; for example, Brian Thompson's (1966) anthology. A number of teachers began to integrate their reading and writing programs to provide more holistic approaches and some of these were also published: Among the best were Barry Carozzi's (1970) *Patchwork Paperbacks*, which included stories, poems, news items, jokes, and puzzles; and Garth Boomer's (1971) *Themes and Images*, based on a series of photographs for stimulating children's writing.

Language experience, which owed much to the work of Ashton Warner (1963), further emphasized learners' contributions to their growth in reading and writing. A popular version was *Breakthrough to Literacy* (Mackay, Thompson, & Schaub, 1970), a kit that enabled young children, with the collaboration of their teachers, to use their own language patterns and experiences to write and illustrate stories which could then be made into books for them and their peers to read. Reid's (1974) analysis of the program endorsed its holistic principles, which she considered had "certainly shown that fruitful ideas from linguistic and psycholinguistic theory can be translated into procedures which teachers can accept and use" (p. 98). Nevertheless, she believed the program promoted writing at the expense of reading. Wilson's *Write Me A Sign: About Language Experience* (1979) was a further advance because she highlighted the interrelationships of listening, reading, speaking, and writing in children's learning. She also relied on the teacher's ability to find books to suit each child's needs rather than using sets of readers.

The contribution of learners' experience and knowledge to their developing literacy was enshrined in language experience: Literacy began where the child was, and the child's ideas and means of expression were accepted, even if not error free, as links between oral and written language were established (Pigdon & Woolley, 1989).

Although the concept of the learner as a source as well as a recipient of knowledge was gaining acceptance, reading was still seen as a receptive process. It needed Goodman's (1967, 1969) model of reading as a psycholinguistic guessing game to make it clear that reading was an active process, a transaction between reader and author in which the reader used a range of cues and strategies to gain meaning from the text. His revolutionary ideas were already making considerable waves among Australian reading educators when I returned to Melbourne in 1974 after 15 years abroad, eight of them in the United States.

It was heartening to find innovative teachers encouraging their students to follow more natural and pleasant paths to literacy, but in some classrooms, advances in literacy instruction came slowly. Learning to read was still equated with recognizing individual words, either by parroting them from lists or sounding them out one by one. Once they could decipher enough words, children were given carefully graded readers to "decode." It was assumed these would be meaningful to them.

Furthermore, reading assessment in the mid-1970s had not yet caught up with emerging developments in the teaching of reading, although Australia had avoided the annual epidemics of standardized testing which exerted such a stultifying influence on reading curricula in the United States. It was disappointing in 1974 to find Victorian teachers still using measures similar to those I had encountered in conservative American schools, from where I had unfond memories of administering batteries of skills tests to children who were struggling with reading.

The majority of reading tests were imported, and local ones mostly imitated them. Commonly used measures included a jumble of word lists that often failed to match readers' needs, a battery of phonics tests, and reading comprehension tests consisting of literal questioning of collections of unrelated paragraphs. Teachers also made informal assessments of children's reading ability from hearing them read, but these tended to focus on precise identification of words and fluency of expression (Long, 1986a). In sum, reading was not being assessed holistically, as a meaningful activity in which readers engaged for a purpose, but rather as a series of fragmented skills apparently considered valuable in themselves.

There were bright spots: The GAP cloze tests (McLeod, 1965) encouraged the use of context clues for meaningful reading, and Clay's (1972/1993) *Early Detection of Reading Difficulties* contained the innovative *Concepts About Print* for assessing young children's knowledge of books. However, by far the most important advance came from Goodman's research for his psycholinguistic model of reading. His tool for this research was the *Taxonomy of Cues and Miscues in Reading*, which enabled him to discover what cues and strategies readers were using to gain meaning from print by examining their oral reading and comparing 18 categories of observed and expected responses (Goodman, 1969).

In 1972 Yetta Goodman and Carolyn Burke developed the *Reading Miscue Inventory* for assessing reading comprehension. This was a simplified form of Ken Goodman's taxonomy for analyzing oral reading, with a retelling and questioning section added. Its publication brought miscue analysis within reach of classroom teachers and exerted a major influence on the teaching of reading because it was more than just an assessment instrument. Its primary purpose was to enable teachers to gain an understanding of the reading process itself. Only when they became conversant with the model which underlay it would they be able to use miscue analysis effectively to assess children's reading ability and plan appropriate instructional strategies.

The *Reading Miscue Inventory* could provide teachers with more information from a single reading of a meaningful unit of text than any other measure available to Australian teachers, who were moving from traditional reading instruction to more holistic approaches, and, as such, it was potentially very valuable. However, it was a complex instrument and many teachers who were drawn to the Goodman model found marking, coding, and interpreting miscues a daunting task. Attempts to simplify the assessment procedures without detracting from their effectiveness were therefore made by a number of educators, including Mark Brennan from Riverina College and Barbara Johnson from the Australian Council of Educational Research.

During this period Ken and Yetta Goodman were invited to visit Australia. Ken's research, which was to have profound effects on the teaching and assessment of reading throughout the country, had already aroused considerable interest among college and classroom teachers, and the Goodmans were received with enthusiasm. At seminars and in classrooms, through interviews on radio and film, they lucidly and vigorously expounded the new model of reading and demonstrated its applications to teaching and assessment, which did much to ensure its widening acceptance.

MODIFICATIONS OF THE *READING MISCUE INVENTORY*

In 1982 I was able to spend a year studying with the Goodmans in Arizona and clarifying those aspects of the Goodman reading model which still puzzled me. That was the beginning of my research on miscue analysis, including some of the simplified versions published in the United States, Canada, the United Kingdom, and Australia.

I was seeking a modification of the *Reading Miscue Inventory* that would increase its usefulness for classroom teachers: One that would be easier to use but would nevertheless give teachers comparable insights into the reading process. My research located 15 modified forms (Long, 1986a), which can be divided into three general categories:

1. Syntheses of the Reading Miscue Inventory (RMI) and the Informal Reading Inventory (IRI),
2. Adaptations of miscue analysis for cloze procedures,

3. Simplifications of the RMI achieved by reducing the number of taxonomy questions and analytic procedures.

Syntheses of the RMI and IRI. The informal reading inventory was developed as a test of ability to read a passage aloud and answer questions about it. Scoring is based on the percentage of errors (words read inaccurately) and from this an independent, instructional, or frustration level of reading is calculated. There appears to be no empirical evidence to support these levels (Goodman, 1976). I found five attempts to synthesize the RMI and IRI: Tortelli (1976), Smith and Weaver (1978), Bean (1979), Christie (1979), and Siegal (1979). These evaluated readers' use of cues and miscues in different ways, but each had definite disadvantages and none provided evidence of field testing.

Combined Miscue Analysis and Cloze Procedure. The cloze procedure is used as a measure of readability, a teaching strategy and an assessment technique in which the reader is asked to read a passage, supplying certain words that have been deleted. Scoring consists of calculating the percentage of replacements that are exactly the same as in the original text. In the combined procedures nonexact replacements are treated as miscues and analyzed according to RMI protocol.

Five miscue analysis-cum-cloze tests were examined: Anderson (1980) and Page (1975) produced cloze tests of silent reading, and Aulls (1979) and McLean (1979) developed combined oral and silent cloze tests. Cambourne (1979) devised the self-deprecatingly entitled CRAP (Cambourne Reading Analysis Procedure), an instrument designed to measure reading comprehension utilizing a silent cloze exercise. However, Cambourne (1992) now doubts the validity of this procedure, although at the time he was "besotted with its potential" (p.11). His more recent research indicates that ineffective readers could slot in the correct word on the basis of minimal syntactic cues and word association (or even random guessing) on enough occasions to lift their scores significantly.

Simplified Forms of the RMI. Attempts have been made to simplify the RMI by reducing the number of taxonomy questions and eliminating some of the procedures without compromising its basic principles. I considered five examples: Those developed by Hood (1975-76), Griffin and Jongsma (1980), and Potter (1980) were limited in scope and did not appear to have been trialed; but two others, Brennan (1979) and Johnson (1979), were more comprehensive and had been field tested.

I finally selected the *Reading Appraisal Guide* (Johnson, 1979) for comparison with the *Reading Miscue Inventory.* The rationale and procedures were based on the Goodman model of reading and *Reading Miscue Inventory*, to which users were referred, and directions appeared to be adequate. An attempt was made to simplify the coding and scoring of miscues by reducing the categories to *Language Maintained* or *Language Lost*, *Meaning Maintained* or *Meaning Lost*, and *Self-Correction*. A retelling was followed by suggestions for modified instruction, illustrated with case studies.

MISCUE ANALYSIS 1983

I studied the effectiveness of in-depth training in miscue analysis, as reflected in the *Reading Miscue Inventory* (RMI), compared with training in the simplified form, the *Reading Appraisal Guide* (RAG), working with 20 teachers undertaking the Graduate Diploma in Special Education in Melbourne (Long, 1986a). All had taught reading at some stage and knew something of the Goodmans' work, which they associated variously with language experience, psycholinguistics, reading for meaning, and whole language. Eleven were aware of the purpose and methodology of miscue analysis in a general way, but none had used the RMI or the RAG.

To begin the study, the teachers listened to taped reading and retelling by two third graders, Tanya and Justin. The teachers each had a script of the story the children read and transcripts of their retelling and were required to write a descriptive assessment of each child's reading strategies and understanding of the story, using any method that seemed appropriate to them.

I then divided the teachers into two equal groups and gave them 16 hours of tutorial in miscue analysis, based on the procedures used by Watson (1982). One group (the RMI group) was trained in the use of the *Reading Miscue Inventory*; the other group (the RAG group) received training adapted to fit the *Reading Appraisal Guide*. After training, the teachers reassessed Tanya's and Justin's taped reading and retelling, but this time both groups of teachers were allowed to use any material related to their training in miscue analysis.

All teachers, regardless of whether they used the RMI or the RAG, were assessed for their expertise in the analysis of miscues and their ability to interpret the children's reading and suggest modifications to instruction. I also sought to gain insights into their perceptions of the reading process and the emphasis they placed on different aspects of reading behavior. Finally, I attempted to assess whether any changes had occurred in these during the two different training programs. Data for the analysis consisted of the teachers' test record sheets and descriptive assessments, my diary of group sessions and individual conferences, and recorded discussions with both groups.

Both qualitative and quantitative comparisons showed that improvements made by the RMI group were significantly greater than those made by the RAG group. Scoring in both groups was affected by marking and coding errors, but the RMI group showed a better understanding of the relative importance of the graphophonic, syntactic, and semantic systems than did the RAG group. In the final assessment four of the latter ignored graphophonic cueing, which is not coded in the RAG; both groups paid more attention to syntactic cueing, largely ignored in their initial assessments, and semantic cueing was generally well understood.

The strategies (prediction, selection, and confirmation) were in general less well handled than the cueing systems, although the RMI group showed good understanding of the importance of self-correction in the search for meaning. A few teachers in each group discussed prediction and confirmation strategies perceptively but most made only brief references to them.

Teachers in both groups handled comprehension assessment well and most made recommendations to help the children improve their reading. All emphasized the importance of reading for meaning, but overall the RMI group's strategies were superior. For example, several of the RAG group believed Tanya needed cloze exercises to improve her already competent semantic cueing. Teachers in both groups suggested some useful instructional strategies for Justin, a more hesitant reader, but some members of the RAG group wanted to improve his syntax, an area of strength, and underestimated his ability to predict meaning.

Teachers' reactions to the program were positive. Both groups expressed approval of the Goodman reading model in principle and reiterated that the study had been worthwhile because it had given them greater understanding of the reading process and better strategies for teaching and evaluating children's reading. When discussing the RMI's practical usefulness, the teachers who had used it expressed qualified approval: The time needed to complete assessments was a major concern, and several teachers found procedures complicated and were unsure of the validity of their findings.

The RAG users were able to complete their assessments more quickly but had a number of problems with their instrument. Some were unsure of the meaning of *Language Maintained/Language Lost*, and most had not noticed that scoring for syntactic and semantic cueing failed to take self-correction into account.

This study showed the *Reading Miscue Inventory* to be a better instrument than the *Reading Appraisal Guide* for two reasons: First, its manual provided clearer and more detailed instructions and examples to help subjects administer and score reading and retelling, and interpret information gained from them; second, the information provided was more clearly related to aspects of the reading process emphasized in the Goodman model of reading. In sum, the *Reading Appraisal Guide* was quicker and easier to use, but its short cuts tended to result in a less well-balanced assessment of cues and strategies, and it did not emerge as an effective alternative to the *Reading Miscue Inventory*.

Research indicates that training teachers in miscue analysis strongly affects their beliefs about reading, and this belief is borne out by the study. The teachers were well-disposed toward the Goodmans' work when they commenced the program but lacked detailed knowledge of miscue analysis and the model of reading that underlies it. Increased adherence to the Goodman model and improved understanding of reading were demonstrated as the program progressed; attention focused more on syntactic and semantic cueing, discriminating self-correction, and use of context (prediction and confirmation strategies) to gain meaning.

Miscue analysis has more subtle uses than most teachers realize. Those who have learned from its use to make in-depth assessments of reading can employ it informally in intuitive assessments. A number of educators have already drawn attention to this (Y. Goodman, 1978; Watson, 1982), and the more experienced teachers in this study were aware that they would not always need to carry out formal coding to assess various aspects of children's reading ability.

The 1983 study demonstrated that in-depth training in miscue analysis could provide teachers with a sound basis for understanding and evaluating children's literacy development. Nevertheless, despite the *Reading Miscue Inventory*'s conceptual superiority to the *Reading Appraisal Guide*, it seemed that it might benefit from further modification. The challenge remained to make miscue analysis an easier process while retaining its effectiveness as an assessment measure.

A new development made this possible. Yetta Goodman and Carolyn Burke, with the help of Dorothy Watson, decided to revise and expand the *Reading Miscue Inventory*, and in 1987 the *Reading Miscue Inventory: Alternative Procedures* was published. This version enables miscue analysis to be carried out at different levels of complexity, depending on whether the user is doing in-depth research, making a rapid, global assessment of a child's reading, or doing something in between. Alternative I is similar to the 1972 *Reading Miscue Inventory* procedures, and three progressively simpler revisions follow. In Alternatives II and III miscues are coded sentence by sentence, instead of word by word, for syntactic and semantic acceptability and meaning change. Alternative III has no score sheet because the coding and scoring are done on the marked reading transcript. Finally, there is Alternative IV, a global version for those who are highly experienced in miscue analysis and can evaluate miscues while the child is reading.

MISCUE ANALYSIS 1985

I was fortunate enough to have access to part of the revised RMI version prior to its 1987 publication because in 1985, Dorothy Watson came to Melbourne, bearing with her a draft of Alternative III. Several of its modifications appeared to make the procedures more manageable for classroom teachers: The coding of oral reading sentence by sentence, instead of word by word, meant that miscues were always seen in context; grammatical function similarity, which my teachers had found difficult, had been removed and only syntactic and semantic acceptability and meaning change were scored. Teachers could use the Alternative II score sheet for formal coding of graphophonic miscues if they needed to do so. Finally, the miscues were coded and scored and the scores totaled and percentaged on the transcript itself, a more immediate method that seemed likely to lessen the number of errors teachers made when using a separate record sheet (Long, 1987).

In order to assess the effectiveness of the draft revision I undertook a second study (Long, 1986b) comparing Alternative III (RMI III) with the Brennan Record for the Inventory of Miscues (BRIM), a modification of the *Reading Miscue Inventory* which had been influenced by Rousch and Cambourne's reading research. In the BRIM, 25 miscues are marked, and if meaning is maintained or they are corrected, they are not coded further. Nonmeaningful miscues are coded for semantic acceptability, grammatical function, and graphic and phonemic proximity. Scores are graphed to demonstrate areas of strength and weakness. Suggestions for interpretation are provided but do not include retelling, which is barely mentioned.

The second study replicated the first one as far as possible. The subjects were 16 teachers undertaking the 1985 Graduate Diploma in Special Education course and, like the previous group, they had a general idea of the Goodman model of reading and miscue analysis, but none had used the RMI or the BRIM.

I again used Tanya's and Justin's reading and retelling tapes, and the initial and final assessments were conducted in the same manner as before. For miscue analysis, one group received training in the use of the RMI III and the other in the BRIM. My evaluations of the teachers' assessments of the two children's reading and retelling were carried out as before, but this time the quantitative analysis was omitted and I rated each assessment category as A, B, C, D, or F (fail) and combined the results in a final letter grade.

Comparisons made after training indicated that the RMI III group had improved their evaluations considerably and outperformed the BRIM group. The RMI III group, who coded miscues sentence by sentence, found the process quicker and easier than the BRIM group, who were coding single miscues. Furthermore, the RMI III group, who coded and scored miscues on their transcripts, made fewer errors than the BRIM Group, who had to use separate record sheets.

There were marked differences in assessment of the cueing systems. RMI III does not score graphophonic miscues, but some of the RMI group used their 1972 handbook to code them, whereas other assessed them intuitively. Syntactic acceptability was assessed and interpreted with reasonable success by the RMI III group, but instead of syntactic acceptability, the BRIM group scored grammatical function, which teachers found difficult to code and interpret. All subjects understood the importance of semantic cueing, but whereas the RMI III teachers realized Tanya's strengths, and tended to underestimate Justin's ability, the BRIM teachers were overly critical of both of them.

The strategies of prediction and confirmation were only referred to briefly, but self-correction was well interpreted by both groups, although it is not scored in the RMI III. In the BRIM, all miscues are scored for self-correction, and the teachers consequently discussed this strategy at some length.

Retelling was competently assessed by most teachers. Because of the paucity of the BRIM's instructions in this area, I used the RMI manual for training both groups, so it is not surprising that their standards of assessment were similar. However, there were differences between the two groups' proposed modifications of reading instruction. In general, the RMI III group's recommendations were more inclined to be directed to reading for meaning. BRIM users tended to be confused by their scoring system, which led them to underestimate the children's ability and suggest unnecessary remedial strategies such as training in phonics, which Tanya did not need and Justin overused.

Both groups stated that they found the program stimulating and gained valuable information about how children read. The RMI III teachers were pleased with their instrument, despite having to work from a draft manuscript and the 1972 RMI manual, and they completed assessments more quickly and easily than the 1983 RMI teachers. The BRIM teachers found directions in their manual "pretty scrappy," especially for the retelling. Some suggested that all miscues should be fully coded and not just the unacceptable ones, as this led them to underestimate readers' ability. They had mixed feelings about the graph for showing readers' performance levels and pointed out that no rationale was provided for it.

The results of this study indicated that the RMI III was a superior instrument to the BRIM. It also appeared to be more accessible than its predecessor, the RMI, and to provide equally valid information about children's reading ability, as well as increasing teachers' understanding and acceptance of the Goodman model of reading. It therefore seemed to possess the qualities that the authors of some of the earlier adaptations were seeking (Long, 1987).

From this time onward I used the Alternative III procedures successfully in my graduate and undergraduate classes in literacy. Working with these students enabled me to compare the effects of training in miscue analysis on the attitudes to reading of both experienced graduates and trainee teachers during a period in which the teaching and assessment of reading were becoming increasingly holistic.

MISCUE ANALYSIS 1993

In 1993, as part of a team, I taught literacy classes for second year B.Ed. (Primary) students. The syllabus was based on whole language principles and practice, emphasizing teacher-pupil collaboration, integration of the four language areas, and a literature-based approach to reading and writing. Each student undertook a child study with a primary school pupil in which the student and pupil developed reading and writing portfolios of the pupil's work, and the student kept a journal of observations of and interactions with the pupil. These, together with a miscue analysis of the child's reading, provided the basis for a final evaluation of the pupil's progress throughout the year.

The students were limited to two 2-hour training sessions in miscue analysis, using Alternative III of the 1987 revision of the *Reading Miscue Inventory*, after which they used the instrument to carry out assessments of their pupils' reading and retelling. I evaluated the assessments and conferred with individual students who needed to do some revision. In a third session we discussed the miscue analysis and retelling procedures and how they informed reading evaluation and instruction; I also sought students' opinions of the usefulness of Alternative III and the training they had been given.

Marking and coding of miscues seemed to present few difficulties. Use of the cueing systems was well assessed: In my previous studies syntactic cueing had been difficult for some teachers, but not for these students, probably because of their language studies in the previous year. Of the strategies, self-correction was well understood. Prediction and confirmation were specifically discussed only by the most competent students, but others used terms such as "made good guesses," "tried to work out what came next," and "knew when it made sense." The retelling was adequately assessed, although discussions and questioning indicated a need for further practice. Recommendations for modifying instruction were limited because most students were concentrating on assessment techniques rather than thinking ahead to teaching, but individual conferences helped them improve their performances. Their final submissions were all satisfactory and some were very good.

In our discussions the students indicated that they were comfortable with the Goodman model of reading, and they agreed that the information gained from interaction with their pupils, the portfolios, and miscue analyses provided a good basis for assessing growth in literacy. Considering their limited experience and the short time allowed for training, their results and feedback were pleasing but not unexpected.

The teachers in the 1983 and 1985 studies were all trained at least 20 years ago and had learned to read long before whole language evolved from Ken Goodman's psycholinguistic model of the reading process. They had to learn both the underlying concepts of miscue analysis as well as the procedures, a strenuous process that required them to unload part, and sometimes a considerable amount, of what they had been taught. The 1993 class had it easier: Most of their schooling occurred during a period in which literacy instruction and assessment were becoming increasingly holistic, and their preservice teacher training in language and literacy was strongly oriented toward whole language. Because they were already familiar with the underlying principles, the practice of miscue analysis followed naturally.

Over the last 20 years a major part of my work has been concerned with training teachers in reading instruction and evaluation and, in doing so, promoting the Goodman model of reading and the *Reading Miscue Inventory*. This has led to research on how the RMI could be made more "user friendly" while retaining its effectiveness. The positive reactions I have had from teachers and would-be teachers have repeatedly demonstrated that training in the Goodman model of reading and miscue analysis influences teachers' beliefs about reading and encourages them to put those beliefs into practice, whether they subsequently apply miscue analysis techniques formally or intuitively.

FUTURE TRENDS

Innovation, informed by particular beliefs about language and literacy, is nowhere more evident than in the assessment of children's growth in reading. In fact, assessment has gradually caught up with instruction by moving away from externally designed tests that measure children's skills against norms and toward holistic, informal classroom assessment (Bouffler, 1992; Cambourne & Turbill, 1990; Daley, 1989).

Read and Retell (Brown & Cambourne, 1987) is a popular example of such in-depth, ongoing evaluation. Developed from the retelling procedure in the *Reading Miscue Inventory* for "something called a whole language/natural learning classroom" (p. 12), it can be used to assess oral or silent reading through speaking, writing, and/or drawing. The procedures become part of a range of ongoing classroom activities which include multiple reading of texts around a central theme and sharing and comparing of retelling. This allows teachers to observe and interact with their pupils as they evaluate their ability to express ideas without interrupting the learning process.

Ken Goodman (1989) believes classroom evaluation should respect both teachers and learners. He urges teachers to become "constant kidwatchers," employing natural language in authentic contexts in ongoing classroom activities and using the knowledge gained to plan and modify programs to provide supportive learning environments that promote literacy growth. Instead of relying on periodic tests, "whole language teachers have pupils fill portfolios with their own writing, records of their reading experiences, and examples of other learning activities" (Goodman, 1986, p. 42).

Many Australian educators (Derewianka, 1992; March & Burke, 1992; Ward, 1992) have also come to regard collections of learners' work, compiled in portfolios, as primary sources of information for evaluation. This fits comfortably with whole language principles, provided that the material is part of student-centered, ongoing classroom activities, and the teachers who compile the portfolios are competent to select and evaluate them (Rivilland, 1992). To do this, teachers must have a sound knowledge not only of the reading process but of in-depth assessment, for which miscue analysis and retelling are still the best available guides. Regrettably, some teachers have been led to believe that less in-depth measures such as running records or their own unguided intuition are all they will ever need.

Ken Goodman's model of reading and whole language are now part of our educational landscape, to which anyone with a sufficiently wide experience of Australian classrooms can attest. Australian professional associations and publishers concerned with reading continue to disseminate the work of whole language teachers and researchers, and there has been strong support from education authorities such as the Victorian Ministry of Education, whose "English Language Frameworks" (Ministry of Education, 1988) have stressed the benefits of whole language principles in the teaching of literacy. Recently, a TAWL (Teachers Applying Whole Language) teachers group was set up in Victoria: It already has representatives in all states and a national Whole Language Umbrella conference was convened in 1996.

However, despite progress in the instruction and evaluation of children's reading, there is no cause for complacency. In 1979, Holdaway warned of authority figures who attempt to dominate teachers and programs and who respond to educational innovations with demands to "go back to basics" (p. 189). In present times there are renewed calls, particularly from conservative state governments, to sound the retreat: To "reinstate the three Rs" (return to traditional styles of teaching reading) and "make teachers accountable for raising children's literacy standards" (introduce statewide standardized testing of reading). Educators must resist these retrograde demands so that advances in the instruction and evaluation of children's reading continue to gain momentum, and enlightened teachers are not hampered by bureaucratic straitjackets in their efforts to meet readers' needs.

REFERENCES

Anderson, J. (1980). *New miscue analysis: A tool for comprehending reading.* Urbana, IL: ERIC (ED198516).

Ashton Warner, S. (1963). *Teacher.* New York: Simon & Schuster.

Aulls, N.W. (1979). A *framework for interpreting silent and oral reading.* Urbana, IL: ERIC (ED 189594).

Bean, T. W. (1979). The miscue mini-form: Refining the informal reading inventory. *Reading World, 18,* 41-45.

Bird, B., Scanlon, A., Falk, I., & Hart, J. (Eds.). (1968). *Trend books.* Melbourne: Cheshire.

Boomer, G. (1971). *Themes and images.* Adelaide: Balara Books.

Bouffler, C. (1992). *Literacy evaluation: Issues and practicalities.* Newton, NSW: PETA.

Brennan, M. (1979). *Brennan record for the interpretation of miscues.* Wagga Wagga, NSW: Riverina College of Advanced Education.

Brown, H., & Cambourne, B. (1987). *Read and retell.* North Ryde, NSW: Methuen.

Cambourne, B. (1979). *Some psycholinguistic dimensions of the silent reading process: A pilot study.* Paper presented at the Australian Reading Conference, Melbourne, 1977. Urbana, IL: ERIC (165087).

Cambourne, B. (1992). Testing times for literacy. *The Australian Journal of Language and Literacy, 15*(4), 261-272.

Cambourne, B., & Turbill, J. (1990). Assessment in whole language classrooms: Theory into practice. *The Elementary School Journal, 90*(3), 337-349.

Carozzi, B. (Ed.). (1970). *Patchwork paperbacks*. London: Cassell.

Christie, J. (1979). Qualitative analysis system: Updating the IRI. *Reading World, 18*, 393-399.

Clay, M. (1993). *The early detection of reading difficulties*. Auckland, New Zealand: Heinemann.(Original work published 1972)

Daley, E. (Ed.). (1989). *Monitoring children's language development*. Melbourne: Australian Reading Association.

Derewianka, B. (1992). *Language assessment in primary classrooms*. Marrackville, NSW: Harcourt Brace Jovanovich.

Goodman, K. (1967). Reading: A psycholinguistic guessing game. *Journal of the Reading Specialist, 6*, 126-135.

Goodman, K. (1969). Analysis of oral reading: Applied psycholinguistics. *Reading Research Quarterly, 5*, 9-30.

Goodman, K. (1982). What we know about reading. In F. Gollasch (Ed.), *The selected writings of Kenneth S. Goodman (Vol. 1)*. Boston: Routledge & Kegan Paul.

Goodman, K. (1986). *What's whole in whole language?* Richmond Hill, Ontario: Scholastic.

Goodman, K. (1989). Preface. In K. Goodman, Y. Goodman, & W. Hood, *The whole language evaluation book*. Portsmouth, NH: Heinemann.

Goodman, Y. (1978). Kidwatching: An alternative to testing. *Journal of National Elementary Principals, 57*(4), 41-45.

Goodman, Y., & Burke, C. (1972). *Reading miscue inventory manual*. London: Macmillan.

Goodman, Y., Watson, D., & Burke, C. (1987). *The reading miscue inventory: Alternative procedures*. Katonah, NY: Richard C. Owen Publishers.

Griffin, M., & Jongsma, K. (1980). *Adaptation of retelling: Two variations on a theme*. Urbana, IL: ERIC (ED 190 984).

Holdaway, D. (1979). *Foundations of literacy*. Gosford, NSW: Ashton Scholastic.

Hood, J. (1975-76). Qualitative analysis of oral reading errors: The interjudge reliability of scores. *Reading Research Quarterly, 11*, 577-598.

Johnson, B. (1979). *The reading appraisal guide*. Melbourne: Australian Council of Educational Research.

Long, P. (1986a). *The effectiveness of reading miscue instruments*. Program in Language and Literacy, University of Arizona, Tucson.

Long, P. (1986b). *Matching teaching and assessment models in reading: New directions in miscue analysis.* Paper presented at the Australian Reading Association National Conference, Adelaide.

Long, P. (1987). The Reading Miscue Inventory: Alternative procedures. *Australian Journal of Special Education, 11*(2), 43-44.

Mackay, D., Thompson, B., & Schaub, P. (1970). *Breakthrough to literacy.* London: Longmans.

March, B., & Burke, J. (1992). A whole school approach to literacy. *Australian Journal of Language & Literacy, 15*(1), 7-26.

McLean, N. (1979). *A framework for the qualitative analysis of oral and silent reading.* Urbana, IL: ERIC.

McLeod, J. (1965). *GAP reading comprehension.* Melbourne: Heinemann.

Ministry of Education. (1988). *The English language frameworks.* Melbourne: Ministry of Education.

Page, W.D. (1975). The post-oral reading cloze test. *Journal of Reading Behaviour, 7,* 383-390.

Pigdon, K., & Woolley, M. (1989). Continuity and change: The development of holistic approaches to language and learning. *Australian Journal of Reading, 12*(1), 57-61.

Potter, F. (1980). Miscue analysis: A cautionary note. *Journal of Research in Reading, 3*(2), 116-128.

Reid, J.F. (1974). *Breakthrough in action.* London: Longmans.

Rivilland, J. (1992). Building profiles. In B. Derewianka, *Language assessment in primary classrooms.* Marrickville, NSW: Harcourt Brace Jovanovich.

Siegal, F. (1979). Adapted miscue analysis. *Reading World, 19,* 37-43.

Smith, L., & Weaver, C. (1978). A psycholinguistic look at the informal reading inventory: A rationale and an easy method. *Reading Horizons, 19,* 13-22.

Thompson, B. (1966). *Once around the sun: An anthology of poetry by Australian children.* Melbourne: Oxford University Press.

Thompson, G. (Ed.). (1978). *Mt. Gravatt readers.* Sydney: Addison Wesley.

Tortelli, J. (1976). Simplified psycholinguistic diagnosis. *The Reading Teacher, 28,* 637-640.

Ward, G. (1992). Observing progress in early reading in schools. *Australian Journal of Language & Literacy, 15*(3), 211-224.

Watson, D. (1982). *Training in miscue analysis.* Tucson: University of Arizona Press.

Wilson, L. (1979). *Write me a sign: About language experience.* Melbourne: Thomas Nelson.

Chapter Thirteen

Bridging the Gap: Bringing Whole Language to ESL and Bringing ESL to Whole Language

David E. Freeman
Yvonne S. Freeman
Fresno Pacific University

INTRODUCTION—FROM FAR AFIELD

Maybe it was because we came directly from Mexico to study ways of teaching English as a second language (ESL) that we were able to spend two years at the University of Arizona without the slightest idea of who Ken Goodman was. In our third year, however, when Yvonne began to look into a doctoral program in bilingual education, she was told that no such program existed, but that she should talk to Ken and Yetta Goodman if she wanted to do advanced study in language learning. That Fall she enrolled in the Program in Language and Literacy and began her coursework. The following spring, because it fit into David's linguistics program and Yvonne's language and literacy program, we both took our first course with Ken Goodman, a seminar on language learning.

In the first class meeting, Goodman touched a responsive cord with a theme that related directly to us. He lamented the fact that most scholars specialize in one field. He pointed out that specialists do not talk to one another across disciplines. Linguists seldom talk with sociologists, psychologists, or anthropologists, let alone educators. Yet scholars from all these fields are interested in how people develop language and literacy, and research in any one field has implications for the other areas. Goodman encouraged us to read from different fields and to engage in cross-disciplinary research as a way to bridge the gaps among the different disciplines.

During the seminar we wrote our first joint paper on the topic of whole language and teaching a second language. That paper was the beginning for us of an ongoing effort to bridge the gap between whole language and ESL and to encourage the specialists in those different fields to begin talking to one another. Eventually we wrote our first book on this topic, (Y. S. Freeman & D. E. Freeman, 1992a).

Both of us wrote cross-disciplinary doctoral theses under Goodman's direction. David took his degree in linguistics and wrote about reading miscue analysis. Yvonne's dissertation on Spanish reading materials became part of a book she co-authored with Goodman, Pat Shannon, and Sharon Murphy on basal readers (Goodman, Shannon, Freeman, & Murphy, 1988) and her chapter in the follow-up book (Y. S. Freeman, 1993). In both cases, Goodman encouraged us to bridge the gap and to try to bring specialists from different fields together.

Ken and Yetta Goodman had always been interested in cross-cultural and cross-linguistic issues. They did an extensive miscue study that included eight populations of speakers of other languages and other dialects. They worked with Barbara Flores to produce a book on reading for bilingual students (Goodman, Goodman, & Flores, 1979). We also learned from them about the writings of other Goodman-influenced scholars working in the area of second language and bilingual education from a holistic perspective including Rosalinda Barrera, Lois Bird, Mark Clark, Carole Edelsky, Sara Hudelson, Pat Rigg, Aurelia de Silva, and Catherine Wallace.

In our studies with the Goodmans, we began to reflect on our experiences of teaching ESL in the United States and Latin America and on our earlier ESL studies at Arizona. Our Master's work in ESL showed us the importance of moving away from traditional, behavioristic, audiolingual approaches to teaching language and toward a more communicative approach. Several of Ken Goodman's ideas, however, helped push us beyond even the newer methods we had studied in second language teaching.

After we graduated and began our work in California at Fresno Pacific University, our focus shifted somewhat. While we continued to work with ESL and bilingual teachers, attempting to help them implement more holistic practices, we also began to work with mainstream teachers who suddenly found their classes filling with students who did not speak English as their first language. These teachers were overwhelmed by a changing population of English language learners. In California alone, the number of second language students rose from around 380,000 in 1980 to 861,500 in 1990. In 1997, the number topped 1.3 million students in classes K-12.

Many of these mainstream teachers knew about whole language and were successfully implementing effective curriculum. However, few of them knew much about bilingual education, second language acquisition, cross-cultural factors, linguistics, or methods of teaching a second language. For these teachers, it was extremely difficult to implement a student-centered approach for second language students without knowledge of second language issues. Our focus for those teachers, then, shifted to trying to introduce ideas about ESL and bilingual education to whole language teachers. In particular, we focused on building awareness of how second language students are labeled and evaluated and on how teacher attitudes toward language minority students play a crucial role in their academic performance (Y. S. Freeman & D. E. Freeman, 1990, 1992b, 1992c; D. E. Freeman & Y. S. Freeman, 1994).

Goodman had prepared us well to work in cross-disciplinary areas with a wide variety of teachers. He had supported us as we learned about sociopsycholinguistics and tried to apply these new ideas to second language learning and teaching. In addition, he always had insisted that theory had to be practical and that the best practice was always theoretical. We quickly realized that we had to help both the mainstream teachers and the ESL and bilingual teachers who faced daily classroom challenges by presenting practical theory. We began to collect examples of successful practices from the talented teachers we worked with as they conducted case studies and tried out practices such as portfolio assessment. We then used these examples to illustrate the whole language principles we were developing. These classroom scenarios helped teachers visualize alternatives so that they could then implement more effective practices (D. E. Freeman & Y. S. Freeman, 1990).

Maybe it was because we had come directly from Mexico to Arizona that we did not know about Goodman and his work. Since we began to study with Goodman, however, wherever we have been—in California, Mexico, or South America—we have tried to share Goodman's ideas with teachers. And each time we share these ideas, we come to understand them more clearly. We came to Tucson from far afield, but now we see more clearly how right Goodman was in stressing that specialists from different fields need to talk with one another to bridge the gaps that separate their specialized worlds.

MAKING LEARNING EASY

As we have reflected on our own work over the last 12 years for this chapter, it has become increasingly clear to us just how much influence Goodman has had. Much of our writing has centered around a series of principles we feel are important for teachers working with second language students. In the sections that follow we draw parallels between our work and Goodman's by showing similarities between our principles for second language teaching and learning and Goodman's list of when learning is easy and when it is hard (Goodman, 1986). We have taken six of the items from his list and applied them to teaching and learning a second language:

EASY WHEN	HARD WHEN
1. It's whole	1. It's broken into bits
2. It's real and natural	2. It's artificial
3. It's relevant	3. It's irrelevant to the learner
4. It's part of a real event	4. It's out of context
5. It has social utility	5. It has no social value
6. The learner has power to use it	6. The learner is powerless

As we considered methods and materials that were commonly being used in second language teaching, we found that many of them landed squarely on the "HARD WHEN" side of Goodman's chart. It is no wonder, then, that people have trouble learning a new language. Through our work with both mainstream and ESL/bilingual teachers, we developed a series of principles for making second language learning easy. Like Goodman, we contrasted these principles with common sense assumptions that we feel make learning hard (Y. S. Freeman & D. E. Freeman, 1992a). Our principles include the following:

Whole Language Principle	Common Sense Assumption
1. Learning proceeds from whole to part.	1. Learning proceeds from part to whole.
2. Lessons should be learner centered because learning is the active construction of knowledge by the student.	2. Lessons should be teacher centered because learning is the transfer of knowledge from the teacher to the student.
3. Lessons should have meaning and purpose for students now.	3. Lessons should prepare students to function in society after schooling.

4. Learning takes place as groups engage in meaningful social interaction.	4. Learning takes place as individuals practice skills and form habits.
5. In a second language, oral and written language are acquired simultaneously.	5. In a second language, oral language acquisition precedes the development of literacy.
6. Learning should take place in the first language to build concepts and facilitate the acquisition of English.	6. Learning should take place in English to facilitate the acquisition of English.
7. Learning potential is expanded through faith in the learner.	7. The learning potential of bilingual students is limited.

Clearly, there are parallels between Goodman's list and ours. In the next section we outline these similarities. They show how we have modified and applied Goodman's ideas to second language teaching and learning.

KEEPING LEARNING WHOLE: TEACHING WHOLE TO PART AND USING ALL POSSIBLE MODALITIES

Goodman begins by saying that learning is easy when language is kept whole and hard when it is fragmented. Most second language teaching methods present language one piece at a time. Someone, usually a linguist, has dissected the language. Many books for teaching a second language use linguistic analysis and feature one aspect of language in each lesson. For example, a typical ESL lesson would focus on the present tense of regular verbs. It would open with a dialog on daily routines to practice present tense and time expressions. ("I get up at 7:00. I get dressed at 7:15. I eat breakfast at 7:30.") If the class is progressive, the lesson might include a chant or a song, but the focus would be on some specific part of the language such as days of the week or parts of the body. In lessons such as these, teachers and textbook writers have taken the language apart hoping to simplify things for second language learners. That leaves students with the difficult job of putting the language back together again.

Sometimes, however, the fragmentation of the language is not entirely the fault of the teachers or the texts. Because of their past schooling experiences, some ESL students believe that the only way to learn English is to master the parts. When they were asked to read a complete text, our advanced international students in Arizona would look up a great many words in their dictionaries. They read so slowly that by the time they finished a page, they had no idea what they had read. They were so focused on the parts that they had difficulty constructing meaning from texts. We talked with them about the importance of getting the big picture, of reading for meaning, and of making and confirming predictions. We found that even those students who had effective reading strategies in their first language did not transfer them to a second language. They fragmented reading and needed encouragement to adopt a more effective and efficient approach to English.

As we began to work with ESL teachers and mainstream teachers of second language students, we developed the principle that learning goes whole to part, not part to whole, following Goodman's point that language is easier to learn when it is kept whole. We pointed out that second language students need the big picture first, perhaps in the form of a preview of the lesson in their first language. If they focus on the whole, they will eventually begin to discern the parts. Rather than trying to simplify their task by taking the language apart for them and teaching grammar or by using simplified texts, teachers should allow students to make sense out of the whole language.

Another way to fragment language is by following a "natural" sequence of teaching to organize ESL courses. First students listen, then they speak, later they read, and finally they write. In many ESL programs there are separate classes for each of the four areas. David remembers being assigned to teach a listening course for Japanese college students. These students had separate speaking, reading, and writing classes at different times of the day. This sort of fragmentation of curriculum is typical. After all, the reasoning goes, babies follow this same sequence and develop oral language before developing literacy. The logic of following this sequence ignores important differences between babies acquiring their first language and adults or school-age English language learners. Babies do not need written language to communicate at first, but older learners, especially in a print-rich society, do need to use written language to function effectively.

With this in mind, we extended Goodman's notion that learning is easier when language is kept whole with our fifth principle: Teachers should use all four modes and not delay literacy until after students develop oral language. Second language learners need to read and write whole stories and talk about them. They need to read, write, and discuss as they study concepts and attempt to answer big questions. Rather than fragmenting language by separating the modalities, we propose that language teachers involve students in activities that enable them to develop oral and written language simultaneously.

KEEPING LEARNING REAL: MAKING LESSONS LEARNER-CENTERED

A second point on Goodman's list—that learning is easier when it is real and natural and hard when it is artificial—again made us look at typical ESL methods and materials. Many language teaching texts look like basal readers. The language they present is far from the real world of use. Most dialogues, for example, are artificial and designed to teach a particular point of grammar. Consequently, no native speaker really says one of those dialogue lines. Yvonne remembers having high school students change "A mi no me gustan las albondigas" (I don't like meatballs) to statements like "A mi no me gustan las hamburguesas con cebolla" (I don't like hamburgers with onion) in an attempt to salvage a dialogue in the textbook that was mandated when she started teaching Spanish. She recognized instinctively the truth of Goodman's second point, "Learning is easy when it's real." But, substituting "hamburgers with onions" for "meatballs" was not really enough to remedy the problem. What was needed was a whole new orientation toward teaching, learning, language, and curriculum.

The principle that we developed which parallels Goodman's is that lessons should be learner centered because learning is the active construction of knowledge by the student. We contrasted this principle with the common sense assumption that lessons should be teacher centered because learning involves a transfer of knowledge from the teacher to the students. In most ESL situations, the teacher knows English and the students do not, so the logical approach is for the teacher to try to transmit this knowledge to the students, usually by having them imitate and repeat.

With a learner-centered approach, classroom language has a greater potential for being real for students. When Yvonne encouraged students to change meatballs to hamburgers with onions, she was attempting to make the dialogue more real by connecting it with her students' lives. Most of the dialogues and exercises in language texts seem artificial because they are so far away from the lives of the students reading them. Of course, the materials are written by people who do not know the students, so this result is not surprising. Real language is the language that connects with the interests, experiences, and needs of individual students. It is hard for students to learn dialogues about meatballs, especially if they do not eat meatballs at home. It is even hard for them to learn terms like "brother" and "sister" if those terms are presented in a lesson about Mr. and Mrs. Brown and their ideal suburban family, especially when students are living in a crowded apartment complex with an extended family that in no way resembles

Mr. and Mrs. Brown's. When lessons are learner centered, the language naturally becomes more real.

Further, a learner-centered approach acknowledges that language is constructed by individuals through a process that the Goodmans have explained as personal invention shaped by social convention (Goodman & Goodman, 1990). Acquisition is a psychological process that occurs in a social context. If students are only involved with artificial pieces of language, they seem to have a great deal of trouble with the construction process. When the use of the second language is real, students acquire language naturally as they use it for real purposes and "invent" forms that are understood by those in their social group. When their new language "inventions" are not understood, students revise their language to follow social convention to communicate successfully.

As we looked at different methods of teaching a second language, we found that not all involve inauthentic language. Widdowson (1978), for example, distinguishes between usage (study of rules of language) and use (actually using language for various purposes) and argues that second language teaching methods should emphasize use over usage. One way to do this, according to Widdowson, is to teach language through academic content. When the focus is on using language to learn history or science, for example, the uses of language become more real and natural. If students learning English need to learn certain academic content, then content-based lessons are also more learner-centered.

Problem Posing (Freire, 1970; Wallerstein, 1987) is another student-centered approach to teaching language. It involves students in identifying concerns and developing the language needed to solve the problems they "pose" or raise. For example, adult ESL students might raise the problem of inadequate housing. In the process of discussing this problem and generating possible solutions, students would develop the language they need for that particular context.

As we work with teachers, we encourage them to follow Goodman's idea that learning is easier when it is real and natural by suggesting they try teaching language through academic content or a method like Problem Posing. We want teachers to emphasize real use over artificial usage. Both mainstream and ESL teachers have found that their students learn both language and content better when it is connected more closely with their lives and needs and, thus, is more real and natural.

KEEPING LEARNING RELEVANT: ENSURING THAT LESSONS HAVE MEANING AND PURPOSE FOR STUDENTS NOW

In his hard and easy list, Goodman points out that learning is easier when it is relevant. This idea is reflected in a principle we often write about, "Lessons should have meaning and purpose for students now." When language is fragmented and artificial, it seldom is relevant. The language in many ESL lessons is almost completely irrelevant. Often, second language students learn little during class. Meanwhile they learn many useful phrases and expressions from their English-speaking friends outside school. Goodman's idea that learning should be as easy inside school as it is outside, certainly applies here. If lessons are relevant they serve students' immediate purposes.

Many ESL classes we have observed involve students in irrelevant learning because the lessons are future oriented. We have seen teachers trying to help students develop the vocabulary and grammatical structures they will (perhaps) need later in mainstream content classes. Further, many teachers stress oral language development as a prerequisite to reading. In both cases, the activities are carried out with the idea that what students do today will help them in the future. We have encouraged these teachers to teach language through content and to involve students with reading and writing from the beginning so that lessons meet students' immediate needs. In fact, we have suggested that ESL teachers adopt many of the practices of mainstream whole language teachers to make the curriculum more meaningful. These practices include using process writing, reading complete texts to and with students, organizing curriculum around theme cycles (Edelsky, Altwerger, & Flores, 1991), and having students investigate content areas by attempting to answer important questions.

At the same time, we have encouraged mainstream teachers who follow holistic practices to ensure that the curriculum is relevant to all their students. This involves being sure that students can understand the lessons, or in Krashen's terms, being sure that the input is comprehensible (Krashen, 1982). In addition, it means extending traditional curriculum to build on the students' cultural backgrounds. When students can make personal connections to what is being taught, learning naturally has more meaning and purpose for them.

KEEPING LEARNING IN THE CONTEXT OF REAL EVENTS

In his list, Goodman also explained that learning is easier when it is part of a real event and harder when it is out of context. This point relates to the previous three because language is kept in the context of a real event when it is whole, real, and relevant. Context is particularly important for students learning another language. Our first three principles, that lessons should go whole to part, be learner-centered, and be meaningful, are all attempts to keep language in the context of authentic use. In addition, our critique of most ESL methods is that they fragment language and present it out of context. Teaching language through content or through methods like Problem Posing helps keep language in context.

We have encouraged teachers to enrich the context for their second language students. One way to do this is by using students' first languages. However, many methods of teaching second language students stress that students must be taught in English to learn English. Although it is true that in the English as a foreign language setting the emphasis must be on using English in the classroom, an English-only approach in a setting where English is the dominant language is logical but not supported by research. In effect, teaching a non-English speaker wholly in English presents language and concepts out of context. If, as Cummins (1981) argues, a common proficiency underlies the languages we speak, then what we learn in one language will transfer to a second language. By teaching students in their first languages, we keep learning in context.

We have written about ways to enrich the context. We suggested that even when teachers cannot speak all their students' languages they can support them by bringing in human resources including parents, paraprofessionals, and older students; they can encourage students to respond in their first language to content taught in English; they can promote students' first language writing; they can supply the classroom with print resources in the first language; and they may even find primary language videos for their second language students (D. E. Freeman & Y. S. Freeman, 1993). In all these ways, teachers keep language and learning in a meaningful context for second language students.

Even when teachers present concepts in English to students who do not speak English, they should be aware of the importance of context. Again, Cummins' (1981) work has been helpful. He points out that language can be seen as context embedded or context reduced. If teachers embed a new language in a rich, nonlinguistic context by using gestures, pictures, objects, and so on, they make learning easier. If teachers use predictable books and have students write complete stories, they also embed language in context. If teachers can preview and review the content in the students' first language, they provide context. Learning is not made easier by simplifying language. Instead, it is made easier by enriching the context (K.S. Goodman & D.E. Freeman, 1993).

KEEPING LEARNING SOCIALLY USEFUL: ENGAGING STUDENTS IN SOCIAL INTERACTION

The fifth point Goodman makes is that learning is easier when it has social utility. This idea connects with Goodman's notion that learning is a process of personal invention and social convention. When learning occurs in a social context, personal inventions are naturally shaped by social conventions. Language that has social utility is whole, real, relevant, and part of a real event.

We have developed a parallel idea: Lessons should engage students in meaningful social interaction. We have observed many ESL classes in which students practice language in isolation. This is particularly true in language labs. Students listen through headphones and repeat words and phrases rather than interacting with other speakers of the language they are learning. More recently, we have seen many computer programs designed to teach language, but these programs serve to isolate students. Often, in mainstream classes with only a few second language students, teachers seat their English learners in front of a computer off in a corner. Computers are wonderful for endless, repetitive drill (Smith, 1986). They are not so good for meaningful interaction, although some creative teachers have had very good results having students work collaboratively on computers as they compose stories.

It would seem natural for second language teachers to involve students in social interaction. After all, the goal of such classes is to help students develop communicative competence. Some ESL methods involve students in activities such as dialogues and role play. However, if the language in those activities is artificial and irrelevant, students do not develop the language they need for meaningful social interactions. This was certainly the case for Yvonne's students who were learning to express their opinions about meatballs.

The problem in most ESL classes is that the teacher is the only native speaker, so students sit in straight rows and answer the teacher one at a time. Some teachers fear that putting second language students in groups will cause them to learn bad habits from one another. In mainstream classes with a few second language speakers, some teachers are hesitant to mix native and non-native speakers in small groups. Even during collaborative activities, language-minority students may be isolated from others.

As we have worked with teachers, we have suggested teaching language through content and methods like Problem Posing because then, language has social utility. Further, we have encouraged ESL teachers to use activities like shared book reading, peer conferencing for writing, and small group investigations of content area questions. In addition, we have encouraged mainstream teachers to establish pen pals for their second language students and to set up peer tutoring programs because all these activities help their students use language naturally in social interaction.

KEEPING LEARNERS EMPOWERED: HAVING FAITH IN THE LEARNER

Goodman's final point is that learning is easy when students have the power to use what they are learning and hard when they are powerless. Teachers can keep students powerless by presenting language that is fragmented, artificial, irrelevant, and out of context. In such situations, students may be so busy learning nonsense that they never develop the language proficiency they need to succeed in school. On the other hand, when language is whole, real, relevant, and socially useful, students can develop the proficiency they need.

The principle that we have developed that parallels Goodman's final point is that teachers should have faith in their students. We contrast this with the common sense assumption that the potential of bilingual students is limited. Teachers who have faith in their students reject labels, such as Limited English Proficient, for their students. They also find ways to build on learners' strengths, including their primary languages and cultures, to engage them in meaningful learning. As teachers show faith in their students, they help them develop faith in themselves. As Goodman (1991) has written, students need to revalue themselves. This is particularly true for language minority students who are struggling to succeed in a new language and culture. They may perceive themselves as failures unless teachers adopt positive attitudes along with methods that promote students' academic and social success (Y.S. Freeman & Y.M. Goodman, 1993).

If Goodman's point that learning is easy when learners have power holds true for native English-speaking students, it applies even more strongly for students learning English as another language. These students are moving between two worlds, and if they are ever to assume power in the English-speaking world, they must have an empowering curriculum. One issue that is central to empowerment for English learners is the use of their native language. In schools in which students' first languages are prohibited and use of the primary language may be punishable, many students are rendered powerless. An insistence that students can only learn English by being forced to use English flies in the face of research evidence in the area of bilingual education and succeeds in ensuring that second language students become second class citizens.

Questions regarding use of students' first language are part of the larger issue of teacher attitude. Cummins (1989) has contrasted two orientations or sets of attitudes that teachers may develop. One of these, the Anglo conformatory orientation, sees students' first languages and cultures as handicaps or hindrances to their learning English; views the involvement of minority group community members in schools as undesirable; adopts transmission style pedagogy; and engages in assessment that serves to legitimize differences between majority and minority group members. The result of the Anglo conformity orientation is to render language minority students powerless by maintaining the status quo.

If, on the other hand, teachers adopt what Cummins calls an intercultural orientation, they view students' first languages and cultures as a valuable resource to build on; encourage minority group community participation in schools; adopt interactive, experiential pedagogical methods; and use assessment techniques, such as portfolios, that show what students have learned and what they can do.

Evaluation is a critical issue when it comes to showing faith in learners and giving them the power to use what they are learning. Collier's (1989) research has shown that it takes students who are learning English at least five years to approach national norms on standardized content area tests given in English. Five years is a minimum, and during that time students can become discouraged and lose faith in themselves. Students who do poorly on standardized tests often receive an impoverished curriculum of remedial classes. Teachers may also lose faith in the abilities of students who score poorly on tests.

Cummins advocates using assessment techniques that reveal student strengths. We have suggested that teachers can focus on strengths by replacing traditional tests with portfolios (Y. S. Freeman & D. E. Freeman, 1992a, 1992c) and have attempted to answer some common questions about the use of portfolios. The following questions and answers highlight the benefits of using portfolios:

- What does a portfolio show teachers and administrators?
  It shows student growth over time, student interests, student strengths in their first as well as second languages, and the effectiveness of the present curriculum for the student.
- What does a portfolio tell students?
  It shows them what they have learned, what they spend time and energy on, and what they need to work on more.
- What does a portfolio show parents?
  It shows parents what their students are learning, what

they are doing in school, what kinds of activities are valued in school, and what kinds of activities they can do at home to support learning.

- What are the advantages of a portfolio over other types of evaluation?
  Portfolios involve students and allow them to both show and see progress over time. Instead of highlighting what students cannot do, portfolios allow students to show what they can do without time restraints.

The result of teachers' using portfolios as part of taking an intercultural orientation is that students are empowered and the status quo is changed. From our perspective, when teachers take this orientation, they demonstrate a faith that all their students can and will learn, and they create situations in which students have the power to use the language they are learning.

CONCLUSION

We came to Tucson from far afield. Our subject was ESL, not whole language. But our studies in Tucson prepared us to bridge the gap between mainstream teachers and ESL and bilingual specialists by developing a set of whole language principles for teachers with second language students. Using these principles, we provide teachers with the practical theory they need to teach all their students in an increasingly multicultural society.

REFERENCES

Collier, V. (1989). How long? A synthesis of research on academic achievement in a second language. *TESOL Quarterly, 23*(3), 509-532.

Cummins, J. (1981). The role of primary language development in promoting educational success for language minority students. In *Schooling and language minority students: A theoretical framework* (pp. 3-49). Los Angeles: Evaluation, Dissemination and Assessment Center, California State University, Los Angeles.

Cummins, J. (1989). *Empowering minority students.* Sacramento: CABE.

Edelsky, C., Altwerger, B., & Flores, B. (1991). *Whole language: What's the difference?* Portsmouth, NH: Heinemann.

Freeman, D. E., & Freeman, Y. S. (1990). Case studies: Viewing new students in new ways. *California English, 26*(3), 8-9, 26-27.

Freeman, D. E., & Freeman, Y. S. (1993). Strategies for promoting the primary languages of all students. *The Reading Teacher, 46*(7), 552-558.

Freeman, D. E., & Freeman, Y. S. (1994). *Between worlds: Access to second language acquisition*. Portsmouth, NH: Heinemann.

Freeman, Y. S. (1993). Celebremos la literatura: Is It possible with a Spanish reading program? In P. Shannon & K. S. Goodman (Eds.), *Report card on basal readers: Part II*. New York: Richard C. Owen.

Freeman, Y. S., & Freeman, D. E. (1990). New attitudes for new students. *Holistic Education Review, 3*(2), 25-30.

Freeman, Y. S., & Freeman, D. E. (1992a). *Whole language for second language learners*. Portsmouth, NH: Heinemann.

Freeman, Y. S., & Freeman, D. E. (1992b). Portfolio assessment and second language learning. In K. Goodman, Y. Goodman, & L. B. Bird (Eds.), *The whole language catalog: Supplement on authentic assessment* (p. 176). Santa Rosa, CA: American School Publishers.

Freeman, Y. S., & Freeman, D. E. (1992c). What are portfolios and how are they used to assess our students? *TESOL Journal, 1*(2), 39.

Freeman, Y. S., & Goodman, Y. (1993). Revaluing the bilingual learner through a literature reading program. *Reading and Writing Quarterly: Overcoming Learning Difficulties, 9*, 163-182.

Freire, P. (1970). *Pedagogy of the oppressed*. New York: Continuum.

Goodman, K. (1986). *What's whole in whole language*. Portsmouth, NH: Heinemann.

Goodman, K. (1991). Revaluing readers and reading. In S. Stires (Ed.), *With promise: Redefining reading and writing for "special" students* (pp. 127-133). Portsmouth, NH: Heinemann.

Goodman, K., & Freeman, D. (1993). What's simple in simplified language? In M. L. Tickoo (Ed.), *Simplification: Theory and application* (pp. 69-81). Anthology Series 31. Singapore: SAMEO Regional Language Centre.

Goodman, K. S., Goodman, Y. M., & Flores, B. (1979). *Reading in the bilingual classroom: Literacy and biliteracy*. Rosslyn, VA: National Clearinghouse for Bilingual Education.

Goodman, K., Shannon, P., Freeman, Y., & Murphy, S. (1988). *Report card on basal readers*. New York: Richard C. Owen.

Goodman, Y. M., & Goodman, K. S. (1990). Vygotsky in a whole language perspective. In L. Moll (Ed.), *Vygotsky and education: Instructional implications and applications of sociohistorical psychology* (pp. 223-250). Cambridge: Cambridge University Press.

Krashen, S. (1982). *Principles and practice in second language acquisition.* New York: Pergamon Press.

Smith, F. (1986). *Insult to intelligence: The bureaucratic invasion of our classrooms.* New York: Arbor House.

Wallerstein, N. (1987). Problem posing education: Freire's method for transformation. In I. Shor (Ed.), *Freire for the classroom* (pp. 33-44). Portsmouth, NH: Heinemann.

Widdowson, H. (1978). *Teaching language as communication.* Oxford: Oxford University Press.

EXTENSIONS

Chapter Fourteen

From Reading Errors and Spelling Errors to Miscues and Invented Spellings

Sandra Wilde
Portland State University

In an article entitled "Reading, Writing, and Written Texts: A Transactional Socio-psycholinguistic View" (1994), Kenneth Goodman speaks of a Copernican revolution in our understanding of written language processes, particularly as illustrated by the change from a discussion of error to the discussion of miscues when looking at how readers construct, process, and make sense of text. Goodman's own work, of course, which first became widely known with his 1965 article, "A Linguistic Study of Cues and Miscues in Reading," has been at the heart of this revolution. A similar metamorphosis has taken place in how educators and educational researchers view the process of children's learning to spell, beginning with Charles Read's "Pre-school Children's Knowledge of English Phonology" (1971; available in expanded form in Read, 1975). Read, who was not an educator but a linguist interested in children's emergent understanding of the sound system of English, showed that preschoolers' spontaneous spellings were not random and were best looked at not as evidence of error but as a reflection of their development as speakers of the language. Read's work was discovered by educators such as Carol Chomsky (1971) who realized its implications for teachers: Young children with knowledge of the alphabet could be writers even before they were readers, and creating their own spellings would indeed enable them to actively think about and manipulate the sound/letter relationships of English. Since then, the work of the late Edmund Henderson and others (e.g., Henderson & Beers, 1980) has shown that as spellers become more mature, their spellings reflect aspects of English orthography beyond the basic correspondences of letters to sounds, while others, including myself (Wilde, 1992a, 1992b), have looked at spelling in the classroom context and explored curriculum implications of the new knowledge base about spelling.

My goal in this chapter is to illuminate the parallels between the transformation in the view of the reading process that miscue analysis represents and the similar transformative view of what spellers do that came with the invented spelling perspective. As a tool for the discussion, I refer frequently to two texts, the coded miscues of a 12-year-old girl, Dessina (Figure 14.1) and the invented spellings of a 7-year-old boy, Kyle (Figure 14.2).

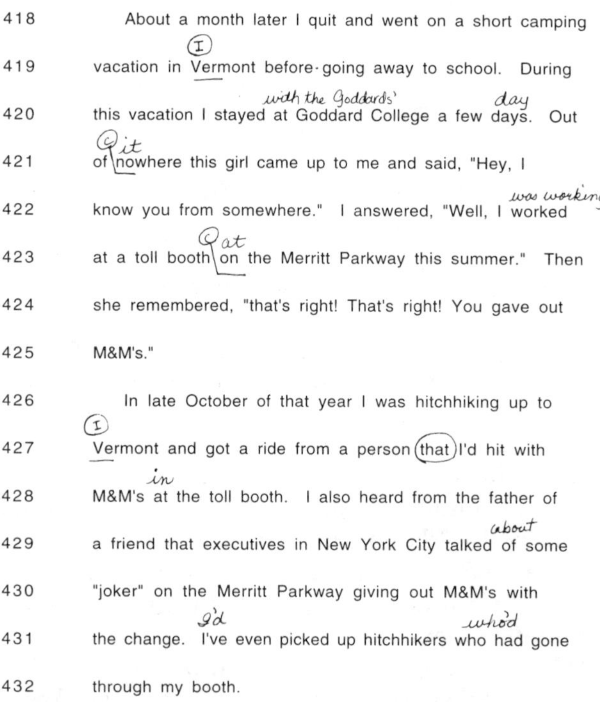

About a month later I quit and went on a short camping vacation in Vermont before going away to school. During this vacation I stayed at Goddard College a few days. Out of nowhere this girl came up to me and said, "Hey, I know you from somewhere." I answered, "Well, I worked at a toll booth on the Merritt Parkway this summer." Then she remembered, "that's right! That's right! You gave out M&M's."

In late October of that year I was hitchhiking up to Vermont and got a ride from a person that I'd hit with M&M's at the toll booth. I also heard from the father of a friend that executives in New York City talked of some "joker" on the Merritt Parkway giving out M&M's with the change. I've even picked up hitchhikers who had gone through my booth.

Figure 14.1. Dessina's reading

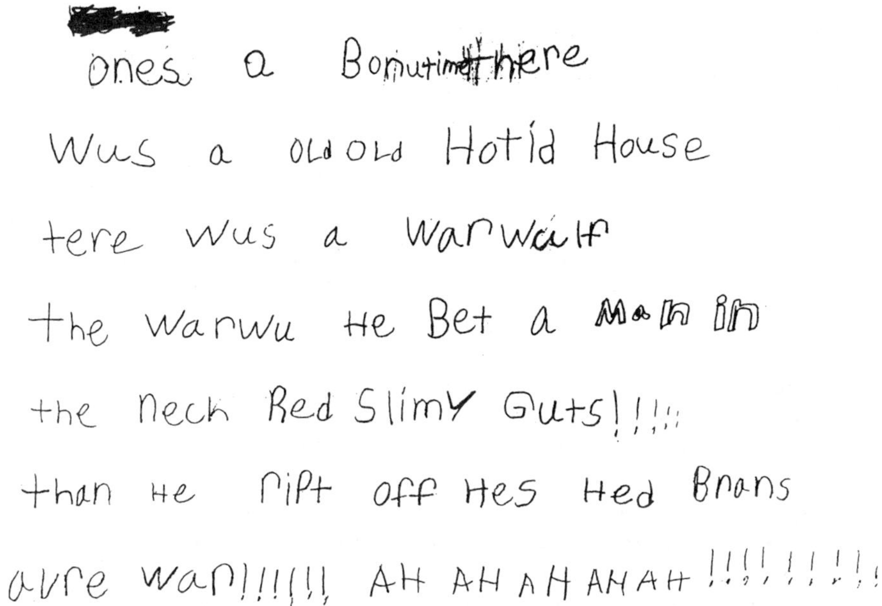

Figure 14.2. Kyle's writing

FROM ERROR COUNTING TO "ERROR" ANALYSIS: A CONSTRUCTIVIST VIEW

One of the unique innovations of Goodman's work in miscue analysis was its departure from the tradition—typical of informal reading inventories—of counting mistakes in reading, and its focus instead on the quality of miscues, defined as observed responses in oral reading that do not match the expected response (Goodman, 1973). Taking the view that "nothing the reader does is accidental," Goodman examined miscues as rule-governed uses of language that provide "a window on the reading process" (1973, p. 5). Similarly, before the discovery of the concept of invented spelling, analyses of spelling error often focused on how spellings fell short of the standard; such schemes divided spellings, for instance, into omissions, additions, transpositions, and substitutions (Spache, 1940), or categorized them as phonetic or nonphonetic (Woolf, 1952). Recent work on spelling, however, focuses almost entirely on what invented spellings reveal about the writer's knowledge of the phonology (the sound system) and orthography (the writing system) of his or her language. (Most studies have been conducted on speakers of English, but Read [1986] summarized the results of comparable research on speakers of other languages.)

These changes in perspective on reading and spelling reflect a constructivist view of literacy (Kamii, 1991). A major contribution of Piaget, the founding father of constructivism, was to teach us that children's thought processes are best understood not as imperfect representations of adult concepts but rather as complete representations on their own terms: organic, evolving theories of the world. Errors must then be seen as representations of the learner's understanding. In the case of reading, miscues are produced in the transaction between the written text and what the reader brings to the text (i.e., knowledge of the linguistic structures of spoken and written language, knowledge about the subject matter of the text, and strategies for reading). Just as young children may make erroneous predictions about the relative capacity of two differently shaped containers in a way that reflects the existing state of their understanding about the conservation of volume, a reader makes predictions about what comes next in a text that may not accord with what is apparently on the page. For instance, Dessina, in line 431 of Figure 14.1, produces the reading "who'd" for "who had," reflecting a more colloquial form presumably found in her speech. Similarly, an American reading of a British author's text may miscue because of a dialect difference, as in Goodman's example of 6 of 21 teenaged Americans who read "headlights" for "headlamps" in a story by Roald Dahl (Goodman & Buck, 1973). The issue here for reading is not so much one of maturity as of a universal process in which the "text" inside the reader's head transacts with the text in the outside world (i.e., on the page). Maturity brings, however, an increasing range of strategies for dealing with increasingly complex written language.

Invented spellings can be defined as the written representations of words that writers create out of their knowledge of written language. For instance, Read (1975) explained young children's occasional spellings like CHRIE for *try* as reflecting their (accurate) perception that *t* before *r* is somewhat more affricated than a *t* before a vowel sound, thus making it similar to the *ch* in *child*. Invented spelling is not merely phonetic, however; it may represent knowledge about orthographic patterns (such as ELBOE for *elbow*, which shows knowledge of silent *e*'s in long vowel spellings), visual memory of individual words (such as LAUHG for *laugh*), or the use of meaning analogies (such as EXCELLERATED for *accelerated*). Researchers of invented spelling can thus analyze writing samples as a way of exploring what a particular child understands about English spelling and also to track developmental progression across children to examine how spelling knowledge develops in general. The main reason why mature writers do not produce as many invented spellings as mature readers produce miscues is that they know the spelling of most words they want to write, whereas every reading of a text, particularly an unfamiliar one, is a new event.

What miscue analysis and invented spelling analysis share at their core, then, is a focus on understanding error as reflective of underlying knowledge and cognitive processes and as capable of enlightening us about how learners conceive of and process written language. This view has transformed classroom practice in both areas: Those who hold a constructivist perspective are unlikely to use an informal reading inventory in which all errors are treated as equal and used to assign a simple reading level, nor are they likely to put much credence in simple right-and-wrong spelling tests.

FUNDAMENTAL QUESTIONS: WHAT CAN WE LEARN FROM MISCUES AND INVENTED SPELLINGS?

The transformed views of miscues and invented spelling that are now an accepted part of how teachers and researchers look at the world are not solely of academic interest: They also have important implications for understanding and working with individual learners, because they tell us how any given individual processes written language. For instance, Goodman's Taxonomy of Reading Miscues (1976) presents 18 categories that provide a variety of lenses for looking at different linguistic aspects of miscues. A number of the categories illuminate aspects of Dessina's processing (see Figure 14.1; the category numbers come from the taxonomy).

1 Correction
The substitution of *it* for *nowhere* (line 421), which was immediately corrected, reflects a prediction based on a common phrase, "out of it," which was presumably corrected because it was so inconsistent with both the perception of the longer word *nowhere* and the meaning of the following text.

3 Graphic Proximity
Dessina's miscue of *day* for *days* (Line 420), one with high graphic similarity, remained uncorrected; the substitution of *it* for *nowhere* (line 420), with no graphic similarity, did get corrected, suggesting that at least some of the time she was disconcerted by miscues that were visually discrepant.

5 Allologs
These are alternative forms of the same item, such as Dessina's *who'd* for *who had,* and they are often a sign that the reader is predicting a natural language form.

10 Semantic Change
Dessina's substitution that created the phrase "with the Goddards' college" rather than "at Goddard College" (line 420) changed the meaning and perhaps resulted from her misprediction that a family's home is where the narrator might have "stayed."

11 Intonation
Dessina's miscue, in which the stress on *Vermont* was shifted to the first syllable, is a word-level intonation shift, perhaps attributable to the word's being a proper name that may have been unfamiliar to Dessina, a Canadian.

The value of such a taxonomy for a teacher is not to assign a score to a reader but as a heuristic device; it is a systematic way of asking questions that will illuminate specific aspects of the reader's use of language. Similarly, invented spellings can be examined on a variety of levels and across a number of features, as shown by several examples from Kyle's writing. (The categories below are not drawn from any formal taxonomy but were chosen to illustrate a number of the linguistic/orthographic features that operate on spelling.)

1 Phonetic accuracy
The substitution of *b* for *p* in the *upon* part of ONES A BONUTIME (once upon a time) shows Kyle writing not the correct sound but one that is phonetically close. Both /b/ and /p/ are bilabial stops, but /b/ is voiced, whereas /p/ is unvoiced. However, unvoiced consonants that are preceded and followed by vowels can easily become somewhat voiced in normal to rapid speech. The spelling of the vowel in WUS (was), however, is phonetically accurate; the "real" spelling of the short *u* sound in this word is an irregular one.

2 Phonetic categorization
The omission of *n* in HOTID (haunted) follows a pattern commonly seen in younger children's invented spelling in which *n* and *m* before other consonants are often omitted because they appear as nasalized vowels rather than fully pronounced stop consonants. (A child who had written *went* with an *n* but then erased it explained it by saying, "It's sort of like there's an *n* there but not really.")

3 Alternative spellings of the same sound
Like many young spellers, Kyle realizes that /z/ is most likely to be spelled with an *s* at the ends of words. We see this not only in his spelling of a plural like BRANS (brains) but in his spelling WUS for *was*.

4 Word boundaries
Kyle's spellings of ONES A BONUTIME (once upon a time) and AVRE WAR (everywhere) show that in a few cases he did not know the conventional segmentation of particular words and phrases. What is remarkable, however, given the unsegmented phonetic nature of the stream of speech, is that children learn to mark word boundaries as well as they do.

5 Morphemic units
Kyle's two spellings of the *-ed* suffix, in HOTID (haunted) and RIPT (ripped), indicate that he did not yet realize that this is a morpheme that is consistently spelled; rather, he spelled it phonetically. Typically, children first spell *-ed* phonetically, then spell it consistently, and finally learn to make changes like *y* to *i* before a suffix.

6 Meaning-based analogy
Possibly Kyle's spelling of ONES for *once* reflects some awareness, whether conscious or not, of the meaning relationship between *one* and *once*.

7 Punctuation and visual features of written language
Kyle has discovered the use of multiple exclamation points and capital letters for emphasis (AH AH AH AH AH !!!!!!!!!).

These detailed examples of some of the questions that have been developed for looking at miscues and invented spellings are just a sampling of how an educated observer can analyze what readers and spellers do; clearly the knowledge base provided by error analysis is tremendously more informative than the one offered by a mere tabulation of correct and incorrect readings and spellings.

STRATEGIES, DEVELOPMENT, AND SOPHISTICATION: ARE THERE "GOOD" AND "BAD" MISCUES AND SPELLINGS?

Part of the power of miscue analysis is the way in which it enables teachers to understand whether readers are using productive or unproductive strategies in reading, with a view to helping the learner build on what is successful and change what is not. Similarly, teachers can track the development of invented spelling over time to monitor how well children are grasping features of spelling like some of those described earlier: alternative spellings of the same sound, the use of suffixes, spelling similarities in words with similar meanings, and so on. We next look at just a few examples from both reading and writing.

The *Reading Miscue Inventory* (Goodman, Watson, & Burke, 1987) defines and models a variety of procedures for using miscue analysis to analyze strengths and weaknesses in a reader's processing of text. For the purposes of this discussion, we use the simplest format, Procedure IV, which consists of asking for each sentence in the reading, "Does the sentence, as the reader left it [i.e., after all corrections], make sense within the context of the story?" In the section of Dessina's reading seen in Figure 14.1, there is only one sentence to which the answer would be "no" (the one reading, in Dessina's rendition, "During this vacation I stayed with the Goddards' college a few day"). The more detailed portraits provided by the more elaborate procedures for miscue analysis provide a rich picture of the reader's strategies, informing us whether he or she overrelies on phonics, produces structures that are grammatical and make sense, under- or overcorrects miscues, and so on. Given this knowledge, the teacher can then plan instruction that helps the reader develop an effective repertoire of reading strategies.

With reading, we often speak of some miscues being "better" than others in that they are more likely to preserve meaning. In spelling, we can talk about levels of sophistication of invented spelling; for instance, of two spellings for the word *people*, PEPOLE is more sophisticated than PEPL because it includes the two silent letters, even if one of them is not in the right place. I have developed a set of questions to ask about invented spellings that can provide teachers with a sense of how spellers grow in sophistication over time (Wilde, 1989); Table 14.1 shows how they apply to Kyle's spellings. (The versions of the questions shown here are highly simplified ones; see the original article for the full forms.)

Table 14.1 shows that most of Kyle's invented spellings reflect a still-emerging sense of how the vowels of many words are spelled, and also a relatively high number of words whose spelling is only off by one letter. The questions are arranged in a rough hierarchy, so that as spellers become more mature, the questions receiving a "yes" answer are more likely to be the higher numbered ones (i.e., those shown toward the right-hand side of Table 14.1). This procedure for looking at invented spellings can, like the *Reading Miscue Inventory*, be both a heuristic tool for teachers (i.e., a structured way of thinking about what is going on with children's spellings) and a way of tracking growth and development over time.

Table 14.1. Analysis of Kyle's Spellings.

Questions:
1. Inexplicable or "weird" spelling?
2. Consonant problems?
3. Vowel problems?
4. Suffix problems?
5. Right letters, wrong order?
6. Off by just one letter?
7. Real word?
8. Punctuation off (word boundaries or apostrophes)?

Word	Spelling	1	2	3	4	5	6	7	8
once	ONES		Y					Y	
upon a time	A BONUTIME		Y	Y					Y
was	WUS			Y			Y		
haunted	HOTID		Y	Y	Y				
there	TERE		Y				Y		
werewolf	WARWULF			Y					
werewolf	WARWU		Y	Y					
bit	BET			Y			Y	Y	
then	THAN			Y			Y	Y	
ripped	RIPT		Y	Y	Y				
his	HIES			Y			Y		
head	HED			Y			Y		
brains	BRANS			Y			Y		
everywhere	AVRE WAR			Y					Y

THE ROLE OF PHONICS IN READING AND SPELLING

A key feature of Goodman's model of the reading process is that the reader uses a number of cues that make up a network of cueing systems, in particular the graphophonic (sound/letter relationships), the syntactic (grammatical), and the semantic (meaning) (Goodman, 1970; in more recent writings he has also stressed the role of personal, social, and pragmatic systems). Because spelling operates almost entirely on the single-word level, and because meaning relationships are a relatively small part of what influences invented spellings, in this discussion I focus on the role of the graphophonic system for readers and spellers.

Bissex (1980), in her study of her son's development as a reader and writer through his early elementary school years, observed that as a reader he tended to begin with the global, a meaning-based sense of the text as a whole and the ideas within it, and only later moved on to make much use of graphophonic information, whereas as a speller his first focus was on sounding out words phoneme by phoneme. These spontaneous choices of focus are, ironically, more or less the opposite of what many traditional school curricula have stressed: There are many advocates of phonics for early reading, and spelling curriculum has emphasized memorizing whole words, along with using teachers or dictionaries as a source for spellings while writing, rather than encouraging children to rely on their own resources.

Research in miscue analysis and in invented spelling analysis has implied the value of curricula that are more in accord with children's spontaneous choice of what to focus on. In reading, miscue analysis shows us the limits and the dangers of an overreliance on graphophonic information. If phonics always worked as a tool for figuring out unfamiliar words, there would be no problem, but it is imprecise enough that miscue analysis research is full of miscues with high graphic similarity in which meaning is lost (e.g., "I'll stay START home HOUSE and keep KEEPING house; Goodman, Watson, & Burke, 1987; the upper case words are substitutions), when readers would often be better off substituting a word that makes sense without even attempting to use phonics (e.g., "I'll light a THE fire . . . and the porridge will be ready in a few minutes FLASH"). Although good readers of an alphabetic language like English surely have a good sense of how sounds and letters are related (giving them tools to come up with a reasonable pronunciation of an unknown word), the inability of beginning readers to produce an accurate independent rendition of a text seems better dealt with by procedures like guided reading, big books, predictable books, taped books, and so on, than by attempting to teach an abstract, formal system that they have little taste for or understanding of.

However, invented spelling is the natural avenue for children to teach *themselves* about phonics, in a way that is developmentally appropriate, because they control the process themselves. It seems obvious that a procedure that children pick up on so quickly, and with such relish, would be a natural one to encourage in schools and for teachers to build on. As we have seen, children's invented spelling tends to become more sophisticated as they grow and develop, and their spellings incorporate increasingly elaborated pieces of phonics knowledge. A number of examples, some taken from Kyle's writing (Figure 14.2) and some from that of other children, provide a sampling of what phonics rules and patterns they apply and suggest what kind of support role the teacher might have in promoting further development. (These are arranged these in roughly developmental order.)

Child and spelling	Phonics principle child is applying	Teacher's role
Kyle: BET (bit) HES (his)	Short vowels are spelled with the letter whose name they most sound like (short i is phonetically close to the letter name *e*).	Provide opportunities to see conventional spellings of short vowels through reading.
Daniel: IZ (is) ANEMLZ (animals)	Consonants (in this case /z/) are spelled with the letter name that includes the sound.	Allow time for awareness of the pattern that /z/ is often spelled *s* to emerge through reading.
Kyle: HED (head) WARWULF (werewolf)	Short vowels are spelled with a single letter (in which *e* stands for short e, *u* for short u, etc.).	Build awareness that there are exceptions.
Kyle: RIPT (ripped)	A single consonant sound /p/ is spelled with a single letter.	Build awareness of double consonants and how they are used.
Johnny: PAKRN (popcorn) BE KAS (because) CARNOS (kernels)	The /k/ sound is sometimes spelled with *c* and sometimes with *k*.	Explore words that use different spellings of /k/ and look for patterns.
Dylan: HELLICOPTER (helicopter)	Double consonants occur after short vowels.	Build awareness of exceptions to and the unpredictability of the double consonant rule.
Carla: PANTE (paint) YORE (your)	Many words, particularly those with long vowels, end in silent *e*.	Explore words with silent final *e* and other spellings of long vowels.

For spelling, then, young writers spontaneously explore the role of phonics in representing words, and teachers can support and scaffold this exploration. Teachers can also help children to realize that a phonetic speller will never be a very good speller and that they need to also learn (largely through reading) the spellings of many individual words, as well as develop resources for finding out the spellings of words they do not know in contexts in which they matter (Wilde, 1992b). For reading, perhaps the most useful role for the teacher is to realize that children will acquire a good deal of internalized, implicit knowledge about the grapho-phonic system of English through reading and invented spelling, and can also learn strategies for dealing with unfamiliar words that include but do not overrely on sound/letter relationships (Wilde, 1997).

LANGUAGE VARIATION AND ITS ROLE IN MISCUES AND INVENTED SPELLING

One final exploration of parallels between recent views about miscues and invented spelling focuses on the nature of how they treat language variation, particularly low-status variations like Black dialect. Probably many teachers would assert that nonstandard dialects, including Black English, are bound to interfere with reading and writing because many people assume both that written language represents a standard (i.e., high-status) version of the language and that encountering language forms different from one's own will create difficulty for the reader. However, the understandings we have gained from both miscue analysis and invented spelling shows that this commonly held perspective is an inaccurate one. (Although my discussion here is primarily a theoretical one, empirical studies and discussions are available elsewhere; see, e.g., Brengelman, 1970; Goodman & Goodman, 1978.)

First of all, it is apparent with a little thought that written language to a large extent represents all dialects, which is why an American reader can read a text written by a British author and vice versa. The differences that do exist are primarily of vocabulary, with occasional syntactic disparities, as well as a few spelling variations that usually do not reflect pronunciation differences. (For instance, Americans and the British pronounce *lieutenant* differently but spell it the same, whereas the reverse is true for *color/colour*.) Therefore, any discrepancies for readers and spellers are likely to be minor ones.

Second, in the case of reading, Goodman and Buck (1973), in an important article, established that proficient readers often deal with language features different from their own by translating them into a surface representation that fits the way they speak themselves. Such a transformation can, of course, only be accomplished by a reader who has processed and understood the underlying meaning. The issue is not, therefore, one of any particular dialect creating special difficulties for readers, but a generic one of developing fluent reading strategies. The African American reader who translates "A word that sounded good," into "A word what sounded good" is in exactly the same position as an American reader who changes *round* to *around* when reading a British writer's, "Look, could you come round at once?" (Goodman & Buck, 1973).

In the case of spelling, young writers' invented spellings tend to be highly phonetic and thus not highly accurate (especially for languages with as much spelling variability as English). But this holds true across dialects. An African American child who writes AXT (or AKST) for *asked* is using the same process as the Anglo American child who writes AST (because the word is not usually pronounced with full articulation as /askt/). Both need to eventually learn to incorporate information beyond the phonetic in their spellings. Similarly, the Cockney child who writes FOT for *thought* is not that much further off than the American child who writes THOT. Different dialects have slightly different sets of homophones, but the differences are minor. For instance, in Oregon, where I live, and also in Canada and many other locations, people tend to pronounce the names *Don* and *Dawn* with the same vowel sound; growing up in New Jersey, I pronounced those two words differently but had identical pronunciations for *Mary, merry,* and *marry*. Yet we have no difficulty in understanding one another. (One of my students, however, told me that until I shared this information in class, she had never understood why her brother Don and her sister Dawn always had so much trouble knowing which one her mother was calling!)

Realizing, therefore, that differences in which version of English one speaks do not create any special difficulties in learning to read or spell is the linguistically accurate way of looking at the situation. It both enables teachers to work appropriately with children of all backgrounds and challenges the still-extant deficit models of language variation.

IMPLICATIONS FOR INSTRUCTION

A great deal has been written about how the knowledge gained from miscue analysis and an understanding of invented spelling is likely to affect instruction; I limit myself here to highlighting a few important points that have to do with the transformed role of the teacher and learner. The constructivist view of reading and spelling that has emerged from the past two or three decades of theory and research has made it clear that we can no longer look at reading and spelling as made up of a collection of "skills" that can be taught in a sequential, cumulative fashion. What learners do at all levels is a holistic process that grows out of their existing knowledge of language and is operationalized by the repertoire of strategies they use for reading and writing. Given this understanding, the role of the teacher changes from dispenser of knowledge to informed coach and provider of opportunities. One of the most crucial changes that has occurred in the approach to literacy education known as whole language is the shift in perception of the teacher's role that it encourages. A teacher who has the knowledge base to look intelligently at miscues and invented spellings in the ways described earlier in this chapter is then able to work with the children in their zones of proximal development (Vygotsky, 1978) to help them expand both their knowledge base and their use of strategies. Returning to the metaphor that introduced this chapter, because of revolutionary changes in how we view reading miscues and invented spellings, teachers can no more see "errors" as simply incorrect than they can convince themselves that the sun orbits around the earth.

REFERENCES

Bissex, G. (1980). *Gnys at wrk: A child learns to read and write.* Cambridge: Harvard University Press.

Brengleman, F. H. (1970). Dialect and the teaching of spelling. *Research in the Teaching of English, 4,* 129-138.

Chomsky, C. (1971). Write now, read later. In C. B. Cazden (Ed.), *Language in early childhood education* (pp. 119-126). Washington, DC: Association for the Education of Young Children.

Goodman, K. S. (1965). A linguistic study of cues and miscues in reading. *Elementary English, 42,* 639-643.

Goodman, K. S. (1970). Psycholinguistic universals in the reading process. *Journal of Typographic Research, 4,* 103-110.

Goodman, K. S. (1973). Miscues: Windows on the reading process. In K. S. Goodman (Ed.), *Miscue analysis: Applications to reading instruction* (pp. 3-14). Urbana, IL: ERIC Clearinghouse on Reading and Communication Skills.

Goodman, K. S. (1976). The Goodman taxonomy of reading miscues. In P.D. Allen & D. Watson (Eds.), *Findings of research in miscue analysis: Classroom implications* (pp. 157-244). Urbana, IL: ERIC Clearinghouse on Reading and Communication Skills.

Goodman, K. S. (1994). Reading, writing, and written texts: A transactional socio-psycholinguistic view. In R. B. Ruddell, M. R. Ruddell, & H. Singer (Eds.), *Theoretical models and processes of reading* (pp. 1093-1130). Newark, DE: International Reading Association.

Goodman, K. S., & Buck, C. (1973). Dialect barriers to reading comprehension: Revisited. *The Reading Teacher, 27,* 6-12.

Goodman, K. S., & Goodman, Y. (1978). *Reading of American children whose language is a stable rural dialect of English or a language other than English* (Research Report No. NIE-C-00-3-0087, U. S. Department of Health Education and Welfare). Tucson: Program in Language and Literacy, University of Arizona.

Goodman, Y. M., Watson, D. J., & Burke, C. L. (1987). *Reading miscue inventory: Alternative procedures.* Katonah, NY: Richard C. Owen.

Henderson, E. H., & Beers, J. W. (Eds.). (1980). *Developmental and cognitive aspects of learning to spell: A reflection of word knowledge.* Newark, DE: International Reading Association.

Kamii, C. (1991). What is constructivism? In C. Kamii, M. Manning, & G. Manning (Eds.), *Early literacy: A constructivist foundation for whole language* (pp. 17-29). Washington: National Education Association.

Read, C. (1971). Pre-school children's knowledge of English phonology. *Harvard Educational Review, 41,* 1-34.

Read, C. (1975). *Children's categorization of speech sounds in English.* Urbana, IL: National Council of Teachers of English.

Read, C. (1986). *Children's creative spelling.* London: Routledge.

Spache, G. (1940). A critical analysis of various methods of classifying spelling errors, I. *Journal of Educational Psychology, 31,* 111-134.

Vygotsky, L. S. (1978). *Mind in society.* Cambridge: Harvard University Press.

Wilde, S. (1989). Looking at invented spelling: A kid-watcher's guide to spelling. In K. S. Goodman, Y. M. Goodman, & W. Hood (Eds.), *The whole language evaluation book* (pp. 213-236). Portsmouth, NH: Heinemann.

Wilde, S. (1992a). Spelling in third and fourth grade: Focus on growth. In Y. M. Goodman & S. Wilde (Eds.), *Literacy events in a community of young writers* (pp. 125-147). New York: Teachers College Press.

Wilde, S. (1992b). *You kan red this! Spelling and punctuation for whole language classrooms, K-6.* Portsmouth, NH: Heinemann.

Wilde, S. (1997). *What's a schwa sound anyway?: A holistic guide to phonetics, phonics, and spelling.* Portsmouth, NH: Heinemann.

Woolf, Sr. M. R. (1952). A study of spelling errors with implications concerning pertinent teaching methods. *Elementary School Journal, 53,* 458-466.

Chapter Fifteen

Retrospective Miscue Analysis: Illuminating the Voice of the Reader

Yetta M. Goodman
University of Arizona

At the end of a workshop on miscue analysis at the York University annual reading conference in Toronto, Chris Worsnop, a reading specialist, came up to me and asked: "Have you ever used miscue analysis with teenagers?"

My off-hand response was that kids would not understand the linguistic and reading process concepts that are necessary in order to use miscue analysis. Chris responded confidently that he had been using miscue analysis with students in a reading clinic in the secondary school where he was teaching. He was pairing students, having one read on tape while the other listened, and then having them both retell. He then rewound the tape recorder and he and the kids listened to the reading again. The kids were in charge of stopping the tape recorder any time they heard a miscue. They then had lively discussions about the causes of the miscues and what readers should do as a result.

Chris said he was writing a report about this work and would send it to me. I was intrigued with Chris' excitement about kids being involved in the analysis of their own miscues. I considered the possibilities and a procedure called *retrospective miscue analysis* (RMA) came into being. Lately, I have been rereading the reports Chris wrote, and I have written articles and a book about retrospective miscue analysis (Goodman, 1996a; Goodman & Marek, 1996). I have realized that encouraging readers to consciously consider the *quality* of their miscues and their reading strategies is an aspect of reading instruction that, for many years, has been inspired by miscue analysis. For nearly two decades, teachers have been encouraged to discuss miscue making and the reasons for it with students (Goodman & Burke, 1980; Goodman, Watson, & Burke, 1996). Dorothy Watson's reader-selected miscues strategies (1978; Watson & Hoge, 1996) also involve kids in selecting their own miscues for analysis and discussion in a classroom setting. This strategy includes readers throughout a silent reading period marking places in their reading where they believe they have problems. They then write the sentences including their miscues on a bookmark. The teacher (often with the students) categorizes the miscues and reading strategies that would be helpful to explore as part of reading instruction in the classroom setting. So it was not talking about miscues with readers that surprised me when Chris approached me with his ideas. Rather, it was engaging readers in the process of analyzing miscues *using the same kinds of questions* that teachers and researchers use during miscue analysis.

After I received Chris's report (Worsnop, 1996), I experimented with his procedures and adapted them to fit readers of various ages and abilities, reading in various settings. I began to use the term *retrospective miscue analysis* (RMA) to refer to this involvement of readers in an analysis of their own reading process. Understanding the power of this instructional strategy has become a major focus of my research since that time.

With graduate students, classroom teachers, and colleagues, I have developed and experimented with a variety of procedures for RMA for both instructional and research purposes (Goodman & Marek, 1989). In miscue analysis classes that I teach, graduate students have planned and carried out instructional projects that involve their students in retrospection of their reading (Stephenson, 1980; Weatherill, 1996; Woodley & Miller, 1983;). Doctoral students have and continue to design dissertation research that examines the role of RMA as an instructional strategy with adults, secondary, and junior high school students (Coles, 1981; Costello, 1992; Flurkey, 1997; Marek, 1987; Raisner, 1977). During the early 1990s, Ann Marek and I were supported by funds from the NCTE research foundation to study RMA with seventh graders. These readers were divided into groups of "good" and "poor" readers, based on standardized test scores and upon teacher evaluations. With graduate students researchers, we studied the reading development of several seventh graders for 1 1/2 years (Goodman and Flurkey, 1996). In the last two years, Prisca Martens, Alan Flurkey, and I have been exploring the uses of miscue analysis with elementary school-aged children (Goodman, Martens, & Flurkey, 1995). Moreover, many classroom teachers have been using retrospective miscue analysis both formally (Costello, 1996) and incidentally within the classroom setting and discussing their procedures and findings with me (Goodman, 1996b). The most significant conclusion from this inquiry is that through RMA, students quite capably and confidently talk about their reading ability and come to value themselves as readers and learners.

For more than 20 years, miscue analysis has been a powerful heuristic tool for teachers and researchers. As Kenneth Goodman predicted years ago, because miscue analysis is a window on the reading process (Goodman, 1973), it can help theorists, teachers, and researchers build and expand a transactional sociopsycholinguistic model of reading (Goodman, 1994). In addition to building a model of the reading process, those of us immersed in miscue research realize that as we change our views about reading, we listen to readers in new ways. We talk about having "miscue ears" or a "miscue head" because instead of hearing miscues as evidence of inadequate reading, we realize that they provide the listener with insights into the reader's knowledge of language cueing systems and his or her proficiency in using reading strategies. Miscues also provide evidence that readers make the text more accessible and meaningful to themselves.

RMA now provides the opportunity for the reading process to become equally accessible to all people learning to read. In this chapter, I explore research on RMA procedures and what we have learned about the importance of organizing experiences with readers to make the reading process conscious and accessible to them.

RETROSPECTIVE MISCUE ANALYSIS (RMA) PROCEDURES

Preparing for RMA Sessions

The initial step in RMA is the same as any reading miscue inventory (RMI) experience: The reader reads orally an entire story or article, without aid from a teacher, and then retells what has been read (Goodman, Watson, & Burke, 1987). The reading material selected for the RMI is always a new text for the reader. However, the language structures and conceptual knowledge of the material are related to the knowledge base and interests of the reader. The reading material is usually somewhat challenging. The teacher/researcher marks the miscues on a typescript that is a replica of the actual reading material.

Following the oral reading, the reader provides an unaided retelling, and then the teacher/researcher asks open-ended questions based on the language and concepts revealed by the student during the unaided retelling. The reading and retelling are taperecorded. It is important to establish rapport with students by honestly explaining to them the purpose of the procedures, what will happen during the subsequent RMA sessions, and the length and number of sessions.

After the collection of the miscue analysis, the teacher/researcher relistens to the reading and retelling, checking the miscues on the typescript, and either transcribing the retelling or noting aspects of the retelling that shed light on the miscues and the reader's comprehension. The miscues are coded using one of the RMI procedures (Goodman, Watson, & Burke, 1987) to profile the reader's use of reading strategies and language cueing systems. It is necessary to be knowledgeable about miscue analysis in order to thoroughly understand the patterns of the reader's miscues and the information from the retelling, as well as to plan for subsequent RMA sessions.

We examined two different types of RMA settings for students. In the first one the teacher/researcher selects the miscues prior to the RMA session and usually works one-on-one with the reader. This procedure, developed by Ann Marek in her study of adult readers (Marek 1987, 1996a, 1996b), is used with students who have been severely labeled or who consider themselves to be illiterate or nonreaders. The second type of RMA places the readers themselves in the position of selecting the miscues they want to examine after listening to a taperecorded reading. This latter procedure is most like the one developed by Chris Worsnop. It is appropriate for most middle school-aged or older readers and can be organized within a classroom setting.

When Teacher/Researchers Select the Miscues

For readers who have strong attitudes about their inability to read, who lack confidence in themselves as learners, and/or who have accommodated a negative view about themselves as readers, the teacher/researcher carefully plans the RMA session. The teacher/researcher initially selects high-quality miscues that reveal the strengths of a reader. After the reader begins to show some confidence, miscues and strategies that interfere with the reader's ability to construct a meaningful text are examined and discussed. High-quality miscues include those that result in syntactically and semantically acceptable sentences, or those that are not acceptable but are immediately self corrected. A second set of miscues might include those that show good prediction strategies but do not fit with the rest of the sentence.

It is important to have all materials carefully arranged at the very beginning of each session. Pencils and paper for marking miscues and taking notes should be readily available. Some researchers have been successful involving students in marking their own miscues on a blank transcript. Tables and chairs should be arranged so that everyone is comfortable. A quiet, separate room for the session aids in obtaining a good-quality taperecording and in having a discussion without too many interruptions. Two taperecorders are arranged. One taperecorder is used to replay the original reading and retelling session in order to relisten and discuss the selected miscues. The second taperecorder is left on to tape and preserve the discussions during the RMA session. The original reading material is on hand, as are two copies (or more depending on the number of participants) of the typescripts of the reading material. One typescript of the text is unmarked, the other is marked with the reader's miscues.

The Retrospective Miscue Analysis (RMA) Session

The RMA session starts with comfortable conversations between the participants to maintain the warm rapport established during the initial meeting. The teacher/researcher advances the audiotape to the miscues that have been preselected. It saves time to mark down the taperecorder's counter number for the selected miscues. The participants listen to the original reading, following along with a typescript of the original text. The typescript may or may not have the miscues marked, depending on the purpose of the sessions and the direction the session will take.

The following are questions that are most often used to guide the discussion about each miscue. Not all of the questions are used during each session, some may prove to be more useful than others. The first group of questions focus on the reader's initial response to the miscue.

Why do you think you made that miscue? Is that a good thing for readers to do? The teacher/researcher keeps in mind the reader's response to these initial questions as the focus of the questions shifts to reading strategies and uses of the language cueing systems.

1. *Does your miscue make sense in this context?* This question focuses readers on the importance of constructing a meaningful text.
2. *Does what you have read sound like language?* This question focuses readers' attention on their use of the syntactic system. It is important for readers to realize that they are

using grammatical or syntactic knowledge as they read and to point out their strengths as they do so. It may be necessary to have readers listen to a particular section one or more times to help them understand the role of language as a system in their reading.

3. *Did you correct what you read? Why did you correct it? Should you have corrected it?* It is important to help readers understand that self correction is a selective process, and only miscues that disrupt the construction of meaning need to be self corrected.
4. *Did what you read look like what is in the text? Did it sound like what is in the text?* The sound and graphic similarity is used not only to demonstrate what readers know about the graphophonic system but also to flag readers who rely on graphophonic information ("Yes, it looks and sounds like what is in the text") to a greater extent than on semantic or syntactic information ("No, it doesn't make sense or sound like language"). Some students need to be helped to realize that overreliance on graphophonic information rather than on meaning is a less productive reading strategy than the focus on making sense. But at the same time, the reader is helped to see how well he or she knows the graphophonic system of language. This is especially helpful for readers who have become controlled by skills-based reading instruction or who believe they do not know phonics.

The purpose of all the questions, which are similar to the ones used by miscue analysis researchers, is to help readers become consciously aware of the strategies they use that show a concern for meaning construction. If the answer to the question *"Does this make sense?"* is "Yes," the discussion revolves around the influential nature of high-quality miscues and the subsequent questions are not asked. It is important to carefully consider the questioning strategies during the RMA sessions. Since the first use of miscue analysis, questions have changed to adapt to the users and their understandings about language and the reading process. Different questions have been used for research purposes and adapted for instructional purposes (Goodman, Watson, & Burke, 1987). The questions guide the reader to consider important aspects of the reading process and, if used appropriately, often move readers toward important insights into their own reading process. Sometimes, the move results in disequilibrium that helps readers reconsider the short circuit strategies that lead them away from their focus on making meaning. If the questions become routinized so that students are responding to them without thoughtful consideration, or if readers do not seem to understand the questions, they need to be adapted. But the adaptations need to be based on a knowledge of reading that is informed by the model of the reading process, which is the foundation for both miscue analysis and RMA.

Following the RMA session, the reader reads another selection and retells. Later the teacher/researcher analyzes the reading using the RMI, and the selection is used for planning the next RMA session. Each subsequent RMA session follows similar procedures. After about six months, teacher/researchers often ask readers to reread the initial reading material. A miscue analysis of the reading and retelling can be used to compare the two readings to show the reader changes across time.

We see such a change in Jeanne, a seventh grader described as a reader in trouble by her teacher and by her score on a standardized reading test. Jeanne made it clear in her initial RMA sessions that the author's language was all important. She believed that it was acceptable for an author to make changes or rewrite his or her own story, but the reader could not make any changes to the language of the text. The following conversation occurred between Jeanne and her teacher/researcher, Joel:

Jeanne: Because, it's o.k. for an author to because he originally wrote the book. But if like somebody else tried to write the book and tried to publish it, the author would get mad and start something. And . . . you know, if you read it differently . . . it's a 100% book and [if you] leave out 25%, the author would make you . . . read it over.

After a number of sessions, she began to show more confidence in the appropriateness of her miscues. Consider the following example:

They leave

Nicky is a baby. That leaves Nicky with us girls.

Jeanne: (listens to herself read) I read *they leave* for *that leaves.*

Joel: Why do you think you did that?

Jeanne: *That leaves Nicky* doesn't make sense. *That leaves Nicky with us girls.* Who's *that?* . . . *That leaves,* who did *that?* There's no purpose. I just think they [authors] made a miscue.

Not only is Jeanne able, at this point during the study, to conceive of the notion that her miscues help her comprehend the text better and that the author may have "messed up," but she is able to discuss her strategies with greater facility than she did earlier.

Another section of a transcript, which took place after Jeanne had a number of RMA sessions, documents how Jeanne was then capable of discussing reading strategies and the language of the text. Joel has selected a miscue that is disruptive to her understanding. Prior to having Jeanne listen to her previous reading, he shows her the place in the story that she will be listening to and asks her to read it aloud first, as follows:

covered
It was the one I always sit at with the big E. L. carved

covered
in an upper corner and the heart carved in the lower one.

Joel blocks out the word *carved* on the reader's copy of the typescript.

Joel: What kind of words would fit in there?
Jeanne: (responds immediately) *E. L. initial? E. L. initialed in an upper corner and the heart covered* . . . I mean . . . umm . . . whatever, *initial . . . initialed in a lower one.*
Joel: What do you mean by *initialed?*
Jeanne: Carved.
Joel: Does *initialed* look like *carved?*
Jeanne: No.
Joel: Does it make sense?
Jeanne: Yeah.
Joel: I think it's a really good word to use in this context. Now I'm going to play the tape where you read that last time and tell me what you think.

Jeanne and Joel listen to the tape as she perseveres in her original reading of *carved*:

4. confused
3. conversed
2. converse
UC 1. con-
It was the one I always sit at with the big E. L. carved
conversed
in an upper corner and the heart carved in the lower one.

The listeners hear that Jeanne leaves her unsuccessful attempt at correction, continues to read, and says *conversed* at the second instance of *carved* in the sentence. The following discussion ensued:

Jeanne: I think it sounded pretty dorky. 'Cause I used *converse . . . conversed* and I just don't think that sounds right.

Joel: Why do you suppose you used *conversed?*

Jeanne: It looked like it.

Joel: What does that tell you in terms of when you're reading? What's important when you read?

Jeanne: To know the meaning . . . the meaning of the story.

Joel: Are the letters important? And the words?

Jeanne: Not as much.

Joel: Is that a surprise to you? (Jeanne nods affirmatively) Do you know what's even more interesting? (Joel erases the penciled covering over *carved.*) Do you know what that word is?

Jeanne: No.

Joel: When we talked about it you wanted to substitute *initialed* and I said what does that mean, and you said *carved.*

Jeanne: That's it! *Carved*!!

In RMA, the teacher/researcher follows the lead of the reader. Readers are encouraged to discover their own answers, but at the same time they are encouraged to consider meaning construction as the heart of the purpose for reading.

When the Readers Select their Miscues

In some cases teacher/researchers involve two or more students in selecting their own miscues for purposes of discussion. This is sometimes done in a setting outside of the classroom, such as in a reading clinic (Worsnop, 1996), or it can be done in the classroom with small groups of students participating in collaborative retrospective miscue analysis (CRMA) (Costello, 1992, 1996).

In these sessions, students focus on the nature of miscues and reading strategies as in the previously described procedure. But teachers/researchers use such opportunities to examine the *kinds of miscues* that readers pay attention to and select as problems for discussion. It is interesting to also note which miscues readers do not notice as they relisten to themselves and others read. In RMA research, we have found that readers often ignore high-quality miscues such as synonym substitutions (*do his job* for *do his work*) or substitutions of function words (such as *the baby* for *his baby*) that make only slight changes to the meaning of the story. Readers often say: "Oh, that doesn't make any difference." Although they are right about the small difference such miscues make to their understanding, these are good miscues for readers to discuss. Discussing such miscues with students reveals readers' sophisticated uses of syntactic and semantic cueing systems. The discussions also establish the principle that all readers make miscues and, further, that many miscues are the result of appropriate reading strategies.

When readers are in charge of stopping the taperecorder when they hear miscues, then the teacher/researcher does not have much planning to do in the preselection of appropriate miscues for consideration. It is helpful, however, to have a marked transcript of the reading for discussion purposes.

In these settings, any of the participants may stop the tape recorder whenever they hear something unexpected in the reading. Readers are not always sure what the term *miscue* means, but the teacher/researcher uses the term consistently. Using terms such as *mistake* or *error* defeats the purpose of helping the reader realize that miscues are necessary and helpful to comprehension and the reading process. Saying, "Stop the recorder every time you hear something as you read that surprises you or is unexpected," may be helpful at the beginning of the RMA sessions. Eventually, through experiences with the teacher/researcher, readers begin to build a concept about miscues that more closely resembles the orientation the teacher/researcher has. All listeners, researchers, teachers, and students have different views about what to expect as people read. These differences are greater among novices who have not thought much about the reading process. Discussions about the different ways listeners categorize miscues often become a part of the RMA sessions as readers become more confident in their role as miscue makers and in their understandings of the process.

Each time the taperecorder is turned off in order to discuss a miscue, the reader is encouraged to explore with the participants what occurred and why. Questions similar to those listed earlier are asked about each miscue. This process of identifying and discussing miscues continues throughout the RMA session. Often the response to stopping the taperecorder is: "Why did you stop the tape recorder?", or "What did you hear?" Often there is an argument and the teacher or another student says, "Let's listen again and see if we agree on what we hear."

The following transcript provides an example from a collaborative RMA session. Costello (1992) researched this procedure with groups of four students in her seventh grade classroom. This example comes after the students have had a number of experiences listening to their miscues. The concepts of miscue analysis and the reading process have been introduced to the class. The group has listened to others read prior to listening to Carolyn read. Carolyn stops the taperecorder so the group can discuss her miscue.

> There was a board that unfolded, revealing a path
> colorful
> of colored squares.

Carolyn: I didn't correct myself because *colorful* is like *colored.*
Kirb: Did it help you?
Terry: *Colorful* is like *colored. Colorful* is better than *colored.*
Kirb: Did you change it?
Carolyn: Did I change it? No, because *colorful* made sense.
Jose: Do you think you should have changed it?

The group continues discussing the miscue and agrees that it is a good miscue—one that makes sense and does not need to be corrected.

These two procedures for conducting RMA sessions have been studied to see what we can learn about readers' abilities to talk and think about their reading processes. The analyses of RMA data on readers' self-confidence and use of reading strategies show dynamic changes. In addition, we know that teachers/researchers are adapting uses of RMA as part of their reading instruction to be used in incidental ways in classroom settings. For example, research with primary age children has revealed the positive impact that conscious awareness of the reading process has on reading proficiency and confidence (Goodman, 1996b).

I encourage teachers/researchers to continue to examine RMA as an instructional strategy to document the changes that occur in readers who are given opportunities to talk and think about their reading. However, the RMA research completed over the last 10 years has already provided a number of significant conclusions.

IMPORTANT CONCLUSIONS AND FURTHER CONSIDERATIONS

Among the most important and theoretically/practically provocative conclusions from RMA research are the following:

Talking and Thinking About Reading. Through RMA, readers have the opportunity to discover and document their strategy use and language knowledge as they talk about their own and others' miscues and consider what the miscues mean. As they listen to themselves read, readers talk and reflect on the process of becoming more effective and efficient. They develop language that is appropriate to the settings in which people talk about reading and the reading process.

All Readers Benefit from Revaluing. RMA is a suitable instructional tool for readers of all ages and abilities. It provides a sociolinguistic context in which readers become consciously aware of their capabilities and what they know about language and reading. Readers build confidence in themselves. They become risk takers as they read and talk about reading. As a result, they revalue themselves as readers.

Demythifying and Demystifying Reading. Through RMA, readers begin to evaluate miscues qualitatively rather than quantitatively and to understand that miscues are often supportive and necessary to understanding what they read. They view reading from a realistic frame as they discover that for all readers, reading is problematic in some contexts and easy in others. Readers come to realize that many of the notions they have about reading are based on myths.

The Good Reader/Poor Reader Distinction. For researchers, the RMA procedure has illuminated the inadequacy of simplistic distinctions between poor and good readers. Although these distinctions have been a common way of designating readers in the reading research community, we conclude that each reader is capable of reading some things well, and each reader in essence is illiterate in specific literacy contexts.

I expand on each of these conclusions in the next sections.

Talking and Thinking about Reading

It becomes abundantly clear through RMA studies that readers of all ages and all ability levels are capable of talking and thinking about reading and the reading process. In other words, all readers are capable of reflecting on language as an object of study. The ability to talk and think about the reading process is sometimes called *metalinguistic and/or metacognitive awareness.* Some researchers conclude that young readers or "poor" readers are not capable of such knowledge or awareness, and it must be explicitly taught (Brown, Campione, & Day, 1980). However, in retrospective miscue analysis, students not only talk about and reflect on their reading and language use, but much of what they have to say reflects sophisticated concepts. Armando, who participated in the RMA study we did with seventh graders (Goodman & Flurkey, 1996), provides an example. He was designated a troubled reader based on test scores and teacher evaluation. Consider the following discussion about Armando's miscue:

"Quite so," added Father, tucking his scarf inside

his coat.

Joel: What'd you hear?
Armando: *His craft.*
Joel: Listen to what you did.
Armando: I went back and corrected it . . . Cause I was reading . . . *Father, tucking his craft* and I said "Whoa" as I started reading, "that doesn't sound right." And I was deciding in my mind what way should I start real quick. And I know I had to go on with the story so I started back here and read again.
Joel: Why do you suppose you miscued on *craft?*
Armando: 'Cause *craft/scarf,* like it ends the same and I guess I got mixed up.

All the readers who participate in RMA, regardless of reading proficiency or ability, articulate not only beliefs about the reading process and their strengths and weaknesses as readers, but they also make statements that reveal their ability to reflect on language. Readers discuss the language cueing systems—pragmatic, semantic, syntactic, and graphophonic—as well as reading strategies: predicting, confirming, and searching for meaning. They often use their own metaphors or terminology to talk about the systems and strategies, but there is no doubt that they are talking about language. Joel's discussion with Terri, a designated average seventh grade reader, provides an example of such talk about language. The text sentence is from a story in which the characters are playing a board game. Terri and Joel listen to one of the selected miscues first:

Lion attacks. Move back two spaces, read Judy.

Joel: What happened there? Any idea?
Terri: Like, yeah. 'Cause *read* [reed] and *read* [red] are the same thing but it's . . . past tense, because you can't put *readed* [reeded].
Joel: So you read *move back two spaces, read* [reed] . . . What happened then?
Terri: That is the present tense. And Judy had already read it so it'd be in the past tense.
Joel: O. K. Why do you suppose you did that? Said *read* [reed] instead of *read* [red].
Terri: ' Cause you know, it's spelt the same. That's why.

Joel: Would that affect your understanding?
Terri: Yeah, 'cause of present and past.
Joel: And did you correct it?
Terri: Yes.
Joel: Should you have?
Terri: Yes.

The environment organized for RMA discussions provides a social and linguistic context for readers to either invent the language they need or to learn the language of the social community as they hear others use language to talk about reading. An example of one such invention occurred during Marek's study of adult readers. Throughout the RMA sessions, Marlene, who described herself as dyslexic, began to realize that prediction was important. In order to discuss her predictions, Marlene invented the term "stopper" to refer to the point in the text that signaled a miscue had been made and correction was necessary (Marek, 1996b).

The talk during these sessions reveals that readers are considering or reflecting about what is happening as they read. Readers are eager to talk and think about reading within RMA sessions because the focus is on their reading. Discussing their reading with an interested teacher/researcher, whose purpose is to help readers observe the strengths their miscues reveal, provides each reader with a context in which language becomes the focus of attention. What is important to the discussion is that the focus is on what the readers are reading, what they are doing as they read, and what they are understanding. Often readers lead the discussion, raising problems or issues in their reading that are of great concern to them. The tone of the discussion makes it clear that all participants are taking what the readers are doing seriously and makes them realize that they have important contributions to make to the process of understanding what goes on as people read. This sense of importance and seriousness places the readers in an inquiry mode in which they have equal power with others in the discussion. The role of the teacher/researcher in such contexts is crucial. He or she sets the tone and organizes the context so that readers come to believe that they make a difference in their own learning.

Teachers/researchers interested in exploring the metalinguistic and metacognitive knowledge of readers have a gold mine of opportunities in the close linguistic analysis that occurs during the conversations among the participants in RMA settings.

All Readers Benefit from Revaluing

Elana was a participant in Sarah Costello's dissertation study, and she was designated as a "good" reader according to standardized tests and teacher evaluation. She initially attributed her substitutions and omissions (which usually were semantically and syntactically acceptable) to being lazy. When Sarah asked her, "What did you do when your miscues didn't make sense?", she replied, "Half of the time I went back." When Sarah proved to her that she regressed and self corrected over 80% of her miscues in a particular story, Elana responded: "Some of them I just didn't go back. Just lazy."

Kirb, another designated good reader, in an initial interview about his reading stated that he read every word on the page. "I do because I'm so slow, not so slow, but I'm pretty slow and I'm afraid I'm going to miss something if I don't" (Costello, 1992, p. 166).

Originally, I believed that RMA discussions were only necessary for students having difficulty with reading in school settings. However, the RMA study we did with seventh graders (Goodman & Flurkey, 1996) convinced me otherwise. We had students in the study who, like Elana and Kirb, were reading in the seventh stanine on the school district's standardized reading test—certainly a commonly accepted indicator of reading proficiency. But these readers did not value themselves as readers as I had anticipated they might. They believed that their miscues were caused because they were lazy or slow. They believed strongly in the efficacy of the text. That meant that readers could make no miscues and needed to read slowly, carefully, and accurately, although some like Kirb, at the same time, were concerned that they read too slowly. Their beliefs about themselves as readers were similar to those of less successful readers and not dissimilar from many teachers and graduate students prior to their study of miscue analysis.

We discovered that all readers benefited from RMA discussions. At the end of the NCTE study, each of the seventh grade readers had a more realistic view of themselves and others as readers. They understood more about the reading process and how people read. They valued themselves more and defined themselves as "good" or "much better" readers. One such shift is seen in Kirb's discussion about the importance of RMA discussions for both good and poor readers. He made these remarks about 6 months after the initial interview in which he focused on how slowly he reads:

> If poor readers know what miscues are . . . they would probably become better readers. They wouldn't worry about stopping and not stopping, but going so slow and trying to be perfect. They wouldn't be

> trying to read perfect and pronounce everything right that they wouldn't get the meaning. These groups [CRMA discussions] . . . help them relax . . . more . . . and help them understand more. It would help them [good readers] too. They might be good readers, they might understand everything, but read real slow . . . They might learn to substitute words and read a little faster and still get the same meaning out of it. (Costello, 1992, p. 183)

I have described a number of ways to discuss reading and the reading process with students involved in evaluating the miscues they make. These various procedures include not only planned experiences for research purposes but spontaneous and incidental classroom interactions that I call *critical moment teaching*. Many teachers/researchers knowledgeable about RMA are exploring such procedures in classroom settings (D. Goodman, 1996; Y. Goodman, 1996b). To help a wider audience of teachers appreciate the possibilities of using RMA as part of reading instruction, we must continue to research and write about the classroom opportunities for involving students in discussions about how reading works.

Demystifying and Demythifying

Providing readers with opportunities to discuss reading both demystifies and demythifies the process. Barbara Flores (1982) uses these terms to suggest that students often build misconceptions about the reading process. These misconceptions are based on the myths that have been popularized through strict adherence to didactic reading programs and the teaching of grammar and phonics isolated from language use. Even proficient readers latch onto such myths. Many readers believe that reading is an accurate word-by-word response to print. They believe that readers have to read slowly and carefully. They believe that if they only had appropriate doses of phonics at the right time and in the right way, they would learn to read easily and quickly. They believe that good readers always read fluently, know all of the words, remember everything that they read, and rarely make miscues. They are unaware of the ways in which their knowledge and experiences positively influence their reading because they do not value themselves as learners or readers. We document these perceptions in our initial interviews and discussions with readers during RMA sessions. For readers who believe such myths, reading is a mystery. They seem to think that so-called "good readers" have discovered a magic potion that leads to proficient reading.

However, in discussing and examining the reading process with others, readers come face-to-face with the strategies they use and the language cueing systems that inform their reading and their miscues. As they raise reading to a conscious level in this personal way, readers build their own realistic views of the reading process. During RMA discussions, it is easy to respond to myths about reading as students explore the range of strategies available for readers to use to construct meaning. RMA provides a vehicle for all readers to examine the myths they hold about the reading process, and through such reflection, reading ceases to be an unknowable mystery.

By exploring these myths, readers who lack confidence become aware that all readers—even the best readers—do things in reading that they always thought marked them as poor readers. At the same time, confident readers come to appreciate the reading of others and to understand that miscues and reading strategies show good thinking and reading proficiency. It is important, therefore, for RMA discussions to take place in heterogeneous groups.

Serious talk about reading permits readers to see themselves as intelligent discussants who have control or ownership over their own reading process. Encouraging students to compare learning to read with such things as learning to swim or ride a bike helps them become aware that all learning involves lots of practice in authentic settings, opportunities to fail and make mistakes (miscues), and the motivation to keep going.

In our attempts to help readers become consciously aware of the reading process, we need to be cautious that we do not turn interesting discussions about reading into didactic lessons that are dull and boring. Research should continue to explore any limitations on conscious talk about reading. There was a time when I believed that consciousness about the reading process interfered with reading for meaning. When people are learning to use miscue analysis and become aware of their own miscues, they report being so focused on their miscues that they forget what they are reading about. So although I am confident and enthusiastic about the use of RMA with students, I call for caution with its use. We have only recently begun to research RMA with young children in clinical and classroom settings because of this need for caution, and we urge others interested in exploring RMA to be cautious as well. RMA discussions are not for the purpose of transmitting a holistic view of the reading process, but rather to help students understand how reading works from their own perspectives.

The Good Reader / Poor Reader Distinction

In RMA research, we have worked most often with readers who consider themselves to have reading difficulties or are labeled in some way established by various diagnostic procedures. Through research in RMA and miscue analysis, we have come to understand that no reader is equally proficient in all settings with all written texts. There are limitations on what all people are capable of reading. All readers are proficient or not depending on the purpose for the reading; the nature of the text being read; and the background knowledge, language, and experience of the reader in relation to the written text.

In miscue studies, we identify readers as having degrees of efficiency and effectiveness based on the patterns of miscues throughout a whole text. Readers whose patterns of miscues result in sentences that are semantically and syntactically acceptable, or if unacceptable are corrected, are considered to be *effective* readers of a particular text. In addition to being effective, if readers also show that they make nondeliberate substitutions, omissions and insertions of function words, have high-quality substitution miscues, shift grammatical units of text without disruption to meaning, and have a good percent of substitution miscues that show only some or no graphic and sound similarity, these readers are considered to be *efficient*. We have defined readers as *proficient* if they show both effective and efficient reading strategies. We also use retellings to corroborate the proficiency of the readers.

Proficient readers are in control of the reading process. They read in order to make meaning; they manipulate text as shown by their miscues; they decide when reprocessing is necessary as shown by their overt regressions and self corrections; they know when they understand and when they do not; and they decide what is important or unimportant by determining what aspects of the text need more attention and what aspects need little or none.

If all readers are proficient in some settings, with some materials, and if, conversely, readers are not always proficient depending on setting and materials, general terms such as "good" or "poor" are not helpful descriptions of readers (Goodman & Flurkey, 1996). In RMA studies, we always identify the specific criteria used to establish such distinctions among readers. We use such designations to make comparisons to the vast amount of research done in reading that compares good and poor readers. Most of this research is based on narrow uses of standardized tests, and the researchers invariably conclude that good readers do whatever is being studied better than poor readers.

The "poor" and "good" reader designations in RMA research are used to demonstrate that all readers have more in common in their reading strategy and language use than most researchers usually admit. Good/poor labels are more harmful than helpful. These labels enable some teachers to build expectations about readers without being responsible for listening to students read, talking to students about reading, or examining students' reading profiles across a range of materials.

Another unfortunate ramification of using these labels is that readers begin to define themselves in these terms, and these views begin to limit their expectations for success. Regardless of the strategies readers use, their personal views of the reading process and their own abilities as readers influence their confidence as readers. In turn, their confidence as readers can influence their actual reading development. I am not arguing that merely believing that one is literate will make it so. But I am suggesting that when students believe they are not readers and writers, they act on their mythical perceptions of what categorizes poor readers, nonreaders, or illiterates, and they define themselves in such ways. And these definitions limit their perceptions about their own potential as language users.

Retrospective miscue analysis is a tool that provides opportunities for students to define themselves as literate members of our society as they explore their transactions with written texts. It is a teaching strategy that allows teachers and students to consider what readers are capable of doing and what work readers need to do to become more efficient and effective at reading the range of written materials necessary to function well in a literate society. It provides the window through which readers see their own thinking and learning processes.

In conclusion, I return to my reasons for exploring retrospective miscue analysis. I want to know how RMA influences readers. Specifically, how do readers revalue themselves? How do they revalue the reading process? How do they talk and reflect about the reading process and their own reading proficiency? Does RMA improve their proficiency as readers? During the past decade, I believe that my colleagues and I have provided beginning answers to these questions by documenting the potential of RMA to help all readers, including proficient readers, revalue themselves, and in so doing help them become more proficient. At the same time, we also learned to value all readers, the nature of the reading process, and the power of language in new and expanded ways. As we disseminate what we have learned, I hope that RMA becomes a vehicle to establish revaluing as a major concept that reading researchers, teachers, teacher educators, and teacher/researchers consider seriously.

REFERENCES

Brown, A., Campione, J., & Day, J. (1980). *Learning to learn: On training students to learn from texts* (Tech. Rep. No. 189). Urbana-Champaign: University of Illinois, Center for the Study of Reading.

Coles, R. (1981). *The reading strategies of selected junior high students in the content areas*. Unpublished doctoral dissertation, University of Arizona, Tucson.

Costello, S. (1992). *Collaborative retrospective miscue analysis with middle grade students*. Unpublished doctoral dissertation, University of Arizona, Tucson.

Costello, S. (1996). A teacher-researcher uses RMA. In Y. Goodman & A. Marek (Eds.), *Retrospective miscue analysis: Revaluing readers and reading* (pp. 165-176). Katonah, NY: Richard C. Owen Publishers.

Flores, B. (1982) *Language interference or influence: Toward a theory for Hispanic bilingualism*. Unpublished doctoral dissertation, University of Arizona, Tucson.

Flurkey, A. (1997). *Reading as flow: A linguistic alternative to fluency*. Unpublished doctoral dissertation, University of Arizona, Tucson.

Goodman, D. (1996). The readers' detective club. In Y. Goodman & A. Marek (Eds.), *Retrospective miscue analysis: Revaluing readers and reading* (pp. (177-187). Katonah, NY: Richard C. Owen Publishers.

Goodman, K. (1973). Miscues: Window on the reading process. In K. S. Goodman (Ed.), *Miscue analysis: Applications of reading instruction* (pp. 3-14). Urbana, IL: ERIC and National Council of Teachers of English.

Goodman, K. (1994). Reading, writing and written texts: A transactional sociopsycholinguistic view. In R. Ruddell, M. Ruddell, & H. Singer (Eds.), *Theoretical models and processes of reading* (pp. 1093-1130). Newark, DE: International Reading Association.

Goodman, Y. (1996a). Revaluing readers while readers revalue themselves: Retrospective miscue analysis. *Reading Teacher, 49*(8), 600-609.

Goodman, Y. (1996b). At the critical moment: RMA in classrooms. In Y. Goodman & A. Marek (Eds.), *Retrospective miscue analysis: Revaluing readers and reading* (pp. 189-202). Katonah, NY: Richard C. Owen Publishers.

Goodman, Y., & Burke, C. (1980). *Reading strategies: Focus on comprehension*. Katonah, NY: Richard C. Owen Publishers.

Goodman, Y., & Flurkey, A. (1996). Retrospective miscue analysis in middle school. In Y. Goodman & A. Marek (Eds.), *Retrospective miscue analysis: Revaluing readers and reading* (pp. 87-106). Katonah, NY: Richard C. Owen Publishers.

Goodman, Y. & Marek, A. (1989). *Retrospective miscue analysis: Two papers* (Occasional Paper No. 19). Tucson: University of Arizona, College of Education, Program in Language and Literacy.

Goodman, Y., & Marek, A. (Eds.). (1996). *Retrospective miscue analysis: Revaluing readers and reading*. Katonah, NY: Richard C. Owen Publishers.

Goodman, Y., Martens, P., & Flurkey, A. (Eds.) (1995). [Special issue]. *Primary Voices, 3*(4).

Goodman, Y., Watson, D., & Burke, C. (1987). *Reading miscue inventory: Alternative procedures*. Katonah, NY: Richard C. Owen Publishers.

Goodman, Y., Watson, D., & Burke, C. (1996). *Reading strategies: Focus on comprehension*. Katonah, NY: Richard C. Owen Publishers.

Marek, A. (1987). *Retrospective miscue analysis as an instructional strategy with adult readers*. Unpublished doctoral dissertation, University of Arizona, Tucson.

Marek, A. (1996a). An accomplished professional: A reader in trouble. In Y. Goodman & A. Marek (Eds.), *Retrospective miscue analysis: Revaluing readers and reading* (pp. 51-70). Katonah, NY: Richard C. Owen Publishers.

Marek, A. (1996b). Surviving reading instruction. In Y. Goodman & A. Marek (Eds.), *Retrospective miscue analysis: Revaluing readers and reading* (pp. 71-86). Katonah, NY: Richard C. Owen Publishers.

Raisner, B. (1977). *Reading strategies employed by non-proficient adult college students as observed through miscue analysis retrospection*. Unpublished doctoral dissertation, Hofstra University, Hempstead, N.Y.

Stephenson, M. (1980). *Using principles of miscue analysis as remediation for high school students*. Unpublished paper, University of Arizona, Tucson.

Watson, D. (1978). Reader selected miscues: Getting more from sustained silent reading. *English Education, 10*(2), 75-85.

Watson, D., & Hoge, S. (1996). Reader-selected miscues. In Y. Goodman & A. Marek (Eds.), *Retrospective miscue analysis: Revaluing readers and reading* (pp. 157-164). Katonah, NY: Richard C. Owen Publishers.

Weatherill, D. (1996). Revealing strategies for a good reader. In Y. Goodman & A. Marek (Eds.), *Retrospective miscue analysis: Revaluing readers and reading* (pp. 143-148). Katonah, NY: Richard C. Owen Publishers.

Woodley, J., & Miller, L. (1983). Retrospective miscue analysis: Procedures for research and instruction. *Research on Reading in Secondary Schools*, Monograph Series 10-11, Tucson, AZ.

Worsnop, C. (1996). The beginnings of retrospective miscue analysis. In Y. Goodman & A. Marek (Eds.), *Retrospective miscue analysis: Revaluing readers and reading* (pp. 151-156). Katonah, NY: Richard C. Owen Publishers.

Chapter Sixteen

Teaching of Reading to Second Language Learners

Catherine Wallace
Institute of Education, University of London

It was 1974. I had never taught anyone to read although, as a teacher of English as a Foreign Language, I had taught reading in a foreign language to those who generally were highly literate in their first language. I was a volunteer in a nationwide adult literacy scheme at a time when periodic concern about the extent of adult literacy in Britain had found expression in the Right to Read campaign of that year. Peter was the student I taught for 1-hour periods twice a week during that year. These were my notes at the time:

> Peter at the age of 38, is a total beginner to reading, never having been to school. He is Anglo Indian. He has a Scottish surname and claims that English is his first and only language. He arrived at the lesson on the first day, knowing his ABC, and then only imperfectly, with no idea of letter/sound correspondence and not knowing how to tackle print on the page. Not only did he not possess even the left-right, up-down orientation but he did not appear to have the concept of what a written word was—in the sense of something on the page surrounded by space on either side.

It is clear from these notes that I was as much a novice in many ways as Peter. I would not now characterize learning to read in the rather deficit-oriented ways indicated here. Peter and I were both learners; much of the work was hit and miss and trial and error. Nonetheless, as the weeks went on and I listened to tapes of our lessons, I saw Peter making progress and I was looking for some way—a set of tools or procedures—to capture the nature of this progress. It is a question that remains central for those of us interested in what our learners are doing. What does progress look like? How can we support the strong but intuitive sense we have of our learners' development with frameworks for description and analysis? Are we as teachers to ignore the evidence available to us from our learners' responses to texts in favor of judgments made on the basis of test results? Tests were, in any case, useless for my purposes; on any conventional test Peter would produce no score at all.

It was around this time that I came across Ken Goodman's (1967) article, "Reading: A Psycholinguistic Guessing Game," which introduced the principles of miscue analysis. The procedure of miscue analysis appealed to me for several reasons.

First, miscue analysis looked at learners and, more particularly, at the process of learning to read. It was an attempt to capture on line what strategies learners were using. Of course, as Alderson and Urquhart (1984) have pointed out, miscue analysis remains an interpretation of what is going on. We have no way of getting inside learners' heads. Nonetheless, although subsequent procedures have been developed which attempt to establish learners' own perceptions of difficulty (e.g., Cavalcanti, 1987), at the time miscue analysis most closely provided us with a "window on the reading process." Moreover, the concept of *miscue* was a way of acknowledging that learners are meaning makers; they are attempting to make sense of the world including the world of print.

Second, miscue analysis saw learners' progress through texts and their ongoing development as readers as patterned and rule-governed. Their behavior is not random: There is a system. This notion of miscue related very neatly—although connections were not to my knowledge generally made—to the work then going on in applied linguistics in the field of error analysis, developed by Corder (cf. 1974). In Corder's work, errors were judged to reflect the approximative system of a language learner en route to mastery of the target language. The term *interlanguage*, originally coined by Selinker (1972), was and still is used to describe this individual grammar, which reflects the learner's current hypotheses about the L2. At the time, this was a new way of looking at what learners (language learners particularly, but the same could be said in principle of any learners) are doing and thinking in the process of making sense of incoming language data. Before then, in the field of foreign language learning, errors of speaking or writing were judged negatively, and attributed either to interference from the first language, straightforward mistakes, or as the result of mere carelessness. Of course, all learners will make mistakes of this latter kind. Corder consequently makes a distinction between "errors" as systematic and "mistakes," which are better seen as slips of the tongue or pen. The connection with reading behavior, and indeed other language learning processes, is clear. The view of language learners as inevitable producers of errors that are systematic, not random, and of learning as essentially a problem-solving process relates well to a view of reading that sees the occurrence of error or miscue as both an inherent part of learning and as having some system or patterning.

Reading as an Aspect of Language Behavior

Most specifically and importantly for my purposes was that miscue analysis characterized reading behavior as a kind of language behavior and miscues, in part, a reflection of the language system which learners are currently operating. The language system of second language readers, that is, their interlanguage, is different from that of typical native speakers. We might therefore expect that departures from the text in reading aloud would reflect this. Occasionally, there will also be some difficulty in predicting unfamiliar constructions; that is, sentence constructions that are not within the learners' existing competence. Goodman's work on miscue analysis offers particular insights into the processing of texts by second language learners, for it acknowledges the possibility of mismatches, at graphophonic, syntactic, and semantic levels, between the standard written version of texts and learners' interlanguage systems. Indeed for all learners, both L1 and L2, the way they understand and use language will have an impact on their processing of texts and the nature of miscues made in reading aloud.

Second Language Learners

In talking of second language learners, just what kind of learner do we mean? Is it not preferable to refer to bilingual learners, thus acknowledging the active role of two or more languages, or possibly language varieties, in language development and learning? Although aware of its inadequacy, and with no wish to deny the range of learners' linguistic resources, I use the term *L2 learners* as a general term in this discussion.

My interest in drawing on miscue analysis has been with very early L2 learners, who have little or no literacy in their first language, and who are therefore acquiring literacy along with a second language. With such learners, miscue analysis is not just a tool for teachers to assess progress in reading and language development through the changing nature of miscues; it offers insight for learners themselves into their own learning and language development processes. First, learners have the opportunity to observe, through the nature of their own miscues, how their current interlanguage differs from the language of the text. Second, they are able to learn more about the structure of English because written language is more consistent and fully structured than typical day-to-day spoken language and, because it is visible as marks on the page, it is also more readily talked about.

I have referred earlier to those who have an evolving interlanguage—who are still in the process of acquiring English. There are other kinds of learners who may have stable systems even if they show considerable departure from most native-speaking varieties. Peter was such a learner. Although English was Peter's first and only language, he had a language system that departed considerably from the typical usage of most standard speakers, particularly in the systematic reduction or replacement of some syntactic features. For instance, he did not produce the DO auxiliary in past tense negative sentences, as in "I didn't—or did not—come" (Peter would say, "I never came"). It will immediately and rightly be pointed out that learners may be perfectly competent to predict structures that are absent from their own production. Indeed, this was one of my questions as I analyzed Peter's miscues, particularly those relating to syntactic features. In other words, how far could Peter predict features of syntax found in simple written language that were totally absent in his own usage, as far as I could judge from extensive conversation with him and careful examination of transcripts of his spoken language?

The answers were not at all straightforward. I note from analysis of Peter's spoken language use and reading and that of other students that although it is true that some learners in the very early stages of reading find it hard to predict items of structure that do not occur at all in their own speech, it is also the case that all readers, reading in L1 or L2, have to cope with language that is remote from their own spoken production. It seems to be the degree of difference that is crucial, a point which clearly has implications for our choice of texts for teaching.

In short, both nonstandard and non-native users of English will have typical language usage that differs from the standard and therefore from the language that characterizes most written texts. They will have a different phonemic system as well as a different syntactic and semantic system. As I have argued, this does not necessarily affect their understanding of texts. "Competence, what readers are capable of doing, must be separated from performance, what we observe them do" (Goodman 1988, p. 13). In other words, performance is not a necessary reflection of underlying competence—and this applies both to reading ability and knowledge of English.

However, L2 and nonstandard learners will produce miscues that reflect a different underlying linguistic system. An example would be:

1. "Life in the village begin at 4am" for
2. "Life in the village began at 4am"

This interlanguage miscue by an L2 learner, Ravinder, is typical of miscues that reflect the current usage of the learner. Ravinder was not yet using the irregular past tense form of BEGIN in his own speech.

Access to standard written language will in itself support L2 learners' development toward more standard English, as learners take advantage of exposure to more fully structured, more "visible" input. However, it is generally not productive to correct interlanguage features in the course of reading itself, for learners are likely to see this as a correction of their language, not their processing of the text (although such miscues may be noted for the purposes of general language development work on another occasion). It is, as has often been pointed out (cf. e.g., Wallace, 1988; Wight, 1976), even less appropriate to correct what are more properly seen as dialect features in speakers such as Peter, who have a stable variety of English.

The fact of systematic differences in English language use by L2 learners will also mean, moreover, that some kinds of literacy instruction may be mystifying to them, particularly work on phonemic awareness. For instance, sounds that are separate phonemes in Received Pronunciation may function as allophones in their interlanguage and therefore not be readily distinguishable for them phonetically. So, "ship" and "sheep" will be pronounced identically by some L2 learners, just as, incidentally, will "cot" and "caught" for Scottish speakers. This has long been demonstrated by sociolinguists (e.g., Trudgill, 1975), which makes it all the more surprising that so little account is taken of language variation in the revived interest in the teaching—and testing—of phonemic awareness. In fact, individual learners (both first and second language users) will operate a whole range of different language systems that signal regional, ethnic, and class identity, as well as nationality, but which can nonetheless be broadly characterized as English. This principle of language variation has always been acknowledged in Goodman's work, making it sociolinguistically as well as linguistically well-grounded.

Looking at Learners: Case Studies

As Goodman's work looks at learners and learning rather than methods, it lends itself to case study approaches. That is, it not only offers procedures that take account of learners' language backgrounds, but it also acknowledges the role of the wider context of situation. In order to interpret as well as merely describe what is going on, we need as full an understanding as possible not just of the learner's language system but of a whole set of cultural and contextual factors. In this sense, Goodman's work on miscue analysis is logically part of the wider and continuing commitment to the Whole Language movement, one of whose tenets is the need to look at the learner in a sociocultural context. Quite consistently in the work of Ken and Yetta Goodman, the initial questions to be asked by teachers are not "What kinds of skills do we teach?", but "What abilities, resources and experiences do learners bring with them?"

In the case of learners who come from minority cultural and linguistic backgrounds, it is even more important to be aware of context. It is not just their experience and use of the English language that will diverge, but in many cases, they will also have different experiences of learning and expectations of education.

Context and Variability

Once we acknowledge the role of context we allow for variability. Ellis (1985) has shown how second language learners' production of certain L2 forms will indicate variable competence in predictable ways depending on the linguistic and situational context. Equally, reading behavior as a form of language production, especially in the case of reading aloud, is variable. Goodman (1988) notes that such variability depends on the semantic background brought to the reading task. But there are a whole range of additional factors which promote variability. This seems an unexceptional point to make, and yet much quantitative research and certain kinds of tests largely ignore the effect of context on reading performance and, therefore, take little or no account of variability. Miscue analysis, on the other hand, by offering the possibility to observe learners' responses to texts in varying situations with varying kinds of texts, can capture both systematic variability and the kind of random variability which is part of all human behavior.

In looking at the impact of context in studies of some adult and child learners (Wallace, 1987), I considered both situational and textual context as variables. I was prompted to do this by my observation—guided by miscue analysis—that features of the situation, including the behavior of the teacher, as well as features of the text, frequently frustrate as much as support the learner.

My interest, therefore, extended beyond the interaction between text and reader (as in conventional miscue analysis) to the kind of miscues made and strategies used in the mediated reading event, which takes account of teacher intervention. Moreover, I also wanted to locate this event in a wider context in order to consider some of the cultural assumptions of both teacher and learner. What, for instance, are their respective views of literacy education in general? What are our learners' expectations and experiences of written texts? How much control are we, as teachers, prepared to relinquish? With these questions in mind, I present two case studies of adult learners. In each case I begin with the wider social context and then describe a particular lesson presented as a three-way interaction among teacher, learner, and text.

HILLYARD

The Wider Context

Hillyard approached the local literacy scheme for help with his reading and writing and, as a volunteer, I was asked to be his tutor. I went once a week to his home in Southall in West London. Hillyard was born in Dominica, was in his early to mid-30s, and had been in Britain for about 16 years. He was a confident and resourceful person. There was little evidence of the low self-esteem that supposedly characterizes those of limited literacy. He worked six days a week. On the seventh he washed his clothes and cleaned his one room, which was immaculate. There was chat over cups of tea and cake, and interruptions by friends and his two young nephews. The television was on throughout but never really attended to. My roles shifted in this setting from casual friend, to a sort of social worker—though intimate or personal matters were never discussed—to a rather formal instructor. Hillyard liked to call me "cheach" (teacher) and though assertive enough as a conversationalist, he tended not to challenge or make suggestions once we were in teaching mode.

Language Background

Hillyard's first language was a variety of French Creole, but English had been the medium of instruction at school, which he had seemingly attended intermittently in Dominica. Because of the circumstances of our lessons, I was able to see Hillyard operate in a range of linguistic settings. When friends came by he would talk in French Creole; with his two young nephews he used a less standard variety of English than he used with me. This opportunity to observe his linguistic versatility gave me richer insight into his language repertoire than I might otherwise have had. The following is an example of a conversation between the two of us, which is incidentally a comment (arguably with racist overtones) on the predominantly Indian community in which Hillyard lived.

H. Mark you, I got them for friend you know, Indian people, some of them you know.
C. What - sorry?
H. I got some Indian for friend.
C. So some of them you get on all right with?
H. Not much . . . just to keep the time goin' you know . . . their culture - I can (= "cannot" in Hillyard's language variety) understand their culture at all. Their culture much different than other people.
C. What about English people?
H. English people and West Indian same culture en it? . . . same culture . . . same rule. No different. Food the same, same language, the same dress. English like dance, West Indian like dance, but Indian no like that . . . just goin' in the pub, drink and come back home. Indian no like English picture, only their own picture they like. That's what they like. But English picture and West Indian no difference . . . we can understand Indian language and it's far for us to go to picture. We have to go out from Southall - West Ealing or in the West End of London . . . But with Indian now, they goin' their picture. Indian no dance. No eat food like we.
C. But you've been into Indian houses.
H. Cheach, I've been already when . . . you find they makin' a cup of tea for you. You have to put the tea and the milk together to boil. I find that is fun - it is fun. So when I tell them that's not the way to makin' tea they tellin' me that we and English people we don't know how to make tea!

An Interaction Around Text

The following extract is from a book entitled *Toussaint L'Ouverture of the West Indies* (Bentley, 1969) about the Haitian slave who led the successful slave revolt against the French.

i) preamble (Hillyard's contributions are in capitals.)

Did you have a look at this? I DOESN'T HAVE MUCH TIME BUT I DOES TAKE IT AT WORK . . . WHEN I GOT THE TIME I DOES. (inaudible) Remember we were talking about er. . this was about Toussaint who lived in - do you remember where he lived? HAITI and in Haiti at that time all the rich men were what? FRENCH and what about the black people, what were they? SLAVE Slaves right, and this means the French people owned the slaves. Do you remember what kind of things grew in Haiti? SUGAR - SUGAR CANE. COFFEE. Good and there were orchards too . . . It goes on to say that the owners were very cruel and used to hit the slaves with whips. Lets see how you got on with this.

ii) the reading (My intervention is in parentheses followed by H's responses.) Words that H. finally reads correctly after hesitation or a miscue are underlined.

Some of the owner were very - very cruel. If they - if they does . . . if they don' T - H- O - U - G - H - T - thought that they - their slave were not workin' hard . . . (start again from the beginning of the sentence). If they thought if they thought that their slave were not workin' hard enough ("enough" you got it this time) they beat them [pauses] (how did they beat them?). They beat them ...f..F - I - E - R - C - E - firstly (It's like "firstly" it means savagely . . . horribly) - [It's clear that H. does not know this word so I give it - "fiercely"] with big hips - whip. In all the West Indies islands (whether) British and French and also in America there were quite a lot . . . a lot of C - R - U - cruel slave owner (So who were cruel? - the owner of the slave). Sometime a slave were beaten so terrible that he decide . . . that he did . . . he die (So why did he die? - because of beatin'). . . . Toussaint owner were not a cruel man. He treat his slave well . . . . Sometime slave run away from the cruel owner and had ("hid") in the wild forest and they and they often dead of hunger or decided (What else can you die of? hunger or - disaster - no that's a good guess; it's another word for illness)- oh disease.

The original text reads:

Some of the owners were very cruel. If they thought that their slaves were not working hard enough, they beat them fiercely

> with big whips. In all the West Indian islands, whether British or French, and also in America, there were quite a lot of cruel slave-owners. Sometimes a slave was beaten so terribly that he died. Even women-slaves were whipped very harshly. Toussaint's owner was not a cruel man. He treated his slaves well. Sometimes slaves ran away from the cruel owners and hid in the wild forests, and then they often died of hunger or disease.

Comments

The text. The text is complex and rather literary and formal (e.g., the reduced subordinate clause introduced by "whether" in line 11). However, Hillyard is engaged with the story, and the general content compensates in part for some of the unpredictable language. Also some potentially difficult vocabulary is within a predictable semantic field relating to the conditions of slavery.

Hillyard. Hillyard's miscues are of two major kinds: one is a frequency of graphophonic miscues, for example, had/hid or hips/whips. Importantly, however, they are usually immediately self-corrected and thus might be defined as slips in Corder's sense. The second are miscues that are attributable to his own use of English; for example, the consistent omission of the "ed" past tense ending (an example in this extract is in line 16) and the omission of plural s. Hillyard, clearly drawing on his experience with earlier teaching methods, uses letter names as a strategy to tackle problem words, with some apparent success, as long as he knows the word (compare, e.g., "thought", "cruel" and "fiercely"). In listening to him on tape, however, it seems that he is not so much using this as a route to meaning (Goodman [1988] challenges the feasibility of this) but of checking out for himself. The letter naming is done very rapidly, as if to suggest, "Yes that's what I thought!"

What is of greatest interest, along with the fairly consistent use of his own interlanguage, is the way he can predict items in the text which would not generally feature in his own language. At a lexical level is the word 'disease'; more significantly, at the syntactic level, is the word 'enough' at the end of a longish subordinate clause. Once Hillyard accepts the advice to backtrack into the text, he readily predicts this word.

CW. It is always worth looking at potential as well as actual points of intervention. So although I now consider that I generally intervene excessively in my lessons with Hillyard, I do not, consistent with the view I take on interlanguage miscues, correct these in Hillyard's reading. However, what is more striking is the degree to which I control the interaction. In the preamble, for instance, Hillyard has no opportunity to claim a more equal role in order to elaborate on the circumstances or background of the story of Toussaint, which he recalled well from an earlier lesson and his survey of the text during the week. I am imposing a rather crude political commentary on the text without providing any opportunity for Hillyard to give his own interpretation. In short, I am positioning him both generally in the reading event and in his stance to the particular text.

AMNA

The Wider Context

Amna was a 19-year-old Pakistani woman who had been in Britain for about a year when I met her at the local Further Education college where I was teaching a small group of beginner learners of English, most of whom had little or no literacy in the L1. Amna, one of this group, asked me for extra help with her reading and we then met, generally once a week, over a period of 18 months. Amna, even with her very limited English, was ready to take the initiative in learning situations, and she saw our sharing of texts as an opportunity for one to one interaction as much as an opportunity to improve her reading.

Language Background

Amna's first language was Urdu, but as she had not been to school in Pakistan she was not literate in Urdu and was therefore acquiring literacy along with English (although she began Urdu literacy lessons shortly afterwards). As she had had little contact with English speakers during her year in Britain, she still was a near beginner in English at the start of her classes. Unlike Hillyard, then, her system of English was evolving, and one of the features I wanted to capture was the progress she made in English along with her progress in reading simple texts in English and how both influenced each other.

Interaction Around Texts

As Amna was in the very early stages of reading, her reading of any continuous text remained hesitant although the changing nature of her miscues revealed both language and literacy development (I discuss this more fully in Wallace, 1989). However, the two examples I offer here focus less on specific departures from the text and more on Amna's spontaneous comment on the text, or more exactly, on text plus picture. Like most early readers Amna attempted to use the visual image to extend and clarify the written text.

Example 1

The text is an extract from a book entitled Doing My Flat Up, which is part of a series written by students at Hackney Reading Centre in London. The page read by Amna has an illustration of a woman standing on a ladder, painting the ceiling with a hand-held paintbrush. The two lines of text above the illustration read:

I paint the ceiling.
You should see me.

Amna	CW
I paint. I paint	What's she painting? Look at the picture? What's this?-"Ceiling"
I paint the ceiling you said . . . "Should"	
You should see me . . . you should see . . . Who telling?	Who's . . . ?
Who's she - who's she telling?	
Your should - this is "your"?	"You"
You should see me.	
Then *who* see her?	Yes, who's she talking to?
Yeh.	Well, she's talking to you the reader - I think. Do you think that's strange?
Yeh, nobody here. Then who talk to her?	That's right. Who's talking to her? Well, she's the writer. She's writing the story for you. She's talking to you.

Example 2

The text is an extract from *The Sly Fox and the Little Red Hen* in the Ladybird *Read it Yourself* series of readers for very young children. The picture of the fox in Little Red Hen's kitchen shows a wall shelf with a plate rack above and cups suspended on hooks below. Amna's attention is drawn to the cups hanging on the wall.

Amna	CW
Then before the fox could move she . . . fly up to the - no	 "could" "move" "high beam"
Miss she er . . . you know . . . cup here in the house . . . cup . . . cup. She no use cup.	 What? Why not? Why can't she use a cup?
No Miss . . . because she . . . she you know she . . . she chicken you know.	 Can't chickens use cups?
No Miss . . . she took and maybe nice . . . she nice thinking, you know.	 But you don't think she uses them to drink out of?
No Miss . . . she eat in the floor. She no use cup and plate.	 Um. But in stories things are different . . . I mean . . . in this story the hen can talk and the fox talks . . .
Yes Miss. No in Pakistan. No him talking and no her.	 . . . not even in stories?
Maybe story.	

Comments

The texts. The text in example 1 was produced as part of a Language Experience approach for adult learners in literacy classes, which include L2 and nonstandard speakers of English. It has—rather confusingly and inconsistently I feel—kept some of the features of speech of the student who originally produced it. The text is apparently simply structured but, as is revealed by Amna's comment, pragmatically complex in that the "True Life" convention of the story is quite sophisticated. Amna is used to narratives in which the action and dialogue remain firmly within the text, but this direct address to the reader by the author/protagonist confuses her. More specifically, it is not the semantic meaning of YOU which causes difficulty but its function in the text. The text in example 2 is obviously written for children and raises different kinds of questions about its suitability for adult second language learners.

Amna. It is typical for Amna to take the initiative in commenting on and challenging both the language and content of texts. Thus she challenges the coy and rather patronizing language typical of children's books, commenting on one occasion on the sentence, 'The little old man'—he no little! Equally, she comments on the language of texts. So, for example, Amna, who never herself uses the DO auxiliary to form past tense interrogatives, in response to a sentence "Did you see the ghost?", comments "Did you" means past?

In the cases quoted earlier, she is challenging more global conventions of texts, in particular, sociopragmatic features related to the functions of language in the written text and of the visuals and the relationship between them. On the first occasion, in interaction one, she is querying the convention whereby the author/narrator directly addresses the reader. Amna has never encountered this exophoric use of "you" in a written text, in which one needs to search for a referent outside the text. As a learner who seeks to make sense of texts she wants an explanation. In the second case her attention is directed to the anthropomorphic representation of animals, and the extent to which they are represented as taking part in human activities like drinking out of cups. It may well be that children for whom this text is primarily intended also find this kind of (not untypical) visual representation bizarre (we can accept talking animals, but cups!) but resign themselves early on to this kind of "cuteness" in certain children's books. Amna has no inhibitions about expressing her challenge to what she sees as the ridiculous or far-fetched. Ultimately, however, the incident is positive, as it offers a useful occasion to talk explicitly about some of the conventions of stories.

CW. Here I am reacting to Amna rather than initiating exchanges in the way I do with Hillyard. In the second case I am clearly playing a falsely naive role. I wanted to use these occasions for Amna to develop language proficiency as well as greater awareness of features of text and stories. In fact, I too gained a greater awareness of some of these. Amna's comments offered new insights into the kind of difficulties that might be raised by culturally unfamiliar features of texts.

We see, then, that in looking at what learners are doing and saying in response to texts and trying to learn in turn from their behavior as readers, we are building on miscue analysis principles to consider not just the kind of miscues made—whether graphophonic, syntactic or semantic, or pragmatic—but what might have triggered them. We need to also consider the role of the text and, particularly, the teacher in supporting or frustrating the learner both during the actual reading of texts and at the margins of the interaction.

Influence in Britain of Goodman's work: The State of the Debate

Goodman's work has remained influential in Britain, as evidenced by the attention to miscue analysis in the Schools Council Report: Extending Beginning Reading (Southgate, Arnold, & Johnson, 1981) and, more recently, in the National Curriculum of 1988 and the Primary Language Record (Barrs, Ellis, Hester, & Thomas, 1988), which offers specific guidance on the evaluation of young children's language and learning development. The latter notes, for example, the way in which even beginning readers bring all their linguistic knowledge and experience of life to the task of processing text. British educators such as Arnold (1982) and the authors of the Primary Language Record (Barrs et al., 1988), have adapted, simplified, or extended Goodman's original work while remaining true, I believe, to its fundamental principles, as I too have wished to do in my own work. The continuing adherence to this way of working should come as no surprise as the procedure fits into the long tradition of learner-centered approaches in British schools—particularly at primary level—which take a very similar position to what has come to be known as the Whole Language movement in the United States.

Nonetheless, some of the key principles of Goodman's work have lately fueled renewed controversy about the way we learn to read. This has partly centered around the research finding that skilled readers, to a greater degree than previously thought, read each word in the text, thus seeming to challenge Goodman's view that good readers are highly selective in their reading and, by implication, that we should encourage such selectivity in learners. Alternative and supposedly more adequate models have been proposed during the years since Goodman's original work appeared. These at first sight appear to give greater prominence to the role of the physical text and less to the linguistic and world knowledge resources which readers bring with them to the text. Stanovitch (1980), for instance, talks of the compensatory view by which "a process at any level can compensate for deficiencies at any other level" (p. 36). Certainly, this is pertinent for L2 learners who need to compensate for weak linguistic knowledge by drawing on other—particularly world knowledge—sources.

Ultimately, however, I am not convinced that subsequent models offer significantly improved, or indeed substantially different, accounts to Goodman's. Harrison (1992), for example, in an excellent comprehensive overview of reading theory and practice, notes that the Smith and Goodman accounts are very close to the interactive-compensatory one of Stanovitch. One criticism directed at Goodman's model, though, is that the approach overly focuses on "top down" processing and neglects so-called "bottom up" features. It is interesting, however, that Goodman himself does not, to my knowledge, use either term and no one—least of all Goodman—has ever claimed that one draws exclusively on knowledge of the world and the grammar without engaging with the text itself. Obviously and necessarily, background knowledge of the world and knowledge of the system of English interact with the evidence supplied by the marks on the page. And yet the accusations of a predominantly or even exclusively "top-down" orientation persist e.g., see Eskey, who describes Smith and Goodman as "top-down advocates" [1988, p. 94].

Eskey (1988), in addressing the issue of L2 learners in particular, argues that what he describes as "simple language decoding" has been neglected in second language reading pedagogy, partly due to the influence of Goodman's work. If Eskey means that L2 learners need to know a particular script in order to read it, that seems indisputable; if he means that they need to know the language encoded in the script, that is equally indisputable. But decoding, or *recoding* as Goodman would call it, can never be simple and exclusively bottom up (i.e., drawn from the marks on the page) as seems to be implied. The L2 reader, along with all readers, needs to go beyond the surface graphophonic features of the text. She or he needs to draw on knowledge of semantic and syntactic constraints on graphophonic knowledge to decode even apparently simple sentences accurately (e.g., "She lead a minute dog into the room").

It is true that learners such as Amna who are acquiring literacy along with English need careful support toward an understanding of the way in which the English writing system represents meaning. However, a far more typical case with early L2 readers, who have some literacy in their L1, as school teachers and literacy tutors will attest, is the learner who recodes fluently and accurately in the main but, as revealed by questioning on the text and certain kinds of miscues, has very limited understanding. In fact, they may well read words such as "lead" and "minute" in the previous sentence as /leed/ and /minit/. More to the point, they may not expect to understand because so much of reading pedagogy with beginning readers—in spite of the claimed neglect of "simple decoding skills"—continues to emphasize success in reading as a mere oral rendering of the written text.

Certainly inherent in Goodman's model, and underlying his claim of selectivity of attention in reading, is the linguistically well-established principle of redundancy. Language, particularly written language, duplicates information sources. For example, plural is marked twice, by inflection on the noun and by the plural form of the verb: "The girls are at home." This kind of redundancy as inherent to language is within the text itself. And it is this principle that partly underlies Goodman's view that it is inefficient to attend to every feature of written text.

In short, some of the comments on Goodman's work have led to the setting up of false dichotomies or rigid polarities that have not advanced the debate about reading pedagogy in very practical ways. Where we might all broadly and more significantly agree, however, is that learner-readers are particularly dependent on contextual clues within the text and this context dependency is part of the developmental process. As far as I am aware few, if any, researchers or practitioners have claimed that readers are actively helped in the early stages of reading if contextual clues are withdrawn. Certainly Adams' (1990) widely quoted and detailed work does not lead one to draw these conclusions. Even though Adams quotes the now well-documented work that shows correlation between reading achievement (although there is rarely ever any full discussion about how this is evaluated) and letter naming and phonemic awareness, she, like others, is not able to claim a causal effect, in the sense that specific and direct teaching of these aspects of literacy in isolation from any others best promotes success. On the contrary, it seems likely that the kind of letter awareness and phonemic awareness shown to correlate with later reading achievement is developed in holistic contexts that involve meaningful interaction around print with adults, in what Heath (1983) calls *literacy events*. Thus, with Peter, for instance, although I had early abandoned futile attempts to teach letter-sound correspondence in isolation from continuous text, once we embarked on shared reading aloud he would himself ask, when he wanted to check whether a word was "let" or "tell", for example, "Is that an L or a T?", drawing on and extending one resource he already had —knowledge of the letter names.

A further criticism of Goodman's work has been the assertion of naturalness: given appropriate conditions learning to read will be as natural as learning to speak. This claim has led to some misunderstanding of Goodman's work, as I understand it. First, it is not suggested that learning to read will just happen. It requires constant support and lots of practice, something that many children get in interaction with caregivers. It must be conceded, however, that for some children, the crucial opportunities for practice are much more easily acquired in the case of speaking than with reading and writing. For yet others, opportunities for all kinds of language development are relatively restricted. There is a danger that in wanting to avoid a deficit orientation we fail to acknowledge the very real disadvantages some learners bring to learning because of social, circumstantial reasons.

The question then arises as to whether there is a need, particularly with some learners, to offer firmer scaffolding and more explicit instruction than some versions of Whole Language pedagogy seem to advocate. In other words, how far should learners' progress as readers and writers be structured? What kinds of intervention are helpful? And what, if any, metalinguistic tools will support learning? Although there is now some general agreement as to the need to make what we are doing explicit to learners, differences of view center around which features of the reading and writing process warrant what kinds of specific focusing in what circumstances.

One of the difficulties with the currently favored focus on the development of phonemic awareness is not the emphasis on explicitness or the practice of skills as such. It is the emphasis on one level of language—the graphophonic—to the neglect of syntactic, semantic, and pragmatic features of texts. In particular, the role of syntactic features such as word order and morphology has been relatively neglected. This is in spite of work which has shown that syntactic awareness, in particular of word order, develops in advance of letter/sound awareness in young children (e.g., the work of Manning, Manning, Long, & Kamil, 1993, who draw on the Piagetian research of Ferreiro & Teberosky, 1982).

My own observations of adult L2 learners suggest that principles of syntactic regularities are much more readily understood than are letter/sound correspondences. Moreover, syntactic features such as morphology (e.g., past tense ed and possessive s) are signaled through visual features alone—not through any consistent letter/sound correspondence. For example, Stubbs (1980), drawing on a classic but little quoted study of the English writing system by Albrow (1972), notes how the English writing system gives consistent information about the grammar of English which is revealed graphically not graphophonically. Thus, the important thing to know about ed on words like "paint," "work," "like," and "use" is not how ed is pronounced (which will vary and may be hard to hear in some contexts) but that the juxtaposition of these two letters at the end of a verbal form invariably signals past time in simple written sentences. L2 students are aware of this and a frequent question is "Miss, ED means past?" And this is the right question to ask;

not, for example, "lD means past?", which it may not, for instance, in words like "livid" or "tepid."

In short, analytical skills are certainly crucial but they need to be anchored to learners' past experience, present stage of literacy and language development, and their own current awareness of language, literacy, and learning. As learners become aware of the differences and similarity between speaking and writing they will, like Amna, seek to develop a metalanguage to capture these generalizations.

CONCLUSION

Why, in spite of continuing debate and controversy, some of which is touched on in this chapter, is Goodman's work still so powerful? Why are we still discussing a model which started out in life as a fairly short article nearly 30 years ago? It is, I believe, because the learner strategies identified through miscue analysis are exactly what teachers want to try and understand. They might find it difficult to understand parallel distributed processing, they might be overwhelmed by the detail of successive experimental pieces of research which are rarely classroom based and very hard to evaluate for any other but a small research community, but they are in the best position to observe what their learners do. Goodman's work has a continuing resonance for them: They can say, "Yes, I saw that happen."

Of course, teachers' observation should not be ad hoc and unsystematic; it should be supported by as rich and diverse a theoretical underpinning as possible. We are not talking of easy options. Teachers need very carefully developed skills as observers and a full understanding of the nature of language and literacy acquisition, particularly if they are teaching bilingual learners.

Many of the teachers I teach at the Institute of Education work in multiracial and multilingual classrooms in London schools and colleges. Their students come into the British education system at different ages with diverse linguistic and literacy resources. The teachers are not looking for methods or basal readers; they do not want schemes or packages, whether based on so-called phonics or Whole Language, or sets of competencies. They want a principled, informed understanding of what their learners are doing as they acquire literacy in a second language. Miscue analysis, along with the related procedures which evolved from the early model, provides a point of departure. It offers not definitive solutions to problems, but ways of asking the right questions. What is the impact on learning to read of a different language system or different, culturally influenced experiences? What assumptions do our learners have about literacy and learning? How might we best acknowledge positive strategies as well as locate continuing weaknesses in their reading behavior? Only when we have posed the pertinent questions can we begin to understand and support the literacy development of second language learners.

REFERENCES

Adams M. J. (1990). *Beginning to read: Thinking and learning about print.* Cambridge: MIT Press.

Albrow K. H. (1972). *The English writing system: Notes towards a description.* London: Longman.

Alderson C., & Urquhart, A (Eds.). (1984). *Reading in a foreign language.* London: Longman.

Arnold H. (1982). *Listening to children reading.* London: Hodder and Stoughton.

Barrs M., Ellis, S., Hester, H., & Thomas, A. (1988). *The Primary Language Record: Handbook for teachers.* London: ILEA.

Bentley, J. D. (1969). *Toussaint L'Ouverture of the West Indies.* London: Hulton Educational Publications.

Cavalcanti, M. (1987). Investigating FL reading performance through pause protocols. In C. Faerch & G Kasper (Eds.), *Introspection in second language research multilingual matters* (pp. 230-250). Bristol: Multilingual Matters.

Corder, S.P. (1974). Error analysis, In J. P. Allen & S. P. Corder (Eds.), *The Edinburgh course in applied linguistics, Vol. 3, Techniques in applied linguistics* (pp. 122-154). Oxford: Oxford University Press.

Ellis, R. (1985). Sources of variability in interlanguage. *Applied Linguistics, 6*(2), 118-131.

Eskey, D. (1988). Holding in the bottom, In P. Carrell, J. Devine, & D. Eskey (Eds.), *Interactive approaches to second language reading* (pp. 93-100). Cambridge: Cambridge University Press.

Ferreiro, E., & Teberosky, A. (1982). *Literacy before schooling.* London: Heinemann Educational.

Goodman, K. (1967). Reading: a psycholinguistic guessing game. *Journal of the Reading Specialist,* 126-135.

Goodman, K. (1988). The reading process. In P. Carrell, J. Devine, & D. Eskey (Eds.), *Interactive approaches to second language reading* (pp. 11-21).Cambridge: Cambridge University Press.

Harrison, C. (1992). The reading process and learning to read. What a teacher using a "real books" approach needs to know. In C. Harrison & M. Coles (Eds.), *The reading for real handbook* (pp. 3-28). London: Routledge.

Heath, S. (1983). *Ways with words* Cambridge: Cambridge University Press.

Manning, M., Manning, G., Long, R., & Kamil, C. (1993). Preschoolers' conjectures about segments of a written sentence. *Journal of Research in Childhood Education* , *8*(1), 5-11.

Selinker, L. (1972). Interlanguage. *IRAL, 10*(3), 219-231.

Southgate, B. V., Arnold, H., & Johnson, S. (1981). *Extending beginning reading*. London: Heinemann Educational Books.

Stanovitch, K. (1980). Towards an interactive-compensatory model of individual differences in the development of reading fluency. *Reading Research Quarterly, 16*, 32-71.

Stubbs, M. (1980). *Language and literacy: The sociolinguistics of reading and writing*. London: Routledge and Kegan Paul.

Trudgill, P. (1975). *Accent, dialect and the school.* London: Edward Arnold.

Wallace, C. (1987). Variability and the reading behavior of L2 Readers. In R. Ellis (Ed.), *Second language acquisition in context* (pp. 165-178). Englewood Cliffs, NJ: Prentice Hall.

Wallace, C. (1988). *Learning to read in a multicultural society: The social context of second language literacy*. Englewood Cliffs, NJ: Prentice Hall.

Wallace, C. (1989). Learning to read in a second language: A window on the language acquisition process. *Reading in a Foreign Language, 5*(2), 277-298

Wight, J. (1976, May 14). How much interference? *Times Educational Supplement*.

Chapter Seventeen

African American Children's Literature: Anchor, Compass, and Sail

Rudine Sims Bishop
The Ohio State University

> . . . a people's story is the anchor dat keeps um from driftin', it's the compass to show the way to go and it's a sail dat holds the power dat takes um forward.
>
> —Camille Yarbrough (1990, p. 21)

It was not until the early 1970s that we began to have a substantial number of books or stories for children by and about African Americans. This is true both in terms of what were then thought of as "library books" or recreational reading, and materials designed specifically for reading instruction. In a now famous article, Larrick (1965) caught the attention of the public as well as educators and publishers by declaring that the world of children's books was "all-white." African Americans, she asserted, were practically invisible in the literature they were expected to read in and out of school. The implication was that if those children did not see themselves reflected in the literature, they might come to see literacy and literature as irrelevant to them and their lives. The same concern was shared by critics of basal readers, which traditionally had also featured all-white characters. By the time Ken Goodman conducted the last of the large reading miscue research studies, almost a decade after the Larrick article, things were just beginning to change.

In that study (Goodman, 1978), Ken and a number of assistants, including myself, examined the reading of eight groups of American children whose language was either a stable rural dialect of English or a language other than English. In addition to testing and refining Ken's model of the reading process, the study sought to develop insight into what aspects of the process were universal, and what aspects might be dependent on linguistic differences. A third objective was to learn what special problems, if any, might be attendant on becoming literate in a second language or when the learner's dialect is divergent from that of the school. Ultimately, we hoped to provide useful insights that could feed into improving reading achievement for children like those in the study.

One of the significant aspects of the study was to reaffirm the idea that, even in relation to reading achievement, *what* students read could make a difference. Children in each group were asked to read two stories, one of which was selected to be "culturally relevant" in terms of the daily activities of the characters, the time and place in which the story took place, the age and gender of the characters, and the language structures and rhetorical styles used by the author. When we were able to select relevant stories, the reading, as judged by an examination of retellings, tended to be better; that is, when there were differences between retellings on the two types of stories, generally the higher score was for the "culturally relevant" story.

Locating and selecting such stories, however, was among the most difficult tasks of the study. Regarding the selection of materials, the final statement of the research report was:

> In conclusion, although there has been a large increase in the amount of materials published for children, there is still a dearth of material for specific ethnic groups which also relates to the times, age level and present background of a young reader. If relevant material is necessary to motivate readers, the publishing and educational establishments have a long way to go to fill this need. (Goodman, 1978, pp. 7-15)

Among the readers in the Goodman study was a group of African American second, fourth, and sixth graders in rural Mississippi, a group in whom I had a special interest. Although my participation in the study involved working with children in rural Maine, as an African American woman with a background in teaching and in studying reading and children's literature, I have maintained a particular interest in the school achievement of African American children and in the development of African American children's literature. It is my view that such literature functions not only as an incentive for African American children to become readers, but as a means of socializing them and of helping other children recognize the ties that connect us all together as humans.

Two decades after the Goodman study, we live in a period when the push towards multicultural education is stimulating the publication of more and more of the African American story, and the stories of other people of color are being made available to our children and to all children who have access to books. Efforts to make available the African American story had begun long before Larrick's attention-getting article and the current focus on multicultural literature. In fact, the effort can be traced at least as far back as 1865. Lydia Maria Child, the white abolitionist and editor of a children's magazine, published *The Freedmen's Book* (1865) as a reader for the schools established for freed men and women after the Civil War. It contained essays, biographies, poems, and miscellany by and about African Americans. African Americans themselves have long been involved in producing and publishing African American children's literature. Associated Publishers, the company founded by African American historian Carter G. Woodson, has been publishing children's books related to African American life and history since early in the 20th century. African American poets Langston Hughes and Arna Bontemps wrote books for children in the 1930s, 1940s, and 1950s. The tradition continues today with publishers such as Just Us Books, run by writer/publishers Cheryl and Wade Hudson.

In 1920, W. E. B. DuBois, the great intellectual and civic leader, launched a magazine called *The Brownies' Book*. It was subtitled "A Monthly Magazine for the Children of the Sun," and DuBois declared that it was "for all children, but especially ours." In his magazine, DuBois wanted to entertain children but also to nurture Black children's self-esteem, to familiarize them with Black history, and to provide them with a code of conduct. Among his expressed goals were: "to make colored children realize that being 'colored' is a normal, beautiful thing;" "to make them familiar with the history and achievements of the Negro race;" and, "to point out the best amusements and joys and worthwhile things of life" (DuBois, 1919, p. 286). At the same time, the magazine was to be entertaining and amusing. Because of financial problems, *The Brownies' Book* lasted for only two years, but in setting out his objectives for the magazine, DuBois expressed some of the philosophy and ideology that underlies African American children's literature today as much as it did then.

DuBois understood very well both the importance of history and the power of story. The African American writers and artists who are producing today's African American children's literature share that understanding. It is from one of them, Camille Yarbrough, that I have taken the title for this chapter. Yarbrough's novel, *The Shimmershine Queens,* features a dark-brown-skinned 10-year old girl named Angela. Angie is having a difficult time at school because some of her classmates are harassing her, calling her ugly because of the dark color of her skin and the texture of her hair. Great Cousin Seatta, who is 90, has come to visit the family, and when she hears about Angie's problems, she declares that the children, including Angie, are confused because the adults in their lives have failed to tell them their story. "'Angie,' she said, 'a people's story is the anchor dat keeps um from driftin', it's the compass to show the way to go and it's a sail dat holds the power dat takes um forward'" (Yarbrough, 1990, p. 21). My intention in this chapter is to focus on some of the ways that African American children's literature can function as anchor, compass, and sail for today's children, and in that way to point out what I think is the importance of this literature not only for African American children but for all our children.

AFRICAN AMERICAN CHILDREN'S LITERATURE AS ANCHOR

In *The Shimmershine Queens,* Cousin Seatta's reference to "a people's story" was actually a reference to African American history. As she expressed it in the novel:

> Today is the child of yesterday
> and the mother of tomorrow
> For all that we know and do today
> from yesterday we borrow. (Yarbrough, 1990, p. 24)

Our todays are anchored in our yesterdays, and if we want our tomorrows to be better, we need to be certain that our children—all of our children—know about those yesterdays. From early in the century, history and biography have been central to African American children's literature. African American writers have consistently tried to convey to children a knowledge of African American history and the contributions of individual African Americans to the struggle for freedom and the social and economic well-being of this nation. Back in 1949, the children's literature establishment honored one of those efforts by naming Arna Bontemps's history, *The Story of the Negro* (1948), a runner-up for the John Newbery Medal. As the Newbery medal is the highest award that an American children's book can receive, that act was an important signal that the history of African Americans is a substantial component of the history of the United States, and therefore significant for all American children. The tradition continues today in works like Walter Dean Myers's *Now Is Your Time: The African American Struggle for Freedom* (1991), which traces African American history from Africa to the present, partly through historical events, partly through the lives of well-known individuals, and partly through the author's own family history.

One of the difficult tasks facing writers who present to children the African American story is to find ways to help them face the painful era when many of the ancestors of contemporary African Americans were captured and held in slavery. In the past few years, more than a few new children's books have centered on the slave experience. Novels about slavery and biographies of freedom fighters like Sojourner Truth and Frederick Douglass have been around for some time, and we continue to see new ones such as Joyce Hansen's *The Captive* (1994). What seems to be different currently is the number of picture books such as Dolores Johnson's *Seminole Diary* (1994) and *Now Let Me Fly* (1993), and the 1995 Coretta Scott King award winner, *Christmas in the Big House, Christmas in the Quarters* (1994) by Pat and Fred McKissack. What distinguishes these books from some earlier ones is their perspective on the people who were enslaved and the experience of slavery. What most of these books have in common is that they portray the enslaved people as intelligent, unique, well-rounded individuals with strong family ties and a yearning to be free. They also stress the fact that many of them made courageous efforts to liberate themselves, or, failing that, to put up whatever resistance they could. What these writers and artists seem to be telling readers, especially African American readers, is that we need to claim our history, learn from it, and with that knowledge as a foundation, move ahead. Walter Dean Myers (1991), in the introduction to *Now Is Your Time,* expresses it clearly:

> Some hundreds of years ago an African was brought to the shores of North America. That African was my ancestor, and will always be a part of my heritage. He was worked and beaten, humiliated and subjected to the will of people willing to exploit him. I claim that work, those beatings, that humiliation, the pain of that exploitation.
>
> I claim the darkest moments of my people and celebrate their perseverance.
>
> I claim the joy and the light and the music and the genius and the muscle and the glory of these I write about, and of the legions who have passed this way without yet having their stories told.
>
> History has made me an African American. It is an Africa that I have come from, and an America that I have helped to create. So be it. (p. X)

In recent years, Virginia Hamilton has taken this notion of claiming history a step further by identifying a subgroup of her writings as "Liberation Literature." This is literature about both unsung and well-known individuals who, against great odds, pursued their freedom. Hamilton contends that these individual sufferers are in some sense freed by the very telling of their stories and the documentation of their oppression. Included in her liberation literature is *Anthony Burns: The Defeat and Triumph of a Fugitive Slave* (1988), a historically accurate reconstruction of the life of the last fugitive from slavery to be taken back into bondage from the state of Massachusetts; *The People Could Fly: American Black Folktales* (1985); and *Many Thousand Gone: African Americans from Slavery to Freedom* (1993), a history of slavery in the United States beginning with the 17th century slave trade and the establishment of the American system of slavery, and ending with the Emancipation Proclamation, related through the stories of enslaved former Africans and their quests for freedom. The contribution of "liberation literature" is that, in addition to freeing the subjects of the works, it also frees the readers who, participating through the books in the experiences of the heroes, become part of the struggle for liberation. In explicating the concept of liberation literature and the idea that, by living through the experience of the story the reader also becomes liberated, Hamilton draws readers of all cultures, particularly those in the United States, into the continuing effort to see that the nation lives up to its promise of freedom and liberty for all of its people.

Traditionally, the anchor that keeps most of us from drifting has been the family, and many modern works of African American children's literature place family at their center. Many African American picture books, for example, celebrate a loving relationship between a parent and child. Wade Hudson celebrates a family reunion in *I Love My Family* (1993). Dorothy Strickland and her son Michael recently published a collection of poems about family entitled, *Families: Poems Celebrating the African American Experience* (1994). Jonathan and His Mommy (Smalls-Hector, 1992) is a story about a 5-year-old and his mother taking a special walk together in the city. *Father and Son* (Lauture, 1992) features a young boy and his father having special times together in the country. In *Tell Me a Story, Mama* (Johnson, 1989), a little girl and her mother together retell one of their favorite stories about the mother's childhood, but even though the child asks the mother for the story, she is the one who really does the telling. *One of Three* (Johnson, 1991) and *Two and Too Much* (Walter, 1990) focus on siblings and the ways they get along—or should get along—within a family. A recent novel by Walter Dean Myers presents the 250-year history of a family whose roots are anchored in a field in South Carolina that they call *The Glory Field* (1994).

Within the African American community, not only has the immediate family been important, but part of the traditional foundation of African American culture has been the extended family—the grandparents and aunts and uncles and cousins who helped to raise the children and who shared with them their homes, their food, their love. In Gloria Pinkney's book *Back Home* (1992), children have an opportunity to relive those days when summertime for many Black families who were living in the North meant sending the children down South—back home—to spend time with the family. Donald Crew's *Big Mama's* (1991) focuses on the same kind of experience.

Many picture books for young children feature relationships between a young child and a grandparent or other elder in the family—Great Cousin Seatta, Great Aunt Flossie (Howard, 1991), who has lots of hats and a story to go with each one; and Uncle Jed (Mitchell, 1993), who dreams of having his own barbershop and perseveres until his dream comes true. In celebrating these relationships, African American writers recognize that older people have much to offer the young in the way of wisdom and unconditional love; that they are the keepers of the story and for that reason alone, it is important to listen to what they have to say.

AFRICAN AMERICAN CHILDREN'S LITERATURE AS COMPASS

Cousin Seatta told Angie that a people's story is not only an anchor but also a compass, a guide to show them the way to go. African American children's literature shares with all children's literature the function of socializing our children, of passing on to them the things that we value, the ways we think they should behave, the kind of people we hope they will be. This is one of the functions African American children's poets sometimes fulfill. Lucille Clifton, for instance, opens *Everett Anderson's Year* (1974/1992) with "January," which begins: "'Walk tall in the world, /says Mama/to Everett Anderson." In one of her frequently anthologized poems ("Listen Children" in Clifton, 1987), Clifton again offers advice:

listen children
keep this in the place
you have for keeping
always
keep it all ways

. . .

we have always loved each other
children all ways
pass it on.

Eloise Greenfield, in *Honey, I Love* (1978), her small collection of poems celebrating love in its many guises, aims to help children recognize that love manifests itself in seemingly ordinary ways. In "Love Don't Mean," for example, she asserts that love does not necessarily have to do with "all that kissing/Like on television," but that it can mean something as simple as a child complying with her father's request to "keep your mama company/till I get back."

Sometimes the guidance function of African American children's literature is manifested in the heroes and "sheroes" that African American writers choose to place before children and hold up for them to admire: freedom fighters from the last century such as Sojourner Truth (McKissack & McKissack, 1992) and Harriet Tubman (Lawrence, 1993); 20th century figures who carried on the struggle such as Fannie Lou Hamer (Walter, 1992), Thurgood Marshall (Haskins, 1992), and Martin Luther King, Jr. (Haskins, 1977); writers and artists like Langston Hughes (Cooper, 1994) and Alvin Ailey (Pinkney, 1993); thinkers like Benjamin Banneker (Pinkney, 1994); and many other men and women who overcame obstacles and persevered in order to achieve some goal and contribute to this society. At least from the time of DuBois' *Brownies' Book*, African Americans who write for children have sought to engender pride in African American achievements and to present biographies of African Americans whose lives and deeds have been considered exemplary. The tradition continues.

The guidance is there in fictional works, too. One writer who is especially adept at telling the African American story in a very powerful way is Mildred Taylor. Not only is she an excellent storyteller, but her themes about the importance of family, community, and self-respect are important for all children to ponder. In Taylor's Newbery Medal winner, *Roll of Thunder, Hear My Cry* (1976), Cassie Logan, the 9-year-old narrator, has a conversation with her father that illustrates my point. Cassie, living in Mississippi in 1933, but fortunate enough to be sheltered from much of the evil of that time and place because her family owned their land, has had her first serious brush with overt racism. When Cassie and her grandmother encountered Charlie Simms, a white man, on a sidewalk in town, Simms knocked Cassie off the sidewalk and then made her apologize to his 13-year-old daughter. To further increase Cassie's humiliation, he insisted that she refer to his daughter as "Miz Lillian Jean." Cassie is not only humiliated, but angry, and determined to seek revenge, a risky proposition in Mississippi at that time. She also does not understand why the adults in her family neither defended her right to walk on the sidewalk, nor confronted Charlie Simms after the fact. Her father has profound advice for her about the importance of survival, and the equal importance of maintaining her self-respect:

> Cassie, there'll be a whole lot of things you ain't gonna wanna do but you'll have to do in this life just so you can survive. . . . If I'd've gone after Charlie Simms and given him a good thrashing like I felt like doing, the hurt to all of us would've been a whole lot more than the hurt you received, so I let it be. I don't like letting it be, but I can live with that decision.
>
> But there are other things, Cassie, that if I'd let be, they'd eat away at me and destroy me in the end. And it's the same with you, baby. There are things you can't back down on, things you gotta take a stand on. But it's up to you to decide what them things are. You have got to demand respect in this world, ain't nobody just gonna hand it to you. How you carry yourself, what you stand for—that's how you gain respect. But, little one, ain't nobody's respect worth more than your own. You understand that?" (pp. 175-176)

Later, in one of the most satisfying scenes in a children's novel, the clever Cassie manages to exact her revenge on "Miz Lillian Jean" without causing any harm to herself or her family.

One of the understandings David Logan seeks to pass on to his daughter is that sometimes it is necessary to make the best of a bad situation. Although a great deal less serious, Dolores Johnson's *The Best Bug to Be* (1992), a book for younger children, provides another example of a parent offering advice about how to cope with a situation that the child perceives as less than ideal. Kelly has been assigned the part of a bumble bee in the school play. All her friends have roles that seem to be more interesting or exciting. Sharon will be the Queen of the Butterflies, and Megan gets to be a cute ladybug and also play the cymbals. Robert will stand out as the only toad in the froggy pond, but as Kelly tells her parents:

> I won't be singing. I won't be dancing on my toes. I won't be hippety-hopping like a toad, or playing music like a ladybug. I won't be Queen of the Butterflies, and no talent scout will see me. I'll just be a good-for-nuthin' bumblebee, 'cause I don't do anything but buzz."
>
> "Whatever you're asked to do, sweetheart, you should do your absolute best," said her father.
>
> "You've got so much talent, and you're so smart, you can make your bumblebee the best role on the stage," said her mother.
>
> "Well," said Kelly, "I'll just have to make a bumblebee the best thing there is to be." (unpaged)

She does, of course, and in so doing steals the show and carries on the tradition of having to make something out of nothing. She does it so well that she transcends the menial role that she had been asked to play. Kelly's parents' advice comes from the recognition that historically, African Americans have found themselves in situations that could be limiting and have had to find ways to rise above those limitations.

In some sense, both *Roll of Thunder* and *The Best Bug* have something important to say about survival, if not in the physical sense, then certainly in the psychological sense. As it is in adult African American literature, this focus on psychological survival is one of the important themes in African American children's literature as well. It is the survival of a people that underlies the metaphor of anchor, compass, and sail that Yarbrough places in the mouth of Cousin Seatta. In its role as anchor and compass, stabilizer and guide, African American children's literature has sought to educate the *heads* of its primary audience by providing them with information about their history and achievements. But equally important, it seeks to educate the *heart,* and because it can do both, it has the power to help children internalize their own compass, their own guide to being the best kind of person they know how to be.

AFRICAN AMERICAN CHILDREN'S LITERATURE AS SAIL

The third function that a people's story fulfills, according to Cousin Seatta, is that it is a sail that holds the power to take them forward. Literature in that sense has the potential to be empowering for children who do not always feel valued in the institutional settings in which they receive their formal education. One of the ways we can empower children is to help them value themselves. As it relates to African American children's literature, this idea has particular significance in a world in which many of the images that African American children see in the media are not always positive, and the standard of beauty that is placed before them is one they cannot possibly meet. Many African American writers and artists know about and speak to that concern.

In 1967, when Virginia Hamilton published her first book, *Zeely,* she described a different standard of beauty. This is her description of the title character:

> Zeely Taber was more than six and a half feet tall, thin and deeply dark as a pole of Ceylon ebony. She wore a long smock that reached to her ankles. Her arms, hands and feet were bare, and her thin, oblong head didn't seem to fit quite right on her shoulders.

> She had very high cheekbones and her eyes seemed to turn inward on themselves. Geeder couldn't say what expression she saw on Zeely's face. She knew only that it was calm, that it had pride in it, and that the face was the most beautiful she had ever seen. (pp. 31-32)

It is hardly a Barbie doll image, and though Geeder, the little girl whose story is told in the book, thought Zeely was beautiful, not all African American children recognize the beauty that is theirs. That is why a book like Tom Feelings' *Soul Looks Back in Wonder* (1993) is a significant contribution to African American children's literature. He states in the foreword, "The artists who came together to create *Soul Looks Back in Wonder* understand that one way to project our positive hopes for the future is for young people to see their own beauty reflected in our eyes, through our work" (unpaged). The book presents several of Feelings' beautiful and loving images of Black children, accompanied by poems that celebrate Black youth.

That African American children have internalized negative images of themselves and their physical features is of concern to a number of African American writers. Rejection of her dark skin coloring and the texture of her hair was one of the problems that Angie was facing in *The Shimmershine Queens*. Nikki Grimes' poem "Sweet Blackberry" from *Meet Danitra Brown* (1994) also focuses on the way some African American children have learned to devalue themselves and their physical features and the ways others have learned to counter such negative attitudes. Zuri Jackson, the child who introduces the title character notes that, although her friend Danitra describes Zuri's skin as "like double chocolate fudge," other children make fun of her by suggesting that her skin is so black that "at night, people might think/ you ain't nothin' but a piece of sky." Zuri's mother 's advice is to hurl back at the teasers one of the common self-affirming maxims in African American culture, "The blacker the berry, the sweeter the juice." According to the poem, words do the trick. The teasing stops, and presumably another fictional little girl (and perhaps the reader of the poem) is on her way to developing pride in herself and a recognition of her own worth.

There is at least observational evidence from a number of studies (e.g. Perkins, 1992; Smith, 1993) that experience with African American children's literature can make African American children feel empowered. An anecdote from a teacher/doctoral student illustrates one example. Janelle (not her real name) was a first grader, about 6 years old. Her teacher had been taking a course in multicultural children's literature, and as part of a class project, she decided to teach the children Eloise Greenfield's poem, "Harriet Tubman" (1978) and have them recite it on videotape. It begins this way:

Harriet Tubman didn't take no stuff
Wasn't scared of nothing neither
Didn't come in this world to be no slave
And wasn't going to stay one either. . .

Janelle learned the poem well. She had been having problems on the playground with a fourth grade boy who had been bullying her. One day, after learning the poem, Janelle had had enough, and when the fourth grader began bothering her on the playground, she stood up to him. Surprised, he asked, "Who do you think you are, girl?" She promptly answered, "I'm like Harriet Tubman, and I don't take no stuff," and followed up with a swift punch that blackened his eye.

The next day his parents arrived at school, threatening to sue the bully who had assaulted their son. They were quite surprised when the principal called in a little 6-year-old girl. The parents decided not to pursue the issue, but the principal and the teacher agreed that Janelle had to accept some consequences for her inappropriate behavior of fighting on the playground. The principal's decision was to have Janelle report to his office during recess every day for a week, with some work to keep her occupied. But his last words were to the teacher: "And don't send any of that poetry!" He understood very well that literature can be empowering.

THE POTENTIAL OF AFRICAN AMERICAN CHILDREN'S LITERATURE

The value—and power—of African American children's literature as anchor, compass, and sail is not limited to African American children. If it holds up a mirror to them and reflects back their lives and their own beauty and affirms them as worthwhile human beings, it also acts as a window that allows other children to enter that world and appreciate that beauty. In so doing it widens horizons and enables children unfamiliar with African Americans and the African American experience to begin to make connections with African Americans as fellow human beings.

African American children's literature reaches out to all children because in presenting the specifics and the particulars of African American experiences, it also presents the universal. Like all good literature, African American children's literature deals with universal human emotions such as love, joy, anger, and sorrow. When Everett Anderson's father dies in Lucille Clifton's *Everett Anderson's Goodbye* (1983), there are always a few adults in my classes who weep, no matter what color they are, because they have known the loss of someone they love. When the father in Mildred Taylor's *The Gold Cadillac* (1987) buys a new car with the money they have been saving to buy a house, and does it without consulting his wife, most of the women, and some of the men, in my classes have no problem understanding his wife's reaction, which is to refuse to ride in the car. When Langston Hughes urges us to "Hold fast to dreams," he speaks to anyone who has ever nourished a dream.

African American children's literature connects with all of us because, like all literature, it nurtures the imagination. When we read, we go inside the book. In our imaginations we live through the experiences that the characters are having in the story. And as teachers and parents, we must not underestimate the power of imagination. Einstein said that it was more important to him than his capacity for absorbing positive knowledge. It is imagination that enables inventors to create things never before seen, and artists to find new ways to help us see our world. We need to remember that imagination is tied linguistically to wisdom; it comes from the same word root as the word *magic*, but also the word *magi*, which is a name for wise men.

James Baldwin once wisely noted that, on some level, literature has the power to change the world because the world changes according to the way we see it, and if a writer can change the way we see the world, even by a tiny bit, then that writer can change the world. A recent incident brought Baldwin's argument to mind and suggested once again that artists, whether visual or literary, can have an effect on the way we envision our world. Ashley Bryan, the African American artist, was in town, and I was invited to join the teachers of the host school at a dinner in a restaurant. I was sitting next to Ashley, so I overheard a conversation between him and a white male teacher. The teacher was holding a copy of *What A Morning! The Christmas Story in Black Spirituals* (Langstaff, 1987), which Ashley had illustrated. He had a question, but he wanted to be sure not to offend either Ashley or me, so he carefully couched his question in the context of the study of Israel and the Middle East that he and his children had been doing. The question, he said, was from one of the children, but it was clearly also his own. As he opened the book to the manger scene, he reported that, in their studies, they had seen pictures of people who live in the Middle East, particularly Israelis. Hesitantly, he then asked, "Why did you make Jesus Black?" Without a moment's pause, Ashley answered, "Because I'm black. People always envision their gods in their own images, and since I'm Black, I made Jesus Black, too." The teacher was thoughtful, and I was left with the impression that he may not have been ready to accept Ashley's answer, but the book—and Ashley's artistic vision—had offered him a new insight, a new way to look at the world, and had given him and his children an opportunity for critical thinking and discussion.

African American literature, then, has the power to raise questions and encourage critical thinking, even when readers who are not African American fail to connect with some specific detail or aspect of the literature. And we need critical thinkers and multiple perspectives to take us into the 21st century. What African American children's literature may do for all of us is to inform us about the past and help prepare us to make a better future. Because African American children's literature tells a story that is part and parcel of the American story, and one that is at the heart of many of our social problems, it can function for all our children as an anchor to keep them from drifting, a compass to show the way to go, and a sail to hold the power to take us forward.

REFERENCES

Bontemps, A. (1948). *The story of the Negro.* New York: Knopf

Child, L. M. (1865). *The freedmen's book.* Boston: Ticknor and Fields.

Clifton, L. (1992). *Everett Anderson's year* (Illus. by Ann Grifalconi). New York: Holt. (Original work published 1974)

Clifton, L. (1983). *Everett Anderson's goodbye* (Illus. by Ann Grifalconi). New York: Holt.

Clifton, L. (1987). *Good woman: Poems and a memoir.* New York: BOA Productions, Ltd.

Cooper, F. (1994). *Coming home: From the life of Langston Hughes.* New York: Philomel.

Crews, D. (1991). *Big Mama's.* New York: Greenwillow.

DuBois, W. E. B. (1919). The true brownies. *The Crisis, 18*(6), 286.

Feelings, T. (1993). *Soul looks back in wonder.* New York: Dial.

Goodman, K. S. (1978). *Reading of American children whose language is a stable rural dialect of English or a language other than English.* Final Report. Project NIE-C-00-3-0087. U.S. Dept. of Heath, Education and Welfare.

Greenfield, E. (1978). *Honey, I love, and other love poems* (Illus. by L. and D. Dillon). New York: Crowell.

Grimes, N. (1994). *Meet Danitra Brown* (Illus. by F. Cooper). New York: Lothrop.

Hamilton, V. (1967). *Zeely.* New York: Macmillan.

Hamilton, V. (1985) (Reteller). *The people could fly: American Black folktales* (Illus. by L. and D. Dillon). New York: Knopf.

Hamilton, V. (1988). *Anthony Burns: The defeat and triumph of a fugitive slave.* New York: Knopf.

Hamilton, V. (1993). *Many thousand gone: African Americans from slavery to freedom* (Illus. by L. and D. Dillon). New York: Knopf.

Hansen, J. (1994). *The captive*. New York: Scholastic.

Haskins, J. (1977). *The life and death of Martin Luther King, Jr*. New York: Lothrop.

Haskins, J. (1992). *Thurgood Marshall: A life for justice*. New York: Holt.

Howard, E. F. (1991). *Aunt Flossie's hats (and crab cakes later)* (Illus. by J. Ransome). New York: Clarion.

Hudson, W. (1993). *I love my family* (Illus. by C. Massey). New York: Scholastic.

Johnson, A. (1989). *Tell me a story, mama* (Illus. by D. Soman). New York: Scholastic.

Johnson, A. (1991). *One of three* (Illus. by D. Soman). New York: Orchard.

Johnson, D. (1992). *The best bug to be*. New York: Macmillan.

Johnson, D. (1993). *Now let me fly*. New York: Macmillan.

Johnson, D. (1994). *Seminole diary*. New York: Macmillan.

Langstaff, J. (Selector). (1987). *What a morning! The Christmas story in Black spirituals* (Illus. by Ashley Bryan). New York: Macmillan.

Larrick, N. (1965). The all-white world of children's books. *Saturday Review*, *48*, 63-63, 84-85.

Lauture, D. (1992). *Father and son* (Illus. by J. Green). New York: Philomel, 1992.

Lawrence, J. (1993). *Harriet and the promised land*. New York: Simon and Schuster.

McKissack, P., & McKissack, F. (1992). *Sojourner Truth: Ain't I a woman?* New York: Scholastic.

McKissack, P., & McKissack, F. (1994). *Christmas in the big house, Christmas in the quarters*. New York: Scholastic.

Mitchell, M. K. (1993). *Uncle Jed's barbershop* (Illus. by J. Ransome). New York: Simon and Schuster.

Myers, W. D. (1991). *Now is your time: The African American struggle for freedom*. New York: Scholastic.

Myers, W. D. (1994). *The glory field*. New York: Scholastic.

Perkins, F. D. (1992). *Response patterns of third grade African Americans to culturally conscious literature*. Unpublished doctoral dissertation, The University of Alabama at Birmingham.

Pinkney, A. D. (1993). *Alvin Ailey* (Illus. by J. B. Pinkney). New York: Hyperion.

Pinkney, A. D. (1994). *Dear Benjamin Banneker* (Illus. by J. B. Pinkney). San Diego: Harcourt.

Pinkney, G. (1992). *Back home* (Illus. by J. Pinkney). New York: Dial.

Smalls-Hector, I. (1992). *Jonathan and his mommy*. (Illus. by M. Hays). New York: Little, Brown.

Smith, E. A. (1993). *The anchor dat keeps um from driftin': The responses of African American fourth and fifth graders to African American literature.*

Unpublished doctoral dissertation, The Ohio State University, Columbus.

Strickland, D., & Strickland, M. (Eds.) (1994). *Families: Poems celebrating the African American experience* (Illus. by J. Ward). Honesdale, PA: Boyd's Mills Press.

Taylor, M. D. (1976). *Roll of thunder, hear my cry.* New York: Dial.

Taylor, M. D. (1987). *The gold Cadillac.* New York: Dial.

Walter, M. P. (1990). *Two and too much* (Illus. by P. Cummings). New York: Bradbury.

Walter, M. P. (1992). *Mississippi challenge.* New York: Bradbury.

Yarbrough, C. (1990). *The shimmershine queens.* New York: Knopf.

Chapter Eighteen

Toward a Critical, Whole Language Pedagogy

Bess Altwerger
Towson State University
Barbara Flores
California State University, San Bernardino

As young graduate students in the late 1970s we came, one from the east and one from the west, to Tucson, AZ, in search of knowledge about an emerging theory and pedagogy that offered hope for the future of the disenfranchised youth we had both taught. Though we were intellectually and academically exhilarated by the profound paradigmatic changes taking shape in linguistics, psychology, and reading, it was the prospect of merging Kenneth Goodman's psycholinguistic theory of reading (Goodman, 1967) with the liberatory vision of Paulo Freire (Freire, 1970) that captured our minds and our spirits. Now, almost 20 years later, we stand firm in our commitment to formulate with our colleagues and co-thinkers (Bigelow, 1994a; Christensen, 1994; Edelsky, 1994a, Saaverdra, 1995) a pedagogy in service of equity and justice for all people. We continue to envision classroom life which embraces critical, democratic ideals through both process and content. And we continue to recognize in whole language a theory-in-practice (Edelsky, Altwerger, & Flores, 1991) rich in liberatory potential.

Over the years, other teacher-scholars have come to recognize the myth exposed by Freire (Freire, 1970; Shor & Freire, 1987) that literacy competence and literacy pedagogy can somehow exist in historical and contemporary isolation from the sociopolitical forces and struggles of our society. We have come to appreciate that all literacy instruction does, indeed embody a social and political ideology actualized in the classroom through the particular personal and social functions which literacy serves each school day. A literacy pedagogy has the power either to link literacy competency and use with compliance and submission to authority, or to personal and social inquiry and critique. With this understanding, and the assumption that neutrality and isolationism is not an option, critical educators have, therefore, deliberately chosen to treat literacy as a means to understand, critique, and even transform society. As critical whole language educators, our challenge lies in finding pedagogical strategies consistent with sound whole language practice that reflect a democratic ideal of social equality and justice. Where do we turn for help?

A large body of scholarly literature and a formidable intellectual community has emerged since the publication of *Pedagogy of the Oppressed* (1970), Freire's seminal work. That body of literature, including work by Aaronowitz and Giroux (1985), Giroux (1983), Lankshire (1987), and Shor and Freire (1987), argues for the necessity of critical pedagogy and critical literacy and urges educators to transform their practice to reflect emancipatory goals. Important theoretical concepts developed by these scholars potentially provide educators with a pedagogical framework for developing critical literacy instruction. But with some important exceptions (Bigelow 1994a; Christensen, 1994; Edelsky, 1994b, Peterson, 1994), the critical education literature is sorely lacking in practical curricular guidelines or suggestions for realizing a critical pedagogy in the contemporary elementary classroom. Much of this literature, as powerful and enlightening as it may be, speaks primarily to inner-circle scholars and theorists. Critical whole language teachers are still left with the challenge of developing a literacy curriculum that combines the vision of critical theory with a sound practical theory of language and literacy learning which will guide their everyday classroom life.

From the beginning, whole language has provided a theoretical and practical basis for developing such a critical literacy curriculum in the classroom. With its view of literacy as a personal and social act of meaning construction, and its conceptualization of readers/writers as active and empowered inquirers, whole language provides fertile ground for generating a critical pedagogy. Its opposition to tracking, standardized testing, and behavioral models of curriculum has always placed it squarely in opposition to a social reproductive model of schooling (Edelsky, Altwerger, & Flores, 1991; Flores, 1990). However, the critical potential of whole language has largely gone unrealized. Until recently, there has been a reluctance (both within the classroom and the pages of professional journals) to openly interrogate texts and subject matter content for social and political perspective, inequity and bias, thereby narrowing the scope and depth of classroom inquiry and limiting the critical potential of whole language. To change this, whole language teachers, teacher educators, researchers, and theorists who embrace the goal of critical and emancipatory education must begin to revision and recast whole language practices as opportunities for social reflection and agency.

We suggest that two well-established whole language practices—Literature Study and Theme Cycles—when reconceptualized from this critical perspective, provide us with the pedagogical opportunities and social contexts we seek. In the following sections these practices are described, placed in historical context, and explored in terms of their potential for actualizing critical literacy in the whole language classroom.

LITERATURE STUDY

Literature study (Gilles, 1990; Peterson & Eeds, 1990; Smith, 1990) is presently accepted as a major instructional practice within a comprehensive whole language pedagogy and represents a major departure from the traditional literature "discussion groups" that have historically dominated reading instruction in elementary classrooms. With the formulation by Goodman (1984) and Rosenblatt (1983) of a transactional model of literacy it became necessary to rethink the goals, strategies, and expectations of literature discussion.

Table 18.1. Literature Discussion vs. Literature Study.

Literature Discussion Group	Literature Study
Evaluation of comprehension	Enrichment of interpretation
Meanings preformulated	Meaning is personally and socially constructed
Teacher as authority/evaluator	Teacher as participant and facilitator
Extension activities	Dialogue, analysis, problem posing/solving
Focus on reading skills	Focus on critical interpretation and literary analysis

Brought under scrutiny were literature "discussions" consisting of teacher-directed question-answer sessions in which students are prodded to "understand" the text in ways that coincide with preformulated meanings. The transactional model rejects a static, singular, and purely text-based notion of meaning in favor of one in which meaning is viewed as dynamic and socially situated. The text, although offering "meaning potential," is only one factor in combination with other, equally critical factors, such as reader predisposition and situational context, which contribute to the construction of meaning. Thus, differences and variations in interpretation are not only accepted but expected. The dialogue that ensues within literature study enables readers to negotiate, extend, and even reconstruct their meanings. This dialogue, rather than predetermined extension activities and assignments, provides the context for literary exploration and analysis and may lead to useful, collaboratively negotiated projects and learning experiences. The teacher acts as both a facilitator and participant in literature studies, demonstrating the types of authentic questions readers ask themselves and others as they construct meaning. Although literature study can generate opportunities for teachers to assess students' literacy authentically (see Harp, 1991; Peterson & Eeds, 1990; Rhodes & Shanklin, 1993), more importantly, it shifts teachers' roles to participants and facilitators during dialogue, supplanting and generally replacing the traditional roles of assessor/judge and authority.

It is clear that literature study represents a major paradigm shift in the theoretical framework and pedagogical approach to literature in the classroom, and provides opportunities for accommodating a critical perspective that was previously unavailable in packaged and preformulated approaches to literature. However, literature study as a potential source of social and political reflection and critique often goes unrealized within even the most sound whole language settings. In order to realize the critical potential of literature study we must obviously direct careful attention to offering literature selections that address relevant and meaningful social and political issues. Less obviously, but perhaps more importantly, is our willingness to reconceptualize our goals for literature study to include the development of critical literacy in our students—to enable them to read the world as well as the word (Shor & Freire, 1987). This requires a conscious willingness on the part of teachers to entertain, as well as encourage, dialogue that examines concepts such as social justice and equity in light of the texts studied. Dialogue within literature study must be broadened to include another layer of inquiry in which personal responses and reflections are considered within social and political contexts. And finally, we must "retheorize" (Edelsky, 1994b) the transactional theory underlying literature study to recognize the sociopolitical relations among authors, readers, texts and contexts through which meaning is constructed. At least three conditions must, then, coexist in order to recast literature study as an avenue for social and political inquiry:

1. A culturally and socially varied and multidimensional selection of literature.
2. A "retheorized" transactional model that recognizes meaning construction as socially and politically situated.
3. A socially and politically conscious teacher, capable of inspiring critical dialogue.

We examine each of these separately and demonstrate their importance for critical literature study.

A Culturally and Socially Varied and Multidimensional Selection of Literature.

Educators (Bishop, 1993; Dyson & Genishi, 1994; Harris, 1993) have long urged teachers and school systems to broaden the scope of literature read by students to include representations of the variety of social, cultural, ethnic, and racial groups present in our society. Publishers over the years have heeded this call for more diverse literature by publishing, in increasing (though not sufficient) numbers, authors and children's books which represent a broader spectrum of society. Also available now are books for children and adolescents that deal with serious social issues such as homelessness and poverty, racism, sexism, immigration, religious and cultural persecution, war and genocide. This type of realistic and provocative literature has been a focus of censorship battles (although so have staples such Blume's *Are You There God? It's Me Margaret* and Twain's *Huck Finn*). Nevertheless, such books are now finding their way into literature discussion and instruction in our classrooms. This should be encouraging news for critical educators who view these books as opportunities for social and political critique and possible activism. But just what happens to these books when they enter the classroom? Does the instruction surrounding these books always result in social reflection and critique?

To answer this, let's consider one instructional example which came to our attention not long ago. A son of a graduate student was asked to read *Number the Stars* by Lois Lowry, the Newbery Award winning book that tells the story of a Jewish girl and her family smuggled to safety in Sweden by her Gentile friends and neighbors during the Nazi invasion of Denmark during World War II. Rich in potential for discussions regarding racism, illegal immigration, cross-cultural solidarity, and heroism in the face of fascism and political oppression, the class, instead, filled out 60 pages of activity sheets (Figure 18.1 provides an example) taken from an instructional manual published through Teacher Created Materials (1991).

Many of the ditto sheets focused on "comprehension skills" such as vocabulary, character traits, sequence of events, and factual recall. Other sheets provided information on totally unimportant facts, events, or places such as Tivoli Gardens (an amusement park in Copenhagen) which are mentioned in the book. Little if any time was spent in dialogue concerning student responses and reactions to the book, nor the critical historical or social content of the book.

Given this example, we must wonder if exposure to socially powerful material such as *Number the Stars* in the context of such unenlightened instruction does more harm than good. Ignoring the social substance of a book, avoiding reflection and dialogue, and sidestepping the uncomfortable parallel to the historical and contemporary events in our country and around the world (such as genocide against Native peoples, the Nazi movement in the U.S., the ethnic cleansing in Bosnia, and the treatment of undocumented immigrants to the U.S.) condones, if not encourages, apathy, passivity, and ignorance. The future looks bleak indeed if students exposed to books of social significance are given no opportunity to search for

1. What is so unique about Tivoli Gardens in Copenhagen?
2. When is the best time to visit Tivoli Gardens?
3. Why did King Christian VIII give George Carstensen permission to establish this park?
4. In what year did the Gardens open?
5. How many visitors each year?
6. When is the park open?
7. What are some of the attractions that appeal to the children?
8. Compare and contrast this park with any amusement parks you have visited.
9. What are the features of Tivoli that you would like?
10. Does the author recommend visiting Tivoli Gardens? What advice does she give about the cost of admission?

Figure 18.1. Questions

lessons and themes of importance to their own and others' realities and use these to envision a more just and peaceful society. As a nation we will be doomed to reproduce the historical and societal circumstances that lead to human suffering and hopelessness. Ironically, flooding classrooms with multidimensional and socially significant books without dialogue and analysis could conceivably work against, rather than support the goals of critical literacy.

A "Retheorized" Transactional Model that Recognizes Meaning Construction as Socially and Politically Situated.

Although the previous example of curricular abuse toward *Number the Stars* is situated within a literature-based approach, it obviously lies outside of a whole language or transactional paradigm in which literature study is a predominant strategy. It might be expected that such negligent treatment toward social and ethical issues would be unlikely or impossible in a literature study in which students engage in dialogue concerning their interpretations, responses, and analyses of the text. However, this is not necessarily the case, even with socially provocative novels. One explanation for this can be traced to the lack of explicit reference to social/political/ideological context in theories of interpretation and literary criticism comprising the foundations for literature study. Though the professional literature emphasizes the role of background knowledge and experience in the interpretive process, with the exception of a few theorists (Bigelow, 1994b; Edelsky, 1994a, 1994b; Taxel, 1988), the social and political realities within which authors and readers develop experience and knowledge about the world receives little attention by whole language scholars (and also by those with more traditional leanings). The interpretive process is idealized as occurring within a political vacuum except for specific interpretive instances involving overtly politicized texts. In these exceptional cases, it is expected that dialogue concerning the social or political content may indeed occur, especially if there is relevance to the readers' own life experiences. But as a general rule, there is little in the theoretical framework that leads teachers to consider social and political critique—unpacking or deconstructing the social/political subtext of a literary work—as a fundamental aspect of literature study. We have, in fact, at various conferences and meetings, often heard whole language teachers of middle-class white students wonder aloud if social critique or even "multicultural" books are relevant or necessary for their students.

Figure 18.2 represents a "retheorized" view of interpretation and meaning construction as socially and politically situated. Authors' and readers' knowledge and experience develop within particular social

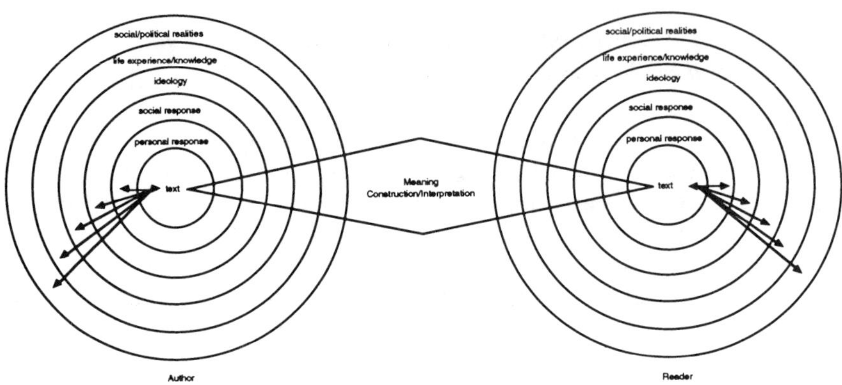

Figure 18.2. "Retheorized model of interpretation

and political realities and are represented through ideological stances and perspectives during the act of meaning and text construction. In this view, all texts, and not only those considered "multicultural" or "socially significant," are generated within the ideological stances of authors and interpreted within the ideological stances of readers. Literature study can provide opportunities for students to discover, analyze, and critique the overt or covert ideological stance of a text, as well as their own interpretation and response to it. Furthermore, they can discover, analyze, and critique the social/political issues and problems embodied within the book in relation to their own beliefs and experiences.

One may wonder whether young readers would be willing, or indeed able, to engage in such socially conscious critique during literature study. Altwerger and Fu (1995) researched this question in a study of the critical dialogue generated during literature studies of potentially socially significant texts (*The Cay* [Taylor, 1969] and *Maniac McGee* [Spinelli, 1990]). The two populations studied were adult college students at Towson State University and intermediate-level elementary students in Karen Brown's Baltimore County resource classroom. Transcripts provide evidence that elementary school students are certainly capable of engaging in socially conscious critique. The following is an excerpt from a discussion among Karen Brown and her students on the book, *The Cay*. They ponder the significance of the character Timothy, an older black man, risking his own life to save Phillip, a blind boy from a racist family whom he has befriended:

T: Phillip was holding on to the tree and he protected Phillip so that the wind and the water couldn't get on him as much.
Ms.B: Yes, remember? Timothy stood behind Phillip and used his back as protection for Phillip.
T: I think that was what changed him. He learned that Timothy loved him and . . .
M: Timothy risked his life for him.
L: It was probably Timothy who was a friend to him and he saved him.
E: He cared about him and he knew he [Phillip] was prejudiced and he wanted him not to be prejudiced.
Ms.B: He wanted to teach him a lesson. Did he really love him? He gave up his life for Phillip. Do you think he thought he would die?
J: I thought Timothy would be saved but he died in the hospital . . . Timothy was old and he had a fever, but he still gave his life up so Phillip could live.
J: [The author wanted us to] understand that blacks and whites are the same and that Phillip actually changed his feelings about Timothy.
T: I think he was trying to make the point that not all black people are bad and you can't just judge a race by what one person does that is bad.
Ms.B: Do you think Phillip learned that black people were bad because of experiences he had? How did he get his . . .
L: From his mother. She wanted to move back to the USA.
J: [His] father didn't want to move back to the USA.
L: Probably because his father and mother were prejudiced and it went back into slavery days—they were really mean to blacks and she learned that . . .
Ms.B: It was in Virginia where she came from. Probably prejudice that went through history.
J: Generation to generation.

Ms.B: Can we break that kind of prejudice that goes from generation to generation? Is it happening now?
T: Yeah, there is not as much intolerance toward blacks, [but there's] still prejudice today . . .
Ms.B: What things have started people . . .
M: Not judge people by their color but by person.
L: Stop racism . . .
T: Go back in history and look at black people and how they helped future contribution . . .
M: Wasn't there black guys in wars—when they stopped slavery back in the Civil War days?

This example shows students and teachers together dialoging about social issues in the text (which we coded as IT) and connecting it to social issues in the greater society today (coded as IG). The other categories of talk that we generated from transcripts of the series of discussions by both groups about the two novels appear in Table 18.2.

These categories include talk that represents interactions among all the layers of context present in our "retheorized" model of interpretation (Figure 18.2). For both adults and children, dialogue indicates an exploration of the social issues represented in the text, in their own lives, and which relates the two. Generalized statements concerning social and political issues and problems such as racism in society (not spoken in direct connection to the text or their own personal lives) also occur. These findings suggest that even for elementary children, literature study can generate a more critical dialogue in which they explore class, gender, racial, and environmental problems and issues that impact their own lives as well as the lives of the characters in their books. But this cannot occur without a teacher who is capable and willing to encourage this type of critique.

A Socially and Politically Conscious Teacher, Capable of Inspiring Critical Dialogue

In the example given earlier for Number the Stars, there is virtually no opportunity to discuss with children the complex and profound issues concerning prejudice, intolerance, and oppression represented by this novel. Is this just an artifact of the theoretical model of reading and reading instruction underlying this type of approach, or do some teachers hide behind worksheets, preformulated questions or activities, and teacher-controlled "discussion" as a way to avoid the socially or politically "delicate" issues that may emerge from more open-ended, collaborative literature exploration?

Table 18.2. Categories of Talk for Literature Studies: Children and Adults.

Category	Description
Text (T)	Statements and questions concerning meaning and interpretation of text
Personal response to text (PR>T)	Personal responses/affective reactions to text
Issues in text (IT)	Dialogue concerning social issues (class, race, gender, culture, values) addressed within the text
Issues in life (IL)	Dialogue concerning social issues (class, race, gender, culture, values) directly related to speaker's personal life
Issues in text/issues in life (IT<>IL)	Talk that connects social issues in the text with social issues in speaker's personal life
Issues-General (IG)	Statements or questions about social issues not directly related to text or personal life of speaker; critical statements about society in general
Critique of Text (C>T)	Dialogue that critiques text or evaluates author's craft
Text to Text (T<>T)	Comparing/contrasting text to other related texts
Life to Text (L<>T)	Statements or questions that relate personal life experiences to aspects of text
Metalinguistics (M)	Talk about reading strategies
Author (A)	Talk about author's life/work

Most teachers today have had few opportunities during their own education to engage in personal and social reflection of literature in collaborative dialogic settings, no less engage in social and political critique. With the exception of instances in which college English professors hammered the established social or political moral of a given novel over our heads so we could regurgitate it on a test (a practice which we in no way support!), schools have traditionally provided few examples of critique. It takes a bit of courage, an inclination toward risk taking, and a fervent belief in the goal of critical and emancipatory education for a teacher to achieve critical literature study in the classroom. For most of us, it takes a conscious decision to engage in social and political critique ourselves, along with our students, in order for it to occur. During a literature study we must be willing to wonder aloud, question aloud, and reflect aloud about the issues and stances suggested by a text, legitimizing this type of dialogue for our students.

And we must recognize in the responses and reflections of our students opportunities to openly interrogate problems and issues in the story world as well as the world around them.

Altwerger and Fu (1995) found that the category of talk generated by the teacher during literature study greatly influenced the children's talk that followed. That is, when the teacher reflected on or posed questions about social issues in the text or in society in general (as Karen Brown did in the excerpt provided earlier), the students were likely to continue the discussion in the same vein. As if needing clearance, or simply examples, once the teacher brought up the topics, young students, too, would begin to discuss racism and discrimination represented by the text and existing around them. However, the students in our study were much less likely to relate social and political issues to their own personal circumstances even when the teacher openly did so. Though capable and willing to examine issues in society and within the story world, students in this group, at least, kept their own private lives private. For some teachers this may come as welcome news, for others it is another challenge. Nevertheless, it is important to understand that invasion of privacy, dogmatism, or imposition of ideology or political position has absolutely no place in the sort of critical literature study we envision. We are convinced that when literature study is based on multidimensional, high-quality literature and a retheorized view of interpretation, and when it is facilitated by a teacher demonstrating social equality and justice in pedagogy, as well as critique, it can be a powerful critical practice.

The Theme Cycle

The theme cycle as a curricular model has been in a process of refinement and elaboration for over 10 years, since we first presented it at a Teachers Applying Whole Language (TAWL) meeting in Tucson, AZ in 1986. The fact that it has undergone an evolutionary and transformational process speaks well for the core assumption underlying the theme cycle: True learning embodies inquiry and change. Although the critical, generative potential of the theme cycle has been present from the beginning (see Figure 18.3; Altwerger & Flores, 1986) this potential could only be realized in an educational context in which social and political critique is a viable curricular goal. As more whole language educators search for ways to link their pedagogy to an ideology of social equity and justice, they look to the theme cycle and other related inquiry-based models (Theme Immersion [Manning & Manning, 1994]; Theme Exploration [Weaver, Chaston, & Peterson, 1993]) for help. In this section, we show how the theme cycle has served

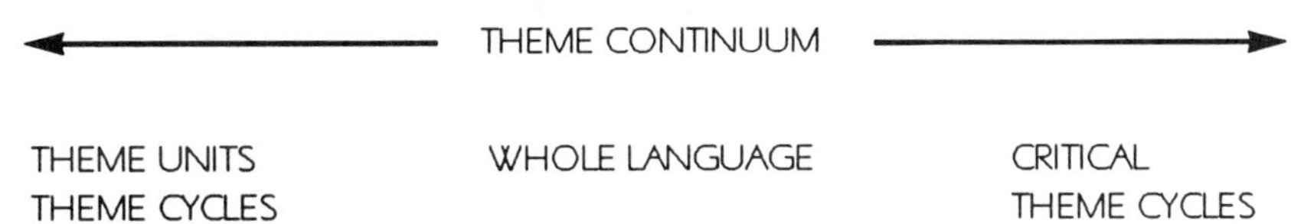

Figure 18.3. A continuum of thematic approaches

as an alternative model of integration and inquiry to whole language teachers and how it can furthermore become a powerful pedagogical tool for critical educators.

The theme cycle was a somewhat unique and revolutionary concept even at the time of its inception when considered in relation to the educational context that existed in the early 1980s. It contrasted most sharply at that time with the teacher-dominated "thematic unit," which was the most widely accepted model for integrated curriculum, even for whole language classrooms. The theme cycle offered teachers a way to reconceptualize the notion of curricular integration, while insisting on collaborative and authentic learning and literacy.

Table 18.3 presents some of the key characteristics that distinguish the theme cycle from the traditional thematic unit model which was and continues to be the most pervasive form of integrated curriculum. Thematic units generally begin with a set of predetermined unit goals and objectives developed without student input. Teachers expend time and effort outside of the classroom collecting resources and developing activities to guide learning. The thematic unit serves as an organizing tool for making curricular connections among content areas. Math, social studies, or science-related "activities" do not necessarily lead to real learning about the content of the unit, even if they are "hands-on" and entertaining. Although thematic units almost always include reading and writing activities, these are often contrived and superficial—more like Edelsky's "exercises" (Edelsky, 1991). Most importantly, underlying thematic units is the view of learning and literacy as the passive acquisition of knowledge and skills. Even when reading material is whole and meaningful, and writing is not limited to isolated sentences and words, literacy lacks authenticity and ownership for students.

It became increasingly clear that an alternative model of integration, consistent with underlying principles of whole language, was needed to replace the thematic unit in whole language classrooms. The theme cycle developed out of that need. Based on a social constructionist view of learning, the theme cycle envisions a collaborative learning environment in which teachers and students

Table 18.3. Thematic Unit vs. Theme Cycle.

Thematic Unit	Theme Cycle
Teacher-determined curriculum	Teacher-student negotiated curriculum
Preformulated learning goals	Goals based on shared knowledge, questions, anomalies, interests
Teacher responsible for planning, organizing, obtaining resources	Teacher-student shared responsibility for planning, organizing, obtaining resources
Activities are focus	Learning experiences, inquiry are focus
Vehicle for learning relevant subject area knowledge	Subject area knowledge used as resources for theme study
Contrived literacy uses	Authentic literacy use

(Based on Altwerger & Flores, 1986, 1992, 1994)

engage together in authentic inquiry and meaning construction. The role of the teacher as a co-learner is to demonstrate and guide the inquiry process, rather than to organize activities based on preformulated content and skills. Together, students and teachers engage in problem and question posing, plan and organize learning experiences, obtain resources, and use language and literacy to facilitate learning. This process of learning and knowledge construction becomes the primary focus of classroom life, not the product of it. Teachers and students learn from each other and from their collaborative investigations, resulting in a cycle of further problem posing and inquiry. Whereas in a thematic unit model the topic of inquiry serves as the vehicle for learning preformulated subject area content, the theme cycle perceives knowledge domains such as the natural sciences, social sciences, and mathematics as resources for the methods of inquiry (see Altwerger & Flores, 1992; Edelsky, Altwerger, & Flores, 1991).

The theme cycle as a pedagogical innovation was warmly embraced by whole language educators eager to enact in their classrooms an instructional framework that put learners, genuine learning, and authentic literacy use at the center. Examples of theme cycles were presented at conferences and in the literature, further fueling the enthusiasm and acceptance of the model. Conspicuously missing, however, from most of these demonstrations of theme cycles was the sort of inquiry that derives from a link to critical and progressive ideology. Even though theme cycles based on bears and dinosaurs could be regarded as an advancement (from a whole language perspective) over thematic units on these same benign topics, how did they represent advances toward critical pedagogy in the classroom? Absent from the dialogue about theme cycles were some important and challenging questions. What is inquiry for? To what end? To serve what interests? To fulfill which social and political goals? And without consciously posing and struggling with such questions, whole language pedagogy, even enriched by the theme cycle, remains subservient to the ideological status quo and impotent to transform the role of school in society. We were still a long way from the "generative themes" we had originally envisioned, in which students and teachers interrogate and critique sanctioned, established knowledge along with their own social/political realities.

The theme cycle grows richer in possibility when it is viewed not only as a theoretically principled practice but as a powerful vehicle for critical practice. Its power lies in its potential to transform life inside and outside classrooms by posing important problems and asking the really tough questions. For this to occur, we must break through the boundaries of sanctioned knowledge, mandated curriculum content, and safe mundane topics, to view the problems and possibilities of everyday life (both past and present) as subjects of inquiry. Table 18.4 identifies the characteristics of the more generative, critical theme cycle we envision, as distinguished from the more apolitical whole language version.

The differences between the two models may best be illustrated by looking into the classroom of one critical teacher, Karen Dockstader-Anderson, a colleague and friend of ours from Albuquerque, NM. For the purposes of this chapter, we discuss only selected aspects of the critical theme cycle she and her students developed, but a full description may be found in Dockstader-Anderson (1994). Karen and

Table 18.4. Whole Language Theme Cycle vs. Critical Theme Cycle.

Whole Language Theme Cycle	Critical Theme Cycle
Negotiated curriculum	Generative curriculum
Personal, social inquiry	Critical inquiry
Purposeful, authentic literacy use	Literacy for personal and social agency
Relevant use of knowledge domains and infusion of literature	Using and critiquing established knowledge, literature
	Constructing new knowledge
	Potential for social action

her students' theme cycle on ecology was generated from a previous study on the environment which had itself been generated from a study of astronomy and the universe. Though selection of these topics grew out of a collaborative, negotiated process, it was the critical issues they discovered during their previous work on the problems in the atmosphere, and then later on the endangerment of animals, which served as the real catalyst for topic selection. The issue which surfaced was a particularly bothersome and socially significant one: "that a minority species was responsible for the destruction of animal habitats and the environment. That species was us" (Dockstader-Anderson, 1994, p. 27). Rather than being satisfied with reading just the mainstream literature on the environment and writing reports about it, Karen and her students researched alternative print sources, such as "Kids for Saving Mother Earth News," and wrote letters for information to the Rainforest Action Network and of protest to the President. By linking authentic literacy to personal and social agency, Karen's class was learning the power of reading and writing to act on and transform their world. As their inquiry broadened and deepened, their determination to plan social actions grew. They wrote a public service message on recycling and the problems of ground water pollution which was broadcast on all the local TV stations. With the help of other students and parents they held an "Earth Expo" at their school, featuring over 20 science exhibits, to inform the community of environmental problems. With the help of a reporter from the *Albuquerque Journal* who had interviewed them about their activism, they wrote and solicited articles about the environment which were then published in the newspaper. They planted trees and gardens in the school community where none had been. They raised funds to purchase trash cans for the playground. They used math, science, literacy, and even the arts to learn and express themselves. But the most important lesson of all they communicated in their own words: "We could talk to people in powerful places, like mayors and newspaper editors; we could write letters and call people and get action and they could work together to make change" (Dockstader-Anderson, 1994, p. 31).

These student activists are more likely to grow into adulthood feeling confident in their ability to transform the world around them and influence the future. Fortunately, they will not be alone. They will find support among a growing number of student activists such as those whose inspiring stories fill the pages of *It's Our World, Too!* (Hoose, 1993). There is Neto and Andy, who stand up against racist football fans; Norvell, a girl who stands up against gangs in Chicago; and the New Mexican students who build a statue for peace at the birthplace of the atom bomb. These are students for whom language, literacy, and inquiry is linked to empowerment and agency. Their work can make a difference, not just for themselves but for all of us.

The Task Ahead

In this chapter, we have explored the critical potential of only two whole language practices which have emerged since Kenneth Goodman turned reading education on its head and Freire offered an ideological framework for looking at education generally. Though each is a revolutionary educator who will leave his mark forever on the world of education, it is critical educators, inspired and informed by the work of both, who must construct a pedagogy which is at once practical, theory-based, and transformative. As students of Kenneth Goodman, we can pay him no greater tribute than to work together as a community of progressive educators to envision a pedagogy that is both whole language and critical. And there is no greater goal than to revision schools and classrooms as sites of hopeful struggle to create a more equitable, just, and peaceful future.

REFERENCES

Aaronowitz, S., & Giroux, H. (1985). *Education under siege*. South Hadley, MA: Bergin and Garvey.

Altwerger, B., & Flores, B. (1986). *Theme cycles*. Symposium presented at Tucson TAWL Conference, Tucson, Arizona.

Altwerger, B., & Flores, B. (1992). Theme cycles. In K. Goodman, L. Bird, & Y. Goodman, *The whole language catalogue* (p. 295). Chicago: American School Publishers.

Altwerger, B., & Flores, B. (1994). Theme cycles.: Creating communities of learners. *Primary Voices*, 2(1), 2-6.

Altwerger, B., & Fu, D. (1995). *The nature of critical dialogue in literature study groups*. Paper presented at American Educational Research Association. San Francisco.

Bigelow, B. (1994a). Getting off the track. In B. Bigelow, L. Christensen, S. Karp, B. Miner, & B. Petersen (Eds.), *Rethinking our classrooms*. Milwaukee, WI: Rethinking Schools.

Bigelow, B. (1994b). Good intentions are not enough: Children's literature in the aftermath of the quincentenary. *The New Advocate, 7*(4), 265-279.

Bishop, R. S. (1993). Multicultural literature for children: Making informed choices. In V. Harris, (Ed.), *Teaching multicultural literature in grades K–8* (pp. 37-53). Norwood, MA: Christopher Gordon.

Blume, J. (1970). *Are you there God? It's me Margaret.* New York: Bradbury.

Christensen, L. (1994). Unlearning the myths that bind us. In B. Bigelow, L. Christensen, S. Karp, B. Miner, & B. Peterson (Eds.), *Rethinking our classrooms.* Milwaukee, WI: Rethinking Schools.

Dockstader–Anderson, K. (1994). Democracy in action. *Primary Voices,* 2(1), 26-32.

Dyson, A.H., & Genishi, C. (Eds). (1994). *The need for story: Cultural diversity in classroom and community.* Urbana, IL: National Council of Teachers of English.

Edelsky, C. (1991). *With liberty and justice for all.* London: Falmer Press.

Edelsky, C. (1994a). Education for democracy. *Language Arts, 71*(1), 252-257.

Edelsky , C. (1994b). *On justice, equity, and petards.* Keynote address, Whole Day of Whole Language. National Council of Teachers of English, Orlando, FL.

Edelsky, C., Altwerger, B., & Flores, B. (1991). *Whole language: What's the difference?* Portsmouth, NH: Heinemann.

Flores, B. (1990). *Whole language: A pedagogy of resistance and possibility.* Paper presented at the California Association of Bilingual Educators Annual Conference, San Francisco.

Freire, P. (1970). *Pedagogy of the oppressed.* New York: Seabury Press.

Gilles, C. (1990). Collaborative literacy strategies: We don't need a circle to have a group. In K. Short & K. Pierce (Eds.), *Talking about books* (pp. 55-68). Portsmouth, MA: Heinemann.

Giroux, H. (1983). *Theory and resistance in education: A pedagogy for the opposition.* Granby, MA: Bergin and Garvey.

Goodman, K. S. (1967). Reading: A psycholinguistic guessing game. *Journal of the Reading Specialist, 6*(4), 126-135.

Goodman, K. (1984) Unity in Reading. In A. Purves & O. Niles (Eds). *Becoming readers in a complex society* (pp. 79-114). 83rd Yearbook of the National Society for the Study of Education. Chicago, NSSE.

Harp, B. (Ed.). (1991). *Assessment and evaluation in whole language programs.* Norwood, MA: Christopher–Gordon.

Harris, V. (1993). *Teaching multicultural literature in grades K–8.* Norwood, MA: Christopher Gordon.

Hoose, P. (1993). *It's our world, too!: Stories of young people making a difference.* Boston, MA: Little, Brown.

Lankshire, C., with Lawler, M. (1987). *Literacy, schooling and revolution.* London: Falmer Press.

Lowry, L. (1989). *Number the stars.* Boston: Houghton-Mifflin.

Manning, M., & Manning, G. (1994). *Theme immersion: Inquiry–based curriculum in elementary schools.* Portsmouth, MA: Heinemann.

Peterson, B. (1994). Teaching for social justice: One teacher's journey. In B. Bigelow, L. Christensen, S. Karp, B. Miner, & B. Petersen (Eds.), *Rethinking our classrooms*. Milwaukee, WI: Rethinking Schools.

Peterson, R., & Eeds, M. (1990). *Grand conversations*. Richmond Hill, Ontario: Scholastic.

Rhodes, L., & Shanklin, N. (1993). *Windows into literacy*. Portsmouth, MA: Heinemann.

Rosenblatt, L. (1983). *Literature as exploration* (4th ed.). New York: Modern Language Association.

Saaverdra, E. (1995). *Teacher transformation: Creating texts and contexts in teacher study groups*. Unpublished doctoral dissertation, University of Arizona, Tucson.

Shor, I., & Freire, P. (1987). *A pedagogy for liberation*. South Hadley, MA: Bergin and Garvey.

Smith, K. (1990). Entertaining a text: A reciprocal process. In K. Short & K. Pierce (Eds.), *Talking about books* (pp. 17-31). Portsmouth, MA: Heinemann.

Spinelli, J. (1990). *Maniac McGee*. Boston: Little, Brown.

Taxel, J. (1988). Children's literature: Ideology and response. *Curriculum Inquiry, 18*, 217-229.

Taylor, T. (1969). *The cay*. New York: Doubleday.

Weaver, C., Chaston, J., & Peterson, S. (1993). *Theme exploration: A voyage of Discovery*. Portsmouth, MA: Heinemann.

Chapter Nineteen

*Common Currents: Yet, Oceans Apart**

Jerome Harste
Indiana University

Recently I had the opportunity to visit whole language classrooms in Hawaii, Indiana, and New York. Although I have no reason to believe these are atypical whole language teachers and classrooms, the fact of the matter is that the sites I visited have long histories of leadership in the whole language movement. In most cases I did more than visit, but I detail the specifics of my experience as I explore trends I see occurring in these settings. Overall, I make a case for why it is that holistic educators can take heart at even this very moment in history when some would have us believe otherwise. Said differently, I had a sabbatical and I used that opportunity to do a status check on what was happening in some very strong pockets of whole language. In this chapter I try to put the patterns I found in perspective as well as set new directions for holistic educators in the future.

*My thanks to Indiana University, the Hawaii State Department of Education, and the teachers and children at Dole Intermediate School, The Manhattan New School, The Center for Inquiry, and The New York Writing Project Schools, without whose support this project would not have been possible.

More and More Holistic Educators are Advocating the Basics of Whole Language: Kidwatching, the Articulation of One's Personal Theory of Literacy, and Teaching as Inquiry. Jimmy Britton once said to me that language educators in the United States had to be proud. Rather than make the mistakes made in England, he saw American educators as working with teachers in helping them develop their own personal theories of literacy. In England, Professor Britton thought that university educators, himself included, gave classroom teachers already developed theories and posed the teaching task as one of implementation.

Despite such perceptions from the outside, the truth of the matter is that with more and more methods books on how to create classrooms for authors, more teachers in the United States have entered whole language through activities ("I do journals"; "I do conferencing") than through the intense study and understanding of children and language. Because so many teachers proclaiming to promote whole language do not have a basic understanding of the cue systems of language nor how it is that children grow and develop as language learners, one trend in the whole language community is a return to fundamentals in an attempt to build a theoretical base of understanding. Indicative of the trend is the fact that I encountered teacher study groups doing exactly this at all three sites on my visit.

Diane Stephens in Hawaii has developed what she calls a "Hypothesis-Test" model of kidwatching. Teachers in her study group keep a 4-column kidwatching journal. In column 1 they record "observations," in column 2 they record "interpretations" (she demands five interpretations for each observation to push thoughtfulness), in column 3 "hypotheses" (these are if-then relationships or patterns they see across interpretations, the function of which is to force teachers to articulate their evolving theory of language instruction), and in column 4 they record "curricular inquiries" (which she defines as new settings in which to test out one's evolving theory). Diane contracts with school systems. Teachers at a particular site are released for a half day during which time the study group meets to share professional books they are reading, work with children who they perceive to be "at risk," and collaborate with each other in making sense of their data and in planning new curricular inquiries. Teachers often work with a single child for more than a year!

Diane's approach is powerful and the results are phenomenal. I do not know when I have encountered a more theoretically grounded group of teachers. These teachers understand the fundamentals of whole language: building curriculum from children, the importance of continually building one's personal theories of language, language learning, language instruction, and teaching as inquiry.

I brought Diane's procedure home to Indiana. As part of my work at the Center for Inquiry in Indianapolis (a new public school that an Indiana study group of teachers developed), we have planned three studies for next year. One hundred and forty-one children make up our school population. Of this number, four children present real difficulties for us—they do not seem to be doing well despite the fact that the curriculum reflects the best of what we currently know about how to support language learning. One study will focus on these four children. Each of us will make weekly observations and then meet to share observations, generate interpretations, identify patterns, and test out new curricular inquiries involving the child. Rather than see these children as problems, we wish to see them as data for what we hope will be a new and more powerful model of instruction.

A second study will use Diane's procedure to track undergraduate teacher education students' evolving theories of language, language learning, and language instruction. In this regard, Dr. Christine Leland and I have asked the Dean of the School of Education to place 20 interns in our school and allow us to be responsible for their complete undergraduate teacher preparation over a 2-year period. Data for this study will include teacher observations of the interns as they operate in their classrooms as well as the interns' own kidwatching journals, which they will keep on children they find personally problematic or anomalous.

The third study is equally exciting. Each of us will fill out a kidwatching entry for every day of teaching on any child or intern that captures our attention that day. We hope to use these entries to study our own changing interests as well as to interrogate the very constructs we are using to make sense of our teaching. True to holistic education, we know that the only thing that assessment can do is help a learner or a community of learners interrogate their values, and we are going to capitalize on this power in explicit ways.

To demonstrate what this return to fundamentals looks like as well as how it gets expressed in kidwatching, the articulation of one's personal theory of literacy, and teaching as inquiry, let me return to Honolulu for a specific example. As part of my extended stay in Hawaii, I visited Diane Yoshizawa's first grade classroom at Wahiawa Elementary during their writing period. Diane was interested in my impression of how her children were progressing. She was concerned about several children, including Jordan who she saw as vulnerable because he has to move on to second grade and is not using invented spelling yet.

> I'm concerned. Rather than move to invented spelling, Jordan is still writing random strings of the letter "b." This is first grade and it is already January! If he doesn't make some progress soon, he is going to be very vulnerable in second grade. They will expect him to be writing. How do I support him?

Critical holistic educators will argue that there are several things wrong with Mrs. Yoshizawa's interpretation of Jordan, as well as her concern in general. For example, what right does any second grade teacher have to hold such expectations for beginning writers? What are the systems of meaning in our society that make such expectations seem right? What other ways of thinking are possible, and what options do these ways of thinking provide for how we might analyze this problem? Who said growth in writing ends in conventional control? Jordan has a sense of story and only one year ago spent all of his time screaming by the easel. Who says story isn't more basic than mastery of the graphophonemic system of language, or even emotional well being for that matter?

Despite the questions that could and in fact have been asked of Mrs. Yoshizawa, one could easily miss the bigger picture. The significance does not come by being right. By articulating what one believes (a true learner always has to believe that at least one tenet in his or her existing theory is wrong), beliefs become open to personal and systematic interrogation.

There have always been intuitive teachers, but I do not believe there have ever been "good" intuitive teachers. Even if they are intuitively doing the "right thing," intuitive teachers are a menace to the profession. It is by articulating what we believe that we open up what we know to reflection, interrogation, and thoughtful future learning. To advocate otherwise is to believe teaching is a matter of getting it right rather than an ongoing matter of inquiry.

Going back to whole language basics is sometimes, unfortunately, related to that other "back to basics." Just at the moment when history offers us new opportunities to understand the roles of immersion and interpretation in learning, there is a growing concern in the whole language community that we may have gone too far in ignoring the skills. Even in whole language classrooms, there is a real skill mentality afloat. Lots of whole language educators have let the skill-and-drill advocates intimidate them. That is why the countertrend of getting back to the basics of kidwatching is so important. What the nay-sayers do not seem to understand is that there truly is no going home. Whole language teachers are much too theoretically strong to go back to a phonics-first approach to the teaching of reading. Even the recent attacks on whole language in California as a result of dropping test scores are, when one gets by the headlines and looks at the substance, a call to keep whole language and to add phonics. California children are reading more books than ever before, and no one is asking whole language teachers to drop what they are doing in the name of writing.

In New York City I visited a kindergarten and a fifth grade classroom that Diane Epstein and Randy Bomer selected for me to observe. Diane is the resource teacher at School 148, which is part of Lucy Calkins' Writing Project. I saw two marvelous beginning teachers. In Suzanne Gonzales' kindergarten classroom, a student in the class, Sara, asked if I would like her to copy her story in my Sketch Journal. I, of course, was delighted. I also watched this teacher read two stories to the children and get them talking and thinking about the craft of writing, specifically what word other than "said" an author might use. In Judy Ballester's fifth grade room I visited a Readers' Club ("four good readers; myself and three of my best friends") as they shared the connections they made between *Sarah, Plain & Tall* (MacLachlan, 1985) and *Journey* (MacLachlan, 1991).

These teachers were part of a New York Writing Project Study Group. This study group was concerned that whole language teachers were not taking the time to make sure children had fundamental reading skills, including how to enter into "grand conversations" about books. Again, it not so much whether or not these concerns are legitimate. What is important is that they are being articulated. Once they are public, interpretations can be pushed and interrogated. I did just that. I spent a follow-up day in a "think tank" with Lucy Calkins, Randy Bomer, Diane Epstein, and other leaders within The Writing Project exploring what it is that they thought they were correcting given a whole language model of reading. The day was extremely generative for all of us. Even I had to articulate why I was not as concerned as they were about issues that interested them and, in that process, I grew.

There is Lots of Interest in, Confusion About, and Hope for Inquiry as a Latent Potential and New Frontier for Whole Language. Inquiry is the growing buzz word in whole language circles, often replacing "whole language" as the term being used to describe a holistic curriculum. In part, the use of the term *inquiry* allows educators to proceed with a holistic agenda while avoiding the term *whole language* which sends up red flags among many constituents. I see this trend as negative because it allows everyone to avoid addressing underlying issues. It is only a matter of time before inquiry, too, will become a problematic term. I don't see the term *whole language* as the problem. What is problematic is the underlying structures of meaning that are in operation in society:

"Teachers need to be told what to teach." "Everyone knows that in order to read you need to know your letters and sounds." Avoiding terms like *whole language* may allow educators to avoid these knotty issues, but the root problem never gets addressed or corrected.

On the other hand, there are instances when the use of the term *inquiry* seems more positive. In these instances, the term reflects a trend toward more integrated study as well as the movement of holistic philosophy across the curriculum. At each site—Hawaii, New York, and Indiana—inquiry was meant to capture more than just an integrated approach to the language arts. Included in the term was an integrated approach to teaching reading, writing, mathematics, science, social studies, and more.

While visiting The Manhattan New School (Harwayne, 1994), I spend the entire day wandering through classrooms, working with children, and talking with teachers. Shelly Harwayne, the principal, spent most of her day giving me a tour, explaining things I was smart enough to see for myself as well as things I was too dense to pick up immediately. In Joanne Henley's third grade classroom, I worked with a group of children who were testing out various student-generated hypotheses about how multiplication and division works using manipulatives. The children in my group verified the principle that a number divided by a number is the same as the answer taken times the number that was divided plus its remainder. When they shared this with Joanne she encouraged them to express their finding in writing. When Edmond and his friends came back to the table, I did the same. Edmond turned to me and rather huffily said, "Will you two give me some time!" "Oh, sorry," I said, "since you were messing with the manipulatives, I thought probably you were thinking about skipping that part." He just looked at me rather disgustedly. So much for my sensitive kidwatching.

In Sharon Takerski's room I watched her enrapture a group of first graders in a content-area trade book called *New Providence* (Von Tscharner, Fleming, & Townscape Institute, 1987). Talk about a master teacher. At one point she turned to Ashley, who was being disruptive, to say, "Ashley, you really should be part of this group. When you're not, you really miss out and so do we." It was an exciting moment: Not only did Ashley begin to attend to the book but also to the conversations of her classmates. Before my eyes a class-focused study (Short & Burke, 1991) was born.

I also spent some time in Judy Davis' fifth grade room. They were in the process of finishing a unit on medieval times, and groups had to decide what kind of building they wished to contribute to a display the class had decided to make. Judy used the problems that came up to stimulate further inquiry and discussion among the group as a whole. Children naturally assumed the perspectives of artists, architects, historians, and city planners.

Despite the growing popularity of the term, for the most part inquiry still needs to be invented from the inside out through the hard work of curricular development, risk taking, and reflection. At Dole Intermediate School in Honolulu, I worked side-by-side with teachers as they explored what an inquiry-based curriculum looked like. For the most part I worked with Jennifer Story and Eda Kaneakua, who with several other teachers team teach a pod of 120 sixth graders. Thanks to the openness of this school to change, I was invited and visited teachers in other pods and attended several school-wide planning meetings. The State Department of Education in Hawaii sees the work going on at Dole as innovative and has underwritten the costs of freeing two teams of teachers to work on inquiry at several all-day staff meetings throughout the year.

One of the problems teachers seemed to be having in understanding inquiry was its closeness to theme cycles and units of study. For some teachers inquiry was just a fancy way of talking about integrating the language arts. They seemed to have missed the point that inquiry is a new philosophical stance on what the whole of education is all about.

In reality I found several competing definitions of inquiry in place. There were teachers who saw inquiry as a form of transmission: Here's the question; here's the answer. In classrooms holding this model of inquiry students were permitted to generate their own questions, but in answer to the question of "What is inquiry?", children were being taught that you answered it by finding the right fact in the right resource book. Questions and answers had a one-to-one correspondence.

Although children's literature dominated all of the classrooms I visited, the use of literature itself was problematic. In terms of inquiry, children in these classrooms often generated lists of questions and then went to library books collected by the teacher to find the answer, a practice that equated research with library research in the minds of children.

There were other groups of teachers who equated inquiry with discovery learning. They know what it is that children are to inquire into as well as learn. It is the child's task to discover what the teacher has decided kids must learn.

By way of contrast, the staff at the Center for Inquiry (CFI) in Indianapolis sees inquiry not so much as answering questions as unpacking issues. In addition to handing future generations problems of some magnitude to solve—hence, an inquiry curriculum—they believe that they must also stop generating simple answers to complex problems. Inquiry for the CFI staff is about understanding the complexity of issues, and in this light taking thoughtful new action. The meaning that one makes of an experience metaphorically must be projected forward to untangle the unfamiliar. It is the projection forward of the known that constitutes inquiry. Inquiry is a philosophical stance on what the whole of education is about and should not be relegated to a time slot in the afternoon in which curricular areas are integrated. CFI teachers want reading to be seen as inquiry, writing as inquiry, curriculum as inquiry, and inquiry as curriculum.

At Mililani Uka Elementary School I worked with Jocelyn Mokulehua, a third grade teacher, on teaching reading as inquiry. I must have been somewhat successful in my efforts to run several literature discussion groups because the kids seemed to approve. One child asked Jocelyn after I left, "When is that old guy going to come back? I liked our discussion."

The literature discussion sessions I did in Jocelyn's classroom were videotaped, and often Jocelyn and several of the other teachers in her curriculum study group watched the videotapes for the purpose of discussing differences between the way I conducted literature discussion and the way they conducted literature discussion. One of the first things they noted is that I, following Carole Edelsky's observation of Karen Smith teaching (Harste & Jurewicz, 1991), "assumed comprehension" and often began the literature discussion by asking the children what they made of this story and the value they saw in it for helping understand our world. These discussions were not easy, but they were powerful in the sense that they involved going beyond the book to a discussion of action and often an interrogation of our personal and social values.

A second thing they noticed was the value of a hard book. Books that the children found difficult to understand and that left the hard work of projection up to them, generated the best discussions. A case in point was the difference between the literature discussion of *Chocolate Fever* (Smith, 1972) and *The Mountains of Tibet* (Gerstein, 1987). *Chocolate Fever* is very explicit. The author states the moral of the tale as well as what it means. *The Mountains of Tibet* leaves the reader hanging. Children have to deal with the concept of reincarnation as well as come to grips with the fact that the main character in the story, a boy, chose to come back as a girl. The discussion that ensued was rich. The children talked about how different cultures have different beliefs, what benefit we could derive from understanding other cultures, and how our own cultural and gender-based prejudices color our interpretations of the story. The agenda is to explore how it is we make whole language critical. Reading as inquiry provides a needed perspective.

I did not get a chance to explore writing as inquiry with elementary or middle-school children, though I did with teachers in several study groups. I am convinced that curriculum cannot move ahead unless teachers begin to write. It is in writing curriculum that our intuitive theories of instruction become articulated, are made public, and become a source of professional growth. Through writing, teaching more easily comes to be seen as inquiry and the role of the teacher, like that of their students, one of inquirer.

In New York, teachers not only write curriculum but have debriefing sessions after school with visitors that focus on observations and concerns that visitors noted during their stay. These sessions are voluntary but attended by as many teachers as can adjust their schedule, and they are the basis of curriculum revision and reflection.

In many ways, inquiry and critical literacy are latent potentials in whole language. The development of inquiry as a major curricular thrust represents a growing understanding of the underlying processes of learning, and specifically, the multiple roles that language plays in learning. Critical literacy, in which children interrogate the systems of meaning that are in place in their society that shape their personal response, extends as well as deepens our understanding of the role of reflection and reflexivity in learning. With these understandings, not surprisingly, more and more educators feel a need to make whole language critical, though how actually to proceed is less clear to them. Issues of equity and justice still make whole language teachers nervous. Front-loading curriculum on issues of equity and justice by preselecting what themes students will or will not study strikes many holistic educators as a return to direct instruction and everything that whole language was meant to reform in the first place. However, even when topics of equity and justice naturally arise, teachers too often retreat to safer curricular ground.

As a theory, education as inquiry is meant to make curriculum more relevant as well as more critical. Although no one had the answer, teachers at all three sites—New York, Indiana, and Hawaii—were beginning to grapple with these issues, trying to build from, rather than retreat from, what it is they thought they knew about language, learning, and children.

More and More Classroom Teachers Actually Expect Academics to be Personally Helpful in Improving Literacy Instruction in Their Classrooms. Said differently, top-down models of professional development are on their way out. In their place are study groups and collaborative teacher education programs.

Over the course of my visits I attended several after-school teacher study group meetings. Topics ranged from how classroom teachers might better support reluctant readers, to assessment, to what it is a specific group of four teachers might want to do next year when they go to a new school that philosophically better reflects their belief system. In some instances we have had dinner meetings that lasted six hours.

One of the side effects of teachers taking charge of their own professional development is that more and more teachers are beginning to explore nonhierarchical ways of involving parents in education. Parents, for the first time since the onset of compulsory education, are being invited to become true partners in their child's education.

At Ka'ala Elementary in Wahiawa, Elaine Tsuchiyama, a second grade teacher, invited me to participate in her parents' program. I not only spoke to the parents about the importance of reading to their child at home, but worked with Sereath, a newly arrived immigrant child from Cambodia, on building a puff-mobile which we tested for distance. Later as a whole group we talked about the virtues of various parent-child designs.

Teachers at the new Center for Inquiry in Indianapolis ran a series of parent meetings in an attempt to incorporate into the Center's philosophy the parents' visions of what education might be. Although we had gained approval from the Indianapolis Public Schools to open the Center's doors by arguing that we wanted to be an inquiry-based, multiple-ways-of-knowing school, it was time to live our model. The staff at the Center divided the two-hour parent meetings into four parts. During the first half hour children took their parents to various centers around the room where they experienced firsthand the kinds of curricular engagements that the children in the school were experiencing and enjoying. During the second half hour the teachers and I talked with the parents about our vision of this school—why inquiry based, why collaboration, why multiple ways of knowing, and the like. We ended this session by explaining to parents that we saw curriculum as a metaphor for the lives we want to live and people we want to be. During the third half hour, we gave parents an opportunity to meet in groups to address three questions: (a) By the time your child is grown, what kind of person do you want your child to be?, (b) What experiences do you think your child will need to get there?, and (c) What role do you see school playing in this process? We assigned a teacher to each group as a scribe with the strict rule that they not direct the conversation, but let the parents speak. During the fourth half hour we posted all the charts that had been generated and the parents became inquirers looking for common patterns and anomalies which we took time to pull out and discuss. We were impressed with what these inner-city parents developed. Although they wanted their children to have basic skills, the bulk of their vision had to do with people who were competent, had a sense of values, and knew how to problem solve. It was enough to give us renewed hope in public education.

What is particularly interesting about this trend is that college professors, classroom teachers, and parents are working side by side. It is not an "Us-Them" relationship, but a "We." It was heartening to see college professors up to their necks in curriculum and the interactional models they lived extended to parents by the teachers who were involved.

At each site, college faculty members were involved as true collaborators in education. Although they still offered more than their share of advice, they also participated in instruction, curriculum development, evaluation, and research. Although they, like other collaborators, could step back to take reflective looks, they no longer were free to step away from their own tangled involvements. If we define morality and ethics in terms of relationships, then clearly whole language has raised the stakes in education.

CONCLUSION

To the extent that the three sites I visited—New York, Indiana, Hawaii—are indicative of what is happening in whole language, I believe holistic educators can take heart. Since 1967—the year in which Ken Goodman published his first article on whole language—the philosophy has worked its way into the very soul of education. As this chapter suggests, some very fundamental changes are afloat. Slogans such as "kidwatching," "teacher-researcher," and "inquiry-based instruction," are not so much bandwagons as they are expressions of a powerful new undercurrent in how we think about education. All of the teachers reported on in this chapter are involved in school restructuring. In very real ways they are writing a new identity not only for themselves but for the profession. If pragmatically we say that what a theory changes says lots about what a theory is and whether it is needed or not, then holistic educators can take heart. Despite geographical distances, whole language has set in motion some new, common currents, any one of which is still enough to trip up the system. The three trends I note in this chapter—back to the basics, inquiry-based education, and university-school collaboration—seem, just like the sites I visited, oceans apart from one another. Yet underneath—at a philosophical level—there are common currents: faith in teachers, children, and the learning process; a commitment to democratic processes, public schooling, and the bettering of both through inquiry; and an expectation that both difference and community propel literacy learning.

REFERENCES

Goodman, K.S. (1967). Reading: A psycholinguistic guessing game. *Journal of the Reading Specialist*, 4(1), 126-135.

Gerstein, M. (1987). *Mountains of Tibet*. New York: Harper & Row.

Harste, J.C. (Host & Developer), & Jurewicz, E. (Producer & Director). (1991). *Literature circles* (Visions of Literacy Series). Portsmouth, NH: Heinemann.

Harwayne, S. (1994). The Manhattan New School. *Talking Points*, 2(2), 8-9.

MacLachlan, P. (1985). *Sarah, plain and tall*. New York: Harper & Row.

MacLachlan, P. (1991). *Journey*. New York: Dell.

Short, K.G., & Burke, C.L. (1991). *Creating curriculum*. Portsmouth, NH: Heinemann.

Smith, R.K. (1972). *Chocolate fever* (Illustrated by G. Fiammenghi). New York: Putman.

Von Tscharner, R., Fleming, R., & Townscape Institute. (1987). *New Providence* (Illustrated by D. Orloff). San Diego, CA: Harcourt.

Chapter Twenty

Learning a First Language for the Second Time: "Goodman Contexts" and "Vygotskyan Zones" in Recovery from Aphasia

Steven L. Strauss
University of Maryland Medical Systems

Aphasia is a heterogeneous disorder of language that affects at least 100,000 Americans yearly who suffer a stroke, traumatic brain injury, or brain tumors (Albert et al., 1981). Its potential for altering an individual's lifestyle is profound because it leads to both loss of independence and an array of depressive syndromes (Benson & Ardila, 1993). Although much spontaneous recovery does occur, patients are often left with residual deficits that resist traditional treatment regimens.

An important, although perhaps overlooked, characteristic of recovery from aphasia is that it represents a type of learning. This is not to say that the patient relearns his or her lost grammatical structures or phonemic inventory. Rather, the successful patient relearns how to communicate linguistically, a purposeful behavior that involves both linguistic competence and communicative competence (Chomsky, 1965; Hymes, 1987).

More specifically, recovery from aphasia represents a type of adult language learning. As opposed to the well-studied "learning a second language for the first time," recovery from aphasia can be considered "learning a first language for the second time." As such, we can ask whether what is known about language learning in nonaphasic situations is applicable to aphasic individuals as well. We may find that it is not, but the question is clearly an empirical one, to be decided by the facts of the matter and not dismissed a priori .

The development of linguistic abilities is remarkably complex and multifaceted. It involves not only the 'growth' of the 'mental organ' for formally representing grammatical structures (Chomsky, 1965, 1975, 1982), but, in addition, the capacity to use linguistic knowledge in the service of creating contextually appropriate meanings (Halliday, 1975). A comprehensive theory of language development must account for facts from both of these domains. Goodman's work represents one of the major steps in this direction because what he has proposed is a general paradigm for understanding the relationship between optimal conditions for creating contextually appropriate meanings and how such use of language leads to growth and development over time.

Although Goodman's most well-known contributions have been in the psycholinguistics and pedagogy of reading (Goodman, 1967, 1985, 1986), both he and his coworkers have investigated important questions about learning to read, in particular, and language learning in general. The unifying principle of the philosophy that has emerged from this work is that all language is learned in natural, meaningful, social contexts. (I refer to these as "Goodman contexts.") This is a neo-Vygotskyan position on learning, applied to the special case of language. It has received widespread support from studies on normal populations of children learning to read (Goodman, Altwerger, & Marek, 1989; Goodman & Goodman, 1979), children learning to write (Ferreiro & Teberosky, 1982; Harste et al., 1982; Harste et al., 1984; Read, 1975), children learning a first oral language (Brown, 1973; Halliday, 1975), and adults learning a second language (Krashen, 1982; Krashen and Terrell, 1983). It has also received support from important studies on special populations, including deaf readers (Ewoldt, 1977) and children with developmental disabilities (Rhodes & Dudley-Marling, 1988). There is increasing evidence that it is applicable to recovery from aphasia in adults.

Though deceptively simple in its form, the Goodman principle of language learning has profound implications for how we conduct language teaching and rehabilitation because it poses an admonition against breaking language and grammar apart into small, hierarchically arranged units and then expecting the learner to master these units in a graded fashion (Goodman,1986). Such units may be appropriate for grammatical theory but are not so readily fashioned into a theory of language learning.

The Goodman principle of language learning is not simply an article of faith. It is based on numerous empirical observations of language events that demonstrate that learning over time is maximized by immersing the learner in those social contexts that optimize individual performance episodes for that learner. This principle is illustrated in Figure 20.1:

Indeed, Goodman's principle can be thought of as one that relates language performance to language learning: His work identifies those contexts for language use that optimize the language user's performance, and then sees language learning as occurring in the Vygotskyan 'zones of proximal development' (Vygotsky, 1978) established by these contexts. Goodman's enduring contribution is that optimal contexts for language use involve purpose and meaning on the part of the language users, as well as natural, authentic texts (Edelsky, 1991). They allow the full complement of cognitive resources to be available to the language user. Suboptimal contexts are created, in vitro so to speak, either by eliminating purpose and meaning from the language activity, or by using "inauthentic" texts; these contexts then become obstacles both to performance and to learning.

Data from adult aphasic language provide striking support for Goodman's notion that language performance is optimized in social contexts that involve authentic texts and prompt language users to have particular communicative purposes. Indeed, the variability of some aphasic language makes this even more apparent than is already the case with normal variability because some aphasic individuals are completely incomprehensible in non-Goodman contexts, yet sound entirely normal in Goodman contexts. This finding establishes the first (i.e., optimal performance) part of Goodman's principle; future studies

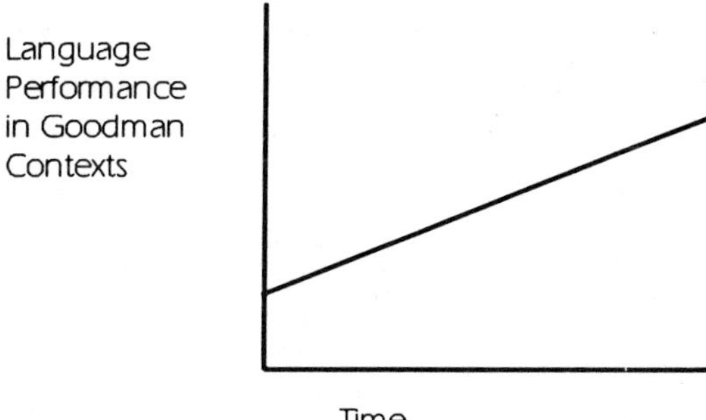

Figure 20.1. The Goodman principle of language learning

of recovery will need to take up the second part, that is, the question of whether language recovery in adult aphasia is itself optimized by immersing the learner in these Goodman-type contexts. If this can be demonstrated, it would represent yet another area in which language development is seen to occur through the conjunction of a Goodman context with a Vygotskyan zone. It would, in fact, demonstrate that recovery from aphasia is truly a kind of language learning. The real, practical need for aphasia rehabilitation demands that we pursue this theoretically important question.

LANGUAGE, MEDICAL SCIENCE, AND THE STAGES OF STROKE

A stroke may be thought of as occurring in three stages: (a) the *pre-symptomatic* stage, (b) the *acute* stage, and (c) the *recovery* stage. Each stage of a stroke has its own medical goals, treatment, and scientific foundations. These are shown in Table 20.1:

Stage 1 is a prophylactic stage aimed at minimizing the risks that increase the likelihood of a stroke (hypertension, diabetes, tobacco, etc.). Stroke is a vascular disease of the brain, and the pathophysiology of vascular disease forms the scientific foundation for rational intervention at this stage.

Stage 2 is the acute stage of a stroke. The goal of medical intervention is to identify the precise location of the stroke to better infer its likely etiology. Neuroanatomy is the scientific foundation on which localization and etiology are based, therefore it guides the rational treatment strategies at this stage.

Table 20.1. The Stages of Stroke and Their Characteristics.

STAGE OF STROKE:	Pre-symptomatic	Acute	Recovery
MEDICAL GOAL:	prophylaxis	stabilization	rehabilitation
INTERVENTION:	control risk factors; aspirin	CT scan; blood pressure control; etc.	speech, physical, occupational therapy; treat post-stroke depression
SCIENTIFIC FOUNDATION:	pathophysiology of vascular disease	neuro-anatomy	theories of learning

Stage 3 is the recovery stage of a stroke. The goal of medical intervention is to maximize recovery. Rehabilitation is the recovery of functional abilities that existed prior to the stroke, though perhaps performed in a different manner. These include communication, ambulation and transfers, feeding, toileting, dressing, and personal hygiene. They are accomplished by active learning on the part of the patient, under the guidance of professional therapists.

Questions about language also depend on the context in which they occur. Thus, questions at Stage 1 will be about normal language, its structure, development, and history. Questions at Stage 2 will be in the service of localization; for over 100 years it has been known that a patient's fluency, comprehension, repetition ability, and naming ability help to localize the stroke to a particular site along the peri-Sylvian fissure of the left hemisphere (Geschwind, 1965). Questions about language at Stage 3 will deal with how language is learned by an organically disturbed brain. The null hypotheses will be those principles of language learning that were discovered at Stage 1. In other words, principles of language learning should be those that form the initial hypotheses for research on rational intervention at Stage 3.

GOODMAN CONTEXTS AND APHASIC LANGUAGE: CASE STUDIES

The following patient cases demonstrate the nature of variability in aphasia: It inclines more toward the normal as the context for use becomes more natural. A natural context (what I am calling a "Goodman context") is one that allows the participants to adopt social roles in which they use language for making meaning. In many cases (if not all), aphasic language remains abnormal despite an optimal Goodman context. Nevertheless, it can still be shown that a Goodman context brings about an improvement in certain key language performance parameters.

Case 1: "Phil"

Phil is a 59-year-old, right-handed white man with a history of hypertension, who suffered a left hemisphere stroke with resultant language impairment. His speech is prosodically and phonemically fluent (i.e., "flowing"), but his comprehension of oral language is poor. Incomprehensible jargon is a frequent feature of his spoken language. On written language testing with the Boston Diagnostic Aphasia Examination (BDAE); (Goodglass & Kaplan, 1982), his written word-picture matching is 100% accurate; oral word recognition 75% accurate; and oral sentence and short paragraph reading comprehension 50% accurate. He failed to show improvement with standard therapies.

Phil was given a series of "authentic" text passages to read aloud (magazine articles, short book chapters, newspaper advertisements, etc.). Following this he was given a set of individual words printed on 3-by-5 index cards, also to read aloud. The individual words chosen were every seventh word from the text passages. All the tasks were completed in a single session.

On the individual word testing, Phil's responses were phonologically fluent, although incomprehensible, jargon. He frequently resorted to a strategy of pointing to individual letters and "counting" or "spelling" in a left-to-right fashion, apparently in an effort to identify the words. This strategy did not improve performance. On the other hand, his spontaneous comments about his own reading produced comprehensible language. Selected items from the word list, and Phil's oral responses, are shown in Table 20.2.

Phil's oral reading of a magazine advertisement for a famous department store again produced incomprehensible jargon. However, there are several semantic paralexias (i.e., semantically based oral reading "errors" or miscues) occurring over phrasal domains,

Table 20.2. "Phil's" Reading of Single Words.

Target Word	Phil's Reading (conventionalized spellings; perseveration on /p/ noted)
him	prectis-bo, say I finished
damaged	pettis-hill, pettis-ho, (points) 1-2-3-4-5-6-7, That hit it
cleaned	fixed, (points) 1-2-3-4-5-6-7
peak	pectis-bo, (points) 1-2-3-4, prapis-bally
have	bravis-body, (points) 1-2-3-4, (Tester: "Now, you don't have to count. What do you think that says?") woman
other	pemult, (points) s-h-a-2-3
And	pretis-bodis, (points) h-a-a, (points again) 1-2-3
were	prenewith, (points) space-h-a-3, (points again) 1-2-3-4
left	prables-oh, Is that correct?
towel	polish-brake, (points) plair-a-o-chris-full, It's wrong isn't it?, (points) 1-2-3-4-5- That's what it's supposed to be corrected, (Tester: "And what does that say?") three helpings

suggesting a certain degree of text processing and comprehension. Furthermore, Phil resorts to an oral "spelling strategy" only once; as a result, his oral reading of the text is more fluent than his oral reading of single words. The advertisement and Phil's reading are shown below (semantic paralexias italicized):

> Advertisement
>
> SALE. It's our biggest sale of the year. A sale unlike any other! Your opportunity to save on new fall fashions before the season begins. You'll find an unparalleled selection for the entire family at the lowest prices of the season. Prices go up August 3. Shop late. Sunday til 7pm. Macy's.

> Phil's Reading of Advertisement (conventionalized spellings)
>
> Plus is all or your spinach and the force. Perot and completed or confederacy to cat helps us you confederacy around the busty sempos day. For the semulance to counterspack, supposed to be, or the plus be, piss a plussy and the *price specials* of the pantidas. *Purchase due to be, purchase is to be over till twentieth 'bout Monday,* semble, coclinus till the twenty-fifth street. And then the plenis-bow is for substernce, f-h-a sen twentieth. Pens to the plenis the pen saterbus. (*Tester: "Very good."*) Thanks.

Finally, in a passage from a book about Mickey Mantle, Phil's oral reading was again incomprehensible jargon. However, on seeing a photograph of the famous ballplayer, he spontaneously exclaimed: "Oh, he's one of the greatest guys that ever lived."

The important generalization that underlies Phil's linguistic performance is the following: The more the speech event is self-initiated, that is, authentically communicative, the more comprehensible and pragmatically acceptable it is; the less the speech event is a component of meaningful communication, the more it becomes incomprehensible jargon. This is shown in Table 20.3.

As long as a certain degree of communicative integrity is retained (examples (1) and (2)), Phil's oral language reflects an attempt at meaning construction. This is evidenced by the production of semantic paralexias in the attempted reading of structurally complex text, and, furthermore, by the fact that Phil's behavior in reading the advertisement is quite unlike his behavior in reading isolated single words. In the former, "spelling" strategies do not play a prominent role. Thus, Phil's overt behavior suggests a strategy of word-identification for the single word reading task, and a strategy of meaning construction for

Table 20.3. Phil's Comprehensibility/Pragmatic Acceptability as a Function of Meaningful Communication.

1. Most Meaningful Communication
   a. Spontaneous response to photograph: "He's one of the greatest guys that ever lived."
   b. Spontaneous response to compliment (e.g., "Very good"): "Thank you."
   c. Questions own performance on word identification task: "Is that correct?"

2. Intermediate Meaningful Communication
   a. "Spelling" strategy on word identification task: 1-2-3; space-h-a-3; plair-a-o-chris-full
   b. Oral reading of cohesive and coherent text (advertisement), but with impaired receptive abilities for complex structures: jargon + phrasal semantic paralexias.

3. Least Meaningful Communication
   a. Acontextual single word identification task: incomprehensible jargon.

the text-reading task. As Goodman has repeatedly emphasized, reading a coherent text is a qualitatively distinct psychological phenomenon from reading isolated single words. The former involves hypothesis formation (predicting) and confirming or disconfirming hypotheses, based on the utilization of both visual and nonvisual cueing systems, whereas the latter involves recognition based exclusively on visual cues.

Of course, even though Phil's apparent focus in this example is on meaningful communication, his impaired psycholinguistic resources have rendered this quite difficult for him. However, insofar as purposeful, meaningful interactions with people and with the environment are evident in his nonverbal behavior (e.g., he successfully and spontaneously ambulates to those rooms in his home that are appropriate for a particular planned or stated activity), Phil's reading problem represents a case of relatively preserved (attempts at) meaning-constructing dissociated from relatively impaired language processes. But the preservation of meaning-constructing behavior is not only the quintessential premise of Goodman's philosophy of language, it is also the sine qua non for cognitive rehabilitation in neurology.

Case 2: "Alice"

Alice is a 68-year-old, right-handed white woman who had a left middle cerebral artery infarct that resulted in right hemiplegia and global aphasia (severe expressive and receptive difficulties). That her speech was rendered incomprehensible is readily apparent from her residual segmental inventory. Her "words" consist almost entirely of the sounds [d], [n], [o], [e], and [i]. Furthermore, [e] and [i] are in complementary distribution, with [i] appearing word-finally and [e] appearing elsewhere. Thus, the phonemic inventory consists of the voiced alveolar stops /d/ and /n/ and the mid vowels /o/ and /e/. All syllables are of the structure (C) V, and "words" contain up to three syllables (e.g., [ononi], [odeni], [odo], [do], and [o). Any syllable can be accented (e.g., ['ononi], [o'noni], [o'do).

Alice was given an oral reading task consisting of 10 declarative sentences, their corresponding Wh-questions, and their corresponding Yes-No questions (e.g., "Sally is here," "Who is here?," and "Is Sally here?". The sentences were presented individually and in random order, with filler sentences. Both audio and video recordings were made of Alice's reading. Fundamental frequency (FO) tracings were generated by Computerized Speech Laboratory software (Kay Elemetrics) using an FFT-COMB algorithm. (Typical artifactual errors [noise and octave errors] were identified in the tracings and eliminated in a principled fashion.) The test stimuli are shown in Table 20.4.

On a separate occasion, Alice was given an oral reading task with test stimuli consisting of uncontrolled, "natural" written texts, that is, plays, stories, nonfiction, and so on. FO tracings were obtained by the identical method used for single sentences in isolation.

The purpose of the video recordings of Alice's readings was to show her pointing to the text words with her left forefinger while reading. Given her incomprehensible speech, it was possible in this way to match printed words and sentences with their oral responses.

Without exception, Alice's FO tracings for isolated sentences demonstrated a falling terminal contour. This was the case even for Yes-No questions, which normal subjects read with the expected rising intonation. On the other hand, rising intonations were obtained for at least some of the Yes-No questions when they appeared as part of a connected text.

For Alice, rising terminal intonations, as demonstrated with acoustic tracings, were obtainable only with Yes/No questions embedded in a text. Thus, for Alice, there is a striking difference between her performance on a sentence task and on a text task: The repertoire of intonation contours for orally read individual sentences is

Table 20.4. Alice: Single Sentence Stimuli.

1	a.	Fred is the mayor of the city.
	b.	Who is the mayor of the city?
	c.	Is Fred the mayor of the city?
2.	a.	Sally is happy.
	b.	Who is happy?
	c.	Is Sally happy?
3.	a.	Baseball can be played in the rain.
	b.	What can be played in the rain?
	c.	Can baseball be played in the rain?
4.	a.	An apple is good to eat.
	b.	What is good to eat?
	c.	Is an apple good to eat?
5.	a.	Flowers can make a garden pretty.
	b.	What can make a garden pretty?
	c.	Can flowers make a garden pretty?
6.	a.	The cat is chasing the mouse.
	b.	What is chasing the mouse?
	c.	Is the cat chasing the mouse?
7.	a.	Louis was the king of France.
	b.	Who was the king of France?
	c.	Was Louis the king of France?
8.	a.	Pink is a pretty color.
	b.	What is a pretty color?
	c.	Is pink a pretty color?
9.	a.	A guitar is fun to play.
	b.	What is fun to play?
	c.	Is a guitar fun to play?
10.	a.	Mary will dance in the show.
	b.	Who will dance in the show?
	c.	Will Mary dance in the show?

narrower than that for orally read sentences in connected text. In addition, the wider repertoire found in connected text reading more closely approximates the normal intonation repertoire.

This finding raises important questions about the phenomenon of text reading versus single sentence reading because it is clear from the data that Alice is not incapable of producing the expected intonation contours. It is just that this capability is revealed only with her text reading. An explanation making use of notions from speech act theory (Austin, 1962; Pratt, 1977; Searle, 1969) seems promising; the falling intonation contour of single sentences, including Yes-No questions, is the expected contour if the sentences are being reported by Alice (i.e.,

"(This is the sentence:) Is Sally here?"), whereas the falling and rising intonation contours of sentences read aloud from text are the expected contours if the usual speech acts signaled by the sentences (e.g., request, query, etc.) are being *performed* by Alice. If the role of speech acts turns out to be a crucial component of the explanation of the difference between single sentence reading and text reading, it will justify the further question of just how much can be concluded about an individual's overall language abilities from studies of their abilities on component word and sentence tasks; text reading and single sentence reading appear to be qualitatively distinct phenomena.

The observations for these two subjects suggest that reading text is a qualitatively distinct phenomenon from reading isolated sentences and isolated words. This raises the following important research questions:

1. For both normals and aphasics, what is the relationship between the processing of written text and the processing of its component parts?
2. What are the unique properties of written text that demand a level of processing that is distinct from word and sentence processing?
3. What aspects of written text processing are typically retained in aphasia?
4. What aspects of written text processing are typically impaired in aphasia?
5. What relationship exists between an aphasic person's ability to process oral text and the ability to process written text?

The fact that language performance deteriorates with the distortion of purpose and the suppression of meaning and text authenticity, and communicative purpose, meaning, and text authenticity are features of spontaneous, uncontrolled speech, suggests that purpose, meaning, and text authenticity represent the default case in human behavior. Diminished performance can be created by imposing external obstacles on the language activity. These external obstacles may be words or sentences devoid of context, or an apparent lack of communicative purpose in the language event.

The third case study, discussed next, demonstrates the need to generalize the category of "performance obstacle" to include internal obstacles as well. These can be thought of as psychological characteristics of the language user that exist independently of the language event. Certain clearly pathological characteristics are unfortunately quite common in patients with stroke (Benson, 1973; Robinson & Benson, 1981; Starkstein & Robinson, 1989).

Case 3: "Ralph" (Strauss, 1994)

Ralph is a 68-year-old, left-handed white man with a history of cardiac disease and Parkinsonian tremor who suffered a left hemispheric stroke with resultant language difficulty. On initial evaluation with the Western Aphasia Battery (Kertesz, 1979), he was diagnosed as having a mild to moderate mixed aphasia (i.e., both expressive and receptive language difficulties). Subsequently, his language problem was predominantly a mild word-finding difficulty in spontaneous speech and a moderate to severe verbal apraxia (difficulty with motor programming for articulation, manifest by effortful "distortions" of vowels and consonant clusters).

The following are samples of Ralph's spontaneous oral discourse:

> Sample 1. U::m...How butterfly goes through...butterfly.... butterfly goes through...butterfu::es... butterfly goes three processes of life...be::fore before before it um before it's an adult...before it big before it big.
> Sample 2. Well he my do::ctor told me when I a::sked him...He doctor um um ... to::ld me I that I didn't have um the Par the some kind of Parkinson's. He said um I but he said it's not Parkinson's disea::se...the tre::mors. That's what he called told me.

These samples contain typical features of Ralph's speech abnormality. There are vowel prolongations (X::) and consonant cluster changes, as well as word-retrieval difficulty and some telegraphic speech. He produces on average 52 words per minute of speech. Ralph is at times visibly frustrated at his speech difficulty, often to the point of tearfulness.

Ralph's wife and daughter reported that he had been having a recurring dream for many years, actually beginning some years prior to the stroke, but continuing even afterwards. The dream is remarkable not only for its content but for the fact that in it Ralph's speech is practically normal. This is a segment of Ralph's dream discourse, audiotaped by a family member as he talked aloud in his sleep:

> Dream Speech. Where the hell you been pop? Man you told me to stand there and wait till you got there and I stood here. I stood here till you got here pop. I stood right here and I said...well I told the man I said if

> my father said he was gonna be here my father will be here. And that's why I stood here and waited. But how in the hell can you get up and down that hill a::nd how high it is but you won't let me go up it? Ma::n that hill is high. Yeah. I know. I know exactly what you're saying. Oh, I know. Now let me a::sk you a question. I wanna a::sk you some questions.

In this corpus, there are only occasional vowel prolongations and no obvious difficulties with consonant clusters or word-finding. Ralph produces approximately 156 words per minute of dream speech, three times the rate of his average awake speech. On the very next day, and indeed every day since, Ralph's awake speech was once again slow, apractic, and anomic.

What could be responsible for this remarkable disparity? Clearly, this is an exceedingly difficult question to answer fully, but I believe that the evidence points to Ralph's affect as the source of his variation.

Ralph suffers from severe post-stroke depression, a sequela of stroke that has been estimated to afflict up to 40% of stroke patients within weeks to months of the stroke (Starkstein & Robinson, 1989). Ralph freely admits to having a depressed mood and states that he no longer finds pleasure in previously enjoyable activities. He reports subjective memory problems and difficulty concentrating, and complains of fatigue, inability to sleep, and poor appetite. These are classic, nonspecific, psychologic, and autonomic symptoms associated with depression.

As a young man, Ralph's first job was as an officer in the local police force. He states that he met regularly with a judge in order to learn to speak "better English." Eventually, he left the police force to run a funeral home, for which he authored all the literature that was distributed to clients. He became experienced at giving speeches to community audiences consisting of hundreds of people.

Now, Ralph avoids shopping in stores because he fears people will take his speech as a sign of "stupidity." Although he denies suicidal thoughts, he asserts that he has "nothing to live for."

In his recurring dream, Ralph goes to a hill to see his deceased father, who is descending from the hilltop. Present with his father are other members of Ralph's family who have passed away. He converses with his father and ends each dream with his father entreating him to accompany him back up the hill, to which Ralph responds that he is "not yet ready to go."

Ralph's dream content was well known to Freud, who analyzed the significance of the "dead father" in his own dreams and in the dreams of his patients:

> I will begin with a few examples in which the absurdity of the dream content is apparent only, disappearing when the dream is more thoroughly examined. These are certain dreams which—accidentally, one begins by thinking—are concerned with the dreamer's dead father. . .
>
> If in the dream the dreamer is not reminded that the dead person is dead, he sets himself on a par with the dead; he dreams of his own death. The sudden realization or astonishment in the dream ("but he has long been dead!") is a protest against this identification, and rejects the meaning that the dreamer is dead. (quoted in Brill, 1938, 409-413)

Ralph's "sudden realization" occurs when he is invited to join his father (and other deceased relatives). In his decision not to join them, Ralph affirms his desire to live. Indeed, the occurrence of the dream itself began at a point in Ralph's life prior to his stroke, during a period when he had already overcome his low self-esteem, as reflected in the negative evaluation he had of his former speech.

Thus, in his dream, Ralph returns to a time in his life when he was more self-assured and when he asserted this self-assurance through his use of language. Now, following the stroke, Ralph is depressed, and he takes his abnormal speech as validation of his mood.

Ralph's present language problem appears to be a severe affective disorder superimposed on a mild aphasia. If the affective problem is eliminated, as it seems to be during the dream, then the language behavior improves dramatically. Thus, affective disorder can be a kind of internal obstacle to optimal language performance. That it is at the same time a well-recognized obstacle to learning (Altwerger & Ivener, 1994; Dulay & Burt, 1977) supports Goodman's notion that learning presupposes contexts that are optimal for realizing a learner's current abilities.

CONCLUSIONS AND PROSPECTS

In the spirit of John Dewey, Goodman has stated that the goal of education is to take the learner from where he or she is now to as far as he or she is capable of going. But internal and external obstacles to performance do not allow us to see where the learner is now. We might inaccurately identify a learner to be merely at point A, when he or she is actually at the more advanced point B (see Figure 20.2). Advancing the learner from point A to a point C partway between A and B has not really taught him or her anything he or she does not already know. This immensely important concept of learning applies equally to recovery from neurologic disease.

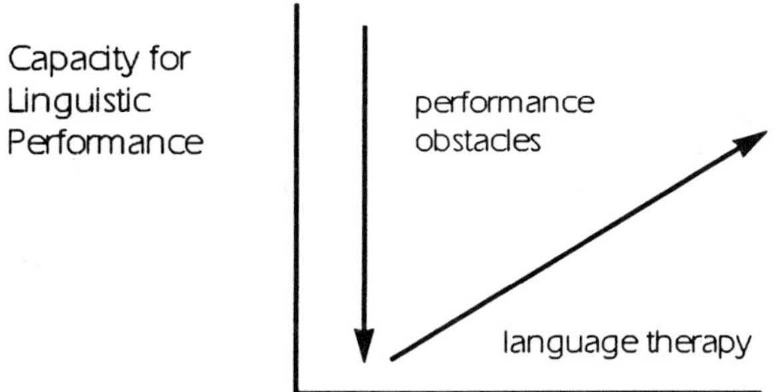

Figure 20.2. Relationship between therapy and performance results

The preceding case studies not only exemplify characteristics of Goodman contexts, but they expand our understanding of them as well. Reconfirmed is the crucial importance of purposeful and meaningful behavior in both optimizing and understanding language use and of authentic texts that permit such behavior to occur. Suboptimal contexts are created by the imposition of obstacles on the purposeful and meaningful use of language. These obstacles may be externally imposed, as seen in the case of inauthentic texts and noncommunicative tasks used for testing or treatment. They may also be internally imposed, as in the case of post-stroke depression confounding the purpose of a language event by adding to it a layer of self-consciousness in which the language user is attempting to avoid a negative public perception of his abnormal speech at the same time that he or she is trying to communicate.

Perhaps the most exciting aspect of the preceding case studies is the realization that the field of aphasiology has available to it a voluminous, well-established body of knowledge and set of scientific principles on language learning that can open the curtains of optimism for millions of individuals and their families. The challenge is for workers in this field to take advantage of this important opportunity.

REFERENCES

Albert, M.L. et al. (1981). *Clinical aspects of dysphasia*. New York: Springer Verlag.

Altwerger, B., & Ivener, B. (1994). Self-esteem: Access to literacy in multicultural and multilingual classrooms. In K. Spangenberg-Urbschat & R. Pritchard (Eds.), *Kids come in all languages: Reading instruction for ESL students*. Newark, DE: International Reading Association.

Austin, J.L. (1962). *How to do things with words*. Clarendon, UK: Oxford University Press.

Benson, D.F. (1973). Psychiatric aspects of aphasia. *British Journal of Psychiatry, 123*, 555-566.

Benson, D.F., & Ardila, A. (1993) Depression in aphasia. In S.E. Starkstein, & R.G. Robinson (Eds.),

Brill, A.A. (Ed. & Trans). (1938). *The basic writings of Sigmund Freud*. New York: Modern Library.

Brown, R. (1973). *A first language: The early stages*. Cambridge, MA: Harvard University Press.

Chomsky, N. (1965). *Aspects of the theory of syntax*. Cambridge, MA: MIT Press.

Chomsky, N. (1975). *Reflections on language*. New York: Pantheon.

Chomsky, N. (1982). *Lectures on government and binding*. Dordrecht: Foris Publications.

Dulay, H., & Burt, M. (1977). Remarks on creativity in language acquisition. In M. Burt, H. Dulay, & M. Finocchiaro (Eds.), *Viewpoints on English as a second language*. New York: Regents.

Edelsky, C. (1991). *Literacy and justice for all: Rethinking the social in language and education*. London: Falmer.

Ewoldt, C. (1977). *A psycholinguistic description of selected deaf children reading sign language*. Unpublished doctoral dissertation, Wayne State University, Detroit.

Ferreiro, E., & Teberosky, A. (1982). *Literacy before schooling*. Exeter, NH: Heinemann.

Geschwind, N. (1965). Disconnection syndromes in animals and man. *Brain, 88*, 237-294, 585-644.

Goodglass, H., & Kaplan, E. (1982). *The assessment of aphasia and related disorders* (2nd ed.). Philadelphia: Lea and Febiger.

Goodman, K.S. (1967). Reading: A psycholinguistic guessing game. *Journal of the Reading Specialist*, 259-271.

Goodman, K.S. (1985). A linguistic study of cues and miscues in reading. In H. Singer & R.B. Ruddell (Eds.), *Theoretical models and processes of reading*. Newark, DE: International Reading Association.

Goodman, K.S. (1986). *What's whole in whole language?* Portsmouth: Heinemann.

Goodman, K.S., & Goodman, Y.M. (1979). Learning to read is natural. In L. B. Resnick & P. A. Weaver (Eds.), *Theory and practice of early reading* (Vol. 1, pp. 137-154). Hillsdale, NJ: Erlbaum.

Goodman, Y.M., Altwerger, B., & Marek, A. (1989). *Print awareness in preschool children: The development of literacy in preschool children, research and review* (Occasional Paper). Program in Language and Literacy, University of Arizona, Tucson.

Halliday, M.A.K. (1975) *Learning how to mean: Explorations in the development of language*. London: Edward Arnold.

Harste, J., Burke, C., & Woodward, V. (1982). *Children's language and world: Initial encounters with print*. Final Report, NIE Project G-79-0132, Washington, DC: National Institutes of Education.

Harste, J., Woodward, V., & Burke, C. (1984). *Language stories and literacy lessons*. Exeter, NH: Heinemann.

Hymes, D. (1987). Communicative competence. In U. Ammon et al. (Eds.), *Sociolinguistics—Soziolinguistik* (pp. 219-230). Berlin: Walter de Gruyter.

Kertesz, A. (1979). *Aphasia and associated disorders: Taxonomy, localization, and recovery*. New York: Grune and Stratton.

Krashen, S. (1982). *Principles and practice in second language acquisition*. Hayward, CA: Alemany Press.

Krashen, S., & Terrell, T.D. (1983). *The natural approach: Language acquisition in the classroom*. Hayward, CA: Alemany Press.

Pratt, M.L. (1977). *Towards a speech act theory of literary discourse*. Bloomington: Indiana University Press.

Read, C. (1975). *Children's categorization of speech sounds in English*. Urbana, IL: National Council of Teachers of English.

Rhodes, L., & Dudley-Marling, C. (1988). *Readers and writers with a difference*. Portsmouth, NH: Heinemann.

Robinson, R.G., & Benson, D.F. (1981). Depression in aphasic patients: Frequency, severity, and clinical-pathological correlations. *Brain and Language, 14*, 282-291.

Searle, J.R. (1969). *Speech acts: An essay in the philosophy of language*. Cambridge: Cambridge University Press.

Starkstein, S.E., & Robinson, R. G. (1988). Aphasia and depression. *Aphasiology, 2*, 1-20.

Starkstein, S., & Robinson, W. (1989). Affective disorders and cerebral vascular disease. *British Journal of Psychiatry, 154*, 170-182.

Strauss, S.L. (1994). *A sixty-eight year-old man with aphasia and somniloquy*. Case presented at the Annual Meeting of the American Academy of Neurology, Session on Unusual Cognitive Disorders, Washington, DC.

Vygotsky, L.S. (1978). *Mind in society*. Cambridge, MA: Harvard University Press.

EPILOGUE

Chapter Twenty–One

What it Means to be a Good Colleague

Roger Shuy
Georgetown University

Every academic comes to realize sooner or later that this work can be a lonely endeavor unless good colleagues can be found to share one's hopes, successes, and struggles. In graduate school we are trained to be totally independent, to work alone, and to display our individual talents and promise. Group work, alas, is generally discouraged because those who evaluate us would then be confused about how to assess us individually. So we write our papers singly, sit in our lonely carrels in the library, take our tests, write our dissertations, and sit for our comprehensives by ourselves, like big people, proving to all our individual worth as scholars.

When we finally secure our first teaching position, however, things look a bit different. We knew how to be students, but now we are in a totally new and confusing ballgame, with unseen risks and tremendously important stakes involving looming tenure decisions. Often we think about sharing our vulnerability with our colleagues but the risks are often too high. We can't let them know what we don't know or what we're afraid of because this might count against us in our climb up the academic ladder.

One would assume that fellow faculty members exchange drafts of their papers and help each other into print, save each other from silly mistakes, and, in general, behave as friends and allies. Sadly, this is rarely the case, for fellow members of departments often see themselves as competitors with us and with each other. Therefore, giving help to the competition is thought to be self-destructive. What I am describing here is, of course, only generally true, not exclusively. Once in a while we find true colleagues in our departments. But more often we seek out colleagues at other universities, where the competition is less threatening, or in other departments of our own university.

Whenever we do find a good colleague, we cherish our good fortune and do all we can to keep the relationship alive. Because few scholars ever achieve a truly collegial relationship, I thought it appropriate to use this forum to outline its characteristics and to describe how my collegial relationship with Ken Goodman instances each point.

I deem the essential characteristics of a good collegial relationship as follows:

1. Good colleagues are hard to find. You have to work at it.
2. Good colleagues trust each other.
3. Good colleagues can differ with each other without affecting their relationship.
4. Good colleagues share their vulnerabilities with each other.
5. Good colleagues suffer together.
6. Good colleagues stay that way.

GOOD COLLEAGUES ARE HARD TO FIND

My personal academic realization, first at Wheaton College and later at Michigan State University, was that if I was going to have true colleagues, I would have to find them outside my own department. Ruminating on this problem, I went to the annual International Reading Association meeting in Boston to present a paper on dialect interference in reading. An hour or so before I was to give my paper, I attended a session in which Ken Goodman was the speaker. His paper devastated me, not because of its quality but because he presented virtually the same speech that I was about to give myself. I rushed up to him after his talk and told him as much and apologized in advance for what might appear to be outright plagiarism. He wasn't a bit upset. He smiled and told me that he really appreciated having a colleague in this work, even an unrecognized one. This began our many years of colleagueship, which is the focus of this chapter.

GOOD COLLEAGUES TRUST EACH OTHER

One of the primary requirements for being good colleagues is mutual trust. When we put our naked ideas in front of another scholar, we become extremely vulnerable. When we find colleagues in another academic discipline who gloat over knowing something we don't know, who hide their knowledge from us by couching it in language that only insiders can comprehend, and who are so insecure about the flaws in their own field that they offer us what appear to be feeble and specious defenses of it, then we have great difficulty becoming colleagues. "Joining," a skill central to being an effective family therapist, has to be done by both participants in the collegial bond. Joining can't occur, however, without the permission of the other to be joined. With Ken Goodman, the door was always open for me to join in his educational quests. He didn't exclude me with jargon or ambiguity, and he was forthright about the problems in his own field, those with which he alleged that I might help.

In fact, our mutual concerns were so similar that we learned a great deal from each other, as good colleagues might be expected to do. As we both prepared for one academic meeting in which we were scheduled to be on the same panel, we concocted an outrageous idea. I usually gave the linguistic perspective and Goodman made sense of it from the educational perspective. This time, we proposed to reverse roles. He would do the linguistic part and I would do the education. We wondered whether or not anyone would notice. We pulled it off with grace and élan. Nobody seemed to be able to tell the difference. We didn't speak of this further. Another of the qualities of good colleagues is to be able to share secrets together.

GOOD COLLEAGUES CAN DIFFER

Like most people without advanced training in education, I was insecure about what my own children were enduring in the public schools. Sometime before I met Ken Goodman, my third grade son was said to have "reading problems" (at least this is what his teacher told me). Like most parents who didn't really know anything about reading, I was more or less willing to accept her judgment. I dutifully went to the parent-teacher conference where I was shown some evidence of his failure. This evidence consisted of several sheets of ditto paper on which Tim had written numbers next to the individual words. The list looked something like this:

LEMON 1
SPIDER 1
BUTTERFLY 2
BOTTLE 1
etc.

Tim's teacher explained that the children were to count the number of syllables in each word and write the total in the space next to it. Tim was one short in most cases. It didn't take genius to figure out, however, that he was consistently one short or, for that matter, that syllable counting had only the remotest possible connection to whatever it was that "reading" was all about. Sadly, I asked the teacher how she defined a syllable. Scornfully, she recited, "A syllable is something that contains a vowel sound; everyone knows that." Puzzled by this, I then asked her what the vowel sounds in these words were. Her scorn turned to anger as she said, "Lemon has e and o, spider has i and e, butterfly has u, e, and y, and bottle has o and e." No amount of reason could persuade her that Tim was hearing sounds, not letters, and that these were letters, not sounds. Failing at this, I called the publisher, who hired me on the spot.

My work as consultant with Ginn and Company highlights a different phase of collegiality with Ken Goodman. He was on a somewhat different track of thinking from my own. Although we agreed on the basics, my theory was that change in the field of reading would be gradual and slow, not revolutionary, and that it would be better to change the system from within rather than to throw the rascals out and start all over again. However right my theory may have been, after 14 years of frustration with the commercial end of reading, I finally threw in the towel. Whatever early progress I was able to make was regularly turned around, based on mysterious evidence from "marketing reports" that I was never allowed to see.

Another theoretical difference Ken Goodman and I had was over decoding. It was obvious that publishers had led teachers to believe that this was very difficult and that decoding instruction should be spread over six to eight years of schooling. Goodman quite correctly observed that this was nonsense. I agreed with him in everything except the amount of decoding necessary. I claimed, and still do for that matter, that some decoding is useful, although instruction was generally ill-conceived, badly executed, and continued far longer than necessary. We kept a respectful difference of opinion on this, highlighting an important characteristic of good colleagues: They can disagree on some issues and still work together. I never felt vilified for my disagreement with him, and I never had a sense that it would keep us apart. Nor did this good feeling prevent Ken from reminding me how wrong he thought I was.

nourishment, which the children needed, with research. The task was to build a sandwich. Each child was seated at a table containing two pieces of bread and a slice of lunch meat while the researcher stood by the table and observed." "Strike two," I shouted. "Tell us exactly what the instructions were," Goodman pleaded. "Well, first we told them to put the lunch meat under a piece of bread and they couldn't do it," continued Engelmann. "Strike three," said Goodman, raising his thumb in the air. "Whoever heard of making a sandwich that way?"

Now Engelmann was annoyed. Dramatically he turned to the audience and asked, "How many in this room believe that these children are cognitively deprived?" Hundreds of hands, Black and white, slowly raised. Smiling, Engelmann then asked, "And how many in this room do *not* believe these children are cognitively impaired?" Two hands went up, both from the speaker's platform. We had been soundly beaten even before we had a chance to give our talks.

I don't remember much else about that meeting, but I know that I experienced a truly significant collegial event. Goodman was willing to go down with the ship for his beliefs. He had a lot more to lose from such a defeat than I did because it was an education meeting and he was a prominent educator. As an outsider, I had less to lose, but I felt the same pain. Until then, we had shared the excitement of kindred minds and goals. Now we also shared the agony of defeat. What more could a colleague ask?

GOOD COLLEAGUES STAY THAT WAY

In the 1980s, my scholarly interests changed rather dramatically. Goodman had moved across the country, making our contacts less frequent. I had decided to focus my attention on linguistic issues involving law instead of education. I stopped attending meetings of the International Reading Association, the National Council of Teachers of English, the American Educational Research Association, and other conferences where we might meet and share collegial thoughts. I also virtually stopped writing for education journals, making me, at best, suspect as a contributor even to this volume. Despite the fact that we haven't communicated in any significant professional way for at least a decade, Ken Goodman remained a faithful colleague, and this qualifies me to tell the world what having a good colleague really means. We found each other, we trusted each other, we differed on a few points, we were vulnerable to each other, we suffered together, and we have remained colleagues despite the changes in interests and the separation of miles. One couldn't ask more than this of a good colleague.

GOOD COLLEAGUES ARE WILLING TO BE VULNERABLE

I never claimed to have a credential in education. I was once certified as a secondary teacher in Ohio, where I actually taught junior high for four years, but this in no way authorized me to make pronouncements about how educational change should be accomplished. Ken Goodman had considerable authority, by virtue of his training and experience, but he had little or no training in my own field, linguistics. This made him cautious about making judgments about language without first checking them out. Because I had become very interested in education and he had become very interested in linguistics, we made a natural pair.

He sometimes asked me to consult with him at Wayne State University in the early formulation of Miscue Analysis. I recall that at first, miscues were referred to as something else, "errors" as I recall. This term bothered us both, for the whole point was to show that spoken language variation, not mistakes, caused different realizations of the written symbols. We wanted to get rid of the harmful notion that such oral renditions were mistakes. Somehow, "miscues" emerged as the compromise term, certainly better than "errors" or "mistakes," but still not perfect. To this day I wish for a more apt term, but I haven't been able to think of one. The collegiality point here is that Goodman never hid the problem from me and I never hid my discomfort from him. Colleagues don't do that. They are willing to be vulnerable to each other, revealing their weaknesses in the hope that the colleague will help them improve things. They don't dismiss each other or each other's fields as uninformed, stupid, or willfully ambiguous. They try to help, if they can.

GOOD COLLEAGUES SUFFER TOGETHER

As it turns out, the linguistic tools that would have been most useful to reading were not yet available either to me or to him. A bit of linguistic history is necessary here. The major thrust, therefore tools, of linguistics in the 1960s and most of the 1970s were phonology, morphology, and syntax. Semantics was an area that we recognized as important but had only a vague grasp of. I can recall a paper, in fact, at a Linguistic Society of America meeting in the mid-1960s in which the speaker, the chairman of a prestigious linguistics department in California, concluded that there was no way that linguistics could deal with meaning. Obviously, linguistics also had no way to address conveyed meaning—pragmatics—either, because it hadn't been invented yet. At that time we confined ourselves, as many linguists do still today, to units of language no larger than a sentence. It wasn't until the late 1970s that discourse analysis began to emerge.

If Ken Goodman and I had met for the first time 35 years later than we actually did, I could have offered him, and the field of reading as well, a much fuller bag of tools to work with, and both of our jobs might have been accomplished more efficiently and quickly. But even with our limited tool bag, he was able to fight an effective, if frustrating, battle against the entrenched reading conventions of decoding without comprehension, standardized testing based on these same reductionist conventions, and the traditional misinformation that children whose spoken language varies from some perceived, but hardly real, Standard English are broken vessels that have to be fixed.

The battle was not always easy. I recall one particular event at which Ken Goodman and I were among the three or four featured speakers before 500 teachers. The meeting was the Michigan Compensatory Education Conference in Grand Rapids, sometime in the late 1960s. The first speaker was Sigfried Engelmann, the controversial author of the famous Distar program, which had gained great popularity. Distar was a paradigm behaviorist program for what were then called "disadvantaged children." The materials scripted teachers rigidly and worked on a strictly Skinnerian pattern. Engelmann began by describing these children, exclusively urban Black as far as I can recall, as having limited language and limited concepts. I, for one, have never been comfortable about what was being called a concept, but I had every reason to believe that inner-city children had a very rich and elaborated language system which varied from that which was expected by the schools. This fact had been made very clear to me from our Michigan State research, The Detroit Dialect Study, in 1966. Bill Labov had also shown this to be the case in New York City, and Ken Goodman had been saying it about Detroit kids as well. A Detroit white teacher, Ruth Golden, had become convinced of Engelmann's position even earlier, claiming that such children needed to wipe out their dialect in favor of the school norm. She produced a set of materials, including the Golden tapes, to remedy this problem. Goodman, Labov, and I, among others, were voices in the wilderness disagreeing with Engelmann and Golden.

Engelmann went on with his observations about the lack of language and concepts of urban Black children until Goodman couldn't stand it any more. Uncharacteristically, he interrupted the presentation just after Engelmann had said, "Black children don't know the difference between over and under." "How do you know?", Goodman asked. "Research," Engelmann replied. "Tell us about it," I chimed in.

Engelmann took the bait and explained that the research was conducted at his laboratory at the University of Illinois. "Strike one," shouted Goodman. Ignoring this, Engelmann continued, "It combined